ENVISIONING SOCIOLOGY

ENVISIONING SOCIOLOGY

Victor Branford, Patrick Geddes, and the Quest for Social Reconstruction

JOHN SCOTT

RAY BROMLEY

STATE UNIVERSITY OF NEW YORK PRESS

The cover illustration is based on "Armageddon (A.D. 1914–16)," originally included in *A Rustic View of War and Peace* (Cities Committee 1918, 10). In its prefatory note, the anonymous author, almost certainly Victor Branford, describes the pamphlet as "propaganda" intended to change public opinion and to be diffused as widely as possible; not attributable to the Sociological Society. The illustration is unsigned, but attributed to Philip Mairet.

In the lower portion, "the War Lords, under mask of their heraldic birds and beasts, are enjoying their Valhalla of combat" seeking pillage, territory and imperial expansion. The combatants are nations and empires, monarchies and republics, represented by one- and two-headed eagles, winged and unwinged lions, a turkey, and a rooster—a panorama of Europe during World War I.

In the upper portion, the Phoenix rises from the burning city—a city that is damaged, but still largely intact. Its skyline includes one major monument and numerous towers, spires, and domes associated with civic, religious, and educational institutions. Commerce and industry are arrayed around the civic core, peripheral rather than central to the great work of social reconstruction.

Published by
STATE UNIVERSITY OF NEW YORK PRESS, ALBANY

© 2013 State University of New York

All rights reserved

Printed in the United States of America

No part of this book may be used or reproduced in any manner whatsoever without written permission. No part of this book may be stored in a retrieval system or transmitted in any form or by any means including electronic, electrostatic, magnetic tape, mechanical, photocopying, recording, or otherwise without the prior permission in writing of the publisher.

For information, contact
State University of New York Press, Albany, NY
www.sunypress.edu

Production, Laurie Searl
Marketing, Anne M. Valentine

Library of Congress Cataloging-in-Publication Data

Scott, John, 1949–
  Envisioning sociology : Victor Branford, Patrick Geddes, and the quest for social reconstruction / John Scott and Ray Bromley.
    p. cm.
  Includes bibliographical references and index.
  ISBN 978-1-4384-4731-5 (hbk. : alk. paper)
  ISBN 978-1-4384-4730-8 (pbk. : alk. paper)
  1. Branford, Victor. 2. Geddes, Patrick, Sir, 1854–1932. 3. Sociologists—Great Britain—Biography. 4. Sociology—Great Britain—History. I. Bromley, R. J. II. Title.

HM478.S38 2013
301.092'2—dc23
[B]
                                                2012027767

10 9 8 7 6 5 4 3 2 1

CONTENTS

LIST OF TABLES vii

PREFACE AND ACKNOWLEDGMENTS ix

INTRODUCTION 1

CHAPTER ONE
Victorian and Edwardian Sociology 5

CHAPTER TWO
Geddes, Branford, and Gurney: Personal Partnerships 25

CHAPTER THREE
Organizing an Intellectual Vision 43

CHAPTER FOUR
Environment, Region, and Social Reconstruction 81

CHAPTER FIVE
Planning the Built Environment: Civics and Conservative Surgery ... 103

CHAPTER SIX
Socialization, Citizenship, and the University Militant 129

CHAPTER SEVEN
Cooperation, Finance, and Capitalism 161

CHAPTER EIGHT
Financiers, the Credit System, and the Third Alternative ... 181

CHAPTER NINE
Failure of a Sociological Project   209

APPENDIX A
William Branford   217

APPENDIX B
The Branford, Gurney, and Geddes families   221

NOTES   225

REFERENCES   243

INDEX   275

LIST OF TABLES

Table 3.1	Executive Committee of the Sociological Society (1903)	56
Table 3.2	Papers for the Present (1919)	68
Table 3.3	Papers for the Present (1921)	69
Table 3.4	The Making of the Future—as announced or planned (1917)	70
Table 3.5	Studies in Contemporary Social Evolution (1923)	74
Table 3.6	Our Modern World: Papers of Victor Branford (1927)	75
Table 3.7	Our Modern World: Papers of Victor Branford (1928)	75
Table 4.1	Class Divisions in Complex Societies	88
Table 6.1	The Stages of Development	136
Table 8.1	Temporal Power Alignments	189

PREFACE AND ACKNOWLEDGMENTS

This book is the first to report on the sociological project of Victor Branford, Patrick Geddes, and their circle. While a number of biographies and discussions of Patrick Geddes have appeared, these concentrate on his work in urban planning. When considered within the wider social sciences he is often considered only as a planner or geographer, and not a sociologist. Mention of Victor Branford has been confined, at best, to the footnotes in histories of sociology, yet he was the leading organizational and intellectual figure in the early days of British sociology. The two stood at the heart of a vast international network of connections within the social sciences. Our book is predicated on the view that an assessment of their ideas and their practical work is long overdue.

The book has been a long time in preparation and many debts have been incurred during that time. John Scott's interest in the area was encouraged by a question raised by Sabita Branford, granddaughter of Victor Branford, at a meeting on British sociology at the London School of Economics. The project has also benefited from the discovery of family papers (now in the Keele University Archive) by Jean Branford, a distant relative of Branford's cousin who settled in South Africa. Much of the early research was undertaken jointly with Chris Husbands, who co-authored some early papers but was unable to continue to be involved in the project. We are immensely grateful to Chris for his continuing collaboration in our discussions. Ray Bromley's interest in the area stemmed from interest in Patrick Geddes's contributions to urban planning and from family connections close to Keele University.

Many archivists, family historians, and fellow social scientists have helped us track down obscure items of information. These are too numerous to name individually, but we have tried to indicate a number of these people in the endnotes of the book. We are grateful to all of them for making this book possible. The book is a true transatlantic and interdisciplinary cooperation, for both the authors and those who have helped us in our task. The two authors have met on a number of occasions but have pursued a largely electronic relationship for the best part of a decade. Each has undertaken library and archival research and the results have been shared for joint discussion and further development. It has been a hugely enjoyable and rewarding process.

The works discussed in the book are very much products of their time. This is especially apparent in the male-oriented language used and in what now seem rather archaic views of gender roles. While we have discussed the substantive biases and prejudices that appear in their work when discussing gender and women, we have not routinely noted or corrected the use of inappropriate pronouns. Despite this gender bias, it is striking that Branford and Geddes were among the few social scientists of their time who did actually regard the question of gender as a major topic for sociological discussion.

Victor Branford came from a large family and we have tried to ensure that the particular Branford we refer to in the text is always clear, either from the context or by explicit use of a first name. Biographical citations to "Branford" are always citations to Victor Branford, unless otherwise indicated, and other Branfords are distinguished by their initials where any doubt could arise. Where any confusion may arise, we cite Victor Branford as "V. V. Branford." Citations to the work of Sybella Branford are made using the name under which she was published at the time, except that papers by "Mrs. V. Branford" are cited as "S. Branford."

A great deal of biographical information has been acquired on the numerous individuals in and around the circle centered on Branford and Geddes. Material concerning the family members of the leading protagonists are included in the two appendices. Appendix A relates the relevant details of the life of William Branford, father of Victor Branford. Appendix B provides briefer biographies of members of the families of Victor Branford, Sybella Gurney, and Patrick Geddes. Other biographical details can be found in the online database at https://sites.google.com/site/sociologysource/thebranfordproject2/thebranfordproject3.

We hope that our readers will enjoy reading this book as much as we have enjoyed writing it.

John Scott, Cornwall, UK
Ray Bromley, Albany, N.Y., USA
June 2012

INTRODUCTION

British sociology has often been seen by commentators on the history of the discipline as the poor cousin of the intellectual developments that took place in other parts of the world. Long and thriving traditions of sociological analysis have been identified and much discussed in the United States, Germany, and France, and numerous social theorists and researchers in these countries have been seen as the architects of the "classical" sociologies that flowered from the late nineteenth century to the middle of the twentieth. A particularly influential commentator on intellectual culture has decried the absence in Britain of any classical sociology (Anderson 1968). While Herbert Spencer has been recognized as a pioneering British sociologist and has had a substantial international impact, he has tended to be seen as having no lasting influence in his own country.

We show the inadequacy of this claim in the following chapters. We show that Spencer's British successors as sociologists were numerous and that they developed his insights in diverse directions. Leonard Hobhouse, in particular, was the focal point for a number of writers who built a mainstream of sociological work along the evolutionary basis laid down by Spencer. We argue that another group of theorists, centered on Patrick Geddes, rivaled this evolutionary mainstream and were especially important in the emerging organizational structure of British sociology. The Geddes group, however, has been forgotten and ignored to an even greater extent than Hobhouse and his school. The task that we undertake in this book is to rediscover the leading ideas of these thinkers and to set them in the wider context of the development of British and American social thought, the building of a professional and disciplinary base for sociology, and the formulation of a political project of social reconstruction. In the final chapter we assess their contemporary significance and discuss why it is that they have largely been forgotten.

In discussing Geddes, his colleagues, and followers, we are dealing with a collaborative circle of writers and activists who, together with their larger network of associates, were active during the first three decades of the twentieth century and aimed to build a broad-based sociological movement that could underpin the establishment of a professional organization and academic community of sociologists within which their own intellectual approach would play a leading part. A collaborative circle has been defined as a set of friends who work together in relation to a shared intellectual vision that guides their work (Farrell 2001). This shared vision defines how the members of the circle feel they should work and how they should relate to others, establishing the possibilities and limits that constrain their larger projects.

The leading figure in the collaborative circle with which we are concerned is Patrick Geddes himself. Geddes worked on the margins of academic society in Edinburgh to set out the core intellectual elements of a sociological and wider intellectual vision that he conveyed to students who then became devoted disciples in the further development of the vision and its wider dissemination from his base in the Outlook Tower. He and his disciples took their sociological view to London and sought to establish it at the center of the academic system. Principal among these disciples was Victor Branford, the key architect of the first professional association for British sociologists (the Sociological Society), its first professional journal (the *Sociological Review*), and the means through which the first Chair in sociology came to be established (at the London School of Economics). Branford's business career generated the financial resources that he put to use in the service of sociology and that enabled him to make a number of intellectual contributions of his own to the Geddesian vision. The third figure in the core of the collaborative circle was Branford's second wife, Sybella (neé Gurney), who contributed a great deal to the practical application of the vision and its spiritual underpinning. Her personal fortune supplemented Branford's and allowed her to contribute to the task of institutionalizing Geddes's conception of sociology and civic action.

Geddes, Victor Branford, and Sybella Branford cooperated in a number of ventures and practical projects. The other members of the collaborative circle included, for various periods and at various times, Branford's younger brother the educationalist Benchara Branford, the New Age Romantic George Sandeman, and the educationalist Gilbert Slater. They influenced a wider network of associates including the communitarian Ernest Westlake, the psychologist Lionel Tayler (see Tayler 1931), the philosopher Mark Wenley, the geographer Andrew Herbertson, the architect-planners Raymond Unwin, Barry Parker, and Patrick Abercrombie, the designers Charles Ashbee and Philip Mairet, Branford's poet nephew Freddie (Frederick Victor Branford), and Branford's clergymen brothers Jack and Lionel. In the sphere of business they had strong financial and intellectual associations with City merchants John Heslop and Vernon Malcolmson, the latter also writing on rural housing (Malcolmson 1920), the financier Charles Mendl, and a raft of railway financiers with Latin American interests. In the United States they maintained close contact with Albion Small and Jane Addams at Chicago, with Small's student Charles Ellwood at Missouri, and with Stanley Hall at Clark University. The latter two developed ideas that both paralleled and influenced the work of those in the circle. Geddes and Victor Branford were on close personal terms with both William James and Thorstein Veblen and they maintained fruitful intellectual contacts with Marcel Mauss. Toward the ends of their lives they attracted the young New York urbanist and architectural writer Lewis Mumford, whose own work developed and articulated their intellectual and practical concerns. Through Mumford, the influential New York–based circle of visionaries known as the Regional Planning Association of America adopted many of Geddes's ideas.

These were the collaborators, associates, and supporters of the intellectual vision promoted by the Geddes circle as the basis for professional sociology in Britain. In the chapters of this book we explore the sociological content of this vision and its influence within both sociology and geography. We also examine the practical application of the vision in civics, planning, and strategies of social reconstruction, uncovering its foundations in ideas of spiritual renewal. In the first chapters we place their work in its international context and we document the little-known biographies of Victor Branford and Sybella Gurney, key collaborators, promoters, and publicists for Patrick Geddes. Crucial to their mission was Branford's view of sociology as an omnibus discipline: the greatest of the social sciences and embracing much of what others considered to be geography, urban planning, economics, and political science.

Branford and Geddes lived and worked in a period when there were very few established chairs in the social sciences, and when sociology was an incipient field, rather than an established academic discipline. Most of the members of the Sociological Society were gentleman-scholars, rather than professional academics, and only a few women were present and involved. The gentleman-scholars were also involved in business, politics and religion, and they often had ties to several formative academic disciplines. They divided their time among a range of different activities, they often funded scholarly activities from their own businesses, and some of the businessmen generously funded impecunious colleagues so that they could continue their intellectual and civic pursuits. Geddes's own career was based largely on his ability to attract followers, donors, and colleagues willing to bail him out financially and to support the publication of his work. Branford's career was largely based on his rather humble origins, his ambition to make money, and his dedication to write, organize, and spend money to promote Geddes's vision.

The early-twentieth-century businessmen associated with the emergence of British sociology tended to work closely together, both in the pursuit of profits and in the pursuit of their intellectual interests. They had strong links with merchant banking, the armed forces, and colonial service, and they relied heavily on social networks, social standing, and personal relationships. In such circumstances, an understanding of the development of sociology as an academic discipline requires a substantial amount of research on business networks. Our discussion of the emergence of British sociology and its links to the schools of sociology emerging in other parts of the world is based on our exploration of business, social, and intellectual networks, and on global patterns of trade, migration, and investment.

ONE

VICTORIAN AND EDWARDIAN SOCIOLOGY

The nineteenth century was a period of massive intellectual change. In both the United States and Europe there was a renewed awareness of the centrality of the "social" and the "cultural" in explanations of individual human behavior. New approaches emerged with a shared concern for establishing rigorous "scientific" methods in the study of social phenomena. Their proponents forged the new university disciplines of economics, geography, anthropology, psychology, and sociology, and they became involved in building a professional infrastructure of journals and associations to sustain this intellectual work. They inspired scientifically informed practices of social change through planning and social reconstruction. It is for these reasons that the last third of the nineteenth century and the first two decades of the twentieth century have been characterized as the "classical" period of the social sciences.

Patrick Geddes and his circle were among those in Britain who contributed to the development of classical sociology. In this chapter we will set out the intellectual and professional context in which they made these contributions, setting the scene for our consideration of their personal and business relations in chapters 2 and 3 and their own intellectual concerns in the remainder of the book.

STATISTICAL SOCIAL RESEARCH

Although a number of the leading social thinkers of the nineteenth century used ethnographic and statistical data in their theoretical reflections, few were engaged in systematic data collection and analysis. There was, however, a parallel development of statistical survey work, undertaken in isolation from theoretical reflection and providing an independent source for a disciplinary sociology.

The earliest attempts at systematic survey work occurred in France and were undertaken in close association with economic investigations into national wealth and resources. Quesnay's *Tableau Économique* (1758) set out a comprehensive model of the relations between production, distribution, and national wealth, and Quetelet (1848) explored the systematic "laws" of association among empirical measures of these. Over the nineteenth century a stream of works on "moral statistics"—statistics on crime and other social problems—were produced and yielded the empirical basis for such studies as that of Durkheim (1897) on suicide. In a different vein, Le Play collected information on household budgets and expenditure as a way of correlating environmental conditions with customary practices.

In Britain, early empirical surveys had been undertaken by Sir John Sinclair and Sir Frederick Eden, who used the clergy as respondents for their *Statistical Account of Scotland* (Sinclair 1791–92) and *The State of the Poor* (Eden 1797). These surveys preceded the work of Quetelet but had little long-term influence on intellectual life.[1] Together with the population theories and predictions of Malthus (1798), however, they led to the establishment of a regular population census that was to be carried out every ten years from 1801. Political economists began to make use of census data alongside Treasury data on financial resources but found the available statistics rather limited and many advocated more systematic data collection along the lines proposed by Quetelet.

The bases for this work of data collection were the local statistical societies, the earliest of which was formed in Manchester in 1833 (Ashton 1934; Abrams 1968).The following year the Statistical Society of London was formed by the British Association and similar societies were formed in Birmingham, Bristol, Glasgow, Leeds, Liverpool, and other major cities. Oriented to investigation into social conditions and such "social problems" as poverty, wages, education, crime, and family disorganization, the social statisticians undertook house-to-house enquiries using rudimentary questionnaires. Much of this statistical work was purely descriptive, but there were some attempts at explanation. A major area in which such explanatory work was undertaken was the investigation of the effects of climate and of employment on health. Edwin Chadwick, a member of the London society, produced data on health and social conditions that informed his reports for the Poor Law Commissioners. William Farr was also a member and ensured that the society's work influenced the development of government statistics on health and the development of the population census. By the end of the 1840s, however, the statistical societies were largely moribund, their purposes seemingly made irrelevant by an improvement in economic and social conditions and a growing reliance on benevolent action on the part of employers: the "Two Nations" depicted by Disraeli (1845) were seen as divided by culture and attitudes rather than by structural economic conditions.

The 1850s and '60s saw a growing involvement of professional expertise in the public policy of an increasingly, but incompletely, bureaucratized state. The National Association for the Promotion of Social Science (the SSA) was formed in 1857 as a discussion forum on the uses of social research in national and local government policy and administration, its proponents aiming to build an informed public opinion and to channel this influence into parliamentary considerations (Goldman 2002, 14–16). The SSA was based on the view that scientific knowledge is empirical knowledge that provides the basis for social reform. Such an approach embodied a positivism of the type espoused by Comte, though this was seen by its members as involving an exclusively statistical—and not theoretical—knowledge (Goldman 2002, ch. 10). The formation of the SSA paralleled similar moves elsewhere, most notably the European (though largely Franco-Belgian) society formed in Brussels in 1862, the American Social Science Association formed in 1865, and the German *Verein für Sozialpolitik* formed in 1872. The SSA maintained close links with various local statistical societies, including the Statistical Society of London (later the Royal Statistical Society), though a proposed merger never came off. The association sponsored and supported a number of investigations, reporting these at conferences and in its journals and *Transactions*.

The prime movers in the SSA were Benthamite liberal politicians, civil servants, businessmen, and social reformers. Apart from limited contacts with Mill and Spencer, the only sociologist to have any significant contact with the SSA was Le Play. Absent or weakly represented were academics other than a few political economists. Goldman (2002, 341–42) has suggested that the practical success of the SSA meant that its leadership felt no pressing need to establish a university discipline to take forward its aims. In France, Germany, and the United States, on the other hand, the social science associations were relatively unsuccessful in establishing liberal agendas and the impetus toward the building of a university discipline of sociology was correspondingly greater.

Awareness of the social problem of class was reflected in a growing literature of social exploration in which ethnographic observation and interviews largely replaced statistical concerns. The journalist Henry Mayhew had undertaken a number of investigations into work and street life for the *Morning Chronicle* in the late 1840s (Mayhew 1849–50; and see Mayhew 1861), but the principal example of this style of research was the radical Marxist study carried out by Engels (1845) on the streets of Salford and Manchester. Where Engels explained working-class demoralization in terms of the economic contradictions of the mode of production under which they live, other social explorers saw demoralization as a moral failure on the part of the workers themselves (Mearns 1883; W. Booth 1890). Mayhew, however, interviewed many of the London poor and aimed to exhibit in his reports the consequences of employment conditions for the moral outlook and way of life followed.

It was this literature of social exploration that lay behind the growth of laborism and socialism in Britain from the 1880s: the SDF, Socialist League, and Fabian Society were all formed in 1884, and the Independent Labour Party was formed in 1893. Discussion in radical circles had stressed the salience of economic conditions and had decried the extent of the poverty that had been allowed to develop in the major cities. The American radical Henry George claimed that a massive proportion of the London population was living in poverty and his view had been taken up in radical circles as an argument for state action to address the problem of poverty. Charles Booth, a Conservative businessman from Liverpool, seriously questioned George's claim and went on to undertake the greatest of the nineteenth-century surveys, concluding, paradoxically, that George had understated the true extent of poverty.

Booth adopted the quantitative methods of the early statistical societies and combined these with the ethnographic methods of Mayhew for his investigation into the extent of London poverty and the causes of its existence (Bulmer 1991a). Beginning with an investigation of East London, he moved on to a comprehensive survey of the whole of London that he published in seventeen volumes (C. Booth 1901–02). His analysis employed a scheme of social classes, defined by the type of work and level of income of their members, and he showed that poverty was to be found in the bottom four classes of the distribution. Although he showed that only just over 8 percent of the population were "very poor," the true extent of poverty was estimated at more than 30 percent. Poverty, he argued, was produced by a combination of disadvantaged economic conditions (low pay, unemployment, and casual employment) and improvident habits. His survey went beyond poverty itself into a huge investigation of work conditions and community life that emulated and advanced upon the principles advocated by Le Play. The influence of Le Play was greatest, however, in a subsequent survey of York undertaken by Seebohm Rowntree (1901) in which household budget data were collected as a way of directly investigating the consumption and savings habits of ordinary working and nonworking families.

THE INTERNATIONAL DEVELOPMENT OF SOCIAL THEORY

Sociology as a theoretically grounded discipline developed most comprehensively in France and Germany and, toward the end of the nineteenth century, in the United States. Each country had its distinctive traditions of social thought, yet social theorists and researchers engaged in a growing international interchange of ideas. Globally, sociology existed as overlapping circles of intellectual concerns, and the sociology that developed in the United States was especially marked by the influence of French and German ideas as well as those that had developed in Britain.

Social thought in nineteenth-century France had its roots in the ideas of Montesquieu, Rousseau, and the Enlightenment encyclopedists. Though strongly influenced by English ideas on the political and intellectual importance of individual freedom, their main concern had been with the origins and character of specifically "social" phenomena. They saw inherited customs and material environmental conditions as the key determinants of individual actions and explored the ways in which action produced and was shaped by legal institutions and the social division of labor. Conservative theorists such as De Bonald and De Maistre set out an account of the "moral constraint" that social institutions exercise over individuals. Henri de Saint-Simon and then Auguste Comte took up this idea of the distinctiveness and autonomy of "social facts" and proposed a new science to study them. This science—to which Comte gave the newly coined name of "Sociology"—was to provide the knowledge and understanding that would make it possible to predict social trends and so to engage in a rational reconstruction of society through enhancing social harmony and establishing a universal brotherhood of humanity.

Emile Durkheim took up this program and established sociology as an intellectual discipline at the heart of the French educational system. Drawing especially on Montesquieu (Durkheim 1892), he explored the division of labor (1893) and individual acts of suicide (1897) from a sociological point of view, and he set out the principles of scientific method (1895) needed in undertaking social studies. His most important work was, arguably, his influential study of the origins of moral values and intellectual ideas in socially organized religious practices (1912). Other thinkers in France had explored the social dimensions of human activity (Espinas 1877; Worms 1896; Tarde 1890) and some had begun to construct a new discipline of geography to explore the effects of material conditions (see the later systematizations in Vidal de la Blache 1922; Febvre 1922), but it was Durkheim's advocacy of the Comtean vision that dominated French thought. Working closely with his nephew Marcel Mauss (Durkheim and Mauss 1903; Mauss 1902, 1904–05, 1925), and with François Simiand and others, he founded a professional journal—the *Année Sociologique*—in 1896, established sociological ideas in the training of school teachers, and, in 1913, became the holder, at Bordeaux, of the key chair in sociology.

German social theory originated in the intellectual innovations of Immanuel Kant (1784), Johann Herder (1784–91), and, above all, Georg

Hegel (1821, 1831). Hegel held that social phenomena could be understood as complexes of ideas that provide the meanings that individuals give to their actions. He set out a theory of society and of history as the continual development of a social purpose through ever more universal stages: from familism through civil society to the nation-state. Wilhelm Dilthey (1883) spelled out the implications of this point of view for the development of the specifically "cultural sciences" emerging as the geography and "folk psychology" of Adolph Bastian (1881), Friedrich Ratzel (1882–91), and Wilhelm Wundt (1912). It was in the hands of Ferdinand Tönnies (1889), Werner Sombart (1902), and Max Weber (see, inter alia, 1904, 1904–05) that there was a specifically "sociological" implementation of this view. Their work focused on the forms and types of social relations in and through which individual actions are able to produce large-scale historical transformations, and they formed in 1910 a German Sociological Society (see Adair-Toteff 2005) as the vehicle through which they could develop an empirically oriented approach to social life. The first chair in the subject, to which Franz Oppenheimer was appointed, was established at Frankfurt in 1918, and Max Weber was given a chair in the subject, at Munich, later that same year.

The socialist movements of Europe were bases for approaches to social theory that were French and German in origin but, by the late nineteenth century, had an international character. The early forms of socialism associated with Charles Fourier and Robert Owen had been transformed by Karl Marx and Friedrich Engels (1848) into a politically grounded social theory of economic life. Though this rarely went under the name of sociology (but see Bukharin 1921), it had a significant influence on the work undertaken in the emerging departments of economics, politics, history, and sociology across the world. Marxism served as a critical foil for much of the work of Weber and as a specifically political doctrine, Marxism shaped most forms of late-nineteenth-century and early-twentieth-century social theory.

The earliest expressions of social thought in the United States drew on ideas from Adam Smith, Montesquieu, and Herder, but systematic statements of social theory first developed in opposition to this liberal mainstream among defenders of the slaveholding system of the South. Henry Hughes (1854) and George Fitzhugh (1854) adapted Comte's sociology to present a view of economic mechanisms as embedded in larger "organic" structures of custom and social solidarity. By contrast, Henry Carey constructed a more materialistic model of human action in which he drew on the work of Friedrich List (1841) to set out a view of social action as the outcome of the forces of attraction generated by the motions of individuals (Carey 1858–59, 1872). Somewhat later, Lester Ward (1883) returned to Comtean ideas and developed an account of the growth of rational social planning. This general approach influenced the theory of patriarchal gender divisions produced by Charlotte Gilman (1898, 1911), though this never received mainstream attention. Sociology was established as a university discipline in the 1870s by William Sumner at Yale, the main influences on his evolutionary theory of the structuring of social inequalities (Sumner 1883) being Harriet Martineau and Herbert Spencer. He later developed this into a theory of the constraining power of customs and "folkways" (Sumner 1906).

It was, however, the establishment in the early 1890s of graduate and research departments at Chicago and Columbia that really established sociology as a professional discipline in the United States. Albion Small was appointed as head of the new department at Chicago, recruiting Charles Zueblin as an extension lecturer, and George Vincent (a key figure in the Chautauqua summer schools), as co-writer for some of his texts. Small brought to Chicago a number of thinkers who began to elaborate a distinctive set of theoretical ideas that they took from contemporary German sociology. John Dewey and George Mead developed a specifically social dimension to the psychology of William James (1890), stressing the interactional basis of self-formation. While systematized only much later (Dewey 1922; Mead 1927), their ideas influenced the sociological work of William Thomas (Thomas and Znaniecki 1918–19) and became the basis of what Herbert Blumer (1937) was to describe as "symbolic interactionism." Empirical work on the city of Chicago itself led to the development of a specifically "ecological" perspective on urban processes that prospered after the appointment of Robert Park in 1914 and was undertaken in conjunction with the geographical work of Ellen Semple (1911) and the ecological studies of Harlan Barrows (1923).

Outside Chicago, Franklin Giddings (1896) developed a distinctive subjectivist approach at Columbia and sponsored quantitative work that he aligned with the work of the New York Charity Organization Society. A major influence on sociology at Wisconsin was Thorstein Veblen, who had taught economics at Chicago from 1892 to 1906 and was one of the few American sociologists influenced by Marx's social theory. At Wisconsin, however, it was German formal sociology that was the principal influence (Ross 1901, 1920; Wiese-Becker 1932).

Small was the central figure in the institutional organization of American sociology. He started the *American Journal of Sociology* in 1895 and used it not only to present the work of his fellow Chicago sociologists but also to make available translations of key works in European sociology. The American Sociological Society was formed in 1905, having formerly been a section of the American Economics Association. This was explicitly intended as an academic association of teachers and researchers, unlike the earlier National Social Science Association, which had been an association of clergy and social reformers interested in the empirical study of "social problems" and social welfare. The close association, at the heart of professional sociology, of the *AJS* and the ASS with the Chicago department lasted until the 1930s.[2]

VISIONS OF SOCIAL RECONSTRUCTION

For many of the late-nineteenth and early-twentieth-century social scientists, the development of social theory was interwoven with an idealistic vision of social reconstruction. They saw this reconstruction as a comprehensive rebuilding of society, requiring the rejection of violence and revolution, the promotion of mass education and participation, and the recognition that social inequalities should be reduced in order to create a broader climate of fairness and opportunity. Reconstruction was to be a grassroots process, based on a growth of awareness, knowledge, and culture through lifelong education and the emergence of a new spirituality. It assumed that all social changes are interdependent and that a truly positive transformation of society would require the consent and involvement of millions of people inspired by education and a vision of a better future.

The roots of this reconstructionism lay in Comtean sociology and the social gospel of the Protestant churches. Among the Comtean theorists and researchers, sociology was seen as providing the theoretical knowledge and understanding that could guide informed social interaction and planning. The predictive capacity of social science was the basis of effective and informed social change. Where Marxists saw social change occurring through revolutionary action, the Comteans saw it as a gradual process led by an informed and enlightened elite. The social gospel inspired a more practical and reformist approach to social reconstruction. Ministers, theologians, and social activists such as Walter Rauschenbusch (1907, 1917) in New York, Jane Addams in Chicago, and Samuel and Henrietta Barnett in London emphasized the moral duty of the middle and upper classes to give charitable donations and to volunteer their labor to educate, train, and support the socially disadvantaged. The most immediate products of their efforts were lay outreach programs such as the YMCA, the Salvation Army, and the settlement house movement, but they linked to much wider movements in arts and crafts, garden cities, cooperatives, and alternative education. Most of the reconstructionists were middle-class visionaries seeking a peaceful middle ground between the opposing ideologies of capitalism and communism, working to build a society free from both exploitation and revolution. The reconstructionists could easily be caricatured as naive idealists, "do-gooders," and "busybodies," but many of the institutions that they were associated with still continue. Typically they advocated social outreach to urban slums and impoverished rural communities, cooperatives, arts exhibitions and performances, handicrafts, credit unions, community development, participatory and lifelong learning, volunteerism, civic activism, grassroots democracy, and the growth of a range of nonprofit organizations. Albion Small was especially interested in the practical applications of sociology, and he worked closely with Jane Addams and her Hull House settlements. He made applied sociology and social work an integral part of the Department of Sociology at the University of Chicago until the formation of a separate School of Civics and Philanthropy in 1904. Social reconstruction was seen as a "third way," neither capitalist nor communist, based on social mobilization and community solidarity.

Comtism, Protestantism, the social gospel, and the Christian socialist movement formed the mainstream of social reconstructionism, but this political orientation was inspired also by other religious movements, one Catholic and the other interreligious. In 1893, with the encyclical *Rerum Novarum*, Pope Leo XIII initiated the social doctrine of the Catholic Church, a call for peace, harmony, and redistribution between rich and poor and between capital and labor. *Rerum Novarum* sought to place national governments at the center of the political process, arbitrating between organized capital and organized labor and persuading both sides to moderate their demands, support humane living and working conditions, engage in collective bargaining, and reach nonviolent compromise. It was a reaction to the rise of communism and militant trade unionism, to the growth of social inequalities, and to the brutal repression of striking and demonstrating workers and peasants. Along with social gospel thinking and the rise of social democracy and political movements such as the Fabian socialists, it laid the basis for twentieth-century welfare states with labor legislation, old-age pensions, disability benefits, and other support systems.

The interreligious current reflected the growing fascination of Western intellectuals with Eastern religions. This was most notable with Buddhism and Hinduism, both of which originated in South Asia, but was also apparent in much newer ideals such as Theosophy, which originated in New York but offered a form of Eastern enlightenment, and the Bahá'í religion that originated in Iran. Typically the Western devotees did not undergo a complete religious conversion. Instead, they opted for meditation and yoga, and for the argument that all great religions ultimately embody the same moral principles and worship the same divine spirit. Many of the figures associated with reconstructionism interacted frequently with Annie Besant and other Theosophists, with Israel Zangwill and other Zionists, and with Rabindranath Tagore, Swami Vivekananda, and other Hindu visionaries.

Social reconstructionism was fundamentally a lay movement drawing on an eclectic set of religious traditions. Many of its adherents were not frequent churchgoers, and some had largely abandoned conventional Christianity. What united the movement was its profound idealism, its internationalism, and its search for fundamental social changes that could forever end the prospects of war and violent revolution. Its advocates referred very often simply to "reconstruction" rather than to "social reconstruction," but their thinking had little to do with reconstructing the physical fabric. Instead, they focused on developing ideas to change socioeconomic and political systems to create permanent conditions of peace, social harmony, and prosperity.

Sociology in Britain developed in parallel with these international trends and in conjunction with statistical, empirical work. Many of the earliest strands in British social theory had influenced the direction taken by social theoreticians in France, Germany, and the United States, and they continued to exercise an influence throughout the nineteenth century. Later developments in British social theory took place through dialogue with the key figures involved in the establishment of sociology elsewhere.

ECONOMIC INDIVIDUALISM AND SOCIAL ACTION

The dominant strand in nineteenth-century British social thought had its origins in the individualistic theories of the seventeenth and eighteenth centuries. Thomas Hobbes and John Locke had laid the foundations for this later work in their philosophical reflections on knowledge, reason, and individual liberty from state interference. The leading figures in the Scottish Enlightenment of the eighteenth century—David Hume, Adam Ferguson, John Millar, Dugald Stewart, and Adam Smith—explored the interplay of rationality and emotion in human action and applied these ideas to construct theories of the historical development of economic exchange, private property, division of labor, and class formation. This work took a more analytical turn under the influence of Jeremy Bentham and resulted in the political economy of David Ricardo (1817), Thomas Malthus (1820), and James Mill (1821). This "utilitarian" economics was based on the assumption that social activities could be explained in terms of individualistic, rational, and calculative actions. Social relations, and most particularly those of the economy, were seen as the outcomes of processes of social exchange among rationally motivated individual agents, each of whom is orientated by calculations of the possible "utility" to be derived from alternative courses of action.

The earliest attempt to broaden this political economy into a more general theory of social life was that of Harriet Martineau. On the basis of her reading of the early ideas of Comte, which she later presented in a summary translation (1853), she sought to unite Comte's "positive" methodology for the social sciences with utilitarian economic ideas (Martineau 1831).

She was among the first of the social scientists to undertake theoretically informed empirical research, investigating structures of social inequality and the divisions of gender and ethnicity. Reflecting on her investigations into social inequalities in American society, she produced a textbook on methods of social research (Martineau 1838; on the basis of Martineau 1837). Somewhat later, Henry Sidgwick (1891) took utilitarian theory into the sphere of political analysis that had initially concerned Bentham (see Bentham 1789).

John Stuart Mill (1865) undertook a deeper philosophical investigation into Comte's methodology. Though he was critical of Comte's own theoretical conclusions, Mill began to construct a sociological theory that recognized cultural diversity but retained a strong individualistic foundation. Mill (1848) saw this view of the social as complementing the economic analysis that he had derived from the earlier work of his father. This theory was, however, only partly developed (Mill 1869). The associationist psychology of Locke held that the ideas, feelings, and sensations that make up the mental worlds of individuals are "associated" with one another through the frequency and recency with which they have been experienced, their similarity to one another, and the implications that they suggest (see Flugel 1933, chs. 2.2 and 3.5; Hearnshaw 1964, ch. 9). James Mill, as a principal advocate of this position, had seen pleasure and pain as mechanisms through which psychological elements become associated with each other. This view had already begun to be abandoned by the early nineteenth century, and John Mill's *Logic of the Moral Sciences* (Mill 1843) was influential in moving psychology away from this cognitive and purely intellectualist basis. His concern was to uncover the motivational factors generating economic and political actions and to recognize the importance of "will," emotion, and purpose in motivating the individual actions that drive social development.

Despite its concern for the moral justifications offered for political regulation and individual liberty, the individualistic approach was largely limited to the abstract analysis of economic activity. It was in this area that Stanley Jevons (1871) and Alfred Marshall (1890) set out ideas that made Britain a leading player in the international development of microeconomic theory. Despite the early promptings of Martineau, it was not until Maynard Keynes (1936) that economic thought adopted more systemic ideas about macrolevel social phenomena.

Comte's work, however, had taken a broader approach than British individualism and he rejected all claims for the foundational status of individual psychology in the social sciences. His argument that societies comprised social systems with distinctive, emergent properties that had to be explained in social terms was developed in Britain outside the framework of mainstream political economy.

SOCIOLOGY AND SOCIAL EVOLUTION

Herbert Spencer was the British theorist who most clearly carried forward Comte's aspiration for a distinctively *social* form of theorizing.[3] Though he was critical of many aspects of Comte's work, and he vehemently denied all suggestions that he was a mere disciple of Comte, Spencer formulated a theory of the structure and development of whole societies. Individual action remained a central element in this theory, but he was the first British writer to properly recognize the power of social phenomena to constrain individual actions. So important and distinctive was Spencer's theory that it rapidly superseded in influence that of Comte, and it was taken up enthusiastically in the United States, in much of Europe, and in the Far East.

Spencer set out a systematic body of comparative and historical ideas that integrated social theory with a mass of empirical data on a wide variety of societies and traced social development from its most "primitive" to its most complex forms (Spencer 1873, 1873–93). Social structures, he argued, must be treated as autonomous and distinctively social facts that are formed through the linguistically mediated interactions that connect individuals with each other. As "social organisms" or social systems, they exhibit a pattern of development or structural change that Spencer referred to as "evolution," though his emphasis on internal, endogenous processes of development was somewhat at variance with the emerging evolutionary theories of Charles Darwin. Spencer saw social evolution as the outcome of a continual struggle for survival among social groups and their individual members. Competition, conflict, and struggle, he argued, are the driving forces in this social development.

The development of a social organism was seen by Spencer as a process of "growth" analogous to the growth of a plant from its seed. It is through growth that specialized "organs" come to be differentiated from the remainder of the social body, much as such physiological organs as the heart and lungs are formed when a human body develops from its embryonic to its infant stage. In the social organism, organs such as markets, churches, states, families, and so on each come to be regulated by specialized social institutions as a generalized structure of customs gives way to a more differentiated normative structure. At the level of the social organism as a whole, development is apparent as distinct "stages" of relative backwardness and advance. Thus, contemporary societies, Spencer argued, had evolved from earlier and more sharply stratified societies that adopted a "militant" orientation in their dealings with their individual members and with other societies. Centralized states play a key role in such societies. The modern social forms that developed from these primitive forms, he held, are "industrial" societies that have a greater degree of social equality and more pacific or civil forms of regulation. Social solidarity in these societies is organized around individual citizenship rights and contractual relations that limit the powers of governments. Thus, the individualistic theories of political economy are particularly appropriate for the analysis of the highly differentiated spheres of economic and political activity found in industrial societies, but less so for studying the social institutions in which they are embedded.

Similar evolutionary accounts were proposed by anthropologists Sir Edward Tylor (1871) and Sir James Frazer (1890). Using evidence from the growing number of travel and missionary reports on "primitive" societies, they recognized an underlying similarity in human nature, which they saw as responsible for similarities of cultural development found in all societies. Spencer relied on a Lamarckian view according to which culture is the repository of acquired knowledge and capacities. Tylor and Frazer, however, remained close to Darwin and recognized the importance of selection processes in determining the outcomes of historical change. They highlighted certain common or universal constraints and conditions under which evolution occurs and concluded that the environmental selection of cultural traits leads all societies to pass through a similar sequence of evolutionary stages. Social development, they held, has run from stone age "savagery" to metal age "barbarism" and, eventually, to the "civilized" stage of advanced productive technology (see also Lubbock 1865, 1870).

A further distinctive twist to evolutionary theory was given by Benjamin Kidd, a self-educated amateur who was fascinated by developments in biology and became a convinced Darwinist.[4] His *Social Evolution* (1894; see also 1898) became a massive best-seller—more influential even than the works of Spencer—and he was invited to write the keynote entry on "Sociology" for the 1902 edition of the *Encyclopaedia Britannica*. Critical of Spencer's reliance on the inheritance of acquired characteristics, Kidd gave even greater emphasis to conflict and struggle than had Spencer. It is, he argued, the struggles among "solidaristic" and internally altruistic social groups that shape overall social development. The members of social groups that build a collective consciousness and institutionalize social solidarity will act altruistically toward each other but will tend to come into conflict with rival social groups. The clash between groups is the mechanism through which occurs the natural selection of cultural traits that give competitive advantages in group struggle.

Kidd saw the rise of Western civilization and its contemporary ideals of collective welfare and social obligation as resulting from the extended solidarity consequent upon the adoption of Christianity. The declining influence of religion in the contemporary Western world, he argued, had weakened social solidarity and was, as a result, increasing individualistic self-interest at the expense of altruism. Kidd rejected the socialist solutions of collective regulation through a powerful centralized state and advocated, instead, a renewal of Christian religion as a means of collective regeneration.

IDEALIST STRANDS IN BRITISH SOCIAL THEORY

By the early twentieth century, a broadly evolutionary or developmental approach had become the dominant form of social theory in Britain. Its implications were pursued, however, in a number of different directions, both idealist and materialist. Idealist interpretations of Spencer's arguments were pursued in the philosophical works of Edward Caird, David Ritchie, and Henry Jones. These writers drew heavily on the German idealism that the political philosopher T. H. Green (1879) had made the basis for a "New Liberalism," but they were particularly inspired by Hegel's social philosophy. They reinterpreted Spencer's concept of the social organism to emphasize the ideal or "spiritual" character of social processes. Where Spencer saw social organisms as constructed from calculative individual acts, the British Hegelians held that the spiritual or cultural integrity of social phenomena was a precondition for these individual actions (Jones 1883).

The most important social theorist to develop this argument was Bernard Bosanquet (1897, 1899), who held that the structure of a society must be seen as comprising webs of communication and interdependence through which individuals are connected into systemic social wholes and within which individual personalities and state activities are formed. The "social inheritance" of a society—its system of culture and social institutions—comprises the shared ideas that sustain social solidarity but are held within individual minds. The individual self is formed through socialization into the cultural heritage. There is, therefore, a "social mind" that exists as a dispersed system of cultural meanings and shared knowledge and is maintained in existence through the communicative acts of socialized individuals. Through this communicative interaction a "general will" can be formed as the basis of the social integration and role behavior of the individual members of a society.[5]

On this basis, the idealists explored the social character of modernity. While all societies that persist must maintain their cultural unity, they noted a decline in traditional solidarities and the slow and partial emergence of new forms of social solidarity in contemporary industrial societies. These new solidarities are not yet fully developed and industrial societies are marked by a breakdown of group solidarities that leaves individuals unrooted and disordered. Thus, the growing individualism of civil society and its associational forms of relationship is not a result of the decline of religion per se, as Kidd had argued. It is, rather, a result of the decay of the traditional solidarities that underpinned the organic communities of preindustrial societies. The task of social policy, the idealists held, is to devise new bases of solidarity appropriate to contemporary industrialism.

They further agreed that in an industrial society the reciprocal interdependence of one individual upon another in a social division of labor is based on individual rights of citizenship and on the corresponding obligations toward others. The idealists saw it as the task of social reform to ensure that state action promotes and enhances these individual rights and obligations (Ritchie 1895; Bradley 1876). Correspondingly, social theory had to explore the contribution that individual citizens can make to social welfare by uncovering the principles of the "social good" that underpin social reform and social work (Jones 1910, 1919). The forms of social intervention and social work that these theoreticians sought to institutionalize were embodied in the work of the London-based Charity Organisation Society (COS). Formed to undertake social service and to provide a proper professional training for social workers, the COS became an instrument for the application of Bosanquet's ideas through a "School of Sociology" at the London School of Economics. Bosanquet's wife, Helen, drew on his theory in her own more empirical studies of inequality, family relations, and community (H. Bosanquet 1898, 1902, 1906) and made these the basis for the novel casework methods that she introduced into the social work of the COS.

The idealist social theorists had a substantial and continuing influence within British sociology and social policy, though their direct influence gradually diminished over time. Their lasting influence was on the philosopher and historian Robin Collingwood's work on Roman society (Collingwood 1923) and Sir Edward Evans-Pritchard's (1937, 1940) interpretation of his fieldwork on the Azande and the Nuer of East Africa.[6]

MATERIALIST STRANDS IN BRITISH SOCIAL THEORIES

The idealist theorists were concerned with the cultural systems of meaning that constituted the structures of social organisms, but a number of materialist theorists focused on the structural conditions themselves and their relations to the material environment. Having many affinities with the political economists, they recognized the autonomy of economic relations from individual actions and examined their interdependence with cultural factors in forming social wholes.

Marxism had far less impact on socialist thought in Britain than it had in France and Germany, and British socialism was strongly rooted in the cooperative tradition of Robert Owen and the communitarian and ecological ideas of John Ruskin and William Morris. Morris, along with Eleanor Marx and other radical socialists, had split from Henry Hyndman's Social Democratic Federation to form the Socialist League in which the ideas of Marx and Ruskin could be fused. This same fusion was apparent in the Fabian Society, whose members included Edward Carpenter, Edward Pease, Hubert Bland, and, a little later, George Bernard Shaw.[7] Fabian membership later grew to include Annie Besant, Graham Wallas, Sydney Olivier, and Sidney Webb.[8] Politically, the society's members were radical Liberals who sought to build a progressive block within the Liberal Party, though its membership also included the Labourite politicians Tom Mann, John Burns, and Ben Tillett and the suffragist Emmeline Pankhurst.

Sidney Webb, the leading figure in the society, met Beatrice Potter in 1890. Potter—soon to become Beatrice Webb—had close family friendships with both Spencer and the Comtean writer Frederick Harrison, and she had worked with her cousin Charles Booth during his research into East End poverty. Her strong intellectual interests in the cooperative movement and its contribution to social change were brought into the Fabian Society. Influenced by Harrison's (1877) interpretation of Comte, however, the Webbs took the view that social policy had to be devised by an elite of administrators armed with a scientific knowledge of relevant facts gained through social research.

A Marx study group was formed within the Fabian Society with a view to formulating a non-Marxist socialism that, nevertheless, took seriously the principal elements in Marxist economic theory. While the society recognized the importance of class divisions in contemporary capitalism, the labor theory of value was rejected in favor of a rent-based theory of exploitation.[9] The influential *Fabian Essays in Socialism* (Olivier 1889) was the first outcome of these discussions and set out the key elements of a non-Marxist social theory of material life in which the growing market power of industrial and financial monopolies within the economy was seen as associated with a growing polarization of social classes.

The London School of Economics and Political Science (LSE) was formed as a Fabian organization in 1895, the Webbs seeing it as the most effective way of advancing the society's theoretical and empirical work.[10] The School organized lectures in economics, statistics, commerce, and political science. It hosted the COS lectures in sociology and soon set up its own department in the subject. Many of its lecturers developed the Fabian interpretation of Marxist theory, and the most important Marxist-inspired work in later years was that of Harold Laski (see, for example, Laski 1919).[11]

TOWARD A TWENTIETH-CENTURY MAINSTREAM

Idealist and materialist theories vied for intellectual influence in the emerging British social sciences of the twentieth century, and Geddes and Branford brought them together within their Sociological Society. These intellectual differences were the subject of lively debate in the society and helped to shape the sociological ideas that Geddes and Branford themselves developed. When a department of sociology came to be properly established at the LSE, however, it was Leonard Hobhouse who was appointed to the chair. Hobhouse produced a powerful form of evolutionism that showed strong influences from both the idealists and the Fabians, and it was his theory that became the basis of the dominant intellectual framework for British sociology through much of the first half of the twentieth century.

Hobhouse studied and taught philosophy at Oxford, working in an environment dominated by the Hegelian thought that helped to shape his major study in the philosophy of knowledge (Hobhouse 1896). Through his involvement in labor politics and the work of the Fabian Society, he produced an early study of the labor movement (Hobhouse 1893) and became convinced of the need for tighter links between trades unions, cooperatives, and municipal organizations. Resigning from Oxford to take up political journalism, he continued to work on theoretical issues and produced a major statement of evolutionary psychology (Hobhouse 1901). Following an invitation to lecture on political science at the LSE, Hobhouse began work on a comparative sociology of mental development through a critical engagement with the work of the idealist social theorists at Oxford (Hobhouse 1906). On the strength of this work he was appointed to the new LSE chair of sociology in 1907.

Hobhouse developed a distinctive understanding of the social world as a network of interacting and communicating individuals who sustain relatively fixed and autonomous structures of relations through the "social mind" that is brought into being by their communication. Like Bosanquet, he recognized that this social mentality is not an actual entity that exists separately from the individual members of a society but is a network of communicated ideas and meanings contained in and circulating among individual minds. Central to the social mind are the "rules" that comprise the major social institutions—the normative factors that regulate social interactions. A population that shares a set of rules is a community, and these rules are embodied in its customs and laws. Simple, undifferentiated societies are organized through a single, cohesive system of rules, but socially differentiated communities are formed into distinct clusters of social institutions that regulate each specialized sphere of activity.

Hobhouse saw social entities developing over time according to definite evolutionary principles. The natural selection of rules and ideas ensures the integration of societies as ongoing organisms and is the basis of their long-term transformation. At a global level, he depicted a general evolution from simple kinship-based societies, through "civilized" societies with centralized, authoritarian states, to modern "civic" societies based around individual principles of citizenship (Hobhouse 1924; see also Hobhouse et al. 1914). Individual citizenship rights are means to social improvement, and Hobhouse saw them as the basis for a new and reconstructed liberalism (Hobhouse 1911).

This view of the evolutionary development of liberal citizenship was a major influence on his colleague Richard Tawney (1921) and was later taken up by Thomas H. Marshall as the basis of his own influential account of citizenship rights (Marshall 1949). Through Marshall, this has continued to influence work in the area of migration, rights, welfare, and citizenship. The main disciple of Hobhouse within British sociology, however, was Morris Ginsberg (1921), who devoted himself to promoting the intellectual inheritance of Hobhouse against all perceived challenges. Ginsberg, however, made no real contribution to developing or enlarging Hobhouse's ideas, and he excluded any other approach to sociology from the LSE—the only significant department of sociology in the country through the middle years of the twentieth century.

The pool of ideas from which Hobhouse drew also inspired others to develop related ideas on society and the social mind. Robert MacIver, a lecturer at Aberdeen University and the first British person after Hobhouse to include the word *Sociology* in his job title, was strongly influenced by idealist philosophy and by the new work of Durkheim and Simmel. He produced an important and influential study of community (MacIver 1917) before leaving Britain for Canada and the United States, where he published a short introduction to sociology (MacIver 1921) that popularized and developed the ideas of his earlier book. This book was published first in England, intended for a university extension audience, and was extremely influential in the sociological debates of the 1920s.[12]

Psychologist William McDougall worked on the anthropological expedition to the Torres Straits led by Alfred Haddon and W. H. R. Rivers (see Herle and Rouse 1998). It was this practical exposure to cultural differences that led to him developing a more specifically *social* psychology. His most important work (McDougall 1908) was produced in the same year as a key work by Graham Wallas (1908) on the same subject, and McDougall's attempts to build a social psychology were further developed in a book published shortly before he left Britain to settle in the United States (McDougall 1920).[13]

During the 1920s, two further strands of theory developed from the work of Hobhouse. These carried forward a similar view of the social organism, but rejected his overarching evolutionary approach. A structural sociology akin to that of Durkheim was developed in the work of Rivers (1924) and Alfred Radcliffe-Brown (1922), while Hobhouse's LSE colleague Bronislaw Malinowski (1922) set out a "functionalist" view in which culture played a central part. These approaches had their greatest influence in the new social anthropology departments of Britain and its colonial territories. Their lasting impact was to encourage the reception of American structural functionalism after World War II.

Geddes and Branford worked at the heart of the intellectual debates discussed in this chapter. Of all the British theorists, they had, perhaps, the most extensive international links to their contemporaries in France, Germany, and the United States. They contributed their distinctive perspective to the general intellectual ferment of the time, and they drew on some of its most advanced expressions. They promoted the cause of teaching sociology through the establishment of lectureships and chairs, and their Sociological Society and *Sociological Review* were among the first in the world to be established. We will examine this project in the remainder of this book, beginning with a consideration of their personal backgrounds and connections in chapter 2 and the intellectual networks associated with their work in chapter 3.

TWO

GEDDES, BRANFORD, AND GURNEY

Personal Partnerships

Three sociologists are central to our account of British sociology and policies of social reconstruction. These are Patrick Geddes, Victor Branford, and Sybella Gurney, who developed complex and enduring personal partnerships.[1] Geddes was the dominant intellectual figure of the trio, influencing a whole generation of writers in sociology, geography, urban planning, and biology. Branford was the faithful disciple and proselytizer, initially a "son" and later a "brother" to Geddes, developing his theoretical and political ideas and giving them organizational form in a sociological society. Gurney met Geddes and Branford through her work on cooperative housing and garden cities. She eventually married Branford and contributed substantially to his ideas and to the ongoing development of the Sociological Society. These interpersonal relations solidified Geddes, Branford, and Gurney as the intellectual leaders and organizers of a larger collaborative circle of writers and practical reformers committed to a particular version of sociology and social reconstruction.

In 1932, the year of his death aged seventy-seven, Patrick Geddes remained the energetic and dominating presence that he had been throughout his life. Wiry in build, yet agile and with piercing eyes, he was also somewhat shaggy and disheveled in appearance: due in large part to his beard and his trademark long hair, parted in the middle, both once dark and reddish. His appearance, perhaps deliberately cultivated, was that of the eccentric professor. In lectures and conversation alike he spoke in a continuous and rapid flow that not infrequently became an indistinct mumble as his disquisition turned into active thought and reflection. At other times, carried by his own enthusiasm and passion, he would burst into high volume and electrifying ferocity. Geddes was sociable and outgoing in company and could be both witty and mischievous, though his enthusiasm and intellectual certainty tended to cow, or to alienate, those who disagreed or misunderstood him. He was, however, a charismatic figure, attracting much support and loyalty, and he was surrounded by disciples who were all too willing to proselytize on his behalf and to abase themselves to his needs.

This devotion he received from others was an essential condition for his work. Geddes was himself chaotic and disorganized. He produced a constant stream of ideas, but had neither the inclination nor the discipline to work them out systematically or in detail. A man of enthusiasms, he flitted from one to another and worked on each only so long as he felt that he was contributing some shaping or directive insight. He was invariably interested in the next project rather than the current one, his mind racing ahead to future endeavors, and he left his disciples to undertake the systematic and detailed work that he eschewed for himself. Some of these disciples, as a result, became closely associated with his ideas and innovations, claiming that all they wrote had been derived from or inspired by Geddes. In practical matters—especially financial ones—Geddes would take on commitments or undertake expenditure with little thought for how the costs were to be met or how they were to mesh with other commitments. In these matters, too, he relied on his devoted followers to sort out his practical arrangements and deliver him from disaster: though he rarely acknowledged their role or recognized their efforts as necessary. His commitment to his projects blinded him to the chaos that he frequently caused.

Agnostic about ultimate religious truths, his interest in religious systems was, nevertheless, as enthusiastic as his interest in scientific projects. He had a deep sense of the importance of spirituality to human affairs and of the contribution that the search for spiritual meaning could make to social reconstruction and moral renewal. Thus, he explored the variety of religious systems of the Victorian and Edwardian new age: Theosophy and Bahá'ísm, for example, he saw as active centers of exploration into the nature of human existence in the world.

When Victor Branford had died at sixty-six, just two years before Geddes, he had only recently lost the energy and dynamism that had previously sustained him. He was short—around 5 feet 5 inches—slight in build, with blue-grey eyes, sharp features, and, in his youth, reddish brown hair. He had been left rather frail and delicate by a bout of consumption in his thirties, but was full of energy in all he did. He was regarded by many who met him as Scottish: he had spent twenty-five years of his life there and must have spoken with a noticeable Edinburgh accent. He was nervous and rather shy: feeling tense in public, he smoked and had the habit of fingering his neatly trimmed beard and biting his moustache. Despite his frailty and nervousness, he threw himself wholeheartedly into a series of major ventures.

Branford's nervousness was the result of an enduring sense of insecurity acquired during a childhood in which he learned to apply himself diligently in his work as a way of proving himself to others. Emotionally, he was rather repressed and he exhibited a somewhat stern self-discipline. He came across as dry and hardheaded, and in public he would probably not be mistaken for anything other than the accountant that he was. Despite the tension he felt in public, he was comfortable and confident in business meetings and at meetings of the Sociological Society, where his expertise gave him a great sense of authority.

There was something of a division between Branford's public and domestic demeanor. In the city he conformed to current dress style and wore pinstripes and top hat, while in the country he preferred ragged tweeds. Indeed, he was completely relaxed at home in the country. To friends and houseguests he offered courteous hospitality and could be both witty and relaxed. He was, however, no *bon viveur,* preferring plain and unpretentious fare. The fond nickname used by those close to him, "Veris," was perhaps a play on his middle name, Verasis, that may have reflected both its root meaning of "true" and a love for the spring. He enjoyed country life and, like his father, was an accomplished horseman. He was a good dancer and an effective skater, winning skating competitions even late in life. He enjoyed golf, and his final home was conveniently located with private access to the first hole of the Hastings golf course. He was somewhat frugal in his personal habits: he had the habit of reusing old sheets of notepaper and of cramming his messages onto every spare corner of paper. He was a competent typist for professional matters, but his personal correspondence was written by hand in an almost indecipherable scrawl. In later life he employed both a personal secretary and a typist who worked from an office in his Hastings home.

Branford had an immense attraction to ideas and intellectual concerns and had a lively inner intellectual life. He became animated in scholarly discussions, enthused by intellectual debate far more than by domestic matters or business concerns. His reflection on his accountancy work was concerned more with its intellectual implications than with the practical tasks undertaken. He was, however, far from eloquent in his writing. His poetic and allusive style failed to convey his intellectual insights: indeed, it tended to obscure them. It was as if he felt the need constantly to demonstrate the seriousness and cultural respectability of his arguments, even if this be at the expense of clarity. His intellectual output was also marked by an overdeveloped sense of loyalty to Geddes that reined in his own originality. He tended to present his own insights as mere glosses on those of his mentor and would effusively praise even the trivial or insignificant remarks of the latter. He perhaps transferred to Geddes some of the feelings that he was unable wholeheartedly to express toward his father.

Branford was a rationalist but not a secularist, holding firmly to the importance of the social role of religion. Though he was probably not a believer in the conventional Christian idea of God, he was deeply spiritual and had a great respect for the religious beliefs of others. Espousal of a spiritual belief was seen as an essential escape from the degradation of human life that he found in contemporary industrial civilization. He regarded himself as a man of vision and thought of his vision as something implanted deeply within himself and as providing his vocation in life. He had listened to the inner voice that had called him to sociology, but he remained, perhaps, agnostic about the ultimate source of that voice.

Sybella Gurney, who had married Victor Branford in 1910, died four years before him after a long illness. At 5 feet 6 inches she was just slightly taller than he and seven years younger. She had a dark complexion, brown hair, and brown eyes. Lewis Mumford (1982, 261) described her as an "ample, buttery sort of woman." From an early age she had lived an independent life. Though she may have been intimately involved with Henry Vivian during the time they were planning and building the Brentham housing estate in Ealing, West London, she lived alone until her marriage to Branford in her mid-forties. She seems to have been thoughtful and kindly toward others, with a "smiling wit" and a "gracious personality" (Vivian 1927). She enjoyed art, games, and dancing.

Gurney provided the intellectual partnership that Branford had not found in his first marriage. Though enthused by Sybella's quick mind, he seems also to have been exasperated by what he regarded as a certain wooliness in her thought. Sybella did, however, make a number of important contributions to their shared intellectual enterprise. She was always the more practical of the two, being especially concerned with housing and community reforms and less likely to engage in wide-ranging intellectual disquisition. Nevertheless, they seem to have had a comfortable and happy life together. She was undoubtedly fond of him, as he was of her. Both enjoyed the garden that they established at their Hastings home.

Gurney was comfortable and welcoming at home though not, perhaps, conventionally domestic. She was attached to their two adopted sons but did not provide them with an intense mothering. In their young childhood the boys had a governess and were later sent away to boarding school. She suffered her long illness during their early adolescent years and the boys were dependent on the secretary, housekeeper, and relatives for routine care while she was abroad in hospital and Victor Branford was traveling on business.

Conventional religion was important to Gurney and she was, like her father, of a High Church persuasion. She remained an active Anglican throughout her life and was committed to the social role of the Church. Her thought and practice brought her close to the Christian socialism that was emerging in the early part of the twentieth century. While living in Richmond she was a member of its Christian Social Council, and in Hastings she joined the Christian Social Service Centre, becoming secretary of its Housing Committee. Victor Branford regarded the refusal of her parish church to display an elaborate memorial tablet after her death as a significant affront to her memory and her Christian beliefs.

PATRICK GEDDES'S EARLY LIFE

The Geddes family originated in the Scottish lowlands, but Patrick's grandfather, a merchant, had settled in the Highlands.[2] Thus it was that Alexander Geddes, Patrick's father, was born a highlander and brought up as a Gaelic speaker. The family moved to Glasgow when the grandfather's business collapsed at the end of the Napoleonic War, and both grandparents were to die there in a cholera epidemic. Alexander was left in the care of an elder brother and joined the Black Watch as soon as he was seventeen. He served for thirty years, joining as a drummer but rising to the rank of Sergeant Major. He refused further promotion, but when he retired to serve in the reserves—the Perthshire Rifles—he took the rank of Captain and may have been on royal service at Balmoral (Stephen 2008, 3, 19). Alexander married Janet Stevenson, from lowland Airdrie, who worked as a regimental school teacher during her husband's military career.

All the children except Patrick had been born abroad while Alexander was on army service. Robert was born in Dublin in 1839, Jessie (known as "Mousie" and the one daughter) was born in Corfu in 1841, and John (known as "Jack") was born in Malta in 1844. A further boy died in infancy two years later aboard a troopship to Bermuda. Patrick (always known as "Pat") was born in 1854 in Ballater, Aberdeenshire, after his father's retirement and shortly before the family settled in Perth.[3] Patrick's brothers were soon to leave home: Jack went to New Zealand in 1860 as a coffee and spice merchant, while Robert went to Mexico in 1864 to work for the London Bank of Mexico and South America (Stephen 2004, 24).

The absence of the older boys meant that Patrick developed an especially close relationship with his father. Alexander was an Elder in the Free Kirk and as such, he took his religion seriously and gave Patrick a strict religious upbringing. The Sunday bible reading bored Patrick, and there was little music in the house. It was through his father, however, that he was introduced to the library and the world of books, and he became a voracious reader. It was through his father, too, that he acquired his love for the countryside. His father enjoyed country rambles, and it was on walks with his father that Patrick developed a devotion to natural history, a knowledge of gardening, and a penchant for field observation. This combination of books and natural history set the course of Patrick's later career and shaped his own views on education. His main childhood enjoyment was to take Saturday rambles in the countryside with friends such as Harry and David Barker, often following the Tay valley from Perth into Dundee. It was in Dundee when in his late teens that he seems to have met Martin White, striking up a friendship that was to last a lifetime and was to prove crucial both for his career and for the development of sociology in Britain.

Patrick attended Perth Academy, where he was a good but not outstanding student. On leaving school he followed in the footsteps of his brother Robert and took employment as a clerk in the Perth branch of the National Bank of Scotland. This was largely to please his parents, who wished to see him enter a safe and respectable career. In due course, however, he was able to persuade his father that he should be permitted to study botany. For three years he followed a course of self-education and in 1874 he entered Edinburgh University. The university proved uncongenial, and after just one week he decided to transfer to London to study in the laboratories of Thomas Huxley at the School of Mines in South Kensington.

While studying in London, Geddes made two trips abroad in the period 1878–79. Seconded to a marine research establishment at Roscoff in Brittany, he visited Paris and encountered the ideas of Frédéric Le Play that were to become the cornerstone of his own theoretical approach to sociology. Later in 1879, he visited his brother Robert in Mexico, where a period of blindness, brought on by intensive microscope work, led him to invent a method of thinking with the aid of folded paper. Thereafter, Geddes was constantly to be found articulating Le Play's ideas while folding and unfolding sheets of paper.

In 1881, by which time his brother Robert had retired back to Britain, Geddes took up an appointment as a demonstrator in botany and lecturer in zoology in the Edinburgh University Medical School, remaining there until 1888.[4] He was an indifferent lecturer, often mumbling into the blackboard, but he inspired his students with his enthusiasm for his subjects. He began to write on scientific matters, presenting a paper on statistics to the annual meeting of the British Association for the Advancement of Science. Later in that year he was invited by Martin White to give a lecture to the Dundee Naturalists' Society, of which Martin and his father had been founder members. White himself had previously presented a paper on research into electricity based on his visit to the Paris Electrical Exhibition (Macdonald 2000, 136).

In Edinburgh, Geddes became friendly with James Oliphant, the head of a girls' school who was interested in social issues and drew him into practical social work. It was through this that he met Oliphant's sister-in-law Anna Morton, the daughter of Liverpool merchant Frazer Morton. The relationship blossomed, and in 1886, following a trip to Greece with Martin White, he and Anna were married at the Liverpool home of the Mortons. They lived initially in Geddes's lodgings in Princes Street before moving into an apartment at 6 James Court in the slum district of the Lawnmarket, where they remained until their move to Ramsay Gardens in 1893. Geddes and Anna had three children: Norah was born in 1887, Alasdair in 1891, and Arthur in 1895. They were brought up in relaxed if chaotic circumstances. Geddes treated them as little adults, talking to them of intellectual matters from an early age. Thanks to Anna, music became important for the whole family and the children played instruments in family recitals.

GEDDES AND THE EDUCATIONAL PROJECT

Geddes never completed his undergraduate degree, and he was unsuccessful in the applications he made for professorships. He applied for the chair in natural history at Edinburgh University in 1882, the foundation chair in botany at University College Dundee in 1884, and the chair in botany at Edinburgh in 1888. Recognizing that Geddes was unlikely to secure an academic post by conventional means, Martin White used funds made available by the death of his father to endow a chair of botany for him at the University of Dundee in 1888 (Macdonald 2000, 143; 2004a, 20). The university had been desperate for funds and agreed to an arrangement under which Geddes was able to spend the bulk of his time on other work in Edinburgh. Living in Newport during his summer teaching term, Geddes could spend the rest of the year in Edinburgh.

In Edinburgh, Geddes set out to promote his ideas through scientific Summer Schools in zoology and botany for teachers and a general public. He became engaged in literary ventures and helped to set up the Old Edinburgh School of Art in order to contribute to a Scottish cultural renaissance of arts and crafts. He also set up student housing cooperatives near Edinburgh University (Leonard and Mackenzie 1989) and became involved in providing practical relief for Armenian refugees in Cyprus.

Martin White's support was crucial to many of Geddes's educational activities. He increasingly took on the role of patron or sponsor in an attempt to shape Geddes's career. He had been elected MP for Forfarshire in 1895, having failed to gain the nomination in the previous year. What could have been an important national base for Geddes and his associates was short-lived, however, as White was forced to resign the following year because of rumors concerning his private life. These rumors never became a matter of public comment, but concerned a longstanding affair with a woman he had known since the age of twelve.[5] The woman—clergyman's daughter Helen ("Ella") Grant—became pregnant and refused the abortion remedies of gin and ergot proposed by White. Ella brought a court action alleging breach of a promise to marry her, but White proposed an out of court settlement and the matter was hushed up. White's political career, however, was in ruins, and he began to spend more of his time in London.

From 1897, Geddes and his family had been spending more and more time away from Edinburgh. While working at Dundee, Geddes took up residence during his summer teaching terms in Newport-on-Tay, across the river and to the south of the city. When not teaching, he spent much of his time at Crauford, a country house at Lasswade just outside Edinburgh. From 1899 to 1900 he spent much time abroad, making two long visits to the United States and being heavily involved in plans for the Paris Exposition. Both of his parents died shortly before what turned out to be the last of the regular Edinburgh Summer Schools. This detachment from Edinburgh was to continue, and from 1900 to 1905 Geddes barely visited Edinburgh at all.

By the turn of the century, Geddes's butterfly enthusiasms, his willingness to take on projects without any consideration for their financial implications, and his persistent interventions in practical administrative matters for which he had no aptitude were leading many of his followers and supporters to lose patience with him and they realized that his aspirations would have to be carried on in his name despite him rather than through him. A further summer meeting was held in Edinburgh in 1903, but this was a mere one-off event. His most successful venture was the launch by Victor Branford of the Sociological Society in 1903. Their educational efforts, however, were soon overshadowed by the establishment of sociology teaching at the London School of Economics. Martin White had been persuaded by Branford to finance a chair in sociology at the School, seeing this as a way of launching Geddes onto the London scene and establishing his vision of sociology firmly in the academy. Geddes, however, made a mess of the interview and the trial lecture, and the appointment went instead to Leonard Hobhouse. Indeed, there is some suggestion that White may have come to see the need for a more philosophical approach to sociology than that pursued by Geddes and that he may not have been unduly disappointed at the outcome of the appointment process (Macdonald 2004a, 25).

Geddes was by this time heavily involved in practical issues of urban planning. In response to an invitation from the Dunfermline Carnegie Trust, both he and the landscape gardener Thomas Mawson submitted proposals to remodel Pittencrieff Park and its surroundings in Andrew Carnegie's hometown of Dunfermline. Geddes built on this experience with a series of planning exhibitions in Britain and abroad. Though the exhibitions were highly praised and many civic leaders expressed interest in hosting one, with the exception of a display shipped to India (see chapter 3), the exhibitions effectively ended with the outbreak of World War I in July 1914.

Geddes had been predicting a European war for many years, seeing it as an inevitable expression of the inherent "Wardom" of the modern age. His writings were increasingly concerned with warfare, but he also faced personal tragedies as a result of the war. He twice traveled to India with Anna and it was during the second visit, in 1917, that he received news that his son Alasdair, undoubtedly his favorite, had been killed in action (Branford 1918), just a few weeks before Anna died in an Indian hospital of enteric fever following dysentery. Geddes was distraught at the double loss and threw himself into a flurry of planning commissions for urban authorities in India. He returned to Scotland in 1919 but only to retire from his Dundee chair in order to take up the post of Professor of Civics and Sociology at the University of Bombay. Simultaneously, he accepted a commission from the Zionist Federation to design a new University of Jerusalem. Geddes remained at Bombay from 1919 to 1923, but in 1924 he shifted his attention back to university reform and started the Collège des Écossais, as a hall of residence for the university at Montpellier.

In 1928 he married for a second time, to Lilian Brown, a wealthy corn-flour heiress from Paisley who had attended his summer meetings during the 1890s and whose father had helped finance some of Geddes's early business ventures. Lilian was some fifteen years younger than Patrick and had begun a correspondence with him in 1921.[6] No doubt one reason for his attraction to her was her willingness to put her money at the disposal of his projects. The marriage was met with disapproval from his children and much consternation among his friends. Nevertheless, Lilian's money proved useful to the causes and her house in Netherton Grove, Chelsea, became his London base. Although Geddes had turned down a knighthood in 1912 "for democratic reasons," he did accept one in 1932. He died that same year on April 17, in Montpellier.

THE EARLY YEARS OF VICTOR BRANFORD

The Branfords[7] were descended from a long line of Norfolk farmers, though Victor's grandfather had been a miller and brewer, and his father, William Catton Branford, was a veterinary surgeon.[8] William trained in London and began his career in Oundle, Northamptonshire, where he set up household with his deceased wife's sister Ann Kitchen, and had five surviving children: Mary (known as "Mollie") was the oldest, followed by Victor (born in September 1863 and known as "Vic"),[9] Lionel (known in childhood as "Willie"), John (known as "Jack"), and Benchara (known as "Ben"). All seem to have been unaware of their probable illegitimacy. William and his family moved to Edinburgh in 1869 when he took up an academic post in the veterinary college. Conflict with his students and the college authorities led to his dismissal and for a time the family returned south, where his common law wife died young. William Branford returned to Edinburgh in 1874, but two years later he took a post as Colonial Veterinary Surgeon in the Cape Colony (now part of South Africa), leaving his young family in Edinburgh in the care of a stern, Norfolk-born housekeeper, Miss Sarah Armes. Mollie may have been expected to help look after her younger brothers when they were not away at school, but her dislike for housework meant that there was little love lost between her and Miss Armes. William Branford returned to Edinburgh after six years in South Africa, following his imprisonment for fraud, and he spent the rest of his life racing, gambling, and evading the numerous creditors created in his property and business deals.

Victor Branford's childhood and those of his siblings could not have been easy. Their father was overbearing but distracted by dubious money-making ventures, though he was undoubtedly a scientific inspiration and was held in affection by his boys. Any sense of security must have come from school. Victor began as a boarder at Oundle School in the years 1874–75, where he won a Classics and English prize,[10] but he spent most of his school years (1875–1881) at Daniel Stewart's College in Edinburgh. All the boys grew up with intellectual interests and did well at school. Both Ben and Jack also studied at Daniel Stewart's College and Edinburgh University. At the college, Ben was the 1882 Medalist in mathematics, the 1884 Dux and Gold Medalist in mathematics, and winner of a £100 college bursary. Jack won a scholarship for free education and board and became 1884 Medalist in mathematics. He played as a forward in the school rugby team and in later life was an active member of the Old Boy's Association. Ben studied mathematics at university and won the First Class mathematics prize in the advanced class of 1888. Jack graduated with a Distinction in 1890, after which he immediately entered theological training and achieved a First Class in the preliminary theological examinations. Lionel studied at the Royal High School. He entered Edinburgh University to study mathematics but transferred to theology, also attaining First Class in the preliminary examinations. He became a deacon and curate in Edinburgh, Glasgow, and Duns before completing a degree course at Durham in 1894. Mollie seems to have attended pre-university classes at St George's Hall, run by the Edinburgh Ladies Education Association, but did not go on to university.

Victor Branford appears to have been a star student. He entered the arts faculty of the university to study history in 1881, a year after his father's imprisonment and return from South Africa, but he soon switched to natural science. He was awarded the Certificate of Merit in the junior class for 1882 and gained a Distinction in the bursary examinations.[11] He graduated in 1886 with the distinction of an honors award (Anon. 1888). This was the year in which his father's problems with his debtors became pressing and Victor, as the oldest son, was closely drawn into his father's difficulties. He jointly signed with his father a promissory note to repay the principal debts, but his income was such that he was unable to meet the commitment. In 1889 he was named as a founding director of his father's South Africa nitrates company, but he was unable to meet the cost of the qualification shares. Fortunately, he lost no money in the collapse of the company, but he was committed to helping his father to repay the shareholders' losses. Victor's income at this time came from private tuition in science for students of the preliminary medical examinations, and he produced some primers for these students (Branford 1888, 1889).[12] Mylne and Campbell WS, the lawyers for William's creditors, reported of Victor that "The poor fellow seems to have a great struggle. . . . He seems to be earning a livelihood from literary work of a very precarious kind."[13] Referring to his primers, Victor informed Mylne and Campbell that "the business operations into which I have recently entered have turned out the reverse of remunerative."[14] Early in 1890, he found some employment as a sub-editor on the *Edinburgh Evening Dispatch*, founded a few years earlier by the *Scotsman*, and under legal advice aimed at preventing his own bankruptcy he entered into an arrangement to covenant one-half of his salary each month to pay off the father's debts. Payments were made for the first month but the proprietors of the *Dispatch* disapproved of an employee being in debt and terminated his employment after a mere two months. Victor took great care to shield his brothers from any knowledge of the true extent of his father's financial problems and even in adult life Benchara was unaware of the difficulties his brother experienced in dealing with them and looked back fondly at his maligned and much-beloved "Pater." For Victor, however, it must almost have come as a relief when his father died in 1891.

BRANFORD'S EARLY CAREER AND FIRST MARRIAGE

By the time his father died, Victor Branford had come to know and admire Patrick Geddes, whose lectures in zoology and botany Branford had attended as an undergraduate. He became a member of the group of acolytes around Geddes and he taught on the Edinburgh Summer Schools from 1892 to 1895, initially covering history and then science. He had also, by this time, acquired some journalistic work for the *Dundee Advertiser*, most probably acquired with the help of Geddes and Martin White, the latter being an associate of Sir John Leng, the paper's owner. Branford's circumstances improved to the point at which he was able to spend some time traveling in France, Switzerland, and Italy.[15]

It was in Dundee that Branford met Bess Stewart. Born Matilda Elizabeth Smith in Aston in 1853, she was the daughter of Isaac Smith

(1822–1868), the manager of Mason's steel pen works and nephew of Josiah Mason himself. Her husband, James Farquharson Stewart, had been a journalist and editor of the *Dundee Advertiser* until his death in 1891. Branford seems to have taken on some of Stewart's editorial work, working from Stewart's office, and, it was through this work that he came to know Bess and her daughter Elsie. Branford was attracted to the young Elsie, whom he taught to ride a horse, but felt that his poor health—he appears to have suffered from asthma or TB—precluded a relationship. However, Bess, ten years older than he, developed an affection for him and, having chosen security over love and sex, he proposed marriage to Bess. They were married in 1897 at the London West End register office, with two unknown clerks acting as witnesses. Neither of Bess's two sons from her marriage to Stewart—Martyn and Arthur—were present at the wedding.[16] Her daughter Elsie was also absent, having married in Argentina to Adam Goodfellow, later a business associate of Branford's in Argentina, in the same year that Elizabeth married Branford.[17]

By 1896, Branford had already decided on a change of career from journalism to business. Despite his unfortunate early experience as a director of his father's company, Branford seems to have had an aptitude for business, and the security provided by Bess's money allowed him to join with his student friend John Ross, a qualified accountant, to form a partnership trading as Ross, Branford & Co in Edinburgh and Westminster. Branford specialized in corporate finance, insolvency, and restructuring (see chapter 7).

In London, the Branfords lived for a time in an apartment at 29 King Street, Portman Square. The address on his marriage certificate, 28 Victoria Street, was his business address, and Branford is known to have slept overnight in his offices when working. Geddes was a frequent visitor to the Branford home, generally arriving uninvited and often staying overnight. Bess tired of this intrusion into her life, and Branford bought Rowan Cottage, in White Lion Road on Amersham Common, an isolated part of Buckinghamshire. The Branfords lived alone in the cottage, but Victor spent much of his time commuting between Edinburgh and London and traveling on business. His interests soon took him to Latin America and he spent much time on business in the United States. What time he had free in Britain, and much of his free time during his travels, was devoted to sociology, and it was in the early years of the century that he formed the Sociological Society and the *Sociological Papers* (see chapter 3).

Victor Branford's travels abroad put considerable strain on his marriage. Bess was often at home on her own and feeling lonely. She was, as her brother-in-law Ben described her, "a once beautiful woman with gentle, sympathetic manners and a loving generous heart" but was "worn and weary" from nursing her first husband before his death and looking after her drunken mother. Rural isolation was, perhaps, the final trigger for her own resort to whiskey. Domestic life for Branford became ever more fraught because of Bess's drinking bouts. His brother Lionel settled Bess in a cottage, The Nook, in Stoke, Hampshire, close to his own home in Lye Binley, hoping that he could care for her and resolve her problems. Seeking a divorce, Branford took advantage of his business interests in the United States to establish a purely nominal residence in the small but bustling gold rush town of Goldfield, Nevada. This nominal residence and an application for American naturalization in November 1907, followed by a declaration of intention to immigrate in April 1910,[18] allowed Branford to file for divorce under Nevada law. The grounds for the divorce given in the petition were that Bess was constantly drunk and unable to control her behavior in public,[19] with the aim of appealing to the judge who heard the case and who took a notoriously unsympathetic view of drunkenness. The divorce was, however, "amicable," and Branford remained on close terms with both Elsie and Bess's brother Martyn Josiah Smith. Branford negotiated a financial settlement for Bess, but he prudently ensured that the Cuban Telephone shares on which it was based reverted to him on Bess's death. By the time of the divorce, the Amersham home had been sold and Victor had moved into an apartment in Chelsea, close to the intellectual center of the Sociological Society.[20] Bess died in Hampshire in 1915.

SYBELLA GURNEY AND COOPERATION

Branford remarried shortly after the divorce. There is some suggestion that he may have been on close friendly terms with Penelope Eyre, a wealthy member of the arts and crafts circle in Chelsea, but the object of his affections, and the immediate stimulus for securing the divorce in 1910, was Sybella Gurney, whom he had met through his involvement in the Sociological Society. Sybella Catherine Nino Gurney[21] came from a Cornish family, very loosely connected to the great Quaker cousinhood (Anderson 1980).[22] For at least three or four generations, members of the family had been Rectors of Tregony, near Truro.[23] Sybella's grandfather, however, had read for the bar and lived the life of a country gentleman in Tregony, Brighton, and London until debts arising from election expenses led him to flee to the continent. The family traveled incognito around the Netherlands, France, Germany, and Switzerland. Sybella's father, Archer Thompson Gurney, who had been born in Tregony in 1820 traveled with his father and became involved in some of his speculative ventures but returned to Britain in 1841 to read for the bar. He was, however, drawn to theological and literary interests: he was actively involved in the Oxford Movement and for a while he planned to stand for Parliament as a Protectionist. He was ordained in 1849 and held church posts in Exeter, Soho, and Buckingham and eventually secured appointment as the first chaplain to the British Embassy in Paris, where he held services on official occasions and for the English-speaking residents of the city.

It was in Paris that he met his wife, Elise Hammett, and where Sybella and her four older brothers were born. The brothers were Gerald, Vivian, Archer Hugh (who died as an infant), and Archer Evelyn.[24] Her birth was in July 1870, the month in which the Franco-Prussian war broke out, and the situation in Paris required that the family flee for Britain. Family tradition holds that they crossed the channel in an open boat on the same September day that Napoleon III was captured at the Battle of Sedan. In fact, a more likely departure date is January 1871, during the siege of Paris. Arriving in Britain, the family lived for a short time in Worthing with Archer's mother-in-law, Sybella Hammett, herself a long-term resident of France. At the time of the 1871 census their household at 24 Marine Parade included four French servants and it is likely that the whole group had fled France at around the same time. Archer Gurney soon took livings in Brighton, Hastings, London, and mid-Wales, and eventually settled in Oxford, where he stayed until his death in 1887.

Sybella Gurney was brought up with academic interests. She moved to London and entered Royal Holloway College in 1887 to study for the Oxford examinations. Although women were, by this date, permitted to study for the Oxford examinations, it was not until 1920 that they were entitled to take a degree. Sybella transferred to Oxford to complete her studies and worked under Leonard Hobhouse—she was his first female student—and became friendly with his wife Nora. While at Oxford she developed an interest in philosophy and social reform, and in 1894 she met the pioneers of the cooperative movement at the home of Charlotte Toynbee, widow of the economic historian Arnold Toynbee (Hubback 1927). Gurney soon became an activist of the Labour Co-Partnership Association, being editor of its journal from 1897. Her commitment to cooperative housing schemes became all-embracing and she was in demand as a speaker at rallies and was an active promoter of schemes in Oldham, Letchworth, Kettering, and many other places. In 1905 she formed the Co-Partnership Tenants Housing Council, under the auspices of the LCA, and in 1911 the Rural Co-Partnership Housing Association. She had been living at South Weirs, Brockenhurst, in the New Forest since around 1901 and was also involved there in housing schemes for rural workers. These rural interests led to her involvement in the work of both the Garden Cities movement and the Arts and Crafts movement.[25]

VICTOR AND SYBELLA BRANFORD: THEIR PARTNERSHIP

Sybella Gurney sailed from Liverpool to New York in the month following Victor Branford's divorce and she married him there at the end of the year.[26] The wedding was held in the Philadelphia home of businessman Samuel Fels, whose brother Joseph was a land tax reformer and was closely associated with the work of Branford, Geddes, and Gurney in London. Though Sybella was an Anglican and the Fels brothers were Jewish, the ceremony was conducted by Father John Krohmalney, a Russian Orthodox priest recently arrived from Poland, who officiated in a private capacity prior to taking up a parish appointment.[27] As a divorcee, Victor would have been ineligible for a regular Anglican church wedding but a ceremony performed by an Orthodox Church priest in the relatively more liberal American context would have satisfied Sybella's religious convictions and would have ensured that any doubts about the validity of an American divorce were in no danger of being tested in the British courts.

From 1911 to 1913, the Branfords spent much of their time in the United States, though Victor had returned to the UK to spend a short while in a sanatorium on the Isle of Wight.[28] In the United States, the Branfords lived in an apartment in Manhattan, Victor using the National Arts Club as his business and professional base. Victor's naturalization was finally granted in 1913, though this seems actually to have been the date from which he began to concentrate his business activities in Britain and the successful divorce and remarriage made the naturalization less important.[29] In his deposition to the U.S. Embassy supporting Sybella's application for a passport, Victor explained that he had lived outside the United States from 1914 because the pressing demands of his business work had caused him to spend much of the winter of 1914–15 in a warmer climate and he had had to spend the midsummer of 1916 in a sanatorium.[30] They had, however, rented a summer home in Midlewater (sic), Connecticut, where Sybella would stay while Victor was in New York.

Their first permanent home in Britain was the newly built Boundary House in Wylde's Close, Hampstead, where Sybella had been involved in the establishment of the new Garden Suburb. The house has been described as "a particularly fine house . . . by Parker and Unwin: brown brick, tall chimneys, steep roof, and very little ornament" It had six bedrooms, three reception rooms, and five bathrooms.[31] They adopted two infant sons born illegitimately to the son of one of Sybella's distant cousins (see Appendix C). Benchara Branford suggested that the adoption had been encouraged by Victor as an attempt to prevent Sybella from traveling with him on his business trips. These boys were apparently christened in Hampstead in 1913 as Archer Robert Francis Branford (Archie) and Hugh Sydney Branford

(Hughie), giving them the additional forenames of Sybella's deceased infant brother.[32] In 1916, the family moved to the main part of Hampstead Garden Suburb, living at Goodways on Heathgate, but in 1920, partly for the sake of Victor's health, they moved to a small cottage at 3 Chisholm Street on Richmond Hill and rented Broadley Farm in New Milton, Hampshire, as a summer home.

Living conditions in the Hampshire farmhouse were deliberately Spartan, perhaps in order to maintain its picturesque and "rustic" character. When Lewis Mumford visited in 1920, he was met at New Milton station by the governess and the two children in a dog cart and was taken to the farm. Showing him around the house, Branford unapologetically referred to the primitive sanitary arrangements and remarked: "Perhaps you will do as I do. . . . We have no neighbours for half a mile, and the gorse is thick and beautiful" (Mumford 1982, 260).

Having established a close business association with Bernhard Binder, Branford joined the Binder Hamlyn accountancy partnership on its formation in 1918, remaining with the firm until his death. Through the 1920s, Branford divided his time between business and the Sociological Society in London and leisure and academic writing in the country. In 1921, shortly after Branford had arranged for the purchase of Le Play House for the Sociological Society, he and Sybella gave up their homes in Richmond and New Milton in favor of a red brick cottage called The Pinders in Clive Vale, Hastings. The two boys were sent to a small preparatory school, Garth Place, in neighboring Bexhill. Archie later went on to the progressive boarding school at Bembridge on the Isle of Wight for a while, but both boys completed their education at a private school in Bletsoe, Bedfordshire.[33]

Both Victor and Sybella Branford were suffering from serious illnesses by the time they entered their late fifties. Victor, always of a delicate constitution, and weakened by the strain of his business work in the early years of the war, underwent a prostate operation in 1921 and suffered from postoperative complications for some time, never fully recovering. Sybella developed a serious cancer of the rectum and underwent treatment in the health resort of Territet, Montreux, where they had both taken to spending large parts of the winter. Sybella died in 1926 and Victor continued to spend recuperative time in Switzerland in the years after Sybella's death. His life cycled through bouts of bad health followed by periods of remission. Arthritis was his constant problem and he resorted to a salt bath treatment at Droitwich. Retaining the house in Hastings, Branford also took a small apartment at 55 Cheyne Court, close to the center of Geddes's London concerns. In his last year, his health improved to the point at which, at the age of sixty-six, he won a prize for figure skating. He became very friendly with a young skater, Elspeth Beadle, and her two brothers, and after his own marriage to a younger woman, Geddes joked that Branford should remarry to Elspeth. However, he was soon hit again by his arthritis and developed serious kidney problems. His health deteriorated rapidly in early 1930 and he was taken into a nursing home. His last weeks were worsened by serious worries over his will and the finances of the Sociological Society. He drifted into unconsciousness, waking only sporadically. His final words were "more executors" and then "damn!" before he sunk again into unconsciousness. He died on June 22, 1930, his brother Lionel reading him the Twenty-Third Psalm during his last moments.[34]

THREE

ORGANIZING AN INTELLECTUAL VISION

The collaborative circle around Patrick Geddes and Victor Branford shared a vision, nurtured in the emerging strands of nineteenth-century thought and the Edwardian New Age, of a society reconstructed according to principles derived from social science. Pursuit of this vision solidified it in the developing social science disciplines and the educational and professional organizations and practices through which these disciplines were being established. In this chapter we will trace the intellectual origins of their vision and disciplinary concerns, and we will sketch the particular disciplinary practices and forms through which they attempted to organize that vision.

SOCIALISM, SECULARISM, AND SPIRITUALITY

The ideas that inspired Geddes and his close associates had their roots in four principal traditions of radical thought: the cooperative ideals and practices of John Ruskin, the anarchism of Pyotr Kropotkin, the secularism of the Comtean positivists, and the diverse explorations of spirituality that flowered in high Victorian and Edwardian Britain. In some senses each of these could be described as a form of "socialism." However, these ideas on collective or corporate organization differed radically from those in the mainstream of the socialist and communist parties of Europe, where Marxist principles had had a considerable impact. Ruskinism, anarchism, and secularism were each founded on a conservative belief in the virtues of medieval, precapitalist and preindustrial, structures. They each held that a return to the past and a renewal of its values through a conscious and deliberate process of social reform and reconstruction could reestablish the positive features of the medieval past while avoiding the negative. Most radical was the anarchism of those such as Kropotkin, who stressed the need for autonomous and self-directing small-scale collectivities of producers and consumers to carry forward the democratic principles of the medieval guilds

(Kropotkin 1899). The power of the state and administrative elites—central to mainstream socialism—was seen as inimical to these more democratic structures of collective organization. Geddes first met Kropotkin during a visit to Edinburgh in 1886 to investigate the self-governing student houses that Geddes had set up. Kropotkin described Geddes's social ideas and social work to his friend the geographer Elisée Reclus (Reynolds 2004, 74), and both Kropotkin and Reclus became involved in teaching on Geddes's Edinburgh Summer Schools.

Ruskin's ideas flowered during his brief career at Oxford. It was these ideas on practical cooperative projects of social change, together with the life of Ruskin's student, the economic historian Arnold Toynbee, that inspired Canon Samuel Barnett to begin his social work and worker education ventures at Toynbee Hall in East London. Ruskin also inspired the architect and designer William Morris in his use of design principles drawn from medieval arts and crafts. To promote his views on cooperation, beauty in craft, and the dignity of labor, Ruskin formed the Guild of St. George at Brantwood on Coniston Water in the English Lake District. The aim of this Guild was to purchase land where small-scale agriculture and handicraft works could be established as worker cooperatives and operated according to Owenite principles (Edith Scott 1931).

Five years after its formation, in 1876, the Guild set up St. George's Farm at Totley, near Sheffield, as an experiment in rural socialism. Disagreements between Ruskin and the artisans working the farm led to its conversion into a more commercial market garden, but the cooperative ideals behind the farm did inspire others to pursue rural schemes. Prominent among these rural utopians was Edward Carpenter, a university extension teacher in Sheffield who had been close to the workers at St. George's Farm. An inheritance from his father allowed him to give up his teaching work and set up a communal small-holding at Millthorpe in Derbyshire. Here, he was able to pursue the radical politics and simple life to which he was committed, and he wrote a number of books in which he explored and promoted self-sufficient cooperation and a radical sexual politics (1884, 1889, 1894; See Tsuzuki 1980; Rowbotham 2008). Active in Henry Hyndman's Social Democratic Federation, Carpenter met fellow SDF activist William Morris and the two discovered the many ideas they held in common. The SDF proved to be an uncongenial Marxist organization for the development of these ideas and they broke away in 1885 to form the Socialist League (see Gould 1988; Thompson 1955). This, in turn, inspired Charles Ashbee's School and Guild of Handicraft in Whitechapel—a community of artists and craftsmen living and working together[1]—and the work of Eric Gill at Ditchling, Sussex, and it later inspired the projects of Leonard and Dorothy Elmhirst at Dartington Hall in Devon.

Also active in the SDF was Havelock Ellis, a doctor and pioneering author on sexuality involved in the Progressive Association with Eleanor Marx and Edward Aveling. His libertarian views brought him close to Carpenter and in 1883 they both joined the Fellowship of the New Life, which had recently been formed to promote self-governing and cooperative colonies of workers and craftsmen.[2] The Fellowship was strongly opposed to centralist socialism and attracted gradualists disenchanted with the SDF. Some such as Edward Pease were committed to a more conventional socialism that led them soon to split from the Fellowship and to form the Fabian Society. Ellis, Carpenter, and Olive Schreiner, however, continued to develop their radical ideas on sex and gender politics within the Fellowship (Ellis 1894, 1889; Schreiner 1899; Carpenter 1908).

Ruskin's Oxford students also included Hardwicke Rawnsley, who aimed to promote Ruskin's ideas on practical design through a School of Industrial Art in Keswick. The school promoted the application of aesthetic principles in industrial production and acquired the Ruskin Linen Industry, originally formed by the young spinning teacher Marion Twelves (Benjamin 1974). Rawnsley was firmly committed to the protection of the historical landscape and country houses of England, and in 1895 he joined with Octavia Hill to form the National Trust to preserve and conserve the aesthetically important elements in the cultural heritage. Hill herself had encountered Ruskin and his ideas during his involvement in her communal housing schemes.

This was the political context in which Geddes had first encountered Ruskin's ideas. He read Ruskin on cooperation and economics in 1877 and immediately began a correspondence with him. A particular attraction was the social content of Ruskin's work, and Geddes wrote a pamphlet on *John Ruskin, Economist* (Geddes 1884b) to discuss the connection of economics to ethics and aesthetics. Geddes drew his students and associates into the work of the Guild of St. George,[3] recruiting a number of Ruskin's followers into his housing and cooperative ventures and subsequently into the Sociological Society. The stress on collective organization in Ruskin's work had a particular appeal to Geddes, who fused this with the anarchist ideas he had already begun to explore in his discussions with Kropotkin and Reclus. Their ideals of autonomy and self-sufficiency resonated with the ideals of cooperation and democracy that Geddes found especially attractive (Geddes 1888).

The combination of Ruskin's medievalism with anarchist and cooperative principles gave a solid social basis to Geddes's work in architecture and town planning. This same set of ideas influenced Ebenezer Howard and Henrietta Barnett, whose Garden Cities and Garden Suburbs were self-conscious attempts to unite aesthetics with the economics of urban development and were to be organized as self-governing communities. Henry

Vivian's experiments in cooperative housing—with which Sybella Gurney was involved—carried forward similar principles, though the housing cooperatives perhaps owed more to Owen than to Ruskin (Zueblin 1899a). Gurney's activism in the housing cooperatives and in Labour Co-partnership made her an ideal partner for the work that the Barnetts undertook in Hampstead Garden Suburb (Creedon 2002; Reid 2000).

Engagement with anarchist thought made Geddes and Branford into self-conscious utopians. Anarchism postulates a future social order that is morally preferable to prevailing social conditions and that can be held up as an ideal or goal to be pursued. For Geddes and Branford, however, utopia was to be no mere abstract possibility. A utopian vision had to be a realistically achievable state—a "eutopia"—and sociology had to produce knowledge capable of mobilizing people to aim for this state and guiding them toward its realization. Eutopia is approached through a scientifically guided process of social reconstruction. Humans are oriented toward the world by the conscious study, scheming, planning, designing, and execution through which they shape and control their environment. The achievement of eutopia requires an appropriate "vision": an imaginative conception of what, realistically, might be. It is

> a concentrated effort of the organism, in an intensity of awareness, to stir and guide the life-impulse to an optimum fulfillment by a provision that can be made to come true. (V. V. Branford 1923, 25)

These eutopian proposals for social reconstruction found their first expression in local urban and community planning in Chelsea, where a small and informal society was formed in 1904. Meeting at the home of Dorothea Hollins in More's Gardens, Cheyne Walk, "The Utopians" included Geddes, Branford, and Hollins together with Shapland Swinny, John Slaughter, Lionel Tayler, and the Reverend Joseph Wood. Members were involved in the eugenics movement, positivism, and secularism and were beginning to make their mark through publication. Wood, for example, was a Congregational and Unitarian Minister closely associated with Frederick Gould's Secular Society in Leicester and was the author of a tract on *Wealth and Commonwealth* (Wood 1895).[4] By the time that they published a collection of their discussion papers (Hollins 1908), the Utopians had renamed themselves as the Chelsea Association.

The British secularist movement had three principal bases: the London Positivist Society, the London Ethical Society, and the South Place Ethical Society. The LPS was closely associated with a group of active followers of Comte. Although Comte's work had influenced Harriet Martineau (1853), George Lewes (1853), and John Stuart Mill (1865), his lasting reputation had been established in a series of translations and commentaries produced by a discussion group formed at Wadham College, Oxford, by Richard Congreve, Frederic Harrison, Edward Beesley, and John Bridges.[5] Congreve, the leading member, had been an early convert to Comte's Religion of Humanity and left Oxford in 1854 to become, at Comte's behest, a full-time advocate for English Comtism. The discussion group subsequently met in Harrison's London rooms, presided over by Beesley, pursuing the Comtean idea of rational, scientifically planned social reconstruction. Though Ruskin never joined the group, the Positivists were close to him and adopted his ideas on medieval organicism. Harrison (1877) saw such organizations as the new Model Unions and the London Trades Council as means of collective action through which a cohesive and organic social order could be attained.

Transformed into the Positivist School and meeting at Chapel Street, the group offered training in history, politics, and philosophy and combined this with the provision of Sunday services and prayers. In 1878, however, Congreve reorganized the school as a Church of Humanity, intending to strengthen the more emotional and devotional aspects of Positivist education. Harrison, Beesley, and Bridges remained committed to a more naturalistic form of positivism and continued to meet as an informal discussion group until, in 1881, they moved into new offices at Newton Hall in Fetter Lane and renamed themselves the London Positivist Society. Their activities included induction rituals and hymns, but not the devotional rituals, robes, and incense that so appealed to Congreve. Instead, they organized lectures, publications, social activities, and clubs. The leading lights in the society were Harrison and his close associates Shapland Swinny and Frederick Gould, and the society attracted independent radical thinkers such as John Hobson. Geddes became involved with the London Positivists from his first encounters with Comtean thought in 1874. He was, at the time, working for Huxley but had not been convinced by Huxley's rejection of positivism. Geddes came to know Congreve well, visiting him frequently at his home. He became a regular attendee at the midweek meetings, where he met and became close to both Swinny and Bridges. Geddes maintained an independent commitment to positivism, associating with both Congreve and the Harrison group while also remaining in close association with Pierre Lafitte's group in Paris.[6] On his return to Edinburgh, Geddes attended Positivist meetings in the city, where he met James Oliphant and Anna Morton. The London Society itself began publication of *The Positivist Review* in 1893, Victor Branford contributing an article to its first issue.

Positivism was a major influence on the secularism that developed in the ethical societies.[7] This secularism had its roots in a small, independent Unitarian chapel in South Place to which the American Mancur Conway had been appointed as minister in 1864. Under Conway the chapel abandoned the final vestiges of theological thinking and when, after twenty-one years, he was succeeded by Stanton Coit—previously associated with Felix Adler's Society for Ethical Culture in New York—the chapel was renamed as an "Ethical Society."[8] The South Place Ethical Society took as its object the cultivation of a "rational religious sentiment" through the comparative study of religious ethics, aiming to uncover universal principles of human orientation and conduct. Active members of the Society included Geddes (who met Adler during a visit to the United States in 1900), Hobson, and Carpenter, together with such academics and social theorists as Graham Wallas, John Robertson, George Romanes, Leonard Hobhouse, and Karl Pearson. The Society abandoned the practice of appointing a minister, relying instead on the intellectual leadership of "Lecturers" such as Hobson, Robertson, and the Theosophist and SDF member Herbert Burrows.

The radical politics of the Society is most apparent in the ideas of Hobson and Robertson. The two men were politically and intellectually close to each other and both made their living from journalism and freelance lecturing.[9] Sharing a radical and unconventional approach to economics, they stressed the consequences of underconsumption, and developed sociological approaches to such subjects as class (Hobson 1891, 1901), finance capital and imperialism (Hobson 1894, 1902), ethnicity (Robertson 1897b, 1911), religion (Robertson 1897a), and politics (Robertson 1912; see also 1904). Their political sympathies were with the development of labor ideas within the Liberal Party as a "Lib-Lab" program: Hobson joined the ILP and Robertson became a Liberal MP. Hobson rejected individual charity, statist planning, and direct equality as remedies for social problems, advocating instead what he called a "practicable socialism" based on equality of opportunity. Robertson (1895) saw social life as conditioned by a material environment that provided the foundations for the systems of economic and political power through which class interests are organized and a balance of power established. He was a particularly close friend of Geddes, having met him at meetings of the Edinburgh Secular Society in the early 1880s.

The rival London Ethical Society had been formed by John Muirhead after a meeting with Coit at Toynbee Hall. Muirhead sought to promote the idealist philosophy of Thomas Green, Francis Bradley, and Edward Caird through meetings at Essex Hall in the Strand and attracted strong support from Bernard Bosanquet, who was then working closely with the Charity Organisation Society. The LES organized classes in philosophy, economics, and social history, from which Muirhead produced an influential text on philosophy (Muirhead 1892). The Society was renamed the London School of Ethics and Social Philosophy in 1897 in the hope that it might be recognized by the University of London as a parallel organization to the new London School of Economics that had recently been formed by the Fabian

Society. Failure to achieve this official recognition led to the closure of the school in 1900.[10]

Neither Geddes nor Branford was conventionally religious, though the precise nature of their personal beliefs are unknown. They were, undoubtedly, rationalists in the Comtean tradition and eschewed formal theology, yet they retained a strong sense of the importance of spiritual concerns in social life and saw the need to engage with religious thought in all its forms. Many of those with whom they were associated were involved with a variety of religious systems. Geddes himself had been brought up in the Free Church but had abandoned its theology in his youth: he claimed that the only lie he told his father was that he would be reunited with his wife after death. Geddes, however, maintained close contacts with freethinking intellectual currents in the Free Church, most notably with Alexander Whyte and the anarchist-inclined anthropologist William Robertson Smith. His own wide-ranging religious interests were reinforced by these ecumenical thinkers; Whyte, for example, was a close associate of Cardinal Newman (Macdonald 2004b: 78). Branford's brother Benchara had abandoned religion early in life but returned to a strongly Christian outlook in later life (B. Branford 1934). His brothers Lionel and Jack were ministers in the Church: Lionel an Anglican and Jack in the Church of Scotland. Sybella Gurney was born into an Anglo-Catholic family and was a staunch evangelical Christian.

An explicit engagement with religion is apparent in the involvement of Geddes and Branford in a Christian project on citizenship undertaken by the Reverend James Hand, a young assistant curate in Chelsea who worked with Toynbee Hall. Hand produced a collection of papers on the "social problem" and good citizenship for the Christian Social Union (Hand 1899) that was destined to be the first of a trilogy. The book brought together clergymen and social thinkers to write on the ethical aspects of contemporary social issues such as housing, pensions, poverty, and criminality in relation to national, municipal, and voluntary policies. The contributors included John Hobson, Samuel Barnett of Toynbee Hall, the idealist moral philosopher Hastings Rashdall, and the Christian Socialist George Russell. Hand got to know both Geddes and Branford—most probably through "The Utopians"—and involved them in a follow-up venture on the relations between science and religion (Hand 1904). In addition to papers written by clergy of various denominations, the book included papers by Branford, Geddes (with Arthur Thomson), Bertrand Russell, Oliver Lodge, and Muirhead. Two years later Hand produced the final volume of the trilogy, on science in public affairs (Hand 1906). Contributors to this final volume included Hobson, Henrietta Barnett, and the Scottish Liberal MP Charles MacKinnon Douglas. Branford, who was due to write a new chapter for the book, had been called to South America on business and his earlier address on "Science and Citizenship" (Branford 1906) was included in its place.

This engagement with evangelical and Christian Socialist thinkers was paralleled by an active search for insights from Eastern religious ideas. Geddes was an early supporter of engagement with Bahá'ísm, attending a talk at the Passmore Edwards Settlement by Abdu'l Bahá, the religion's founder, during a visit to London in 1911 (Macdonald 2004b). This was the beginning of a dialogue with the Society of the Eager Heart, formed to promote and produce Alice Buckton's Christian morality play *Eager Heart*. The Society's vice president was Jane Whyte, wife of Alexander Whyte, and it was she who sponsored Bahá's visit to Edinburgh the following year. During this time he visited the Outlook Tower and held several meetings there. Margaret Noble, who had converted to Hinduism and taken the name Sister Nivedita, met Geddes during his first visit to the United States and became a committed adherent to his views. She advised her friend Josephine MacLeod to meet him on his second visit and it was through MacLeod that Geddes met Swami Vivekananda in Chicago. Nivedita, MacLeod, and Vivekananda all met Geddes again at the Paris Exposition, reinforcing his syncretic outlook. It was while visiting India that Geddes met the poet Rabindranath Tagore and had extended discussions with him on how to unify Eastern and Western philosophical systems. Branford was later an active participant in the sessions on comparative religion jointly organized by the Sociological Society and the School of Oriental Studies for the British Empire Exhibition in 1924.

Geddes and Branford were also involved with movements of thought such as Theosophy and spiritualism that grew out of late-nineteenth-century concern for spirituality. Eastern religious ideas were central to the Theosophical Society, formed by Helena Blavatsky in New York and attracting the particular interest of Geddes. This esoteric society had as its aim the promotion of the Universal Brotherhood of Humanity. Blavatsky had once been involved with Bakunin's anarchist group, but the focus of her Theosophy was the view that a comparative study of religion, and especially Eastern religion, could uncover the underlying spiritual truths common to all religions (Pearsall 1972, 217; and see Guenon 1921). The mainstream of the British branch of the Theosophical Society played down the esoteric elements and stressed the more routine comparative study of religion, and had given its active support to some of Bahá's visits to London. Geddes became involved with Society meetings during the 1890s, though it is not clear how active he was in his membership. In India, he renewed his friendship with the prominent Theosophist Annie Besant, having earlier tutored her in London after she had been refused entry to University College (Mavor 1923, Vol. 1, 77). Besant had become more influential in the Society during the first decades of the twentieth century, heralding the great "World Leader" Krishnamurti as the harbinger of a New Age (Pearsall 1972), and she introduced Geddes to Krishnamurti. In its approach to spiritual renewal and social reconstruction Theosophy shared a great deal with the positivism and secularism that inspired Geddes and Branford. The political doctrines of leading Society members, stressing the need to build an organic society of universal brotherhood (Guest 1912; Besant 1916),[11] were developed through debates in the *New Age* political and cultural magazine. Alfred Orage, editor of the *New Age* magazine, subsequently abandoned his editorship to study with Georg Gurdjieff and eventually became a Swedenborgian.

A most striking example of the Victorian and Edwardian concern for spiritual matters was spiritualism itself, which prospered in Spiritualist churches and through popular theatrical performances by spiritualist mediums (Nelson 1969). Spiritualism took a highly rationalized attitude to belief, regarding the existence of spirits and an afterlife as things to be discovered and explained scientifically. This rational attitude also underpinned the work of the Society for Psychical Research, formed by Frank Myers and Edmund Gurney in 1882.[12] Under the presidency of the political philosopher Henry Sidgwick, its members included Ruskin, Oliver Lodge, and Arthur Balfour. Balfour was the brother-in-law of Sidgwick, a future prime minister, and a future president of the Sociological Society (Gauld 1968). Lodge, a physicist who wrote extensively on science and religion was principal of Birmingham University at the time that Branford had applied for its chair of commerce and social science. He set out some of his ideas on spirituality in his contribution to Hand's tract on science and faith and became a convinced spiritualist during World War I as a result of spirit messages he believed to have come from his dead son (Lodge 1916; see also Jolly 1974; Root 1978).

Geddes, Branford, and their close associates were involved, to varying degrees, in these interlinked circles of Ruskinism, secularism, anarchism, and New Age spirituality. These influences were linked by Branford to a positivist commitment to scientific method and social change. The development of a scientific orientation since the European Renaissance, he argued, had established an instrumental and technocratic outlook that disconnected factual knowledge from wider moral and spiritual issues (V. V. Branford 1923, 14, 36, 38; 1924). The alternative humanist movement of thought that underpinned contemporary spirituality pointed toward a broader view in which scientific and spiritual concerns could be reunited. The wider sources of this humanist orientation he found in William James, Piotr Kropotkin, Maria Montessori, Henri Bergson, and Friedrich Foerster. It was in the sociological approach of Comte, however, that a science oriented to humanity in which cultural and natural forces were combined was developed. While Branford recognized the earlier contribution of Joseph de Maistre and the general influence of

Hegel on the idealization of "humanity," it was Comte he saw as providing a comprehensive program that the Geddes circle was to implement. Comte's sociology, he argued, had, however, been a largely abstract theoretical exercise as he had not undertaken the patient and systematic empirical work that was necessary in order to develop the discipline (Branford 1903b).[13]

Comte's sociology involved a eutopian view of what humanity could become if scientific ideas informed social change. This eutopian vision of what *could be* rested on a deep attachment to the ethical principles underlying medieval society and the conviction that they were of universal relevance and application. These principles needed to be adapted to the material conditions of modern industrialism and pointed to new forms of fraternity and democracy. Branford concluded that a spiritual renewal could inspire planned social reconstruction that would bring these forms of life into existence on a scientifically informed basis.

Branford recognized a number of British writers who had contributed to the sociological ideas that he and Geddes sought to promote. He mentioned in particular Robert Owen, Thomas Carlyle, John Stuart Mill, Herbert Spencer, and John Ruskin. Lesser influences on this sociological humanism were George Eliot and Matthew Arnold. Particular importance was accorded to Mill's (1843, 1865) reflections on the methodology of the new discipline and Spencer's (1873, 1873–1893) construction of a system of substantive sociological knowledge, but Branford noted the weakness that characterized sociological work in Britain during the nineteenth century. It was in the work of Geddes, he argued, that the sociological orientation was properly united with the empirical research that had been developing in the research undertaken by the statistical investigators. This sociology was to be a culmination of earlier tendencies.

PROMOTING SOCIOLOGY: THE SOCIOLOGICAL MOVEMENT AND THE SOCIOLOGICAL SOCIETY

Having become committed sociologists, Geddes and Branford aimed at building an organizational base for its development in Britain that could match those emerging in the United States and in continental Europe. Their initial efforts to promote social theory and social reconstruction began in Edinburgh in practical programs of community action. Committed to the practical application of social science, Geddes had been inspired by Octavia Hill's efforts to improve working-class housing, and in 1884 he formed an Environment Society. Working with James Oliphant, he sought material improvements in the Edinburgh Old Town, where he lived and where the university was located. Renamed the Edinburgh Social Union the following year, the Environment Society bought, improved, and rented out apartments, beginning with the purchase of the large part of a tenement block in James Court (Leonard 2007, 139 ff.). Geddes followed no coherent plan but simply bought apartments adjacent to his home and set these up as a cooperative housing scheme and a "University Hall" for student residence. University Hall formally opened in 1887, and further renovated student residences were added over the following decade. He hoped that a population of students living in the area would ensure a cultural renewal through their encouragement of education and uplifting entertainment and the application of aesthetic principles of design. This, he held, was the key to the regeneration of the district. Socially aware students would participate in the social reconstruction of the region in which they lived.

Geddes next bought the old observatory on Castle Hill, in 1892, and began its conversion into an "Outlook Tower" that would serve as a regional civic museum and a base for training students and local residents in social science, helping them to understand their locality in its regional, national, and global context. This enterprise was central to the developing work in university extension teaching that he had begun through the University of St. Andrews. The Chautauqua meetings that had been organized in the United States for some years had come to Geddes's attention and were the immediate inspiration for the summer schools for school teachers that he started at Granton Marine Station in 1885. These summer schools moved to Edinburgh in 1891 and the range of subjects covered was gradually extended into a curriculum organized around geographical study and social evolution. Open to all, they included large numbers of women student teachers from St. George's Training College in Edinburgh, which was the only college providing training for women wishing to pursue a teaching career beyond elementary level. They achieved their peak attendance in 1893, when there were 120 participants, and the last of these summer schools was held in 1899 (Meller 1990, 96).

Geddes used the Outlook Tower in the summer school program to demonstrate the practical implications of geography and evolution. This came from reflection on what was happening in American museums such as the Philadelphia Commercial Museum, which had been set up by the University of Pennsylvania botanist William Wilson following the 1893 World's Fair (Branford 1902; Conn 1998, 115–50).[14] The Philadelphia museum was organized around principles of indexing and cross-referencing, and Geddes hoped to establish the Outlook Tower as an observatory and sociological museum on a similar basis. This would exemplify the approach he had taken from Le Play and that he came to call the "Index Museum." Hatching a plan to implement Reclus's project for the building of a large globe to display at the 1900 World Exposition in Paris, he hoped to establish the Outlook Tower as the base for a world museum. The Tower was visited in the late 1890s by the Chicago sociologist Charles Zueblin, who subsequently wrote an influential and laudatory account of Geddes's work (Zueblin 1899b).

Failing to raise the funds required to build in Paris or to establish a World Museum, Geddes reconceived the Outlook Tower as the base for a geographical institute and soon involved the political writer and MP James Bryce in his idea for a National Geographical Institute for the promotion of all the social sciences. His principal associate at the Tower was a former student and resident of University Hall, Andrew Herbertson, who worked closely on the geographical work with the cartographer John Bartholomew. Geddes's plans for a national institute faltered when the Royal Geographical Society decided to support the establishment of a Geographical Institute at Oxford—where Herbertson had moved in order to work with Halford Mackinder—and he attempted instead to persuade the Royal Scottish Geographical Society to support a parallel venture in Edinburgh.[15] There was, again, a lack of support and progress, and it was Branford who eventually formulated a plan to bolster the case through the formation of an Edinburgh School of Sociology.

This school was officially launched as the "Edinburgh School for Promoting the Study of Ethical, Social, and Economic Subjects," perhaps on the model of the London School of Economics and the London School of Ethics and Social Philosophy. Branford, together with fellow Geddes disciple John Ross, undertook the main tasks involved in founding and running the School from the Outlook Tower, though it was nominally registered at the parental addresses of two of its young administrators. Initially listed with the home address of its secretary, George Elder (whose father was the Keeper of the Scott Monument), its nominal base then moved to the Meadowbank home of Edward McGegan, who was Geddes's assistant at the Tower.[16] Geddes took the position of president and two prominent Edinburgh academics—the political economist Joseph Shield Nicholson and the ethical philosopher James Seth—were recruited as honorary presidents. Organizing roles in the committee were taken by former students and associates of Geddes, including McGegan, Elder, and a Miss J. M. McDonald who acted as treasurer.

The purpose behind the School was the building of a base within the Edinburgh academic community to support the establishment of a strong sociological presence within the university. The School became the springboard for launching the Geddes Lectureship Fund, through which Branford and Ross hoped to finance a lectureship in sociology—to be held by Geddes—at Edinburgh University. This attempt was unsuccessful. Although a small amount of money was raised, it was insufficient for a case to be made to the university. The activities of both Geddes and Branford had, by this time, shifted more firmly toward London, and it was there that they now focused their attention.[17]

Seeking to build a larger professional base for promoting sociology, Branford convened a small meeting at the Royal Statistical Society in the Adelphi Terrace on May 16, 1903, to discuss the possible formation of a national Sociological Society.[18] Bryce was invited to take the chair and other attendees were the Liberal MP Charles Douglas, the anthropologist Alfred Haddon, the psychologist James Sully, Charity Organisation activists Charles S. Loch and Edward Urwick, the administrator of the University of London Extension Board R. D. Roberts, and Martin White. Bryce was particularly significant as a legitimizing figurehead for the Society within the larger intellectual establishment. The involvement of Sully was of particular importance as he had convened a similar meeting two years previously in order to set up the British Psychological Society. It was agreed to launch the new Sociological Society with an academic conference the following month and notice of this conference and an invitation to support the Society were circulated to both academics and practitioners, together with copies of a position paper by Branford on the origins of the word *sociology* (Branford 1903b).[19]

The proposal floated by Branford was for the formation of a broad and inclusive society that would bring together a wide range of those concerned with sociological matters, both theoretical and practical, but would also promote the specific views of Geddes. His efforts were remarkably successful: around 180 people were signed up as members of a "Provisional Committee," and around fifty people attended the launch conference on June 29. Those who had attended the May meeting were reformed into a "Sub-committee" charged with considering a detailed constitution for the Society. Bryce and some others were unable to participate in the subcommittee and were replaced by four new members: Leonard Hobhouse and Sidney Webb from the LSE, Scott Keltie, a friend of Kropotkin and secretary of the Royal Geographical Society, and the prominent amateur sociologist Benjamin Kidd. This constitutional subcommittee set out the intellectual aims of the Society in a pamphlet. They proposed to set subscriptions at the rate of one guinea a year and to offer a special life membership at ten guineas.

The Provisional Committee was convened again on November 20, 1903, to consider these proposals, though attendance at the meeting was only about half of the full membership. The meeting approved the proposed constitution and elected an executive committee that comprised the subcommittee and eight new members (see Table 3. 1). The task of this executive committee was to publish an official statement of the agreed constitution and a list of the membership, the latter showing that the membership stood at around four hundred by the end of 1904. Like most professional societies

Table 3.1. Executive Committee of the Sociological Society (1903)

EC member	Professional background
Edward W. Brabrook (Chairman)	Folklore Society
Victor Branford (Secretary)	
Patrick Geddes	
Martin White	
John H. Bridges	physician and leading Positivist
Clara E. Collet	social researcher
Alfred C. Haddon	physician and anthropologist
Leonard T. Hobhouse	sociologist, LSE
John A. Hobson	economist
John Scott Keltie	Royal Geographical Society
Benjamin Kidd	sociologist
Revd. Alfred L. Lilley	Rector of St. Mary's, Paddington
Charles S. Loch	Charity Organisation Society
R. D. Roberts	University of London Extension Board
Shapland H. Swinny	London Positivist Society
Edward J. Urwick	COS School of Sociology and Economics
Graham Wallas	politics/psychology, LSE
H. G. Wells	novelist and Fabian Society

of the time, the membership was overwhelmingly male, though the lists show that more than sixty women had become members.[20] Initially run from Branford's offices in Westminster, in 1907 the Society secured rooms at 24 Buckingham Street, just off the Strand. It was here that the business of the Society was undertaken, though many of its professional events were held in the larger premises of other professional associations.

Analysis of the initial membership list of the Society shows that a core of nonacademic members was drawn from those in the personal circles around Geddes and Branford and from people active in various Ruskinian groups and enterprises. Geddes's associates included the natural historians J. Arthur Thomson and John C. Medd,[21] businessmen Henry Beveridge of Pitreavie and Henry Coates of Pitcullen, and the Reverend John B. Booth of the Ruskin Union. Core membership also included Victor Branford's three brothers and his brother-in-law Martyn Smith (a Governor of Birmingham University), Benchara Branford's brother-in-law Otto Siepmann (head of modern languages at Clifton College), and Dorothea Hollins of the Chelsea Utopians.

The wider rank and file membership included many academics from cognate disciplines such as philosophy, history, economics, psychology, geography, anthropology, and medicine. Most prominent among these academic members were the moral philosopher and COS activist Bernard Bosanquet, the social psychologist William McDougall, the geographer Halford Mackinder, the psychiatrist Henry Maudesley, and the economist James Mavor. Mavor, who had recently moved from Glasgow to Toronto, was an old friend of both Geddes and Bryce and spent the summers of 1904–06 in London.[22] Academic sociologists were, at this time, very few in number, but numerous social researchers and independent writers supported the Society. Hobhouse and Edvard Westermarck, both of whom were actually teaching sociology at the LSE, were, of course, members, while other social researchers in membership included Benjamin Kidd, John Robertson, John Hobson, Howard Collins (index compiler to Herbert Spencer), Lionel Tayler, Seebohm Rowntree, and Charles Booth. Intellectual debating societies such as the London Positivist Society and the South Place Ethical Society were represented by Caleb Saleeby, John Bridges, Stanton Coit, and Francis Galton, while other prominent intellectuals included Hilaire Belloc, George Bernard Shaw, and H. G. Wells. The academic ranks were strengthened by the nominal membership of a number of prominent overseas sociologists, including Emile Durkheim, Franklin Giddings, Ludwig Gumplowicz, Achille Loria, Adolfo González Posada, Albion Small, Ferdinand Tönnies, Michelangelo Vaccaro, and René Worms.

The overall membership of the Society was, however, very diverse and was by no means dominated numerically by its academic members. There were numerous members of parliament (MPs), mainly Liberals: Herbert Asquith, Leverton Harris, Charles Douglas, Alfred Emmott, Sir Charles Welby, Munro Ferguson, Sir Walter Foster, and Herbert Samuel. Ramsay Macdonald—not yet an MP but a member of the London County Council—was also a member. The numerous clergymen involved in the Society, such as T. C. Fry and James Hand, were mainly associated with settlements and social work. The Toynbee Hall settlement was represented by its head Canon Samuel Barnett and by the LSE academics and settlement workers Richard Tawney and William Beveridge. A particularly large section of the membership was involved in women's education and university extension work, including Lady Aberdeen, Henrietta Franklin, Charles Hecht, and Norman Wyld.

Geddes also became heavily involved in practical affairs outside the Sociological Society. A number of these ventures took place close to his London home in Chelsea. Charles Ashbee, living at 37 Cheyne Walk, had hatched a plan to buy land on the embankment close to Battersea Bridge where he could build flats and artists' studios. When this scheme fell through, John Ross proposed that the Town and Gown Association (see chapter 7) should buy the land as a site for a new University of London hall of residence. This was opposed by Thomas Cobden-Sanderson, a shareholder in the Association and other Geddes ventures, who had become greatly concerned over Geddes's management style. A new team of architects were brought in to develop the land as a conventional—and more commercial—apartment block. The building did eventually become the More Hall university residence, and in 1908 Geddes proposed a radical extension to this. A controversy over the demolition of historic Crosby Hall in the City of London led him to conceive the idea of moving the hall to Chelsea so as to operate it as an extension to More Hall. Working with the Earl of Sandwich and the Utopians, he secured private financial support from Mrs. Mary Wharrie to dismantle the old hall and to remove the materials for rebuilding in Chelsea (Saint 1991). Geddes used the hall for a series of public "masques" that built on the reenactments of history that had been a feature of the Edinburgh summer schools. A "Masque of Learning" had first been performed in Edinburgh in 1912 in celebration of the twenty-fifth anniversary of University Hall, and this was transferred to Crosby Hall, where it was performed in two parts (Geddes 1913a, b). These dramatizations of history were attempts to popularize and disseminate Geddes's sociological view of the development of contemporary culture. Through the Masques he made contact with the theatrical writer Amelia Defries, who became a convert to his ideas and avidly presented them in popular form (Defries 1927, 1928).

Philanthropic ventures in Birmingham and York, together with the Garden City movement and housing co-partnership schemes, had led to a growing interest in planning issues (Ashworth 1954; Cherry 1979), and through his writings on civics, Geddes became more involved in practical urban planning. His first venture was a study of Dunfermline carried out for Andrew Carnegie and the Carnegie Trust. His expanding planning work brought him into contact with Raymond Unwin and Barry Parker, the architect-planners of Letchworth[23] and Hampstead, who had been strongly influenced by Edward Carpenter in the Socialist League. Through groups concerned with the preservation of rural England, Geddes met and influenced Patrick Abercrombie, professor of civic design at Liverpool University. Abercrombie took up the civics framework as a useful sociological basis for his architectural work. Although he built these alliances with prominent architects and planners, Geddes never secured recognition or support from Thomas Horsfall of Manchester and John Nettlefold of Birmingham, who became his great rivals in planning matters.[24]

Geddes and his associates organized a series of touring urban planning exhibitions—under the general title of the "Cities and Town-Planning Exhibition"—in London in 1910, Edinburgh, Dublin, and Belfast in 1911, Ghent in 1913, and, on the verge of World War I, a further exhibition in Dublin. The London exhibition was held at Crosby Hall as part of an

International Town Planning Conference organized by the Royal Institute of British Architects. The Dublin exhibition was sponsored by his friend Lord Aberdeen, the viceregal representative in Dublin, and included a prize competition won by Patrick Abercrombie (Bannon 1999). It was intended that the exhibition would visit major cities in Canada and the United States, and Geddes contacted Charles Zueblin and a number of other intellectual contacts for support. Though Branford, then resident in the United States, acted as an intermediary with New York planners and architects, nothing came of this. However, the exhibition did go to India at the invitation of Lord Pentland, the governor of Madras and a former Secretary of State for Scotland, who was an admirer of Geddes's planning work. The materials for the Indian exhibition were packaged aboard the *Clan Grant*, but the ship was sunk en route by the German cruiser SMS *Emden*. The exhibits were lost, and Geddes had failed to take out any insurance for them, but thanks to Anna Geddes, John Ross, architect Henry Lanchester, and other disciples and associates, new exhibits were hastily arranged and an exhibition was run in India several months later than originally planned. Geddes and his son Alasdair sailed to India under wartime conditions on the SS *Nore*, disembarking at Bombay and traveling on to Madras and Calcutta. These exhibitions were fields of interaction and discourse in which networks of researchers and practitioners could come together in transnational relations to exchange ideas on civics and planning (Chabard 2009; and see Hysler-Rubin 2009).

A Cities Committee to promote civics and town planning had been organized within the Sociological Society in 1907, operating almost as a society within the Society. In 1911, Branford and Geddes had considered forming the Cities Committee into an independent society, as had happened some years earlier when eugenists within the Sociological Society had formed a separate Eugenics Education Society. Though it remained within the Society, the Cities Committee developed close links with other associations formed to promote Geddes's ideas, most notably the Regional Association and the Civic Education League.

The Regional Association had been formed in 1913 as the British Association for Regional Survey, following the success of Geddes's traveling exhibition on planning. Run by Mabel Barker and George Morris, and independent of both the Sociological Society and the Royal Geographical Society, the Association was especially concerned to encourage the use of surveys as teaching devices in schools and universities. The Association was soon to adopt the new name of the Provisional Committee for the Development of Regional Survey but in 1918 settled on the simpler name of the Regional Association. Surveys carried out for the Association included those by schoolteachers Morris in Saffron Walden and Valentine Bell in North

Lambeth, by Charles Fawcett in Teesdale, and Christopher Fagg in Croydon (Asquith 1924, 136; Levi 2006).

The Civic Education League had originally been formed in 1897 as the Moral Instruction League, under the intellectual leadership of Frederick Gould. Its aims were to promote the moral ideals of citizenship through religious and moral education and to improve the quality of teacher training colleges. The League saw history, geography, and sociology as means for the development of "character" and a sense of civic responsibility. Alexander Farquharson was appointed as secretary to the League in 1915 and, together with his professional and personal associate Margaret Tatton, he developed the idea of "Training for Citizenship" and aligned the League more closely with both the Regional Association and the Cities Committee.

Geddes hoped to enhance his growing international influence and took further work in India, carrying out surveys and planning reports for a number of large cities such as Madras, Bombay, Dacca, Indore, and Lucknow (see the extracts in Tyrwhitt 1947). He and Anna visited India twice during 1915–17, meeting the distinguished scientist and inventor Jagadish Chandra Bose about whom he later wrote a book (Geddes 1920c). In 1919, Geddes was appointed by one of his admirers to the foundation chair in sociology at Bombay and departed for this major venture with his son Arthur. Crossing the channel and traveling overland to Marseilles, they sailed on the SS *Etna* to Haifa to consult on some planning work in Palestine and then sailed on from Port Said to Bombay through the Suez Canal and the Red Sea (Boardman 1978, 312). Geddes combined his university work in India with work on a town plan for Haifa and plans for the new Hebrew University of Jerusalem. His appointment at Bombay had been planned as an iconic appointment to inspire town planning and the development of social science in India. Although he delivered a short series of general lectures on sociology (Geddes 1920a, b), his time in Bombay did little to advance sociology in the country. He left India in 1924 and spent the final part of his academic career at Montpellier, where he established the "Scots College" as a hall of residence for Scottish students at the university.

Branford's heavy involvement in business prior to 1918 meant that the Sociological Society drifted with little sign of overall direction until he was able to take a more active role after the war. It was at this time that the Society moved into rooms at the LSE, though conditions there proved too cramped and uncongenial, and in 1920 Branford secured the ownership of a mid-Victorian house in Pimlico, transferring this to the ownership of a Sociological Trust and renaming it Le Play House.[25] Office space in the building was provided for both the Regional Association and the Civic Education League and all three organizations were run on a day-to-day basis by Farquharson. In 1924 a legally separate organization named Le Play House was formed and this new organization subsumed the activities of the Cities Committee, the Regional Association, and the Civic Education League. A division of labor was established whereby Le Play House undertook responsibility for practical survey work and the Sociological Society took responsibility for the promotion of the theoretical works that Branford referred to as "pure sociology" (Evans 1986, 28).

Branford had become somewhat concerned that Geddes's strong support for the activities of Le Play House would result in the development of regionalism and the survey method at the expense of a pure sociology based on his vision of a scientific approach to city life. This rather belated expression of independence from Geddes led Branford in 1927 to approach Morris Ginsberg and seek closer cooperation with the sociologists at the LSE. Farquharson insisted that he, too, be involved in any negotiations and his presence—as a staunch advocate of Geddes's regionalism—fueled Ginsberg's suspicions concerning Branford's intentions and led him to suspect that the approach was a mere ploy to increase the influence of Geddes over the development of British sociology. Ginsberg insisted that the LSE could cooperate with the Sociological Society only if Geddes and Branford both stood down—something that even the seriously ill Branford could not contemplate (Evans 1986, 31; Rocquin 2006, 18).

Reorganization of the Society came about just a few months before Branford's death and when Geddes—spending more of his time in Montpellier—could be quietly marginalized by those working in London. On January 24,1930, an Institute of Sociology was established to incorporate the Sociological Society, and the Oxford anthropologist Robert R. Marett was persuaded to serve as an independent president and as a focus for its academic and intellectual credibility. However, both Ginsberg and Alexander Carr-Saunders (professor of social science at Liverpool University) refused to join the Institute unless Geddes was totally excluded. There were, nevertheless, some glimmerings of cooperation: the LSE and Liverpool sociologists agreed to speak at Institute conferences and, after the death of Geddes, they joined the revamped editorial board of the *Sociological Review*. Meanwhile, however, Geddes's own concerns at his increased marginalization had led him to join with Margaret Tatton in setting up the Foreign Fieldwork Committee of the Institute as a separate "Le Play Society" (Beaver 1962), though this, too, became an increasingly peripheral organization in the development of British social science.[26]

After Branford's death, and even more after Geddes's death two years later, Farquharson played the central role in managing Le Play House, the Sociological Society, and their various associated organizations. Disputes with the LSE sociologists, intellectual turmoil, financial difficulties, and personal conflicts around his management style and romantic attachments ensured that this was a period of institutional decline. Farquharson moved with his wife Dorothea to her home region, taking the organizational apparatus of the Institute to Malvern in Worcestershire and then to Ledbury in Herefordshire. Initially justified as evacuation from wartime bombing, and subsequently associated with the desire to focus on peripheral regions, the rural obscurity signed the death warrant of the Institute in a highly centralized London-focused Britain. The Institute became increasingly irrelevant to academic sociology and the Farquharsons eventually transferred its assets to Keele University. The Institute (and so the Sociological Society) was formally wound up in 1955.

TRANSATLANTIC CONNECTIONS

The internationalism and cosmopolitanism that Geddes and Branford derived from Comte's sociology led them to look to the United States, as the most advanced industrial society of the era, for insights into the problems of present-day society and its potential for radical, democratic reconstruction. Geddes made his first visit to the United States in the early spring of 1899, sailing from Liverpool and landing in New York where he accepted invitations to visit Chicago and Philadelphia on a second visit at the end of the year. This second trip was a three-month lecture tour financed by Sir Robert Pullar, the Perth dyer and a friend of Geddes's father, and was intended to build international support for his project of constructing the huge globe to represent Reclus's geographical ideas. His academic sponsors during the visit—all associated with the Edinburgh School of Sociology—were Charles Zueblin at Chicago and his expatriate friends James Mavor at the University of Toronto and Mark Wenley at the University of Michigan at Ann Arbor. At Chicago he established a close friendship with Jane Addams, whose university settlement at Hull House had emulated Toynbee Hall and Geddes's own work in Edinburgh.[27] He also got to know Albion Small, head of the university department of sociology, and established friendly relations with a number of other members of the university. Most notable among these academic contacts were John Dewey and the radical and eccentric Thorstein Veblen, the latter visiting Geddes in Dundee in 1902. Veblen became a close friend and intellectual influence on both Geddes and Branford: they adopted and cited his analysis of contemporary business and he, in turn, cited Branford's work (1914a) in his book *The Higher Learning in America* (Veblen 1918). At Harvard, Geddes secured the support of Robert Ely for his project and found himself in sympathy with the ideas of William James, who subsequently visited him in Dundee. It was during this second trip to the United States that Geddes met Stanley Hall, the psychologist who was to be such an influence on the social psychology of both Geddes and

Branford. In Washington, Geddes met the American Comtean Lester Ward, and it seems likely that his contacts with Ward and with Addams would have brought him into contact with Charlotte Perkins Gilman.

Geddes's most significant American contact was with Joseph Fels, whom he met in London in 1904–05 and who was to be of importance in many of the practical activities undertaken by Geddes and Branford. The profits from his family business had allowed him the opportunity of pursuing a range of political reform programs. Interested in the secularist movement, Fels joined Felix Adler's Society for Ethical Culture in the mid-1890s and discovered the radical economic ideas of Henry George (1879), who advocated land reform and a "single-tax" system. Fels became a committed and prominent Georgist (Dodson 2005). His advocacy of small-scale, self-sufficient land ownership—a proposal that had great similarities with the anarchist ideas of Kropotkin—led to his involvement in the Philadelphia Vacant Lots Cultivation Association, which made allotments of land to the unemployed and drew up plans to encourage this system in other parts of the United States and in Britain. From 1901 until his death in 1914, Joe Fels visited Britain frequently, where he made London his principal base and where he set up a business office at 39 Wilson Street. In London, he became associated with the Fabian Society and met Labour Party politician George Lansbury, with whom between 1903 and 1908 he launched a number of allotment schemes and farm colonies in which unemployed "settlers" were able to work their own small holdings. The best-known of these were at Laindon and Maryland in Essex and at Hollesley Bay in Suffolk, but other allotment schemes were set up in Birmingham, Edinburgh, Bristol, and Northampton.[28] When Ashbee's Guild of Handicraft in Chipping Campden ran into financial problems after 1905, Fels funded the purchase of land in neighboring Broad Campden that allowed some of the craft workers to resettle on small holdings.

After he settled in England, Fels attended meetings of the London ethical societies and it was probably at these meetings that Geddes first met him.[29] Through 1905 they corresponded about small holdings and planning matters, and Fels attended meetings of the Sociological Society. Geddes and Fels had a mutual friendship with Kropotkin, then living at Bromley in Kent, about two miles from Fels's large house, "Elmwood," at Bickley.[30] The two were on very close terms by the end of 1906, and Geddes put Fels in touch with Branford later that year. Both Geddes and Branford were frequent visitors to Elmwood during 1906 and 1907.[31]

Sometime during 1906, Fels met the Zionist activist Israel Zangwill, who had formed the Jewish Territorial Organisation in 1905 to recruit experts to investigate various overseas possibilities for Jewish settlement, including Libya, Angola, Canada, Mexico, and Siberia (Wohlgelernter 1964). Fels offered to help finance a Jewish colony on Georgist principles and proposed a settlement on land he owned in Paraguay (see chapter 7). This possibility led Geddes to encourage cooperation between Fels and Branford, whose involvement with a Paraguayan railway gave him a common interest in the economic development of the country. It is possible that Fels knew of Sybella Gurney through his earlier labor colony schemes and that he introduced her to Branford; he was certainly a sponsor on their marriage license and the wedding took place in his brother's house in Philadelphia.

Branford was due to travel to Paraguay in early 1907, and Fels proposed joining him there after a meeting with the Argentinean businessman Manuel Rodríguez in London in early December 1906, when the prospects for a Jewish settlement in Paraguay had been discussed. Though the settlement plan was eventually rejected by Zangwill, the relationship between Fels and Branford in relation to Paraguayan development continued and Fels invested directly in the production of tropical produce. Their joint business ventures involved schemes set up by Marcel Hardy, who was involved in a number of labor colony projects in the country. In 1910, Fels backed plans for a new labor colony, investing £15,000 in a scheme run jointly by Hardy and John Slaughter. Slaughter was an American psychologist and first chairman of the Eugenics Education Society, who worked in London from 1905 to 1909 and served for a time as secretary of the Sociological Society. A heavy drinker, Slaughter was imprisoned after the accidental shooting of his cook and a rift developed between him and Hardy.[32] By the end of 1913, Fels was involved in a serious dispute with both men and was also arguing with directors of the Paraguayan railway. Branford was able to put together a rescue operation for Hardy, but Fels was unable to disentangle himself from Hardy's disastrous scheme until 1919.

Following his marriage to Sybella Gurney, Branford spent a great deal of his time in New York on business, living close to the National Arts Club in central Manhattan and using this as his academic base. He undertook an American lecture tour during 1913, presenting a number of papers that he published in *Interpretations and Forecasts* (Branford 1914a). His main sponsors on this lecture tour were associates from the Edinburgh summer schools, most notably William Bailey at Yale and Mark Wenley at Michigan. Bailey, who worked on demography and social statistics (see Bailey 1906), taught political economy and, later, Christian sociology and practical philanthropy at Yale. Wenley began his career at St. Margaret's College in Glasgow and had been a teacher on the 1895 Summer School. He had been teaching philosophy and psychology at Michigan since 1896 and was the author of an influential book on anarchism (Wenley 1913). Branford's ideas found a receptive audience in the United States—some of his essays had already been published in the *American Journal of Sociology*—and he made a firm friend in Charles Ellwood, who was also developing a Comtean view of social reconstruction (1917, 1922). Another close contact in the United States was John Hecht, an economist who contributed to the *New Age* magazine and wrote on issues of social reconstruction (Hecht 1920). Branford was also in contact with Charles Ferguson, a Christian sociologist and advocate of social credit whom he may have met in New York—both were members of the National Arts Club—and Ferguson's ideas on university organization and outreach extended and influenced those of Branford and Geddes (Ferguson 1911, 1900; see Johnson 2006). Branford's achievements in sociology were recognized by the American Sociological Society in 1917, when he was awarded honorary life membership in the Society: he is the only British sociologist ever to have been accorded this honor.

Lewis Mumford was to become a significant associate of both Geddes and Branford, and he developed ideas on urban and industrial development that advanced on theirs.[33] Mumford was largely self-educated and discovered Geddes's biological work in late 1914. Through correspondence with Geddes's son-in-law Frank Mears (working at the Outlook Tower), Mumford obtained copies of Geddes's papers on civics and became totally committed to the ecological approach to the city region, regarding *Cities in Evolution* (Geddes 1915a) as a particular inspiration. This led him to begin a correspondence with Geddes himself, and it was through this that he discovered the writings of Ebenezer Howard on garden cities and George Russell on cooperatives, becoming wholly committed to the Geddes project. He found employment on the short-lived radical magazine *The Dial*, where Veblen was an important intellectual mentor, and in 1920 when closure of the magazine was imminent, he wrote to Geddes and Branford offering to help them with their work in Britain. Branford invited him to help editing the *Sociological Review* and to take free accommodation at Le Play House, and so Mumford worked with Branford for five months in 1920—Geddes was in India at this time—and visited again briefly in 1922. He first met Geddes when the latter made a visit to the United States in 1923, hoping to persuade Mumford to take on the secretarial work of compiling his notes and papers into a systematic work of social theory. Mumford was concerned, however, that Geddes was treating him as a surrogate son—a replacement for Alasdair who had been killed during the war—and he sought to avoid an overly close relationship. He did, however, remain intellectually close and visited Geddes in Edinburgh in 1925 (Miller 1898, 115–33, 219–30).

THE INTELLECTUAL WORK OF THE GEDDES CIRCLE

The professional activities of Geddes and Branford were the base from which they and their circle produced and developed a corpus of work in which they articulated their sociological vision of reconstruction. Central to this work was the Sociological Society, where they grounded their own ideas in a wider disciplinary conception of sociology. In its initial years, a series of symposiums were held and the presentations and discussions were reported in a new publication, the *Sociological Papers*, which appeared as three annual volumes between 1905 and 1907. The published volumes of the *Sociological Papers* reflected the deliberately broad strategy taken by Branford, who wanted to ensure that the Society was not simply a vehicle for Geddes's ideas. Published papers included historical and theoretical statements on the origins and nature of sociology by Branford and by Durkheim, and views on the relationship of sociology to ethics and the philosophy of history. Wenley wrote on the establishment of sociology as an academic discipline in the United States, while Beatrice Webb wrote on observation, interviewing, and the use of documents as methods of social research. The largest single group of papers were on eugenics, reflecting the influence of Francis Galton. Other papers considered agricultural villages, the school, magic, unemployment (by William Beveridge and with comments from Hobson and Rider Haggard), the Russian revolution of 1905, and (by Westermarck) the position of women in early civilizations. Geddes's own contributions (1904b; 1905a), in which he explored civics in relation to city planning and utopianism, were the sole examples of papers specifically on this topic.

The Society was initially very successful in recruiting a diverse range of people who identified in varying ways with what they understood "sociology" to be. Many of its academic activities were organized through study groups, and among the first to be formed were a Social Psychology Group in 1912 and a Group for the Study of Women in Society in 1914, the latter having twenty-eight members. Somewhat later, a Group on Social Finance was formed. The most active group was the Cities Committee, formed in 1907 to promote Geddes's vision of a regional social science through town planning and to undertake regional social surveys.

The success of the *Papers* led the executive committee to draw up plans for a full professional journal to be launched in 1908 under the title, *The Sociological Review*. The first appointee as editor was Hobhouse, though he came to feel that Branford and others in the Geddes circle were exercising an undue influence over the contents of the journal. His resignation after the first four years of the *Review*'s life led to the appointment of Sam Ratcliffe as "Acting Editor," an office he held for the next four years as nominee of the Geddes group. In 1916, Branford felt that his scaled-down business commitments would allow him to take a more central role in the journal and he slimmed down the editorial board and took on the editorial role, holding this until his death in 1930.

The issues under Hobhouse's editorship included a diverse range of articles on such topics as religion, crime, and the family, these generally taking a comparative approach. Authors included such people as Harrison, McDougall, W. H. R. Rivers, Urwick, and Wallas, with Volume Two including rival articles by Bosanquet and Sidney Webb on the Poor Law report of 1908.[34] There were, of course, numerous pieces by the eugenists and also by Geddes. Sybella Gurney's first paper for the *Review*—on the Garden City movement (Gurney 1910)—appeared in Volume Three.[35] Volume Four carried a piece by Branford (1911) commenting on H. G. Wells's critical paper on the nature of a sociological society. A similar pattern of publication was followed under Ratcliffe, with papers on the general election, socialism, the psychology of William James, Australian totemism, black emancipation, and scientific management. There were comparative studies of India, Canada, and China, and on "primitive" cultures and technologies. Authors included Hobson, Wallas, Robertson, Tawney, Robert MacIver, and such foreign luminaries as W. E. B. Du Bois.

It was under Branford's editorship that the balance of articles shifted strongly toward issues of regionalism (in papers by Mumford, Herbert Fleure, and Clifford Darby) and to related issues of civics and urban planning (in papers by Geddes, Unwin, and Abercrombie). One of Branford's first ventures under Ratcliffe had been to launch a symposium on social finance (Branford 1914b) to which his now-wife Sybella had contributed (S. Branford 1915). These articles were followed by other papers on finance, credit, and economic power, including papers on pure economics by such international figures as Irving Fisher. Though there had been a definite shift in content after 1917, this was by no means an exclusive takeover by the Geddes circle. In this period, the *Review* carried papers by Rivers on social psychology, Christopher Dawson on race and nationalism, and other contributions on crime, education, welfare, and public health. Harry Elmer Barnes and Paul Fauconnet contributed articles on the history of sociology. Even Hobhouse was still willing to publish in the journal during 1921. The high point of Geddes-circle dominance was, perhaps, the period from 1923 to 1925, when numerous draft sections from Branford's books were published as articles.

After Branford had once again taken a more active role in the Society and the *Review*, he projected a series of pamphlets and books to draw out the social and political themes of social reconstruction and communal renewal. It was in these publications that Geddes and Branford began to concretize their own view of social reconstruction. Central to this program of publication was a pamphlet series entitled *Papers for the Present*, produced through the Cities Committee and going through various incarnations as it developed. A full outline for the series was initially announced in 1919 with the actual and projected titles shown in Table 3.2. Table 3.3 shows the ultimate, almost complete, form in which the series was published.

Many of the papers appeared in alternative form in the *Sociological Review*, some appearing there first and others being later reported in the journal. The great bulk of the papers appeared under the collective authorship of the Cities Committee. Most of these, however, seem to have been written by Branford, though Geddes produced *Public Health in an Industrial Age* and George Sandeman produced both *Spirit Creative* and *A Gardener of Paradise*. The psychological study of education announced as *The Play Way* seems to have been intended as a contribution from Henry Caldwell Cook, who had published articles on this topic in *The New Age* during 1914 and later brought these together as a book (Cook 1917). *The World Without and the World Within* was to be a reprint of earlier articles by Geddes (1905b),[36] though a work along these lines eventually appeared outside the series as a book by Theodora Thompson (1928).

Table 3.2. Papers for the Present (1919)

	First Series: Morals and Economics
1	*The Modern Midas* (1918)
2	*The Banker's Part in Reconstruction* (1918)
3	*Spirit Creative* (1918)
	Second Series: Art and Education
4	*The Re-education of the Adult* (1918)
5	*A Citizen Soldier* (1918)
6	[*Mars and the Muses*]
7	[*The Play Way*]
	Third Series: Politics and Civics
8	*A Rustic View of War and Peace* (1918)
9	*The Drift to Revolution* (1918)
10	[*Masters of Our Fate*]
11	[*Eutopia or Hell*]
12	[*The Free City in the League of Nations*]
	Fourth Series: Religion
13	[*The World Without and the World Within*]
14	[*An Old Saint in a New Garment*]

Note: Titles in square brackets were unpublished at the time of the announcement. Published titles are shown with the date of their publication.

Source: Advertising trailer in Branford and Geddes (1919b).

Table 3.3. Papers for the Present (1921)

	First Series: Morals and Economics
1	*The Modern Midas* (1918)
2	*The Banker's Part in Reconstruction* (1918)
3	*Spirit Creative* (1918)
	Second Series: Art and Education
4	*The Re-education of the Adult* (1918)
5	*A Citizen Soldier* (1918)
6	*Public Health in the Industrial Age* (1919)
7	*The Third Alternative, Part 1: Business and Philanthropy* (1919)
	Third Series: Politics and Civics
8	*A Rustic View of War and Peace* (1918)
9	*The Drift to Revolution* (1918)
10	*A Gardener of Paradise* (1920)
11	*Sir Ronald Ross's Story* (1920)
12	*The War Mind, the Business Mind, and a Third Alternative* (1920)
	Fourth Series: Religion
13	*[Theology, Civics and Poetry]*
14	*A New Year's Message: Earth, Hell, and the Third Alternative* (1921)
15	*Body, Mind, and Spirit* (1922)

Note: The title in square brackets was unpublished. Published titles are shown with the date of their publication.

A book series paralleled the topics of these pamphlets, dealing with them at greater length. Under the general title "The Making of the Future," this series was to build on the fusion of regionalism, humanism, and civism that Geddes and Branford had seen as the basis of contemporary sociology and that had begun to be set out in *Cities in Evolution* (Geddes 1915a) and *Interpretations and Forecasts* (Branford 1914a). The series was launched with two introductory volumes in 1917 and was projected to include an eventual eight titles, though two further titles are also associated with the series. These are shown in Table 3.4.

The two introductory volumes were intended to set the scene for the series as a whole. *The Coming Polity* outlined the ideas of Geddes and Branford on social development and social reconstruction, making more concrete their eutopian vision. *Ideas at War,* produced from a symposium held at King's College, London, applied these ideas to the particular implications of World War I.[37] The volumes by Fleure and by Peake et al. were supposed to focus on the general principles of regionalism, though only

Table 3.4. The Making of the Future—as announced or planned (1917)

The Coming Polity: A Study in Reconstruction (Branford and Geddes 1917, 1919a)
Ideas at War (Geddes and Slater 1917)
Human Geography in Western Europe: A Study in Appreciation (Fleure 1918)
Social Finances—John Ross
University and City: A Study in Personality and Citizenship—Patrick Geddes and Victor Branford
The Land and the People: A Study in Rural Development—Harold Peake, Herbert Fleure, Sybella Branford
Westminster Temporal and Spiritual: An Interpretative Study—probably Patrick Geddes and Victor Branford
Science and Sanctity: A Study in Spiritual Renewal—Patrick Geddes and Victor Branford

Added later to the series:
The Provinces of England (Fawcett 1919)

Intended as part of the series:
Health and Conduct (Brock 1923)

Note: Titles eventually published are shown in bold. Unpublished titles are shown with their projected or assumed authors.
Source: Announcement in the first volume in the series.

the Fleure volume actually appeared and Branford felt that this was too much of a textbook and was not properly in accordance with the practical aims of the series.[38] By 1919, the projected books on the university and on Westminster had been combined into a single volume under the title *Our Social Inheritance* (Branford and Geddes 1919b) and the proposed book on *Social Finance* had been abandoned, as Ross had been unable to work on it. *The Coming Polity* appeared in a revised edition two years after its first publication; the original edition had been divided into two parts discussing "The Science of the Future" and "Method," but chapters 11 and 12 were substantially reworked to form a third part on "Practice" for the new edition.[39] It was announced that there were "other volumes in preparation," but the only addition made to the series was that by Charles Fawcett on the political organization of the English regions. *Science and Sanctity*, envisaged as a jointly written work on spiritual renewal, eventually appeared under the sole authorship of Victor Branford, though not as a part of the then defunct series (V. V. Branford 1923). It seems that Arthur Brock's *Health and Conduct* was originally intended for the series, but it was completed only after the series was abandoned and appeared simply as one of the "Le Play House Papers."

A major project for Branford and the Sociological Society was the organization of a conference on religion in which they explored the question of spirituality and modernity. Loftus Hare of the School of Oriental and African Studies proposed a review of "Some Living Religions within the Empire," in association with the British Empire Exhibition to be held at Wembley in 1924. This was seen as a continuation of a series of conferences that began in Chicago in 1893 and had continued irregularly in Paris, Basel, Oxford, and Leiden until interrupted by World War I. The Wembley conference was to be a prelude to a full resumption of the series in Paris later in the year. Hare drew in Sir E. Denison Ross, the principal of SOAS, as chairman, and it was during the detailed planning that they decided to approach the Sociological Society as co-organizers. Branford and Sir Francis Younghusband (president of the Society) joined the executive committee of the conference, Branford becoming a vice chairman.

The Living Religions Conference opened at the Imperial Institute in South Kensington in September 1924 with speakers drawn from the major religions of the British Empire, excluding Judaism and Christianity. Branford saw this as a major step toward religious understanding and eventual spiritual unity and pushed ahead with the publication of his own book on the subject (V. Branford 1924), as a general commentary on the implications of the discussions, which were themselves published the following year (Hare 1925). Sociological Society contributors to the symposium included Branford, Geddes, and Arthur Thomson, together with Fleure, Rachel Annan Taylor, Younghusband, and Christopher Dawson.

The various publications of the Sociological Society set out a broad disciplinary program, in which they involved a large and diverse group of social thinkers, and a core vision of social reconstruction. In and around these publications, the various members of the Geddes circle produced their separate and interlinked publications.

Geddes himself was a prolific, if disorganized, author. He threw out loosely connected theoretical statements as his ideas evolved and was constantly engaged in discussion over related ideas, always ready to move in new directions. Though he claimed only to be developing his core ideas, these were often presented in a very simple and didactic form or in dense and overcomplex schemes, and he was ever-reliant on collaborators such as Thomson and Branford to bring some order to his work. Geddes noted the difficulties that readers would have in understanding his work, which "might appear perplexing and discursive," since at one time critical and at another constructive; now general, abstract and classificatory, yet again concrete; and ranging in presentiment from graphic summaries to concrete illustrations, examples and allusions, even anecdotes. (Geddes 1920a, 15)

Geddes's earliest publications were in botany and led on to explorations in biology, where his work did eventually achieve completion. Working with Thomson, who managed to give Geddes's ideas some organization, he produced *The Evolution of Sex* (Geddes and Thomson 1889) and *Chapters on Modern Botany* (1893) and went on to produce general accounts of *Evolution* (1911), *Problems of Sex* (Thomson and Geddes 1912), and *Sex* (Geddes and Thomson 1914). The two went on much later to produce the massive *Life: Outline of General Biology* (1931) as a comprehensive summation of Geddes's ideas.

Geddes saw his work in biology and in sociology as complementary to each other, but he never achieved the systematic statement of sociological principles to which he aspired. When he visited France in 1878, he encountered not only the environmentalism and regionalism of Le Play—as presented by Henri Demolins—but also renewed his enthusiasm for the Comtean positivism he had already encountered in London. On his return to Britain, he began to construct a materialist social science in papers for the Royal Society and the British Association for the Advancement of Science. He began with a discussion of Ruskin's philosophy for the view that labor could be seen as a form of mechanical energy (Geddes 1881, 1884a,b, 1888; and see Studholme 2007), some of these ideas also being presented in his 1886 university extension classes for St. Andrews University. He went on to explore the relationship between the physical environment, labor, and social life, establishing the basic principles in papers on civics for the Sociological Society (1904b, 1905a). These ideas were elaborated in his most famous book *Cities in Evolution* (1915a), and in a series of essays in which he sought to clarify and systematize them. He regarded the essays he published in India (Geddes 1920a,b) as a summation of his thought, but amplified them very slightly in later essays (1924a,b, 1927a,b). He intended that his work on sociology would complement and complete the project set out in *Life* and had planned a companion volume to be called *Social Life. Outline of Sociology*. However, this book never appeared and the final version of his sociological framework appeared only as a lengthy appendix to his last work (Geddes 1931).

In parallel with these general theoretical reflections, Geddes worked on applications of his theory to issues of urban and regional planning and architecture. His first such venture was a short-lived magazine called *The Evergreen*, launched in 1895, in which he brought together a number of literary and historical writers to explore Scottish Celtic culture to develop a romantic sense of "place" as the key to a more cosmopolitan outlook and vision. His most important statements in urban studies were an early report on Dunfermline (1904a) and later reports on Indore (1918) and Jerusalem (1919), though shorter reports were produced on Edinburgh, Chelsea, and some other districts, and some general principles were drawn out in *Cities in Evolution* (1915a). Geddes's numerous political projects were actively promoted in papers on Cyprus and Armenia (1897a,b), on university reform (1890, 1906), and in his contribution to the discussions of the Utopians (Hollins 1908).

Victor Branford's earliest publications were two crammers on biology and chemistry for medical students (Branford 1888, 1889), produced while tutoring in Edinburgh[40] Once engaged in his accountancy business, he produced a series of articles on economics that paralleled the investigations that Geddes had been developing from Ruskin (Branford 1901b,a, 1903a).[41] Branford's publications in sociology proper began in the early years of the twentieth century with articles on the history and nature of sociology (Branford 1903b, 1904) and the relationship between sociology and citizenship (1905, 1906). His developing business career prevented any rapid furtherance of this work, and the brief investigations that he was able to carry out appeared with later lectures and addresses in a compilation produced on the eve of World War I (1914a). His major work of the first decade and a half of the century, however, was his psychobiography of St. Columba (1912), a study in which he began to construct a social psychology of cognitive and moral development.

Toward the end of World War I, Branford persuaded Geddes to allow him to work up the joint books in which he set out the elements of their sociological theory and the political strategy of the Third Way (Branford and Geddes 1919a,b; and see Geddes and Slater 1917).[42] It was in these works that they diagnosed the crisis of "wardom" and the need for peaceful social reconstruction. In the postwar period he furthered these ideas through investigations into the spirituality of what he called the "Larger Modernity" (V. V. Branford 1923, 1924). During this later period, Branford produced numerous articles for the *Sociological Review,* many of these—as already noted—becoming pamphlets in the series of *Papers for the Present.*

Branford constantly sought to reorganize and recast his works into notional series that he felt would give them a greater coherence and impact. The various plans he produced, complete with newly projected titles and the renaming of already published works, illustrate his vision of his own work. His first exercise in intellectual reconstruction was in 1923, when he retrospectively assigned some of his earlier works to a series of "Studies in Contemporary Social Evolution" (see Table 3.5) that brought together

Table 3.5. Studies in Contemporary Social Evolution (1923)

Interpretations and Forecasts (Branford 1914a)
Papers in Banking and Finance (1915–1921)
Westminster: An Interpretative Survey (1916)
The Coming Polity (Branford and Geddes 1919a)
A Citizen Soldier (1917)
A Rustic View of War and Peace (1918)
Our Social Inheritance (Branford and Geddes 1919b)
Whitherward? Hell or Eutopia (V. V. Branford 1921)
Body, Mind and Spirit (1922)*
Science and Sanctity (V. V. Branford 1923)
The Visionary of Life (projected for 1924)

*Most likely intended as a compilation of articles from *Sociological Review*.
Source: Advertising trailer in Branford (1923).

a number of pamphlets and compilations of articles, as well as full-length books. A book to be called *The Visionary of Life* was projected for this series, though its ideas appeared only in part within *Living Religions* (V. V. Branford 1924). In this book, produced for the Wembley Conference, Branford explored the "larger Modernity" of spiritual power that he had discovered through his engagement with religious spirituality. Branford also promised a further volume on *The War Demand and Afterwards*, but this was never completed. It is likely that many of the ideas intended for this book appeared in the discussions of the coal industry that he produced at the time of the general strike (Branford 1926b, a).

Branford was not satisfied with this arrangement and was unhappy with his own ability to rework his papers into more developed studies. He felt that much of his work had been spread across numerous short articles and needed to be pulled together and reworked into more systematic studies. Business commitments and his failing health made it difficult for him to commit sufficient time to this task and he began to hope that someone else would undertake the task after his death. His will included a bequest to the institute to finance the compilation and republication of his works, and he intended that his friend Lewis Mumford would undertake this editorial task. In two codicils to the will he set out frameworks to guide this republication. His initial suggestion was for a series based on manuscripts filed in a "green portmanteau" at his home in Hastings, as shown in Table 3.6.

His revised plan involved a compilation of his unpublished papers into new books, to be followed by the reprinting of his existing works—this time excluding those written jointly with Geddes. A year later, however, he was proposing the immediate reprinting of his published works (in modified

Table 3.6. Our Modern World: Papers of Victor Branford (1927)

1	The Theory of War and Peace
2	The Visioning of Life
	(i) Impulses to War and Presuppositions of a Militant Peace
	(ii) Ideals and Realities (incorporating "A Gardener's Paradise," written with George Sandeman)
3	The Dedicated Life
4	Westminster: Temporal and Spiritual
	Reprints:
5	*Science and Sanctity* (V. V. Branford 1923)
6	*Living Religions* (V. V. Branford 1924)
7	*Whitherward? Hell or Eutopia* (V. V. Branford 1921)

form), which were then to be followed by published versions of his unpublished manuscripts. A final volume was to bring together his key essays on sociology and citizenship (see Table 3.7). This extensive editing and republication was never undertaken. Although Mumford spent some time working on the manuscripts he concluded that they were too diverse and disorganized to be brought together through mere editing. A comprehensive task of reworking would be needed and Mumford was unable to commit the time and effort that this would involve.

The works of those in the wider Geddes circle around the Sociological Society and Le Play House were diverse but they shared a number of core

Table 3.7. Our Modern World: Papers of Victor Branford (1928)

1	*Science and Sanctity* (V. V. Branford 1923)
2	*Whitherward? Hell or Eutopia* [including "A Rustic View of War and Peace," "The Bankers Part in Reconstruction," "A Citizen Soldier," "The Third Alternative," "The Sciences and the Humanities"] (e.g., V. V. Branford 1918, 1919b,a, 1920)
3	*The Coal Crisis and the Future* [including his contribution to *Coal: Ways to Reconstruction*] (V. V. Branford 1926b,a)
4	The Religious Approach
	(i) *Living Religions* (V. V. Branford 1924)
	(ii) *St. Columba* (V. V. Branford 1912)
5	*Our Social Inheritance* (Branford and Geddes 1919b)
6	*The Coming Polity* (Branford and Geddes 1919a)
7	*The Sociological Movement* [essays on sociology from 1903–1928 and essays on citizenship from 1905–07]

ideas that they saw as aspects of a unified paradigm of research. Of course, not all members of the Society can be considered members of the circle, and not all members of the circle were members of the Society. The boundaries of the circle can be established only on the basis of the personal, business, and intellectual associations that we trace in this book.

Principal among these associates, of course, was Sybella Branford, whose first publication was a history of cooperation produced while she was secretary of Labour Co-partnership (Gurney 1896). Her interests in co-partnership were further developed in a paper on co-partnership in housing delivered at an International Congress of Women in Toronto (Gurney 1909), a reflection on the relationship of co-partnership to the guild idea (S. Branford 1923), and a posthumous publication on cooperative principles (S. Branford 1927). The fundamentals of reconstruction and garden city planning were explored in one of her final papers before her marriage (Gurney 1910) and were elaborated in later papers on village development and housing (S. Branford 1913, 1921). In a paper for the *Sociological Review* she examined some of the general ideas of the arts and crafts movement that underpinned these planning proposals (S. Branford 1916–17). Along with Victor Branford she developed an interest in ideas of social credit and contributed a number of discussions of these principles and their relation to communist ideals and spiritual concerns (S. Branford 1915, 1924, 1925). In a minor reflection on educational practices, she discussed Geddes's work for the new university in Jerusalem (S. Branford 1919). Her major sociological publication, however, was a key statement of the methodological principles involved in the Le Play approach to sociology that she co-wrote with the Secretary of the Sociological Society (S. Branford and Farquharson 1924).

Another central figure in the Geddes circle was Benchara Branford who, like his brother, had been inspired by Geddes when an undergraduate student at Edinburgh University. Ben Branford taught mathematics in Yorkshire College and at the university in Leeds, but was appointed as director of education and founding principal of the technical college in Sunderland from 1901–05 before becoming Divisional Inspector of Education for the London County Council. His first publication on the teaching of mathematics (B. Branford 1908) used the developmental psychology of Stanley Hall and anticipated some of the ideas later developed by Piaget. In the early 1890s he had begun work on a major study in philosophical anthropology that he called *Orpheus and Eurydice* and that he completed, in draft, in 1912. Continuing to work on this book, he published works that drew on various of its elements, leading to a book on wardom and the world crisis and on the role of the university in resolving this crisis, publishing this in the midst of World War I (B. Branford 1916). This book proposed a federal constitution for the advanced societies, which he elaborated in *A New*

Chapter in the Science of Government (B. Branford 1919). His final published book, *Eros and Psyche* (B. Branford 1934), was an attempt to set out the philosophical anthropology that underpinned his work and was the only form in which a substantial part of *Orpheus and Eurydice* ever appeared.[43] Apart from his book on mathematics, Benchara Branford's works sold few copies during his lifetime, but the French social philosopher Jean Izoulet was a great admirer and ranked him, somewhat excessively, alongside Newton and Darwin (1927).[44]

The physician Arthur Brock had encountered Geddes during his time as a medical student in Edinburgh and became a convert to his sociological ideas. A specialist in psychiatry, he worked during World War I with Rivers on the treatment of shell shock at Craiglockhart War Hospital in Edinburgh, where one of his patients was the poet Wilfred Owen (Cantor 2005; Hibberd 1977). Brock worked closely with the Outlook Tower throughout this time and developed the thesis that disease—physical and mental—is a result of detachment from the environment and can be treated through sociological practice aimed at social reengagement. He was commissioned to write for the *Papers for the Present,* but Branford felt that the manuscript was in need of considerable stylistic editing and the book (Brock 1923) appeared only after the series had been abandoned.

A number of teachers were active contributors to the evolving framework of ideas. George Sandeman worked as a jobbing editor and writer and ran a private school and printing shop at Ernest Westlake's colony at Godshill in the New Forest, though he spent much time traveling around the countryside in his horse-drawn caravan. His early work included a primer on biology (1896) and the editing of two sets of encyclopedias. For the Sociological Society he wrote articles in the *Sociological Review,* a book on *Social Renewal* (Sandeman 1913), and pamphlets on work and community (Sandeman and Sandeman 1919, 1929). He also developed his ideas in two social novels of family and community (1909, 1915). Henry Caldwell Cook, a teacher at the Perse School in Cambridge, developed innovative educational ideas about the role of play and creative work in his book *The Play Way* (Cook 1917). Theodora Thompson, who also seems to have worked as a teacher, produced an anthology of antiwar writing (Thompson 1918) to which Oliver Lodge wrote a preface, and a psychological study using Geddes's ideas on *The World Without and the World Within* (Thompson 1928). Sister Nivedita investigated Indian family and community life and, under the influence of Geddes, wrote a study on *The Web of Indian Life* (Noble 1904). A further figure in the circle was Gilbert Slater, principal of Ruskin College, Oxford, from 1909 to 1915 and involved in the production of *Ideas at War* (Geddes and Slater 1917). Slater produced, among other things, studies on cooperative housing (1901, 1902), general works in economic and social history (1915, 1930), and, while working with Geddes in India from 1915 to 1922, a major investigation of Indian society (1918, 1924).

Branford and Geddes maintained very close relations with a number of the thinkers on the progressive wing of the eugenics movement who developed ideas that connected with and engaged with the core principles of the Geddes circle. Lionel Tayler trained in medicine at St. Thomas' Hospital, London, and lectured on extension courses in sociology and human biology. His work centered on the biological basis of psychological temperament (Tayler 1904), which he applied specifically to questions of gender difference (Tayler 1922), though he also produced a work on crowd psychology (Tayler 1921). Caleb Saleeby (1909, 1911) wrote from a similar perspective on issues of "race" and gender (and see Freeden 1979), and he produced the first British textbook on sociology (Seleeby 1905). John Slaughter, too, took much from the eugenic argument—he was the first chair of the Eugenics Education Society—and set out a view of women's biological inheritance as the basis of their distinctive role in social life (Slaughter 1909–10; see also Richardson 2000).

Integration of science with art was a major theme in the intellectual work of those in the Geddes circle, and Geddes saw his settlement and planning work as artistic endeavors in support of the Celtic revival and Scottish nationalism. He met the artist and Theosophist John Duncan in Dundee in 1891 and involved him in the work of the Edinburgh Social Union. Duncan produced friezes and murals for Geddes's houses, together with Charles Mackie he decorated Henry Beveridge's home at Pitreavie (Fowle 2004, 41), and he was associated with Geddes in the founding of the Edinburgh School of Art. In 1900, Geddes secured an appointment for him as a lecturer in the Chicago Institute (Ferguson 2004; Young 2004). A major venture for him was his involvement in the production of *The Evergreen* literary magazine, for which Mackie designed a front cover. Contributions to the magazine included stories by "Fiona McLeod" (the pseudonym of William Sharp), the poetry of Duncan and of Rachel Annan Taylor, and explorations of the romanticism of place. The poet F. V. Branford, Victor Branford's nephew, must also be mentioned. Freddie Branford was deeply affected by his wartime experiences and serious disability—he was treated at Craiglockhart—and wrote dark metaphysical poems, a number of which reflected on individual experiences of war. His best-known poems are collected in *Titans and Gods* (F. V. Branford 1918) which contains the autobiographical "To D. C. B," dedicated to his aunt Dorothy, *Five Poems* (F. V. Branford 1922), and *The White Stallion* (F. V. Branford 1924). Some of his poetry originally appeared in *The Dial* magazine at the time when Mumford and Veblen were associated with it.

Geddes's ideas had a huge influence within the developing university discipline of geography and, through this, in urban and regional sociology.[45] A key channel for this was his own son, Arthur, who taught geography at Edinburgh University for many years and wrote an important regional study of India (A. Geddes 1927). Marion Newbigin was a teaching assistant to Arthur Thomson and became a prominent geographer using the Geddes approach (Newbigin 1912; 1914; see also 1924). The cartographer John G. Bartholomew and other members of the prominent Edinburgh map and atlas publishing firm had close relations with Geddes, and Bartholomew and Geddes pushed for new publications, academic programs, and institutions of geography in Scotland. Most important, however, was Andrew Herbertson, who worked for Geddes as a demonstrator in Dundee and then taught geography at Oxford. Herbertson's first major book, an introduction to human geography, was published jointly with his wife Dorothy (Herbertson and Herbertson 1899), and he went on to write more generally and influentially on the regional perspective (Herbertson 1905). Dorothy later produced a life of Frédéric Le Play (D. Herbertson 1897–99) that was eventually edited by Branford and Alexander Farquharson for publication through Le Play House.[46] One of Herbertson's students at Oxford was Charles Fawcett, who wrote pioneering studies in the political geography of frontiers and imperial expansion, including a classic statement of federalism that appeared in "The Making of the Future" and took what Geddes called the "conurbation" as the focus for the major regions he identified (Fawcett 1919; and see 1918, 1933).[47] Most prominent in this sphere was Herbert Fleure, who trained as a zoologist and, influenced by Geddes, taught geography and anthropology at Aberystwyth from 1904. Fleure worked with Geddes and Branford on the Cities and Town Planning Exhibition in Dublin and his *Human Geography in Western Europe* (1918) appeared in the "Making of the Future" series. He worked principally on issues of migration and settlement (Fleure 1922; see Gruffadd 1994) and, with the Newbury-based amateur archaeologist Harold Peake, he produced an extended series of studies in social evolution (Peake and Fleure 1927–1956). Fleure summarized his interpretation of Geddes's position in *Some Problems of Society and Environment* (Fleure 1947).

Geddes's planning activities in Dunfermline were discussed by his colleague John Whitehouse (1905). His ideas on urban design (1909) had a strong influence on the work of Raymond Unwin (1909), Henry Lanchester (1925), and Thomas Adams (1934, 1935), as well as on Patrick Abercrombie (1926, 1934). Abercrombie became the preeminent British planner of the mid-twentieth century, coordinating many major plans, most notably the scheme for the rebuilding of Greater London with a Green Belt and a ring of new towns, prepared before the end of World War II and briefly involving

Lewis Mumford as a consultant (Abercrombie 1944). These geographical and planning arguments were developed among a second generation of students in the regional work of Fawcett's student Robert Dickinson (1934, 1947) and also had an impact on the regional sociology developed in the United States by Howard Odum, who had studied under both Stanley Hall and Robert MacIver (see Odum and Moore 1938).

The major influence that Geddes and Branford had in the area of urbanism, however, was on Lewis Mumford's critical studies of the development of cities (Renwick and Gunn 2008). Mumford's first publication was *The Story of Utopias* (1922), published shortly after his visit to Branford in London. This book set out the politics of a "Third Alternative" based on regional principles, and stressed the importance of artists as contributors to communal renewal by creating images of what *could* be. In the later 1920s he produced a number of works on American literature and culture, but in the early 1930s he launched a series of books to which he gave the generic title "The Renewal of Life." The series began with *Technics and Civilization* (1934) and *The Culture of Cities* (1938), the former originating as a lecture series given at Columbia University at the invitation of Robert MacIver.[48] Mumford later added *The Condition of Man* (1944) and *The Conduct of Life* (1951) to the series.[49]

FOUR

ENVIRONMENT, REGION, AND SOCIAL RECONSTRUCTION

The sociological approach initiated by Geddes and developed by those in his circle of associates aimed to combine the materialism of Le Play's investigations into environmental conditions and work patterns with a recognition of the ways in which the spiritual phenomena of culture were able to shape social life and forms of work. Geddes saw the materialist focus of this work as resonating with the ecological ideas that he had already adopted in his biology and botany and as allowing the construction of an evolutionary theory that could avoid many of the problems of the evolutionism of Spencer. The ideas that he and Branford took from Le Play were characterized as a "regionalism" that stressed the need to understand human life within the personal context of place—the milieu of family, neighborhood, and locality—seen in the context of its material relations with nature. By drawing on Comte's recognition of the universal spiritual unity of humanity, they aimed to reconcile the local orientation of regionalism with the global orientation of humanism.

ENVIRONMENT AND REGION

It was through lectures by Henri Demolins in Paris that Geddes had encountered the ideas of Le Play and he immediately discerned a connection between the environmental focus of Le Play's work and his own ecological orientation. Although Le Play died in 1882, four years after Geddes's visit to Paris, the two men never met and, unusually for Geddes, there was no correspondence between them. Le Play had worked as a mining engineer and occupied the chair of metallurgy at the École des Mines (Herbertson 1897–99). During his travels around the various mining districts of Europe he observed considerable variations in family organization and way of life and decided to resign his chair in order to concentrate on the compilation of social science data on these variations. He devised a method of studying households through the family budgets that organized their activities. Budgetary data were supplemented by observations of family size, physical circumstances, religious practices, housing, and leisure, and the results of these investigations were presented as narrative reportage in Les Ouvriers Européenes (Le 'Play 1855). Le Play went on to provide an interpretation of the variations discovered, arguing that occupational conditions and their historical development were the key determinants of family form: there is a natural congruence between mode of occupation and family life, such that social strains and dislocations arise whenever family relations differ from this natural form. Through responses to these strains, Le Play argued, there is a gradual adaptation of family life to occupational conditions. Occupations, in turn, are determined directly or indirectly by the geographical environment—a view already envisaged by Montesquieu (1748)—while other social phenomena, such as religion and morals, develop around the family form. The historical sequence of occupations followed in a society or social group shapes the development of its "spirit" or culture.[1] These ideas were to be taken up and developed by Demolins (1897), Vignes (1897), and De Tourville (1904).

Geddes and Branford worked hard to elaborate and disseminate the theoretical framework implied by Le Play's work. Le Play, they argued, had emphasized a "rustic process" through which the physical environment conditions rural social life via the causal sequence place-work-family. He also recognized that cultural factors become increasingly important as societies become more complex and urbanized. They proposed, therefore, that there was a need to develop an account of the "civic process" through which culture shapes urban life in a causal sequence of polity-synergy-art. The overall process of social development is a combination of the rustic process and the civic process through the interaction of the material environment and cultural conditions.

For Geddes and Branford the rustic process must be studied through a method that starts out from the material environment (or "place") in which a people (or "folk") live and its attempt to understand the effects of the physical environment in Darwinian terms. Branford held that

> [w]hat exists in the districts in which people live—seas, mountains, plains, forests and the like—determine what occupations are possible, and the occupations demand certain qualities in the people following them, and by a kind of natural selection, enforce the attainment of the qualities on the people. (V. V. Branford 1923, 63)

The place where a people live is the physical, spatial environment within which humans must act and comprises the ultimate conditions to which their patterns of work must be adapted. The scientific description of a region must start with its geology and physical geography, showing its physical structure and its potential for specific patterns of transportation and habitation.[2] Technology and the mode of production are always and necessarily located in a particular environment, and the material conditions within that place constrain the choices that can be made about occupations and forms of labor. Work is productive activity that draws on environmental resources to make them available for human purposes. The work activities of a people, in their turn, condition their social institutions and way of life, forming them into a distinct folk community with particular institutions, customs, and laws. Geddes argued that

> given any habitable region, the characteristic resources of this will determine its occupations, and so its affairs. Furthermore, these essential kinds of occupation will determine various types of family; and these then respectively develop characteristic types of institutions, customs and laws, morals and manners. (Geddes 1920a, 27)

Regional analysis must show how particular occupations arise within the region and how the way of life associated with these generates certain cultural dispositions, values, and traditions among those who follow it. These are the "habits of mind" and typical ways of behaving found in a community, and form what Bourdieu (1972) was later to refer to as the "habitus." The emphasis on Darwinian adaptation to the environment and the active and creative "work" that mediates between environment and the way of life was seen as avoiding the crude environmental determinism that marked the earlier views of Montesquieu and Buckle (Geddes 1905a, 130, 142). A "region" is a unity of place, work, and folk, and the adjective *regional* refers to all those features that comprise the spirit of place: all the customs values, and cultural traditions associated with a specific locality. This emphasis on the autonomy of the environmentally embedded city reflected a commitment to the anarchist and cooperativist views of Reclus and Kropotkin (Law 2005). The final step to be taken in a regional description is to grasp the cultural unity of a community through its members' aesthetic appreciation of the landscape and its myths and histories:

> [T]he regionalist sees the world not merely as landscape. In his survey, the river valley appears next as clothed with characteristic vegetation, varying with soil and subsoil, with contour and slope,

with rainfall and sunshine, and with man's influence above all. (Branford and Geddes 1919a, 84)

Le Play had developed his own regional orientation on the basis of a sectoral classification of occupations and employment relations. He distinguished gathering, pastoral, fishing, forestry, mining, farming, manufacturing, commercial, and professional occupations, and saw these as crosscut by differences in occupational grade. Thus, there were servant, laborer, tenant, owner, and master grades in most occupations. Le Play fully recognized the importance of variations in these employment relations, noting the existence of forced labor, permanent wage labor, and temporary or casual labor.[3]

The various regions and localities of Europe, Le Play argued, were characterized by variations in occupational characteristics that reflected their geographical environments. Demolins summarized Le Play's argument in a discussion of the simplest types of society. Thus, grassland, coastal, and forest environments were associated, respectively, with shepherding, fishing, and hunting, and these occupational differences were associated with, respectively, the patriarchal family in which elders dominate, the stem family (*famille souche*) in which the eldest son inherits, and the unstable family in which all children move away to set up their own homes. These environmentally conditioned ways of life develop into various forms of agriculture from which farming activities and peasant families arise, and in western Europe Le Play saw the stem family as preponderating in areas of peasant farming. Finally, industrialization produces manufacturing occupations that require an occupational and geographical mobility that undermines stable family forms and results in the predominance of the unstable family.

Geddes recognized the didactic importance of this typology and sought to capture its central principle in his idea of the "valley section" (Geddes 1904b, 77–78; Branford and Geddes 1919a, 82 ff.). This was intended as a deliberately simplified model of human social development, though it was repeated ad nauseum in his and Branford's writings. The valley section—probably inspired by Geddes's memory of childhood walks on Kinnoul Hill and the Tay Valley (Geddes 1925)—depicts seven basic types of occupation comparable to the various occupational sectors in the Le Play scheme: miner, woodman, hunter, shepherd, peasant, gardener, and fisherman. Each occupation was seen as a generic category of work that depends on the particular skills cultivated in a population and the environmental conditions under which they live. As occupational types, they encompass a wider range of actual occupations than these labels imply and go beyond Le Play's own scheme. The "miner," for example, stands for the geologist and metallurgist and all who depend on the extraction and processing of natural resources. Similarly, the "hunter" includes the soldier and all militaristic pursuits, the "peasant" includes the botanist and the doctor who depend upon plants and the products of agriculture, and the "fisherman" includes sailors and all seagoing occupations. The valley section, then, attempts to summarize the correlations between "work" and "folk" under varying environmental conditions. Its presentation by Geddes and Branford was simplistic because of the didactic and pedagogic purposes to which they put it. They were attempting to illustrate sociological principles to the uninitiated in the simplest and most direct way, often using magic lantern slides to illustrate their points. Their overuse of the simple model, however, alienated many of their more sophisticated readers who failed to see beyond the simplifications to the more complex understanding of the rustic process that they were trying to draw out from Le Play.

Geddes and Branford used these general principles in the model of the rustic process to develop the idea that people have a complex range of natural instincts and tendencies of behavior that are differentially encouraged under varying ways of life. The "social heritage" built up through their social activity is an outcome of the shaping of an "ancestral heredity" by their environment and way of life (Branford 1926b, 59).[4] Particular occupations and ways of life encourage the differential expression of human dispositions. Engineering occupations involve the cultivation and expression of the woodcraft skills and dispositions found initially in the forester, militaristic occupations are based around the spirit and dispositions developed among hunters, and so on. Any particular society, therefore, comprises a specific mix or balance of the various skills and dispositions that form its social heritage, which are held in a state of interdependence if not harmony (Branford 1926b, 41 ff.). Societies based around intercommunity conflict, for example, cultivate "combatant" dispositions that may become the basis of a "militaristic" way of life. Wherever particular dispositions are overemphasized relative to environmental conditions, there are likely to be social dislocations and the dispositions may come to be seen as "defects" of character in individuals. Normality and difference in personality are, therefore, to be seen as social products.

In complex and urbanized societies, it was argued, a "civic process" becomes the complement to the rustic process. Social life in urban areas reflects the particular mix of dispositions and traditions that residents bring to them through migration and movement from their rural backgrounds to market centers. Towns acquire the character and customs of those who settle there. The town acquires a life and social heritage of its own, combining that of its members as it draws in the diversity of life from its region. The town is a place where a dynamic mix of occupational dispositions becomes adapted to the new urban structures. There is, therefore, both continuity and transformation of what went before. Thus, a town comprises various distinct occupations and social classes, each with its particular way of life and social heritage, but all existing as mere fragments of the social heritage of the city as a whole (Branford 1914a, 28). The overall cultural life of a town is something in which all participate, to a greater or lesser degree, and from which all can learn.

A town becomes a city when it has a strongly developed spiritual life that unites its residents as "citizens" of an "ethical polity" (Branford and Geddes 1919a, 145). Such cities serve as foci for their regions and are the basis of the growth of a civic life—of "civility"—that is inadequately expressed in the word *civilization*. It is central to what it is to be human, embodying all the specifically human characteristics.

Once urban life has been established, there are new possibilities of social evolution. Within the city, cultural or spiritual factors have a far greater autonomy than is the case in rural villages, and they exercise a stronger reciprocal influence on material factors. Where a rural society can be understood through the categories of the valley section, urban life must be understood through a complementary "city section" that depicts "a long street of shops, dwellings, and public buildings . . . parallel to . . . and linked up to the valley section." The city section shows the zoning of urban life into the various places—the specialized markets and quarters—that process, distribute, and sell the products of the region (Geddes 1920b, 274–75). Geddes here was formulating an ecological model of the city similar to that of the Chicago sociologists (Park and Burgess 1925).

Urban societies have a relatively greater autonomy from their physical environment, and the purely rustic process is supplemented by the civic process. The civic process institutionalizes the "spirit creative" made possible by urban life (V. V. Branford 1923, 105; Sandeman 1916–17). In the urban milieu, folk and work are organized into a "polity" with a strongly developed cultural life. The city "accumulates and embodies the cultural heritage of a region, and combines it in some measure and kind with the cultural heritage of larger units, national, racial, religious, human. It stamps the resultant product upon each passing generation of its citizens" (Branford and Geddes 1919a, 156). The polity is the instrument of *gemeinschaftslich* regional memory and community, but organizes this in relation to larger and more abstract values and ideals. As such, it articulates the region with the larger structures of "humanity."

Continued expansion means that cities, in turn, are the basis for nation development, nations being built around a higher unity of the imagined community:

> A people conceive themselves a nation when united by common memories and by aspirations extending even beyond regional

ENVIRONMENT, REGION, AND SOCIAL RECONSTRUCTION   87

boundaries. In a very real sense there is a national spirit. It receives embodiment . . . in characteristic acts and institutions. Language is commonly but not invariably its chief vehicle. (Geddes 1915a, 154).

This national spirit comprises the social heritage, social inheritance, or tradition of those who live within a national territory. The cultural tradition is to the community what memory is to the individual (Geddes 1905a, 139): it constitutes the collective memory. The tradition has both intellectual and emotional dimensions, and it is in its emotional or motivational sense that it constitutes the creative process of "social energizing" that expresses the universal human spirit in nationally specific mental and moral habits or customs and the cultural forms of art, literature, religion, and philosophy (Branford and Geddes 1919b, xxiii, 131).

The rustic process was summarized in the formula place-work-folk. The corresponding formula for the more "subjective" aspects of human life in the civic process is polity-synergy-art (Geddes 1905a, 136–38; Branford and Geddes 1919a, Part 2, Chs 1 and 2; V. V. Branford 1923, 66). The civic organization of city life is the polity, "a community fully realizing, and nobly acting on, the group heritage of aspirations and ideals" (V. V. Branford 1923, 67). Polity organization enables the self-conscious collective reproduction and transformation of the social heritage through the "mental work" of those now able to pool their creative energies through "vital communication" and collective solidarity. This "synergy" is "an impassioned working together of individuals, groups, classes, moved to voluntary execution of purposive schemes deemed worthwhile" (V. V. Branford 1923, 67). Bringing people together in purposive schemes, this is the basis of "art" or the aesthetic improvement of the place in which people live. In consequence, the environment is transformed from a merely built place into a *designed* object of beauty.

TEMPORAL AND SPIRITUAL HEMISPHERES

This view of the regional interdependence of the rustic and civic processes was the cornerstone of a larger theory of society that Branford and Geddes adapted from the ideas of Comte. They took the view that any society, "social formation," or "sociosphere" is a superorganic system comprising two analytically distinct subsystems or "hemispheres," which they call the "temporal" and the "spiritual" (Branford and Geddes 1919b, 37). Temporal systems are those through which economic and political powers are structured as a political economy and that organize the directive and executive functions relating to work and social control. Spiritual systems comprise the culture spheres of thought and expression that constitute the social inheritance and are the basis of forms of power that relate to the social expression of subjectivity and emotionality. This distinction between technical, instrumental activities and "humanistic" activities relates back to one drawn by Coleridge (1830) between the "civilization" of material progress and the "cultivation" of the qualities of humanity. It has some similarities with the distinction made by Alfred Weber (1920–21) between material "civilization" and spiritual "culture."[6]

The internal functional differentiation of each subsystem generates axes of occupational differentiation. Comte had developed his account of the occupational—or "class"—differentiation of a social formation from the medieval distinction between barons, serfs, priests, and monks, generalizing this into a distinction between chiefs, people, emotionals, and intellectuals. These four "social types" or categories were the basis of the social classification used by Branford and Geddes, though they often preferred to use a terminology introduced by Arnold Bennett in his account of life on the Clyde. Thus, they distinguished between organizers, workers, energizers, and initiators (Branford and Geddes 1919a, 23; 1919b, 37).[7] Organizers and workers are the differentiated agents of temporal power, concerned with politics, business, and industry. Energizers and initiators are the agents of spiritual power and motivation, concerned with education and advice, religion, and research. Any society can be analyzed in terms of the relations among these four social categories and their various subdivisions (Branford 1914a, 25–26; Branford and Geddes 1919a, 22–25; 1919b, 36–38; V. V. Branford 1923, 71; B. Branford 1919, 12–13). Table 4.1 shows the various parallels between the Comtean categories used by Geddes and Branford, the earlier categories of Plato and Aristotle, and the contemporary distinctions drawn by H. G. Wells and Bennett.

Table 4.1. Class Divisions in Complex Societies

Branford and Geddes	Plato	Aristotle	Wells	Bennett
Chiefs	Guardians	Citizens	Active kinetic	Organizers
People	Artisans	Laborers	Passive kinetic	Workers
Emotionals	Poets	Teachers	Active poetics	Energizers
Intellectuals	Philosophers	Philosophers	Passive poetics	Initiators

Note: The references are to Plato's *Republic*, Aristotle's *Politics*, Wells's (1905) *Modern Utopia*, and a wartime essay by Arnold Bennett.
Source: Adapted from Branford (1921b, 113, n.1).

The organizers or "chiefs" of temporal power are those involved in direction and executive decision making within structures of economic and political power. They comprise the executives and the "directing classes" (Branford 1920, 65; 1923, 69–70). The workers, operatives, or "people," on the other hand, occupy the subordinate social positions that carry out these decisions and so comprise the "working body" of a society. The temporal activities they undertake comprise the mechanical, vital, and social crafts of engineering, manufacturing, mining, building, agriculture, forestry, fishing, medicine, legal, domestic, and state work, all of which are variously organized into commercial, scientific, administrative, or financial sectors. It is through the work activities of the organizers and workers that the environmental constraints inherent in a place have their effects on a folk. They are the agents of the rustic process and its extensions in complex societies. Spiritual power is rooted in the creativity of the civic process. It comprises the creative and imaginative effects that a people are able to bring to bear through their work. The spiritual or subjective aspect of social life is the means through which there is the emotional formation of active imaginative personalities able to formulate personal and social purposes (Branford 1930, 205). The initiators or intellectuals are seen as the carriers and developers of philosophical and scientific thought. They are the contemplative and informative thinkers concerned with theoretical matters and with providing rationales for action. The energizers, emotionals, or expressionals are said to be responsive to cultural ideals and so specifically concerned with music, writing, praying, art and design, guidance, and advising. They are concerned with expressive matters and it is their enthusiasm and charismatic leadership that shapes the impulses and aspirations that inspire and motivate people in such areas as art, music, education, religion, and even science. This view of the emotionals and the intellectuals parallels Coleridge's view of the "clerisy" as the guardians of humanity's cultivation, the cultural elite who stand in the vanguard of cultural development and oversee social change.

The overall power system of a society comprises a shifting balance between temporal and spiritual subsystems of power (Branford 1928).[8] This interdependence may be such that the subsystems work in mutually reinforcing ways. Under some circumstances, however, one subsystem may be overdeveloped and its operations may therefore undermine the other. When the system of spiritual power has a high degree of autonomy and is the dominant social force, initiators and energizers can provide a sense of purpose that motivates people to act in pursuit of societal goals. A culture of art and knowledge has the capacity to evoke the "latent capacities" of a people and to focus them on "the daily needs of life" (V. V. Branford 1924a, 58). It is also able to legitimate and sustain the coercive systems of temporal power, establishing a sense of community, vitalizing education, and inspiring the temporal chiefs. However, when the system of temporal power is liberated from spiritual control and becomes a self-propelling force the temporal organizers can displace the intellectuals and emotionals. They may then usurp the powers of initiation and energizing and use them to systematize and disseminate the principles that underpin their temporal power. People may then be mobilized to act in purely instrumental terms, with no consideration for the larger moral context of their actions.

The regional and the occupational dimensions crosscut each other in complex patterns of social differentiation and social integration. The dimension of "regionalism" defines a series of nested structural levels that run from the domestic household through the village and the town to the region and thence to the national and international levels of organization, creating a "vast geographical circuit of social solidarity." The dimension of "occupationalism," on the other hand, defines a structural division of labor in society, comprising a series of interdependent and functionally divided positions (B. Branford 1919, 17). Social solidarity depends upon the ways in which these two dimensions of social structure articulate with each other, and the social heritage will tend to be differentiated along the two dimensions.

THE SOCIOLOGICAL VISION AND SOCIAL RECONSTRUCTION

For Geddes and Branford, a sociological understanding of the development of agricultural and industrial societies was the basis on which they could understand contemporary social change and foresee future developments. Sociological understanding enables interpretative forecasts—predictions—of the future consequences of tendencies of change that are inherent in the historically formed circumstances of the present and so makes planned social change possible. This is why its prescriptions for change are "eutopian" rather than "utopian." Planned social change does not aim at a fanciful ideal but at something that is actually "rooted in evolutionary tendencies" (Branford and Geddes 1919a, 12; Geddes 1904b, 89) and is realistically achievable. A sociological vision highlights improvements in the light of the actual material and cultural conditions of a society. Social policy must be geared to implementing feasible change by building the conditions under which it is no longer held back by prevailing social conditions.

Although they sought to learn from and to recruit medieval principles of social life, the view of Geddes and Branford was thoroughly modernist. Their critique of contemporary modernity held that it was only partially or one-sidedly modern. Temporal modernity had undermined human spirituality, which meant that an autonomously modern character structure had not developed. The cultural sphere had become a mere reflex of the temporal structures of power. Where many political reformers looked back to the medieval period as a golden age that was to be reestablished, Branford and Geddes saw it as a stage from which humans could learn how to be more fully modern. A revitalized spirituality—learning from the successes of medieval Christianity—could be the basis of a "larger modernism," a more complete and more fully human modernism.

Social reconstruction is, therefore, seen as progressive, as bringing about an improvement in people's relation to nature and to temporal power through a revitalized sense of community. While stressing the importance of the rural, agrarian community, this view was no backward-looking or reactionary stance. Branford and Geddes stressed the crucial importance of the urban community as a focus of true humanity. The city is a characteristically modern community and it is the focus for the building of the larger modernity to which sociology was to contribute.

They saw the "contemporary" era of European industrialism as having evolved from ancient and recent predecessors. The "ancient" stage had primitive, matriarchal, and patriarchal substages, while the subsequent "recent" stage had classical, medieval, and renaissance substages. The sequence of ancient, recent, and contemporary paralleled Comte's "law" of the three stages of history stretching from the militarism of the Middle Ages through a stage of statist and mercantilist organization, to the contemporary industrial stage of modernity (Geddes 1904b, 82).

In what Geddes and Branford called the "paleotechnic" stage of industrialism—the "old" technical age of steam and coal—urban areas were forged into "conurbations," generally based around coalfields and coal-based technologies.[9] Geddes cites such large city regions as Pittsburgh, Greater London, and Sheffield, along with "bi-polar" conurbations or more complex city regions such as New York-Boston-Philadelphia, Liverpool-Manchester, Leeds-Bradford, Birmingham-Black Country, Cardiff-Swansea, Tyne-Wear-Tees, and Glasgow-Edinburgh (Geddes 1915a, 34 ff).[10] Many of the inhabitants of these conurbations enjoyed a degree of affluence and high levels of private consumption, and there were some considerable fortunes. However, this private affluence did not result in high levels of public provision and had no real impact on public life. City life was marked by growing class differences of income and wealth, and the great conurbations had areas of massive poverty and slum housing. The social life of the masses, especially that of the young, became disorganized and "degenerate." Geddes and Branford diagnosed a strengthening of temporal power vis-à-vis spiritual power and a consequent undermining of civic solidarity and growth in alienation and demoralization. Sociology shows, they argued, that the spiritual solidarity and synergy of the cities had been undermined with the development of industrial cities (Geddes 1915a, ch. 6; Branford and Geddes 1919a, 168; 1919b, 303–306).[11]

A "neotechnic," or new technical age, was beginning to emerge as a result of the "second industrial revolution" of electricity and oil. This second industrial revolution would establish the material potential for a renewal of city life and for the full development of the civic polity. For this to be achieved, however, a new political form was needed to nurture and develop the spiritual life. The task of sociologists, as intellectuals and emotionals, is to identify and help to build this political form through social change oriented toward the common good of humanity. A strategy of planned change, Branford and Geddes argue, must be multipronged, bringing about the material "reconstruction" of social relations, the "re-education" of individual character, and the spiritual "renewal" of human life (Branford and Geddes 1919a, xiii). A strategy of reconstruction, re-education, and renewal builds a "new vitalism" in which there is a full development of the civic qualities of life, personality, citizenship, community, and collective endeavor. In the immediate situation following World War I, Branford and Geddes hoped to capture the wartime spirit of working toward a common goal and so bring about a "social synergy" that would achieve this reconstruction and renewal (Branford and Geddes 1919a, 216).

Frances and George Sandeman developed this idea in their view of an industrial system organized around class and the cash nexus that has undermined the solidarity of communities. They argued for the building of the good life as a process of "healing," seeing spiritual renewal as the means to cooperation and social cohesion shaped by "Brotherhood" and love. Social renewal is "a deliberate *realisation* of the love of the divine perfections of our brothers" (Sandeman and Sandeman 1919, 33). This had to be built from the bottom up, from particular places of work that could be humanized as "the community of work" and so become the seeds for larger transformations. George Sandeman (1913) took his cue from de Tocqueville, highlighting the decline in intermediate groups and, thereby, the communal bonds that can form people into structures of "organic cohesion." This was the view later taken up in the communitarian philosophy of John Macmurray (1935, 1957, 1961) and in Robert Putnam's arguments about the implications of the decline in social capital (Putnam 2000).[12]

Sociology is not, therefore, a detached and completely "value-free" discipline, but neither is it an ideologically committed doctrine. It is an autonomous discipline with a responsibility to engage in public discourse and involve a wider public in its own deliberations. Branford and Geddes's view of the discipline sees it as what Burawoy (2005) has called a public sociology. Their public sociology does not pursue its practical vision and strategy of reconstruction in the manner of the bureaucratic expert, and they rejected the Fabian reliance on the centralized temporal power of state politicians and administrators. They called, instead, for a "resorption" of the powers of government from the state to the individual and the community (Branford 1914a, 319–23), with sociologists promoting their ideas in cooperative and participative endeavors.

The sociologist must combine an intellectual role of understanding with the energizing role of the statesman or educator, mobilizing human energies in the pursuit of social ideals. Sociologists must join with other intellectuals and emotionals to renew spiritual power by mobilizing cultural skills and abilities that have been distorted and suppressed by the dominance of temporal power. They must challenge dominant or mainstream thinkers and actively involve those who are engaged in spiritual tasks and so can best contribute to spiritual renewal: "These are the marching torchbearers of our social inheritance. It is theirs, in the onward and upward movement of civilization, to lead the way and light the path" (Branford and Geddes 1919b, 93, 87, 92). They have the capacity "for exalting well-being, quickening the spirit, dignifying labor, beautifying cities, ennobling personalities" (ibid., 93). They include artists, poets, musicians, novelists, architects, and scientists: "The sociologist has now to search out the fragments of spiritual powers which have been growing up spontaneously and in isolation" (Branford 1914a, 307), bringing them together in a coalition for social reconstruction.

This was the basis on which they founded their arguments about education and community development (discussed in chapter 6). These arguments were underpinned by their advocacy of specific mechanisms of engagement. Principal among these were dramatization and social survey. Dramatization is the idea that sociologists could join with playwrights, poets, and other artists to write and present sociological knowledge and understanding in a way that is both accessible to a general public and could motivate them to join in a strategy of social change. The arts are agencies of social transmission and for the inspiration of utopias; they "create or evoke visions of life," and the artist is the "giver of dreams; and thus inspirer of dreams" (Branford 1914a, 197, 203). The arts are, therefore, central to the ideals and aspirations that motivate or energize people.

Dramatization had been central to Geddes's Edinburgh Summer Schools, and Branford set out the principles behind this method in a talk to the Incorporated Society of the Eager Heart, a religious society devoted to the production of Christian morality plays (Branford 1914a, 140 ff.).[13] Drama, he held, is a "play-rehearsal for life at its intensest" (ibid., 161). Through dramatic play, people are able to anticipate and explore the experiences and emotions that they may sometime encounter in their real lives. Branford highlighted the innovative ideas of theatre critics Gordon Craig and Huntly Carter, linking both to the idea of the "civic theatre" set out in the United States by Percy MacKaye (1912): "By plays and pageants, festivals and processions, by folk drama and culture drama, the Civic Theatre is to achieve the uplift of the people through the redemption of leisure" (Branford 1914a, 366).[14]

Branford saw a model for sociological dramatization in the medieval mystery or miracle plays and the court masques of the sixteenth and seventeenth century. The medieval miracle play, he argued, was a dramatization of history that embodied a particular philosophy of history and was, therefore, a proto-sociological outlook. As a means of entertainment it was also a means for developing and transmitting culture. The mystery play was, he said, "the people's University" (Branford 1914a, 147). It made history real to people and allowed them to put their own lives in a larger context. The medieval miracle and masque must be renewed for a contemporary role in spiritual renewal. Miracle plays such as those performed by the Eager Heart could document the "miracle" of "the conversion from material and selfish to spiritual and altruistic prepossessions" (Branford 1914a, 151).

The principal dramatizations in which Branford and Geddes were involved were the performances of the Masques of Learning by the "Edinburgh Masquers" at University Hall in Edinburgh and at Crosby Hall in London (Geddes 1913a,b). These dramatizations of history and the development of knowledge were seen as central to the cultural role of social reconstruction. They were presented in the style of a mystery play, with members of the Geddes circle playing the parts of great historical figures and personifying larger social groups and cultural movements to depict the progress of cultural understanding and scientific knowledge.

While Geddes and Branford explored literary and poetic forms of expression, dramatization was the artistic venture to which they gave greatest attention. It was, however, developed in only a very limited way and had little lasting impact on sociological practice. It did, nevertheless, influence the documentary film movement of the 1930s and 1940s. The key figures in this were Humphrey Jennings and John Grierson, who were involved in exploring the potential of the new technology of film to develop new forms of public engagement.

Grierson had studied philosophy at Glasgow University under Alexander Lindsay, who inspired him to read Charles Ellwood's (1922) work on religion and the current issues of Mumford's *Dial* magazine. A Rockefeller scholarship allowed him to study public opinion and the news media under Robert Park and Harold Lasswell at Chicago, and while in the United States he became interested in film technology and its implications (Aitken 1990, 36). His analysis of socialist realism in Eisenstein's *Battleship Potemkin* (1925) persuaded him that the new technology of film made possible the "documentary" representation of social reality. He came to believe that documentary film could be a means of providing people with the knowledge and understanding that would enable them to participate more effectively in democratic decision making. Working toward this goal, he began work at the Empire Marketing Board in 1926 and then, from 1933, worked at the GPO Film Unit.[15]

Jennings was born in the artistic colony of Walberswick on the Suffolk coast, the son of an architect and a potter who inculcated in him a commitment to the ideals of Ruskin and Morris (Jackson 2004). A family friend and fellow guild socialist Alfred Orage persuaded the Jenningses to send Humphrey to the Perse School because of its head's advocacy of these same ideals. At the school Jennings was strongly influenced by the English master Caldwell Cook, who was working on his book *The Play Way* (Cook 1917) that was originally intended for the *Papers for the Present*. Cook used dramatization in his teaching and Jennings came to appreciate its educative power. After university, Jennings joined the GPO Film Unit, where he worked with Grierson.

Documentary film is "actuality-based film as a means of public education and as an art form" (Swann 1989). By contrast with newsreel, documentary filming gave a more prominent role to the director in establishing appropriately dramatic shots and using editing techniques to cut from close-up to distant focus and to change scene. In *Drifters* (1929) and *Industrial Britain* (1931), Grierson and his colleagues presented the heroism of labor and the importance of craft skills, seeing these as elements in a division of labor transformed by industrialism. Their use of film advanced from the filming of work to the use of interviews and reenactments, through such films as *Housing Problems* (1935) and Jennings's *Spare Time* (1939). These techniques were combined with the poetry of W. H. Auden and the music of Benjamin Britten in Grierson's famous *Night Mail* (1936).

SOCIAL SURVEY AND SOCIAL PARTICIPATION

The social survey for Geddes and Branford was more than a mere technical instrument of sociological investigation. It was an essential tool of vision and eutopian reconstruction and renewal by virtue of its uniting of theory and practice (Geddes 1904a, 3; and see Fleure 1919b). Social surveys were seen as the specific means for generating knowledge and understanding through the direct participation of those most affected by contemporary conditions and whose involvement would allow them to participate in the formulation of social policies. If each village, town, and city surveys its own environment and builds up resources for enhancing its residents' understanding of their own history and circumstances, they can better formulate plans for the future (V. V. Branford 1921a, 82).

Social survey had been pioneered in the United States by Jane Addams (Residents of Hull House 1895; see Sklar 1985; Strobel 2002), its success persuading Susan Wharton to sponsor the study of Philadelphia by William DuBois (1899) and the Russell Sage Foundation to sponsor the Pittsburgh survey.[16] In Britain, Charles Booth, Seebohm Rowntree, and a number of local research workers undertook studies in London (Booth 1901–02), York (Rowntree 1901), Middlesbrough (Bell 1907), Norwich (Hawkins 1910), and the London districts of Soho (Sherwell 1897) and West Ham (Howard and Wilson 1907). A study cited by Branford as an exemplar of the approach is Maud Davies's (1909) study of the Wiltshire village of Corsley. The most sophisticated developments of these pioneering surveys were the later poverty studies undertaken by Arthur Bowley (Bowley and Burnett-Hurst 1915; Bowley and Hogg 1924), who used rigorous sampling methods to study large populations. Geddes and Branford sought to build on this survey work through their advocacy of more comprehensive methodological techniques and the involvement of the researched as researchers.

Branford and his associates always stressed the importance of visual inspection as the starting point for any social survey. It was important to choose, wherever possible, a high point such as the top of a hill so that an overview of the whole district can be obtained through a synoptic gaze (V. V. Branford 1924b). It can readily be assumed that, if they had been more easily available at the time, Branford would have advocated aerial surveys and filming as logical extensions of the use of the camera obscura at the Outlook Tower. He stressed that this visual inspection can be taken further by walking through the district and observing physical landmarks and the totality of the region from different physical locations. All such techniques give a firm sense of place from which to begin.

Surveys can be reported in purely literary form, as in those of Hilaire Belloc (1902; 1904) that were regarded as exemplars of their type (Branford and Geddes 1919a, 69). As set out in later overviews (S. Branford and Farquharson 1924; Fagg and Hutchings 1930; Dickinson 1934; and see Fleure 1928), however, the social survey was seen as a more systematic and structured report. A full regional survey combines two elements corresponding to the two constituent processes—the rustic and the civic—of the social process. A "rustic survey" follows through the logic of the place-work-folk scheme. In contemporary societies it must be concerned particularly with the rural hinterlands of the cities and with surviving areas of purely rural activity. A "civic survey," on the other hand, follows the logic of the polity-synergy-art scheme and explores communal life within the city and its role in regional and national culture. Taken together, rustic and civic surveys place an urban area within the full regional context of an environing countryside.

A "rustic survey" investigates environmental conditions and patterns of work activity from the basis of an investigation of place. Places are to be studied in terms of the geophysical, geological, and climatological conditions affecting plant and animal distribution, including the effects of the human transformation of the environment. Branford cited the physical surveys of Scotland carried out by Marcel Hardy (1906) as exemplars of a basic environmental description. The survey would comprise an investigation into the distribution of arable, pasture, and woodland, of sandpits, quarries, and water supply, of the pattern of roads, railways, and other patterns of transportation and settlement, and of systems of landholding and land use. These topographical conditions are to be seen in relation to human work patterns through investigations into the conditions, hours, and earnings in various types of industries and their division of labor, the patterns of consumption and family budgets, and patterns of savings, credit, and insurance, extending the concerns of Le Play and his followers. Finally, the habits and customs of the people, the history of their involvement with their place, their demographic patterns and associational involvements are to be investigated, together with a "psychological survey" of their shared mentality, habits, and customs (S. Branford and Farquharson 1924).

A civic survey comprises a community study of the cultural life of a particular city, including its political and associational life as a civil society, its built environment, and the range of cultural activities pursued by its residents. As examples, Branford (1914a, 84–85) cites Geddes's studies of Edinburgh (Geddes 1902; 1911) and Dunfermline (Geddes 1904a) and the program for a survey of Chelsea (Geddes 1908). The civic survey should be linked to a civic museum that acts as a laboratory and for which the Outlook Tower in Edinburgh provides a model. In the tower itself, the successive floors were arranged as progressive moves from the global to the local, each organized as displays and indexes, and culminating in the camera obscura that allowed field investigations of the immediate locality.

The sociological survey advocated by Branford and Geddes is not, however, purely descriptive. It is to be guided by utopian ideas and must suggest practical ways of implementing these (Branford 1914a, 78). To ensure this, and to pursue the democratic principles of the methodology, the residents of the area being surveyed must be involved in the survey, not simply as subjects or respondents but as active participants. It is a means of academic outreach and citizen involvement. In this way, the social survey makes an essential contribution to the development of the polity. The methodology is similar to what is now termed participatory action research (McIntyre 2007).

Branford presented the topographical maps of the Ordnance Survey as providing a model for the outcome of a social survey (Branford 1914a, 64). The Ordnance Survey, with which he was familiar through Fawcett, undertook systematic physical and settlement surveys to compile its topographical maps. Branford held that the systematic use of the place-work-folk framework could provide a whole new dimension, transforming it into a "Sociologist's Chart" (Branford 1914a, 67; Cities-Committee 1911). Such a chart would combine the basic physical map with land use and vegetation mapping and the results of social enquiries into the ways of life followed by the people living in the places charted. Branford also emphasized the need for a comprehensive social survey to go beyond geographical and demographic studies to include the investigation of culture, such as Booth had begun in his investigations into the religious life of London. To the basic chart could be added photographs, lantern slides, relief models, and documents as illustrations and educational devices. The sociological chart is, in effect, a variant of the museum-cum-observatory that had been organized at the Outlook Tower.

Herbertson's work (see Herbertson 1905) was seen by Branford as having explicitly begun this comprehensive task on a physical basis, and he pointed to its emergence in fragmentary forms in the Population Census, the Census of Production, the Reports of the Factory Inspectors and Medical Superintendents, and the various specialist surveys carried out by social investigators. He argued that this work needed to be extended on a comprehensive basis for all official statistics and on a regional basis through systematic indexing and cross-referencing. The ideas conceived by Branford were difficult to implement and are only now becoming possible through the use of GIS and post-code mapping and Internet-based hyperlinked maps and documents.

This idea of the systematic survey built on an initial suggestion by Hugh Mill (1896), who had conceived a scheme for a systematic geographical survey of the British Isles. Fleure, Herbertson, and Arthur Geddes (see Maclean 2004, 97 ff; Wrigley 1950) enthusiastically supported the idea. Mill himself had produced a sample survey of part of Sussex (Mill 1900). One of Herbertson's students, Lavinia Hardy, later a prominent geographer (Bell and McEwan 1996), produced a pioneering study of the one-inch Ordnance Survey map of Salisbury for her Oxford thesis, and Osbert Crawford carried out a study of the Andover map.[17] While a few such studies were published (Smith 1910; Matthews 1910), the project as a whole was too daunting to be carried through. A partial realization was achieved in the British Vegetation Survey, but this, too, was incomplete and, after 1913, it adopted a more analytical approach than the original idea of areal description (Schulte Fischedick 2000). The closest that this project came to achievement was in the land use surveys undertaken by Dudley Stamp (1931, 1948).[18]

In his discussion of the early emergence of the survey method, Branford cited as examples a number of surveys undertaken by members of the Geddes circle. These included a North London survey undertaken by Lionel Tayler (partially reported in Tayler 1904; see Branford 1914a, 72), a survey of Manchester by Thomas Marr (1904), and a survey of Dundee by Mary Walker (Walker and Wilson 1905).[19] Mona Wilson, co-worker with Wilson, was later involved in the well-known West Ham survey (Howard and Wilson 1907). An early manual for these kinds of local studies was produced by Maria Penstone (1910). A regional survey section of the South Eastern Union of Scientific Societies was formed in 1915 by Christopher Fagg to coordinate the work of a growing number of local surveys, including those on Croydon and Saffron Walden, and important late products of the work of the section was a study of Stockbury in Kent (Pugh and Hutchings 1928) and Bishop's Stortford in Hertfordshire (Wood 1929).[20] Branford himself was involved in rustic surveys in Paraguay, carrying out his sociological work while traveling on business for the Paraguay Central Railway, though these reports were unpublished.[21] His work related to more comprehensive surveys undertaken by William Barclay (Barclay 1909; and see Branford 1909) and further unpublished surveys by Marcel Hardy.[22]

The fully developed social survey became a standard instrument in sociological investigation during the interwar years, though not quite in the full-blown version envisaged by Branford and Geddes. A review for the Institute of Sociology undertaken by Alan Wells (1935; see also Caradog Jones 1941) highlighted important surveys of Tyneside (Mess 1928), Brynmawr (Jennings 1934), and Portsmouth (Ford 1934), and the nationally significant investigations in London (Llewellyn Smith 1930–35) and Merseyside (Caradog Jones 1934). A late and sophisticated example of a survey carried out through a Workers' Educational Association course is the classic study carried out in Banbury (Stacey 1960). Survey methods also had a major influence in schoolteaching, where surveys were enthusiastically taken up by large numbers of geography teachers for their field investigations (see Matless 1992).

A further indirect influence of the survey idea was that on the work of the Mass-Observation research organization, set up by Humphrey Jennings and his university friend Charles Madge in 1937 (see Calder 1985). Based at Blackheath in London, and with a parallel operation overseen by anthropologist Tom Harrison in Bolton, their aim was to carry over Jennings's documentary film ideas into actual survey work in which nonprofessional observers would record their observations and impressions of the everyday lives of their families, neighbors, and workmates. In this way, it was believed, they could document the lives of ordinary people more authentically than was possible in professional social science reports. They encouraged the artistic and literary skills of their observers and used their own artistic skills to distil and present observers' reports in published form. Their most important published studies were *May the Twelfth* (Jennings and Madge 1937), *Britain* (Mass-Observation 1939), *The Pub and the People* (Mass-Observation

1943a), and *War Factory* (Mass-Observation 1943b).[23] These observational surveys from Mass-Observation were paralleled in Jennings's wartime films *Listen to Britain* (1942) and *The Silent Village* (1943), and the postwar *A Diary for Timothy* (1946).

CONCLUSION

Geddes and Branford sought to bring unity to the social sciences, though they recognized that there was no consensus among those who study economic, political, and other processes as to the methods, purposes, or boundaries around their intellectual activities. Even in 1923, Branford could recognize the truth in the jibe that "if a dozen inmates of an asylum were each given a spade, taken into a two-acre field and left there in the hope that they would dig and plant it, the resulting confusion could hardly be greater than at present prevails among the cultivators of the field called Social Science" (V. V. Branford 1923, 35). As practiced, he claimed, the social sciences are in a state of confusion. Boundaries are unclear and there is a proliferation of specialisms. Much work in social studies is to be found in the older humanities such as history and jurisprudence, while other work arises as new specialisms. There is a "riot of studies" in a state of "seething turbulence" marked by sectarian commitments to particular intellectual paradigms (V. V. Branford 1923, 92).

They were, however, clear in their own mind about the nature and character of the various social sciences and proposed an intellectual mapping that they hoped would be the basis for a new vision of academic disciplines. Following Comte, they saw sociology as the most general of the social sciences and as the unifying discipline behind geography, economics, anthropology, and other specialisms (V. V. Branford 1923, 89). They carefully defined the respective domains of the various social scientists, using their revised version of Le Play's scheme.

"General sociology," they argued, comprised both "objective sociology" and "subjective sociology." Objective sociology consists of the materialistic investigation of the "rustic" processes of place, work, and folk. Within this overarching social science, geography is the science concerned with the effects of the material environment, while economics is concerned with work patterns, production, and consumption, and anthropology with human communities. Objective sociology is the body of theory that integrates and coordinates these specialist sciences. Branford argued, furthermore, that "Geographer, Economist, and Anthropologist are learning to march in step with each other, and with the Sociologist, towards a common goal" (V. V. Branford 1923, 93).[24]

Subjective sociology consists of the spiritual investigation of civics and involves investigations into polity, culture, and art (Geddes 1905a, 136–38; Branford and Geddes 1919a, Part 2, chs 1 and 2; V. V. Branford 1923, 95–96). Ethics is said to be responsible for investigations into polity organization, social psychology is concerned with culture, and aesthetics explores issues of art and design. In a similar vein, Benchara Branford recognized a tripartite division of the spiritual sciences of human history into theology, psychology, and "esthetology." Theology was seen, in its broadest sense, as the study of practical "priest craft" and forms of ethical intervention. Psychology was seen as the study of "culture craft" or education, while esthetology was seen as the study of the practical activities of art and creative play. Where Victor Branford described the synthetic science of spirit, integrating and coordinating the civic disciplines, as subjective sociology, Benchara Branford limited "sociology" to the study of the interrelation of the rustic, temporal processes and termed the spiritual discipline "Cosmology" (B. Branford 1916, 11, 177).

Where Geddes increasingly focused his attention on the applications of sociology to urban issues—on "civics" as an applied sociology—Victor Branford developed his own concerns with a "pure sociology." This pure sociology was understood as the general body of theory relating to both the objective and the subjective aspects of the social process and within which the social survey method was to highlight the rustic and the civic processes.

FIVE

PLANNING THE BUILT ENVIRONMENT

Civics and Conservative Surgery

Many academic disciplines could claim Patrick Geddes as a pioneer and early inspiration. Sociology was always Branford's priority, just as biology was J. Arthur Thomson's, and during his long career Geddes floated back and forth between these two fields and collaborators. Just as often, however, he delved into other fields, notably education, geography, and city and regional planning. To complicate the disciplinary panorama even further, Geddes promoted and contributed to art, literature, and theater, and he had strong interests in architecture, landscape architecture, psychology, and comparative religion. He was an intellectual omnivore, and despite all Branford's promotion of his image and reputation as a sociologist, he was never willing to concentrate his efforts on sociology.

From 1888 till 1919, Geddes's primary academic position was professor of botany at University College Dundee, a convenient nominal appointment that enabled him to spend most of his time in Edinburgh, then in London, then globetrotting, with extended periods in India. From 1919 till 1924, Geddes held the title of Professor of Civics and Sociology in the Department of Sociology at the University of Bombay. While based in India, both during and after World War I, he traveled extensively within and outside the country and he took numerous small consultancies focusing on city planning.

Of all the disciplines with which he was associated, it is planning, rather than sociology, where Geddes's name is best known, and where he has had the most impact. He was a Renaissance scholar, rather than a narrow specialist, and his contribution to planning came from the social and environmental sciences, rather than from architecture and design. He did not pretend to be an architect or an engineer, but he often drew on the skills of his architect son-in-law Frank Mears, and on the work of a number of architect-planners with whom he worked through Crosby Hall and the Cities Committee of the Sociological Society. Most notable were Charles Ashbee, a leader in historic preservation and the arts and crafts movement, and Raymond Unwin and Patrick Abercrombie, the two leading figures in twentieth-century British planning.

Geddes used maps, diagrams, sketches, and photographs extensively in his publications, and he was fascinated by classifications, lists, and inventories. His notes and publications were often illustrated by matrix typologies, which he called "thinking machines": graphic versions of his folded sheets of paper that were intended to illustrate the relationships between different concepts and entities. In his writings, Geddes usually erred on the side of excess detail, excess illustration, and frequent repetition, so the sheer volume of his output presents a problem to anyone seeking to identify his principal ideas. Despite all his failings, however, a number of major ideas have resonance and lasting significance in city and regional planning. Most of those ideas gained wider prominence through the agency of Lewis Mumford and his associates in the Regional Planning Association of America (RPAA), and a few have regained prominence recently in the literature on engaged universities, university-community partnerships, and sustainability. Most important of all, however, are the ideas that he developed on urban neighborhood upgrading in India. These were communicated to a broader audience through the writings and work of Jaqueline Tyrwhitt and John F. C. Turner, and are now part of a global conventional wisdom on self-help housing and spontaneous settlement in developing countries.[1]

Geddes's major ideas on city and regional planning focused on six major concepts: regionalism, civics, surveys, decentralization, pacifism, and conservative surgery. Through his portrayal of paleotechnic and neotechnic cities, he also pioneered another concept, without actually using the term—sustainability—and his work is often considered an inspiration to later writings on environmentalism, ecology, and bioregionalism.[2]

REGIONALISM AND PLANNING IDEAS

Though few of his ideas on regionalism were in any way surprising or innovative to geographers, who had long considered broader spatial contexts and human-environment relations, Geddes had a significant impact on architect-planners and on some budding sociologists, who tended to view urban buildings and neighborhoods in isolation from their broader contexts. Geddes was obsessive in emphasizing that broader context, arguing that the quality of the built environment has a major impact on social conditions, that neighborhoods should be considered in the context of cities, that adjacent cities may fuse together into conurbations, that cities should be considered in the context of their surrounding regions, and that nation-states should be studied through the identification and description of subnational regions. He emphasized the concept of "region," not as an arbitrary entity envisioned for a specific purpose, but rather as an obvious feature of world geography, multifaceted, multidimensional, and essentially organic, setting human activity in an environmental context. As we showed in chapter 4, his simplistic model of "the valley section" and his "place-work-folk" thinking machine, repeated and reprinted again and again, argued that livelihood is, and should be, determined by topography and natural resources, and that human activity is substantially influenced by environmental conditions. Thus, mining is located where mineral deposits are found, fishing villages are located beside water bodies containing fish, and agriculture is most viable on fertile and well-watered land. His more important contribution was to encourage interest in rural-urban interactions and complementarities, seeing rural areas as major sources of food, water, power, and migrant labor for cities, and cities as service centers for the people of surrounding areas. Thus he emphasized interdependencies, linking together different parts of a region, different regions of a country, and the different countries of the world.[3]

Because of the breadth of his scholarship, bridging environmental sciences, social sciences, and the arts and humanities, Geddes was acutely conscious of the role that nature plays in the human environment. He had a strong interest in forestry, crops, and livestock, and in the role of parks and gardens within the city. His first major book on *City Development* (1904b) was written for the Carnegie Dunfermline Trust and was subtitled *A Study of Parks, Gardens, and Culture-Institutes*. He described this monograph as "at once naturalistic, horticultural, architectural, educational, and social, and in all these respects having to utilize past history and present resources." The book was really a consultancy report for the trust, providing recommendations for the improvement of Pittencrieff Park and surrounding historic areas of Dunfermline, but Geddes inserted his own priorities and an extraordinary number of projects. The work was immensely detailed, proposing how to make a private park into a public amenity, how to clean the polluted stream that runs through the park, how to preserve and adaptively reuse all the historic buildings in the area, how to upgrade slum areas, how to landscape the park, and how to create a wide range of local amenities. Among the projects were social institutes, a central institute, a children's park, a men's gymnasium, a women's pavilion, an open air theatre, an orangery, a Japanese teahouse, numerous gardens, a zoo, a nature palace, a nature museum, a labor museum, a smithy, a crafts village, a hall of medieval history, technical schools, an art institute, a music hall, and the settings for city hall, the historic abbey, and the cathedral. Street trees, sidewalks, statues, conservatories, and sanitation issues figured prominently, as did the choice of plant species for landscaping. The book had many "before and after" pairs of photographs, contrasting the contemporary landscape with the future landscape that would result from implementing his proposals. The primary emphasis was the careful blending of nature, buildings, and human activity, emphasizing recreation, culture, and education for the general public. The images emphasized the historic architecture of Scotland, blended with romantic landscape designs similar to those of such great pioneers as Calvert Vaux, Frederick Law Olmsted, and Joseph Paxton.

Like *City Development*, Geddes's best-known book, *Cities in Evolution: An Introduction to the Town Planning Movement and the Study of Civics* (Geddes 1915b), uses a case study approach. Instead of focusing on one case, such as Dunfermline, however, he took the reader on an esoteric ramble through his ideas, projects, and an eclectic set of examples. Several editions of *Cities in Evolution* have been abridged to cut the length of the volume, but even in abridged form it does not make easy reading. The book combines overviews of world urbanization, economic globalization, and housing policy with a detailed survey of German urban policy before World War I, a review of the state of town planning and civic exhibitions, a treatise on how citizens and planners should be educated, and synoptic essays on "the spirit of cities" and "city betterment." Frequent jumps from global to local, and vice versa, combined with esoteric examples and questions posed but left unanswered, can leave the reader confused or bemused. After a brief paragraph comparing the emergence of conurbations on British and U.S. coalfields, for example, comes the following:

> Of the needful water supplies of all these potential conurbations we leave engineers to speak; but food supplies are conceivable enough, and at all standards, from the too generous dietary of the American hotel to those innumerable costermongers' barrows of cheap and enormous bananas which range through the poorer streets of New York, and grimly suggest a possible importation of tropical conditions, towards the maintenance and multiplication of an all too cheap proletariat. What, in fact, if our present conditions of food supply and of mechanical employments be tending to produce for us conditions hitherto only realized, and in simpler ways, by the teeming millions of China? And what of China herself, already so populous, when her present introduction of Occidental methods and ideas has developed her enormous latent resources of coal, of cheap water communications, as well as railways and the rest? (Geddes 1915b, 49–50)

Despite its evident failings, *Cities in Evolution* inspired the young Lewis Mumford. He adopted many of Geddes's ideas and terms, diffused Geddesian thoughts on planning in his famous books *The Culture of Cities* (1938) and *The City in History* (1961), and emerged as one of the world's foremost writers on urbanism and technology. Largely because of Mumford's enthusiasm, Geddesian regionalism became central to a relatively informal and short-lived "think tank" of U.S. urbanists, a group of about twenty-five activists based in New York City and calling itself the Regional Planning Association of America (RPAA). The senior convenor of the group was the architect Clarence Stein, and other leading members included Henry Wright, Benton MacKaye, Edith Elmer Wood, Catherine Bauer, and Alexander Bing (Parsons 1994). The group met only for ten years from 1923 to1933, but its influence was felt for a much longer period through model neighborhood and new town schemes such as Sunnyside Gardens (Queens, New York) and Radburn (New Jersey), through MacKaye's grand vision for the Appalachian region, focused around his flagship project for an Appalachian Trail (Anderson 2002), and through New Deal projects such as the Tennessee Valley Authority, and the Greenbelt Towns.

One of the RPAA's projects, the 1926 regional planning proposals for New York State, largely authored by Henry Wright, used a Geddesian approach in developing long-term strategies for land-use, urban development, and transportation investments (New York State 1926). Wright and his RPAA colleagues analyzed and organized the state according to the principles of the valley section, identifying prime areas for agriculture, fishing, mining, and forestry, designating areas of landscape and natural resource conservation interest, and concentrating transportation infrastructure and urban development along the L-shaped corridor from New York City northward to Albany, and then westward to Rochester and Buffalo on the Great Lakes. They focused on the state's territory, rather than on the great concentration of population in and around New York City, and they envisioned a growing integration between urban and regional development across the northeastern United States. They followed the logic of Benton Mackaye's original vision for the Appalachian Trail, not just a recreational path along the crest of the mountain range, but the symbolic centerpiece of a mountainous region devoted primarily to cooperative forestry (Mackaye 1921). The trail and forests were intended to provide city dwellers with opportunities for work, recreation, and experiential learning, and to create a permanent green belt to prevent the fusion of expanding urban areas into giant conurbations.

The RPAA's intense period of intellectual activity and community building paralleled a much grander initiative in New York, the preparation of the Regional Plan of New York and its Environs. This was a massive collection of research studies followed by the publication of the plan itself in two volumes (Regional Plan of New York and its Environs 1929, 1931). The plan was prepared by and for the business community of the Tri-State New York Metropolitan Region, and it led to the establishment of the Regional Plan Association (RPA), a research and advocacy organization, which has continued in existence ever since. Most of the funding for the 1929–1931 Regional Plan came from the Russell Sage Foundation, a charity founded in 1907 by Margaret Olivia Sage in memory of her late husband, Russell Sage, a financier and railroad entrepreneur. The foundation was promoted and advised by Robert De Forest, president of the New York Charity Organization Society, and it provided support for the development of social work, social surveys, and improved urban environments. It funded the Pittsburgh Survey directed by Paul Kellogg, long-term editor of *The Survey* and *Survey Graphic,* key U.S. journals promoting activist sociology and publishing articles by Geddes and other members of his circle (Chambers 1971). The foundation also supported the development of Forest Hills Gardens, a garden suburb in the borough of Queens, initiated in 1908, designed by Frederick Law Olmsted Jr. and Grosvenor Atterbury, and reproducing many of the features of Hampstead in London (Klaus 2002).

The key coordinator and author in the preparation of the 1929–1931 Regional Plan of New York and its Environs was Thomas Adams (1871–1940). Born, brought up, and educated in the Edinburgh region, Adams migrated to London in 1900 and later became the first full-time secretary of the Garden City Association, and the first president of the Town Planning Institute. Though never a prominent member of the Geddes circle, Adams was a close associate of Ebenezer Howard, worked with many of the members of the Sociological Society's Cities Committee, and was very aware of Geddes's ideas on regional planning, town planning, and civics. When Adams was elected president of the Town Planning Institute in November 1913, Raymond Unwin and J. W. Cockrill were elected vice presidents, and Geddes was elected honorary librarian. By February 1914, the institute was negotiating for the acquisition and permanent display of Geddes's Cities and Town Planning Exhibition, and it was campaigning to protect Hampstead Garden Suburb from encroachment by new railways (Simpson 1985, 64–66). In the autumn of 1914, however, Adams left Britain for Canada, and in 1923 he was appointed as General Director of the Regional Plan of New York and its Environs. He divided the remainder of his career between Canada, the United States, and the UK, mixing planning practice with university teaching and the publication of numerous reports and several significant textbooks (e.g., Adams 1935). As his career advanced, Adams continuously emphasized pragmatism, willingness to work with those who held wealth, power, and influence, desire to create plans that would be implemented, and desire to influence legislation to facilitate plan implementation.

The 1909 Plan of Chicago (Burnham and Bennett 1909) and the 1929–1931 Regional Plan of New York and its Environs are probably the most famous metropolitan plans ever prepared in North America (Bromley 2001). The New York plan was the subject of numerous critiques by members of the RPAA, synthesized in an exchange between Mumford and Adams in the *New Republic*. In one of the most famous polemics in U.S. planning history, Mumford (1932) argued that the plan was insufficiently regional, did not take adequate account of New York's hinterland, and failed to propose garden cities in the metropolitan region. He also portrayed it as top-down, elitist, and insufficiently conscious of neighborhood communities. In contrast, Adams (1932) argued that the plan represented "the art of the feasible"—what could realistically be achieved in the current socioeconomic and political system. Superficially, at least, this seemed like a clash of Adams, the pragmatist, and Mumford, the Geddesian visionary. Ironically, though, both Mumford and Adams were writing in the immediate aftermath of Geddes's death, and both sought his mantle. Drawing on his Edinburgh roots, Adams claimed a much deeper knowledge of Geddes than Mumford had, arguing that Geddes was more pragmatic than Mumford, and that Geddes would have supported the Regional Plan of New York and its Environs. In the end, portions of the 1929–1931 Regional Plan were implemented, notably much of the proposed highway and park systems, while other portions, notably the strategy for railroads and mass transit, were largely forgotten. The New York Metropolitan Region already had some garden suburbs, and more were built, but it never got a true garden city. The RPAA had launched its own garden city project at Radburn, New Jersey, in 1928, but construction was paralyzed after the Wall Street crash of 1929, and all that remains are two model neighborhoods, surrounded by post–World War II suburban sprawl (Stein 1951, ch. 2).

Despite Adams's claims that Geddes would have supported the 1929–1931 Regional Plan, Lewis Mumford and his RPAA colleagues continued as the prime promoters of Geddes's ideas in North American urban and regional planning. Mumford was forty-one years younger than Geddes, and although he met him only twice, and then very briefly, he had an extended correspondence with him from 1917 till his death in 1932 (see Novak, ed. 1995). Mumford (1948) considered Geddes to be his greatest inspiration, ranking Victor Branford and Thorstein Veblen second-equal, behind Geddes. Mumford's relationship with Geddes was very problematic on a personal level, because Geddes tried hard to persuade Mumford to become his literary assistant and to somehow take the place of Alasdair, his elder son who had been killed in action in World War I (Mumford 1966). Understandably, Lewis Mumford wanted independence and refused to take on such roles. His respect for Geddes was so high, however, that he and his wife Sophia named their only son Geddes. In a grim sequel to the Geddes family's tragedies during World War I, the young Geddes Mumford was killed in action during World War II (Mumford 1947).

CIVICS AS PRACTICE

Throughout his adult life, Geddes was a keen advocate for continuing education, museums and exhibitions, cultural activities such as art and theatre, and cooperative and communitarian solutions to social problems. He deplored idleness, poverty, and squalor, and he saw great potential in involving people in positive programs to improve their education, promote cultural activities, upgrade living conditions, and generate incomes. His civic work, as we showed in chapter 4, began in Edinburgh in 1884 with the formation of the Environment Society, soon renamed the Edinburgh Social Union, a group of civic-minded Edinburgh University lecturers and students and some concerned citizens, who sought to improve social and living conditions in Edinburgh's tenements, promoting window boxes, painting walls, and sometimes adding murals. With his marriage to Anna Morton in 1886, Geddes's civic endeavor became a joint project, living with his wife in Edinburgh's Old Town and promoting many small efforts to improve living conditions, spread education, and build a sense of community (Mairet 1957, 44–81). Patrick and Anna took a special interest in the housing problems of Edinburgh University's students, and they launched University Hall, the first cooperative student hostel in Scotland. Geddes gradually built a following of loyal students, many of them living in University Hall. After the acquisition of the Outlook Tower in 1890, to be developed as a regional museum and sociological laboratory, he was able to launch more ambitious community surveys and development efforts in Edinburgh's Old Town tenements. Eventually, he was able to launch the construction of Ramsay Gardens, a larger student housing cooperative located beside the Outlook Tower, and to publish the four issues of *The Evergreen* in 1895–96, corresponding to the four seasons and promoting a Celtic cultural revival. To Geddes, who saw interconnectedness everywhere, all these various activities were "civics," increasing the links between town and gown, fostering the education of Edinburgh University's students through community engagement, supporting a wide range of cultural and educational activities, conducting research on community problems, and physically building the fabric of Edinburgh University and Edinburgh's Old Town (Geddes 1906; Kitchen 1975, 112–56). The Outlook Tower provided a symbolic centerpiece for all this activity, envisaged as "a laboratory" to teach about and research on the universe, the world, the British Empire, the Scottish nation, the region, and the City of Edinburgh. Charles Zueblin (1899) described it as "the world's first sociological laboratory." The stockholding company established in 1896 to manage Geddes's Edinburgh projects was fittingly called the 'Town and Gown Association Limited,' symbolizing the community-university partnership that Geddes held so dear (Boardman 1978, 147).

Gradually, from 1900 onward, as the Geddes household spent more and more time away from Edinburgh, the civic activities with which Geddes was associated in Edinburgh declined in significance. He was already becoming something of a celebrity, with invitations to visit, lecture, and serve as a consultant to numerous projects both in Britain and overseas. He held a successful Summer School in Paris coinciding with the 1900 World's Fair—the *Exposition Universelle*—but he failed to consolidate a much larger project called the "International Index Museum." This was intended to create a permanent global studies center in Paris, based on donated exhibits from all the nations participating in the World's Fair (Meller 1990, 110–16). Unable to create a permanent global center, Geddes refocused his efforts on regional museums and traveling displays, intending to promote civics and city and regional planning.

Starting with a collection of materials that he contributed to the Town Planning Exhibition held at the Royal Academy in London in 1910, Geddes gradually built up his "Cities and Town-Planning Exhibition," taking it to Dublin, Belfast, and Edinburgh, and eventually to the International Exposition in Ghent (Meller 1995). Geddes used this exhibition as a consciousness-raising tool in his civic agenda, intended to educate the public and to foster an international movement for civics and town planning. To many observers, however, the exhibition was simply a static and eclectic collection of clippings, postcards, photographs, and maps. The significance of such displays diminished rapidly in the 1920s and 1930s with the development of sound and imaging technologies, creating new opportunities to project ideas to the public through radio, gramophone, cinema, and television.

In 1914 the expanded exhibition was shown in Dublin as part of a major effort to develop a new city plan, and then Geddes accepted an invitation from Lord Pentland, the governor of Madras, to take his exhibition to India. Despite the loss of his original exhibition materials at sea, the exhibition was successful and allowed him to spend most of the decade from 1914 to 1924 in India, working there on civics and city planning.

In the late nineteenth and early twentieth century, civics was an emerging field of social activism in both Europe and North America, being particularly associated with the Settlement House movement, the international YMCA movement, the Red Cross, and other nongovernmental organizations. These movements quickly internationalized, and Geddes was one of many who carried pioneering civics initiatives to new lands. The range of priorities and services provided in civics programs varied between countries and cities, but the emphasis was always on voluntary and charitable action through nonprofit organizations. Civics promoted volunteerism, community development, counseling, and popular and continuing education, and it provided day care, counseling services, and food pantries. In America, at a time of mass immigration, it often included English-language classes, and it encouraged voter registration and knowledge of citizens' rights and responsibilities. Geddes was a leader in applying civics to city planning in Britain, Ireland, and India, and he was well aware of comparable work being done in the United States in association with the Settlement House movement, progressive education, the Plans of Chicago and New York, and the emerging urban survey movement (see Dole 1899; Moody 1912; Chambers 1971).

SURVEY THEN PLAN

Probably the best-known Geddes phrase is, "Survey then plan," a maxim that has been repeated thousands of times to generations of planning students. The idea seems logical, but Geddes's passion for detail and comprehensiveness could turn surveys into an obsession, postponing action rather than facilitating it. Sometimes, planners face emergency situations, and it may be necessary to take quick decisions in order to prevent a disaster, minimize its impact, or bring immediate help to its victims. Sometimes, also, problems are simple, rather than multifaceted, and the answer may be known and ready for implementation. For most issues, however, "Survey then plan" is a good maxim for planners.

Though Geddes recommended surveys as a first stage in the planning process, he would not have wanted "Survey then plan" to be his best-known message to the world. He advocated surveys both as data sources for planning and as worthy projects in their own right. For him, as we have shown, surveys are crucial elements in education and community development. Designing and conducting a survey is a means for citizen-students to learn about neighborhoods, towns, cities, and regions and to observe firsthand how different social and environmental variables interrelate with one another. Gradually, a network of Geddes-inspired survey educators emerged, working through schools, the Civic Education League, Le Play House, and other organizations, keen to promote surveys for their educational value: providing a purpose for field trips, a focus for learning, and topics for scholarly debate. Examples of such figures included Valentine Bell, Mabel Barker, Margaret Tatton, Christopher Fagg, and Geoffrey Hutchings. The results of surveys were often published in the *Sociological Review* and other journals, or as monographs, and Le Play House accumulated a massive collection of archived surveys, many of them still held in the archives at Keele University (see Matless 1992). Though nowadays, in a world of remote sensing, geographic information systems, and vast digital databases, the old surveys may seem quaint and bulky, they are often the only data sources available to give clues to local conditions at the time they were conducted.

During the 1920s and 1930s, and especially after the deaths of Branford and Geddes, and with Alexander Farquharson directing Le Play House and editing the *Sociological Review,* community and regional surveys became less sociological and more geographical or ethnographic in character. Large numbers of surveys were conducted, both in Britain and on short organized field trips—often organized by Margaret Tatton—to different parts of Europe, but the emphasis shifted from understanding social dynamics, family structure, and labor markets, toward interpretations of the relationship between culture, economy, physical environment, and settlement morphology. "Muddy-boots geographers" were well represented, following in the scholarly paths of such Geddes and Branford associates as Andrew Herbertson, Charles Fawcett, Herbert Fleure, and Francis Younghusband. As academic sociology came to focus more on questionnaire surveys, rather than community and regional field surveys, Le Play House lost much of its sociological content and membership.

DECENTRALIZATION AND PACIFISM

Throughout their careers, Geddes and Branford were fascinated with peaceful anarchist ideas about decentralization, local democracy, community development, and cooperatives. They did not declare themselves to be anarchists, and they certainly did not support any violent revolutionary movements, but on many occasions they wrote about these topics. Both were very familiar with the writings of Robert Owen and with the British Cooperative Movement, and they had ties to Horace Plunkett and Henry Wolff, leading figures in the International Cooperative Alliance and the rural reconstruction movement (see chapter 7). Two of Geddes's earliest publications were lengthy pamphlets called *John Ruskin: Economist* (1884b) and *Co-operation versus Socialism* (1888a), and both Geddes and Branford had strong links to the Arts and Crafts Movement. There was a strong cooperative underpinning to Geddes's Cyprus work with the Eastern and Colonial Association (Geddes 1897a) and to Branford's work with the West Indian Cooperative Union. Sybella Gurney had helped organize rural and urban cooperative housing programs through Labour Co-Partnership, and probably at her instigation, the Sociological Society published through a cooperative press in

Leicester. Both Elisée Reclus and Peter Kropotkin, two of the world's most famous anarchist intellectuals, visited the Edinburgh Summer Schools in the 1890s, and Geddes and Branford had a thorough grounding in the history of utopian thought.[4]

Above and beyond links to famous anarchists, Geddes and Branford had many other reasons to be suspicious of big governments and imperialism. First and foremost, of course, Geddes was intensely Scottish, a Zionist, and a Francophile, and while he was in India he had strong links with advocates of Indian independence such as Rabindranath Tagore, Margaret Noble (Sister Nivedita), and Annie Besant (1925). Though not overtly or devoutly religious, both Geddes and Branford had a fascination with spirituality, and particularly with Celtic traditions and oriental religions. The recognition of a spiritual domain was crucial to their understanding of community, city, and nation, and to their concept of "the cloister"—the intellectual heart of the ideal community, "a culture-developing set of institutions . . . where the citizen could withdraw himself from day-to-day work and see the whole system" (Clavel 1968, xv). Just as Geddes had emphasized historic, cultural, and religious buildings and institutions in his plan for Dunfermline, he emphasized the synergy of education, culture, and religion, and the role of religion in developing great works of art and music.

In reasserting the importance of spirituality, Geddes and Branford emphasized that there are fields of human endeavor that are, and should be, beyond the reach and control of nation-states, empires, and capitalist corporations. Branford spent most of his life working as a financier and businessman, but he still had time to write many books, pamphlets, and articles on sociology. One of his best works is *St. Columba,* an eighty-three-page monograph first published in 1912. In his Prefatory Note Branford acknowledges the inspiration of "the Comte-Le Play-Geddes formulae, which resume the sociology of the past two generations, and . . . the Lange-James-Hall formulae, which . . . have done a similar service for psychology' (1912, 7).

The story of St. Columba formed the basis for the epilogue scene in Geddes's *Masque of Ancient Learning,* performed in 1912 and 1913 (Defries 1928, 41–48). St. Columba was an AD sixth-century Irish monk, who from a base on the island of Iona organized missionary activity to Scotland, and who turned Iona into a model community with many economic and technological innovations. Iona was self-governing, productive, and prosperous. St. Columba was, in Branford's words,

> at once a priest, a philosopher, a statesman and an educator. It was his task and his ambition to transform his region into a heaven on earth. His monastic settlement he aspired to build into a city dispensing with both the policeman and the lawyer. In fact, he anticipated a modern sociologist in the discovery of Eutopia.

Columba's work in Iona looked to the care both of the place and the people. He conserved the forest. He introduced the culture of fruit trees and of bees, and improved the stock of the island. He shortened the time between seed-time and harvest. He organized the fishing and navigation. He drained the bog between the observatory and the cemetery hills, dammed up the water in a lake and ran it down the ravine to turn the millwheel of his monastery. . . . He tended the sick, comforted the afflicted, admonished and advised the erring, and was a holy and wholesome terror to evil-doers. . . . But the chief purpose of the island monastery was to train the successive bands of missionary monks who sallied forth—often with Columba at their head—into the islands and mainland of Pictish Scotland, and established therein a network of monastic settlements (i.e. radiating foci of practical idealism). (Branford 1912, 61)

In many essays, Geddes and Branford praised small towns, rural areas, and provincial cities, and they advocated community and regional development efforts that were clearly decentrist in character. They did not advocate sweeping central government programs or massive public works. Geddes's planning was local, for a community, neighborhood, campus, town, or city. Through his merchant banking work, Branford was interested in extending railroads and telecommunications in the Americas, and in stimulating new investments in plantations, ranches, and agro-industries, but he saw these tasks as suitable for corporations supported by local and foreign investors, rather than the subject of giant national governmental plans and investments.

World War I had a traumatic impact on Geddes and Branford, and on almost all their social and intellectual circle. As early as 1911 they had warned of the dangers of imminent world war (Mumford 1926, 126), but nothing could prepare them for the daily toll of distressing news during the war itself, or for the traumas of the battlefield survivors who returned home. Geddes lost his exhibition, his elder son, and his wife during the war, and he and Branford saw the world war as a collective insanity.

During World War I, as described more fully in chapter 3, Branford responded to global crisis and Geddes's personal tragedies with the launch of the series of *Papers for the Present* and *The Making of the Future*, trying to lay the foundations for a peaceful postwar reconstruction. By "reconstruction," Branford and Geddes meant something much more profound than reconstructing or replacing the infrastructure and buildings destroyed in the Great War. They were following the concepts developed by Christian Socialists and Social Gospel theologians over the previous forty years, imagining a moral and spiritual "reconstruction" of society. This was the ultimate mission for an activist sociology, finding the way to end war, poverty, and misery by introducing a new spirituality and community value structure (Branford and Geddes 1919b, 365–79). The utopian society that they imagined would have to be democratic, with a combination of individual responsibility and community solidarity. And for such a society to exist, they idealized the old world of the Greek city-state, and peaceful, progressive communities like St. Columba's Iona. The problem, of course, was finding a way to get "from here to there": to transition from a violent and unjust contemporary reality to a much more functional future. Many of the ingredients of their reconstructionism—cooperatives, alternative education, lifelong experiential learning, community development, arts and crafts, credit unions, social credit, engaged universities, and the resurgence of regional and local cultures—are reviewed elsewhere in this volume, but some elements are especially linked to urban, regional, and national planning.

The key planning idea was decentralization and subsidiarity: moving as many government activities as far down the hierarchy of governmental units as possible, creating new units at the lowest levels, and giving much greater powers and autonomy to the lower units. Nation-states might remain in existence, or they might be loosely federated, but the real power would be at a much lower and more localized level, where popular democracy could function effectively. Since the 1890s and their work with the Eastern and Colonial Association to resettle Armenian refugees in Cyprus, Geddes and Branford had been meeting peace and human rights advocates from across Europe. During and after World War I, ideas were beginning to emerge for some form of united Europe, the most coherent possibility being represented by Coudenhove-Kalergi's Pan-European Movement (Coudenhove-Kalergi 1943). More specifically, though, Branford had extensive experience of American federalism and local government, most poignantly with his Nevada divorce and Philadelphia remarriage. Meanwhile, Geddes was traveling extensively in India, serving as a consultant to numerous princely states whose maharajas and their *Durbars* (assemblies of nobles and officials) had invited him to make plans for towns and campuses within their domains. After World War I, with the defeat and breakup of the Ottoman Empire, Geddes was seeing at firsthand how Zionist colonies were emerging in British-administered Palestine.

Small appeared to be beautiful, and decentrism seemed to have many advantages, but Geddes and Branford were very familiar with "the capitals of capital" and the power of military-industrial-financial complexes. To develop their proposals they worked with the economist Gilbert Slater, principal of Ruskin College before its closure at the onset of World War I, and Professor of Indian Economics at the University of Madras from 1915 till 1921. Geddes and Slater (1917) identified the major cities of Europe as "war capitals." London, Paris, Berlin, Istanbul, and Vienna were the most striking examples, but Madrid, Lisbon, Amsterdam, Rome, Budapest, Moscow, and St. Petersburg all had some of the same traits. A "war capital" was a giant city where business, government, and military elites were all concentrated, and where those elites interacted, intermarried, and continually collaborated. Realizing that building a larger colonial empire would give the nation additional captive markets, wealth, and prestige, these elites were happy to go to war with other countries so as to capture portions of their empires. In brief, nation-states went to war to expand their global market shares and supply chains, and to debilitate their competitors.

In the long term, the problem of "war capitals" might be solved by a global decolonization movement of the kind that actually took effect between the late 1940s and the 1990s. In the shorter term, Geddes, Branford, and Slater advocated the solution that Thomas Jefferson and some of the other founding fathers of the United States had advocated in the late eighteenth century. This was to make small cities close to the center of territories the seats of government (Geddes and Slater 1917, 225–49). This would separate government from the military and business elites, and assuming a spread of population across the territory, it might well make the government more accessible to overland travel by average citizens. They envisioned the new small city capitals as more independent from business and military interests, and less susceptible to bribery and corruption. They also envisaged that governments located in such places would be more sympathetic and open to rural and small town interests.

The aftermath of World War I never produced the comprehensive reconstruction of society and values that Geddes, Branford, and Slater had called for. Victory, defeat, mourning, high postwar unemployment, and the punitive revenge of the Treaty of Versailles all distracted public attention from more idealistic and long-term proposals. Few had read the reconstructionists' proposals, and the world moved on. The Spanish Flu pandemic took a horrific toll, the breakup of the German and Ottoman empires gave Britain and France new territories to administer, and the Russian Revolution led to civil war between Reds and Whites, and traumatic changes as the Reds gained control. The example of the Russian Revolution inspired a worldwide upsurge in political radicalism, and many persecuted radicals emigrated from Europe to the Americas. Internationalism quickly foundered in the bitter arguments about the League of Nations, with the United States refusing to join. Red scares, flappers, American Prohibition, and other distractions quickly gave way to the emergence of Italian and German fascism, the Great Depression, and the Spanish Civil War. The moment was lost, and the reconstructionist dreams faded as the authors aged and became more preoccupied with their own medical and family problems.

CONSERVATIVE SURGERY

Despite all the problems of World War I, including the loss of his exhibition, his eldest son, and his wife, the time that Geddes spent in India between 1914 and 1924 was probably the most productive and least well documented of his whole life. He was a prestigious consultant, resident in India, who could help local officials improve their cities and create parks and campuses. He wrote fifty planning reports (Stalley 1972, xii) for the local maharajas who were allowed to rule large portions of India providing they maintained order and guaranteed tax payments and obedience to colonial laws. His reports were detailed and lengthy, supplemented by appendices and folded maps. Some were published, but most were submitted in manuscript form and never had widespread diffusion. Regrettably, now many have been lost, but enough survive to give a clear picture of Geddes's methodology and priorities.

The basic idea that Geddes applied in India was one that he had already tried and tested in Edinburgh, and to some extent also in his plans for Dunfermline. He called the idea "conservative surgery"—preserving all the good elements of the existing urban fabric, and especially buildings and places of historical and religious significance, while repairing or replacing inadequate and hazardous structures, encouraging local improvements through community efforts, and carefully creating, preserving, or enhancing city and neighborhood public spaces. The tenements of Edinburgh and the polluted waterways of Pittencrieff Park had posed challenges, but those challenges were nothing compared with the overcrowding and sanitation problems of many low-income Indian neighborhoods, with their cubicle tenements, shacks, tent-like structures, pavement dwellers, contamination by human and animal excrement, and vulnerability to fire and flooding. The British colonial administrators were often obsessed with density and the problems of epidemic disease, and advocated mass demolitions and cutting wide, straight avenues through existing urban areas. Their cantonments and civil lines, built for their military communities and civilian administrators, reflected low-density suburbanism, with wide straight streets, many bungalows, large lots, and plenty of open spaces. They contrasted dramatically with the dense, crowded "native quarters" in the old towns, with many alleyways and dead ends. The most famous illustration of this contrast was Delhi, where portions of Old Delhi had been totally cleared after the "Mutiny" of 1857, so that British troops could be garrisoned there, and where Lutyens and Baker's New Delhi was under construction as a low-density "city of magnificent distances" contrasting dramatically with the surviving high-density sections of Old Delhi (Irving 1981; Mehra 1991).

When Geddes received a commission to prepare a local plan in an Indian city, he and his assistants prepared a "diagnostic survey," walking every street and alley, sketch-mapping every lot and structure, and classifying the structures by use, historical significance, and quality of construction. His sketch maps also included details of the open areas, including the presence of shrines, trees, and wells (Geddes 1917; and see Mitchell 2010, 1). A typical plan would propose the demolition of between 5 and 20 percent of the structures, and new construction on the edge of the neighborhood or settlement so as to rehouse displaced families. The aim was to remove the worst structures, including any that might collapse or burn down, and to increase the amount of open space. Open space was valued, not just for vehicle and pedestrian circulation, but as fire breaks, and as community areas for meetings, social activities, and childrens' play. Shade trees were particularly valued as focal points for community activities, and Geddes usually proposed planting additional trees and establishing community gardens. In preparing such neighborhood plans, Geddes also looked closely at drainage, sanitation, and garbage disposal, extolling the community to keep ditches and watercourses clear from construction and debris, and to carefully manage their wells and other water sources. Geddes was anxious to preserve historic temples and mosques, and to clear away the lean-to structures that often surrounded religious buildings, protecting their architectural heritage and reducing the risks of fire. He sought to provide space for schools and community centers, and to ensure that every neighborhood had such basic services.

As well as planning for the improvement of existing neighborhoods in Indian cities, Geddes sometimes received commissions for more ambitious projects, most notably his plan for a University of Central India in the city of Indore (Geddes 1918). Though much less well known than the 1919 plan for the Hebrew University of Jerusalem that he prepared with Frank Mears, his vision for a university in Indore was more comprehensive and complete. He focused the projected university on a central library, museums, indoor and outdoor theatres, and an outlook tower. The museum would feature culture, art, urban development, agriculture, and health, with a particular emphasis on the city of Indore and the surrounding region. His recommended selection of academic disciplines to be taught in the university, and his layout of the campus, were all framed around the central roles to be played by the library, museums, theatres, and tower. Thus, for example, Geddes (1918, 36) justified philosophy as "the complemental need of inlook beside outlook," proposing a windowless corner turret of the tower as a quiet meditation room with a narrow shaft of light in the ceiling. With characteristic breadth and detail, he proposed degree regulations to prevent narrow specialization and to promote a broad understanding of the liberal arts and sciences, and he sprinkled his justification for the university structure with the names of famous scholars, including the Humboldt brothers, Goethe, Comte, Bergson, Darwin, Spencer, Huxley, Pasteur, Stanley Hall, and William James.

Linking universities to cities, Geddes (1918, 57) wrote: "The true University blossoms from its Culture-City, great or small; hence the significance not only of Athens or Paris aforesaid, but of Edinburgh or Boston (Harvard), or Leyden, Jena, Aberdeen, and a hundred more, and here conspicuously is the rational hope which lately initiated the University of Benares." The University of Indore would have replicated and extended the great initiative taken in the city of Benares, now known as Varanasi, where what is now known as Banaras Hindu University (BHU) was founded in 1916. That university, which includes an impressive regional museum, was heavily supported by Indian intellectuals and members of the Indian National Congress, and built on the success of the Central Hindu School, which Annie Besant had founded in Benares in 1898.

Though Geddes's university proposals for Indore were not implemented, his ideas for a university helped to justify Rabindranath Tagore's project for Visva Bharati University in Santiniketan, Bengal. Founded in 1921, and building on a community school, Visva Bharati literally meant "communion of the world with India." In its early years, Visva Bharati was dedicated to community outreach, experiential learning, and rural reconstruction, exemplifying many of the ideals and visions that Tagore shared with Geddes. The link to British, Irish, and American ideas on rural reconstruction and decentralized development was further emphasized by Tagore's decision to recruit the English agricultural economist Leonard Elmhirst to lead the rural reconstruction effort (Das Gupta 2006, 194–214). Elmhirst worked at Visva Bharati for the first three years, and after marrying his American sponsor, the wealthy widow Dorothy Whitney Straight, he and his wife purchased Dartington Hall in Devon. Dartington Hall emerged as a leading British institution for alternative education, experiential learning, and rural reconstruction, and the Elmhirsts and Tagore built an ongoing rural reconstruction partnership. During the same initial three years at Visva Bharati, Arthur Geddes, Patrick and Anna's younger son, also worked at Santiniketan, furthering the cause of experiential learning and rural reconstruction.

Many ironies and paradoxes were built into Geddes's Indian neighborhood plans. He was a man of the people and an advocate for the community, but traveling from region to region in a land of immense linguistic complexity, he needed translators to help him communicate with the neighborhood residents. He had a genuine interest in improving the living conditions of poor people, but he was working for elite maharajas, some of whom were immensely rich, and who held their wealth by taxing the poor and ensuring a flow of revenues to the British colonial administration. And Geddes, the Scotsman, was in British India under an administration that tolerated his commissions and proposals, even though those proposals often contradicted the schemes of the administration's own staff. Geddes walked a tightrope, opposing the administration's schemes, the extensive involvement of Indian troops in World War I, and postwar atrocities such as the Amritsar Massacre, but avoiding wartime internment, the fate imposed on more vociferous British dissidents such as Annie Besant.

Geddes's plans for India's densely populated old town neighborhoods, the "native quarters," have been enormously influential since World War II, gradually emerging as a mainstream perspective on "third world housing policy." Nevertheless, very few planners have actually read Geddes's Indian plans. Few copies were produced, they were delivered to local maharajas and *Durbars,* and very few were ever cataloged into libraries and archives or republished with any significant circulation. The key agent, who brought the plans and associated methods to the world's attention, was Jaqueline Tyrwhitt, a British planner who had studied Geddes's writings and visited Edinburgh to explore the Geddes heritage in the 1920s, and who taught planning for the Association for Planning and Regional Reconstruction (APRR) in London in the late 1940s and early 1950s. Tyrwhitt was closely associated with the International Congress on Modern Architecture (CIAM) in the 1940s and 1950s, and from 1955 onward, with Constantinos Doxiadis, the central figure in the Ekistics (science of human settlements) movement, edited or co-edited the widely circulated planning journal *Ekistics* from its first issue in 1955 till her death in 1983 (Shoshkes 2006, 2009). In 1947, with help and encouragement from Geddes's surviving son, Arthur, from Henry Lanchester a member of the old Sociological Society Cities Committee, and from Lewis Mumford, Tyrwhitt published a slim edited book called *Patrick Geddes in India,* explaining the Geddesian approach and providing very brief extracts from Geddes's voluminous writings on India. In his preface to Tyrwhitt's collection, Lewis Mumford extolled Geddes's Edinburgh projects, his "civic surveys," and his "diagnosis before treatment" approach, and his intellectual links with the pioneering American environmentalist George Perkins Marsh and the Russian anarchist Peter Kropotkin. Mumford emphasized Geddes's opposition to colonial bureaucracies:

> This mode of planning challenged the idols of officialdom; it was conceived in terms of primary human needs, not of current business and engineering conventions. . . .
>
> To the town planners' art, Geddes brought the rural virtues; not merely respect for the land and for agricultural processes; but the patience of the peasant, and the sense that orderly growth is more

important than order at the expense of growth. He saw both cities and human beings as wholes; and he saw the processes of repair, renewal, and rebirth as natural phenomena of development. His ideal of the best life possible was always the best that was latent in a particular site and situation, at a particular moment in the development of a particular family, group, or community; not an abstract ideal that could be imposed by authority or force from the outside. . . .

In his early reaction against the cult of the state, Geddes anticipated the modern generation's reaction against totalitarianism. The very thought that his thought remains post-Marxian will, perhaps, link him more closely with the oncoming generation who, in both war and peace, have discovered the limitations of military and bureaucratic organisations, no matter how well-meaning and beneficent their purposes may be, and who—without relapsing into a defeatist laissez faire—will seek for counterpoises to the present tendency to over-concentrate power and authority. (Mumford 1947b, 11–12)

Tyrwhitt's career is enigmatic in many senses, sometimes promoting grassroots planning and community engagement, but also working with leading modernist architects whose grand schemes were the antithesis of such approaches. In editing *Geddes in India,* however, she brought Geddes's Indian heritage out of the shadows, and she presented it directly to a new generation of students in the APRR, a special program for British World War II veterans who sought to enter architecture and planning during a period of vigorous worldwide activity associated with postwar physical reconstruction of bombed cities, the Marshall Plan, the independence of many former colonies, and the ambitious international development rhetoric of the newly formed United Nations and World Bank. Among Tyrwhitt's students was John F. C. Turner, who subsequently worked on British aid projects in Peru, focusing on the squatter settlements (*barriadas*) of Arequipa and Lima. Through a series of articles published in the 1960s and early 1970s (e.g., Turner 1967), and in his highly influential book *Housing by People* (Turner 1976), Turner emerged as the world's leading spokesperson for "conservative surgery," re-baptized as the "neighborhood upgrading" of slums and shantytowns. There was little new in Turner's approach, which built on Geddes and also on the work of Jacob Crane, a mid-twentieth-century American housing policy specialist, but Turner's work came at an opportune time for the major aid agencies and international organizations concerned with "third world development" (Harris 2003; Bromley 2003). Development specialists were seeking an alternative to expensive public housing projects, a means to activate market forces among the very poor in rapidly urbanizing nations, and a means to overcome the highly visible squalor of the burgeoning shantytowns ringing most major cities in Africa, Asia, and Latin America. The result has been the publication of hundreds of articles, reports, and books on upgrading (e.g., Payne 1977; Brakarz 2002), and the implementation of many thousands of neighborhood upgrading projects around the world. Though few are aware of Geddes's inspiration to these efforts, the intellectual link is very clear (Turner 1982, 100).

PALEOTECHNIC, NEOTECHNIC, AND VISIONS OF "SUSTAINABILITY"

In his writings, Geddes frequently created neologisms and typologies, and his terms and typologies sometimes helped to explain new theories and interpretations of reality. He adopted the terms *paleotechnic* and *neotechnic* to summarize a general theory of urban and regional development. This terminology was frequently used by Victor Branford and other disciples, and it was developed into major works and much more sophisticated terms and theories by Lewis Mumford. Geddes had a fascination with Ancient Greek ideas on the *polis* (city) and utopias, and he delighted in developing new words to describe variants on the *polis* and utopia. Branford, Mumford, and Doxiadis all shared this fascination, and so their writings are peppered with neo-Hellenic expressions such as *parasitopolis, tyrannopolis, necropolis, kakatopia, subtopia,* and *ecotopia*. While the great variety of *polises* and *topias* can be irritating or confusing to contemporary readers, at least two of the terms that Geddes introduced to the planning literature have genuine utility: *conurbation,* the fusion of adjacent urban areas while maintaining distinct downtowns, and *megalopolis,* the interlinking of adjacent metropolitan areas into one continuous metropolitan region.[5]

Geddes's general theory of urban and regional development is quite crude and simple. He looks back to a predominantly rural preindustrial world, with villages and small market towns, and idealizes that world as one signifying an intimate working relationship between place, folk, and work, a cradle for the arts and crafts, and a harmony between mankind and the natural environment. Despite the occasional ravages of pandemic disease and invading armies, which he was certainly aware of, he saw these societies as representing wholesome traditions. He also saw them as representing a durable interdependence of nature and human activity, what in twenty-first-century terms we would call "sustainability": a pattern of development that uses renewable natural resources and maintains the fertility and biodiversity of the natural environment, and thus enables future generations to enjoy the same environments, lifestyles, and life prospects as current generations.

Into this simple world came the agricultural and industrial revolutions, with their increasingly intensive use of drainage, irrigation, hybrid crop and livestock varieties, and fertilizers, and the gradual development of canals, railroads, steamships, electricity, telephone, telegraph, motor vehicles, aircraft, radio, television, pesticides, antibiotics, nuclear power and weapons, remote sensing, computers, the Internet, global positioning systems, space exploration, robots, and drones. Geddes only saw part of this vast and accelerating technological progression, but it was enough for him to make a simple two-part division of urbanization, industrialization, and globalization: the identification of paleotechnic and neotechnic cities and civilizations.

Paleotechnic for him was unsustainable, a world based on fossil fuels, industrialization, automation, materialism, and greed. Enormous capitalist wealth was created at the cost of a depleted natural environment, impoverished rural areas, growing rural-urban migration, and the mushrooming of squalid, polluted urban areas characterized by poverty, ignorance, and deprivation. In many senses, it was a materialist industrialized world gone mad. It was gradually destroying the environmental and social conditions, and the cultural traditions and institutions, that enabled free-thinking, self-managing communities to better themselves and maintain sustainability.

To Geddes, many of the new technologies available to humankind were not damaging, and what was needed more than anything else was a high degree of selectivity, consciously favoring clean and environmentally friendly technologies, preserving ecosystems and biodiversity, and maintaining vibrant local societies, economies, and democracies. He described this ideal world as Neotechnic: taking advantage of the progress of science and technology, but constantly selecting the best options and avoiding any developments that would encourage resource depletion, environmental deterioration, increased social inequalities, or social pathologies such as crime, delinquency, alienation, and suicide. Crucial features of the neotechnic world were interdependent relationships between regional cities and surrounding rural areas, the continued vigor of rural societies, the enrichment of human life by the arts and humanities, and the dispersal of urbanization to a variety of small to medium-size cities, rather than concentration in one giant metropolis.

Geddes's neotechnic order offered multiple eutopias in technology, society, politics, and most poignantly in life itself: what Geddes called, following Bergson, "vitalism." In one of his most powerful illustrations (Geddes 1926), he sprinkled the names of inspiring authors into his neotechnic vision: Ruskin, Morris, Wundt, Durkheim, Kelvin, Ferranti, Plunkett, Pasteur, Galton, Haeckel, Comte, Westermarck, Tolstoy, Nietzsche, Eucken, Bergson, James, Schiller, Papini, Gide, Ingram, Hobson, Lamarck, Driesch, Le Play. His selection was curious, very personalistic, and tied to visions of the Recovery of Parnassus, the Recovery of Olympus, and a world based on conservation, electric power, geotechnics, sociology, and social psychology! Geddes, as usual, was complex, leaving the reader bemused, but offering many snippets of what others, most notably Mumford, could build into a more coherent theory and vision.

The simple contrast between paleotechnic and neotechnic alternatives, as presented by Geddes, seems to pose easy choices between bad and good futures, yet the alternatives are rarely so simple. The quest for increased wealth in the short term often imposes longer-term social and environmental costs, and elites often enrich themselves while displacing or impoverishing some poorer social groups. Food shortages and excess abundance of food cause different health problems, but they both cause unnecessary morbidity and mortality. New transportation technologies and growing international trade facilitate the spread of high-value tree species, food crops, and livestock varieties around the world, but they also facilitate the spread of weeds, parasites, vermin, and diseases. Some cities emerge as "world cities," command and control centers in the global system, and the centrality of those cities contrasts dramatically with the marginalization of many regional cities, especially in smaller and poorer countries and regions. Geddes was well aware of the complexity of such issues, and his writings were full of pleas for balance, moderation, and harmony. Without even using the term *sustainability*, he was a pioneer in examining sustainability issues: seeking paths and patterns of environmental, social and economic development that could continue in the long term.

In many senses, the Geddesian vision of the relationships between civilization, urbanism, and technology was fulfilled by Lewis Mumford in his monumental four-part book series called "The Renewal of Life." Mumford drew on the paleotechnic/neotechnic distinction, but his treatment of the underlying issues was much more sophisticated than Geddes's version. Mumford began with *Technics and Civilization* (1934), published just two years after Geddes's death, continued with *The Culture of Cities* (1938), and completed the project with *The Condition of Man* (1944) and *The Conduct of Life* (1951). These were works of hope and progress, setting out a broad humanistic vision of how technology could be harnessed to improve the human condition. Soon after completing the series, however, and depressed by the loss of his son Geddes in World War II, by the cold war, by the dangers of nuclear capabilities, and by the spread of consumerism, individualism, and environmental contamination, Mumford began to develop equally monumental, but much more pessimistic works. *The City in History* (1961) emphasized the horrors of Coketown, Necropolis, and banal suburbs, and the two-volume *Myth of the Machine* (Mumford 1967 and 1970) presented Faustian visions of megamachines, pathologies of power, imperialist misadventures, and the ever-present possibility of nuclear disaster.

GEDDES AND BRANFORD: SOCIOLOGY AND PLANNING COMPARED

This chapter has focused more on Patrick Geddes than on Victor Branford. Though he convened the Cities Committee of the Sociological Society, and though his wife Sybella was active in the Garden Cities Association, Branford never described himself as a planner. His mission was always to promote sociology; to pursue a broad, activist Geddesian version of sociology, which, in Branford's view, subsumed planning, community development, and large portions of education and social work. Branford grouped these fields together as "civics," applied sociology to promote social reconstruction. In contrast to Branford, Geddes did write plans, most notably for Dunfermline, for numerous neighborhoods, cities and institutions in India, and for Tel Aviv and Jerusalem. His plans were full of vague pronouncements, and many were not implemented, but nevertheless they were landmark schemes advocating historic preservation, community development, and environmental conservation. For the period in which they were written, and in comparison with the works of architect-planners, they were socially, environmentally, and historically sensitive and visionary.

Though he chose other words to describe his ideas, Geddes was a pioneer of neighborhood upgrading, community development, and sustainability. Not surprisingly, therefore, his work has been more heavily profiled and praised in planning than in other disciplines. Most notable are Helen Meller's biography, *Patrick Geddes: Social Evolutionist and City Planner* (1990), Volker Welter's *Biopolis: Patrick Geddes and the City of Life* (2002), and Noah Hysler-Rubin's *Patrick Geddes and Town Planning* (2011), but most of the other books published on Geddes give substantial attention to his planning work. All the book-length works on Geddes focus more on his social science and civic activism than on his scholarship in biology, and most of the books comment quite specifically on Geddes's rather disorganized life and scholarship, and the difficulties that many experienced in understanding his lectures, notes, and thinking machines. He was a man of bounding interests and many projects, most of them frustrated, and he lived in troubled times and suffered several personal tragedies. He worked in and on several different countries, and he made two major changes in country of primary residence; from Britain to India in 1914, and from India to France in 1924. Not surprisingly, his many biographers have found it hard to summarize his works and impact. Paddy Kitchen (1975) summarized Geddes wonderfully in the title of her biography, *A Most Unsettling Person: The Life and Ideas of Patrick Geddes, Founding Father of City Planning and Environmentalism.*

As an inspiration to twenty-first-century planning, Geddes had a pioneering role in civics, university outreach, and community partnerships, historic preservation, and community development and neighborhood upgrading. His broader approach emphasized what we now call "sustainable development," focusing on the significance of nature in the city, the interdependence of cities and rural areas, community food security, biodiversity, renewable energy, civic institutions, spirituality, and the importance of a balanced and dispersed urban system, avoiding heavy concentration on a few giant metropolitan areas or conurbations.

In the early debates of the Sociological Society, as exemplified by the articles in the three volumes of *Sociological Papers*, including most of the works presented to the founding meetings of the Society in 1904, 1905, and 1906, the primary debate is between eugenics, as advocated by Francis Galton, Benjamin Kidd, and others, and civics, as advocated by Patrick Geddes, Victor Branford, and others.[6] It was apparently a classic "nature versus nurture" debate in which the two explanations of the human condition are genetics and culture. In reality, however, Geddes's position was much more nuanced, combining the biological and social sciences and focusing on ecology, environment, and culture. To Geddes, the human condition had three major features: our biological nature as mammals within ecosystems; our social nature as the species uniquely possessed with powers of speech, culture, and spirituality; and, our activist nature, as a species, like ants, possessed with a tremendous capacity for social organization, construction, and improvement in the physical and social environment. This was the grand idea that Geddes and Branford sought to bring to sociology, a multifaceted vision of an activist society in its cultural and biological context.[7] Their idea was grander and more sophisticated than eugenics, but they never managed to make it fit into universities because twentieth-century academia had more restrictive concepts of disciplines and expertise. Instead, a much narrower concept of sociology took root, a much narrower version of planning emerged as a separate discipline, and biology, psychology, anthropology, and education all took their separate courses. Meanwhile, civics, the centerpiece of Geddes and Branford's sociology, failed to find a meaningful place in universities or in most sociopolitical systems. Though civic consciousness and spirit would seem desirable attributes of every nation and society, there is little evidence that they are growing or dominant forces in the contemporary world.

SIX

SOCIALIZATION, CITIZENSHIP, AND THE UNIVERSITY MILITANT

The approach taken by Branford and Geddes to society and social reconstruction was complemented by a psychological theory of the socialization of individual personalities as citizens able to undertake the task of social reconstruction. They adopted advanced psychological perspectives and promoted these through their involvement in the emerging progressive school movement. Educational formation at school was seen as a process both of socialization and civilization, and they placed particular emphasis on the education of youths and the role of youth movements in the formation of informed and socially responsible citizens committed to social reconstruction. Education was, however, to be a lifelong task, and the university was to play a key regional role in educating citizens and allowing them to participate in the development of their region. The university was also to look beyond the region to a global context of reconstruction, and they pursued the idea of the "university militant" as a means of cosmopolitan citizenship and global cooperation.

PERSONALITY, SOCIALIZATION, AND CONVERSION

It is now commonplace to recognize the cultural formation of personality, but at the time that Branford and Geddes were writing it was more typical to see mental capacities as biologically conditioned. Few nineteenth-century psychologists would countenance the idea that social forces had any effect on personality, and Branford and Geddes were among the first to see the need for a social psychology. They were committed to an evolutionary perspective according to which the development of any living entity had to be seen as an adaptation to its environment. Humans, they argued, are born not only into a physical environment and material heritage but also into historically specific social relations that comprise their "social heritage." To develop a distinctively social psychology they avidly explored the emerging psychological and educational theories for insights into the socialization of individual human beings. In doing so, they pioneered an approach to understanding individual behavior that reached fruition in Sigmund Freud's psychoanalytic theories of emotional development and Jean Piaget's cognitive developmental theories.

Their starting point was to see the general character, temperament, and aspirations of children as shaped by their inculcation into the cultural outlook formed in their specific class and national heritages. Social differences are produced by the education received within the home, the school, and the larger "social milieu," and it is from this social context that people acquire a specific "code of manners, customs, habits and outlook" (Branford 1914a, 21):

> Education . . . is the complex of means by which a particular social heritage is transmitted to the individual. Out of the past history of his own and allied groups, the individual has his present and his future made for him by his parents, his teachers, his associates, his wife and his children. (Branford 1914a, 22)

Branford held that two infants with similar genetic endowments would grow into socially distinct adults if brought up by families in different social classes but within the same nation. They would learn common national ideas and values but each child would also learn distinct class ideas and values and would be exposed to a different and distinctive set of experiences. As a result, he argued, a child brought up by a peer (an aristocrat) and one brought up by a porter will develop into markedly different individuals by the age of twelve. Despite their initially similar biological endowment, they will develop in different directions because of the effects of their social relations:

> Assume a similarity of stock and a similarity of temperament, the difference that has now intervened between the plebeian and the aristocrat is a social one, (Branford 1914a, 21, 169)

Socialization is an ongoing process within which differences of class and nation can structure the human life cycle. The stages of the life cycle reflect biological processes of growth and maturation as well as social processes of learning and experience. Biological maturation and aging have their effects on individual personality only through the socially shaped conditions of human life. The socialization of individual personality has to be seen as an interaction between the social heritage and the biological heritage. As a result, each stage in life is marked by particular and distinctive opportunities and crises:

> [M]ental habits, like bodily ones, undergo modification, as in going from home to school, falling in love, getting married, becoming a father, making new intimacies of friendship, changing one's occupation, party, religion, and so forth. Throughout life there goes on an incessant process of mental habituation, dehabituation, rehabituation. Each crisis of change is a product of interaction between inner impulse and outer circumstance. (V. V. Branford 1923, 20)

A key influence on the elaboration of these basic assumptions was the American psychologist G. Stanley Hall, whom Geddes had met on his second visit to the United States in 1900 (Boardman 1978, 175; see also Hall 1923). Hall had studied with William James, becoming the first American to obtain a PhD in psychology, and following his doctorate he studied in Germany at Wilhelm Wundt's innovative psychology laboratory. In 1880 he was appointed to a chair in psychology at Johns Hopkins University, where he began to develop an evolutionary approach to psychology that he used in a child study program undertaken during the 1890s (White 1990; Smuts 2005).[1] Hall's psychology identified a number of phases of childhood development and was a pioneering and sophisticated approach that served as a bridge between older faculty and instinct theories and the more rigorously developmental views of Freud and Piaget (Leary 2009, 1987).[2]

The child study movement with which Hall was involved was closely associated with the foundation in 1874 of the Chautauqua Lake Sunday School Assembly, a residential educational community within the Social Gospel movement that began as a regular Summer School and rapidly inspired similar ventures in what came to be called the Chautauqua Circuit (Rieser 2003).[3] Chicago sociologist George Vincent, son of the founder of the Chautauqua circuit, became the director of the Summer School in 1888 and brought many academics from Chicago and Johns Hopkins into its work. It was the success of the Chautauqua movement that had encouraged Geddes to begin his own Summer Schools in 1887, but it was not until some years later that he took up the educational psychology behind it. Child study was a major theoretical and applied topic at the Educational Congress held during the 1893 Chicago World's Fair, and it was there that three female teachers from Britain, including a Miss Clapperton of St. George's Training College in Edinburgh, were inspired to form the British Child Study Association on their return to Edinburgh. They launched its journal—*The Paidologist*—a few years later, in 1899 (Wooldridge 1994, 36; Armytage 1976; Schlossman

1973; Brehoney 2009). Miss Clapperton may well have been known to Geddes, as she was a niece of Jane Hume Clapperton, eugenist and social reformer (see Clapperton 1885), who had corresponded with Geddes about *The Evolution of Sex*. Geddes certainly took a close interest in St. George's, whose principal, Mary R. Wilson, was one of his correspondents, and he read widely into child study research.

It was through the Educational Congress and the British Child Study Association that Geddes and Branford first met many of the leading figures in child psychology. A key contact was Earl Barnes, an educationalist from Stanford who had been head of the Chautauqua organization in Philadelphia and worked in university extension lecturing in London from 1897. Barnes and Geddes first met through the Sesame Club, a revisionist Froebel association for which both men lectured in educational policy and practice (Griggs 1935; see Barnes 1896, 1902). Barnes himself wrote for the *Paidologist* (Barnes 1899, 1901). The secretary of the Sesame Club was Margaret Noble, later Sister Nivedita, who had become head teacher of the Ruskin School in Wimbledon (Read 2003; Brehoney 2004).[4]

It was as a result of his involvement in child study that Hall, along with John Slaughter and Thomas Clouston, invented the term adolescence to describe the period between early childhood and adulthood: from age fourteen to twenty-four in males and from twelve to twenty-one in females, but having its fullest expression around the age of fifteen or sixteen. Hall introduced the word in 1894, and his ideas were given their most forceful and influential expression in his book *Adolescence* (1904).[5] Geddes, who had met Hall on his visit to Worcester, Massachusetts, in 1900, engaged with this book on its publication and wrote an enthusiastic review of it for the Ruskin house journal (Geddes 1904a). This review was later reproduced in *The Paidologist*. It was this enthusiastic review that brought Hall and Geddes into contact with each other and led to Hall visiting Edinburgh in 1906.[6]

Central to Hall's argument, and enthusiastically taken up by Branford and Geddes, was the idea of "recapitulation," based on the evolutionary theory set out by Ernst Haeckel. Hall had encountered Haeckel during his studies in Germany in the early 1880s and Geddes had met him in Jena in 1886, subsequently inviting him to teach at his Edinburgh Summer Schools. Haeckel held that individual biological development, in the womb and during childhood, is a condensed replay of the evolution of the human species. His principle that "ontogeny repeats phylogeny" refers to the maturation of human anatomy and physiology as it repeats the stages of biological evolution and was widely accepted within biology (see Balfour 1880; Haddon 1887). Following this principle, Hall's colleague Alexander Chamberlain (1903) held that human embryos are initially similar to fish and amphibians and he saw the process of learning to crawl as recapitulating the movement of animals from water to land. Hall was the leading figure among those who sought to extend this principle to the psychological level and to see the mental development of individuals as repeating the stages of *social* evolution. This view appeared in varying forms in the work of George Romanes (1889; see also 1885) and Alfred Haddon (see Kuklick 1998) in Britain and James Baldwin (1893) and educationalist Estelle Appleton (1910) in the United States.[7] Geddes and Thomson summarized this as the view that the lifetime of an individual involves "a recapitulation of racial history," though they added that there should be no "exaggerating it into a fallacy" (Geddes and Thomson 1931, 1262).

In his landmark study of adolescence, Hall (1904: 1, viii; 2, 648 ff.) held that the powers and interests of the individual mind develop through various stages that repeat the phases through which human societies have gone during their evolution from primitive to more civilized forms. What he meant by this was that human infants are born with the same biological and psychological equipment as the earliest humans and in order to become a fully socialized member of their particular society they must learn to channel and convert these instincts and dispositions just as their predecessors had done in producing that society. This view was enthusiastically taken up by those in and around the Geddes circle. Branford himself summarized the argument in his assertion that man is "fated to climb afresh each generation his ancestral pedigree" (V. V. Branford 1923, 24; and see Tayler 1921b, 57 ff.). The psychotherapist and educationalist Theodore Faithfull argued that

> [i]n the same way that the human embryo goes through all the stages of its evolution from amoeba to human being, so also the mind, before, but especially after birth, is continually developing and evolving from a lower stage to a higher, by means of experience. (Faithfull 1933, 54; see also Faithfull 1927, 44).

Similarly, Dorothy Revel, a senior teacher at Faithfull's Priory Gate School, held that

> [h]e [sic] is born at the stage of development approximately corresponding to that of early man, and in his growth from birth to adult life he follows out roughly the history of the development of mankind up to the present day. (Revel 1928, 38)

This developmental view was underpinned by Lamarck's view of the inheritance of acquired characteristics, which suggested that the social characteristics acquired at any particular stage of cultural development are inherited genetically rather than simply being passed on through cultural transmission. Hall argued that the behavior and way of life followed by "primitive" hunters and gatherers are inherited as cultural traits that are subsequently overlaid by those acquired at more "advanced" stages of evolution. Human character, therefore, comprises an accumulation of instincts, habitual responses, and dispositions appropriate to various stages of social evolution. The behavior of the young child and "childish" behavior in the adults of "civilized" societies are an expression of "primitive" thought and behavior. As a child in a civilized society matures into adulthood, its various instincts are channeled by the culture in which it lives and many of its "primitive" instincts may be suppressed. Primitive instincts are adapted to the specific conditions of hunter and gatherer societies and are no longer relevant to contemporary "civilized" life. If persisting unchecked into adulthood, these childhood instincts can have pathological consequences—though if they are completely refused expression they may also generate pathological effects:

> [N]early every act, sensation, feeling, will, and thought of the young child tends to be paleopsychic just in proportion as the child is let alone or isolated from the influence of grown-ups, whose presence always tends to the elimination of these archaic elements, and in all cases makes havoc with them, over-repressing some that should have their brief fling. (Hall 1909, 47)

If prematurely repressed, Hall argued, the instincts may be expressed in unacceptable or criminal forms. This was the case, he held, whenever adolescent sexual instincts are either arrested or overdeveloped.

The influence of the cultural environment is strongest in childhood and adolescence, when the developing psyche is most malleable, but the crucial opportunities for environmental influence are biologically determined by maturation and growth. Thus, the adult mind is a complex, layered series of structures of instincts and tendencies of action, the deeper structures operating unconsciously (Hall 1904: 2, 60).

It was on this basis that Branford argued that those who live in contemporary industrial societies are "uprooted rustics" (1926b, 41). They retain the instincts and predispositions of the rustic occupations of hunter, fisherman, forester, and miner, and these instincts need to be "converted" to civilized use. If they remain "unconverted" or undergo "reversion," they will find their expression in the predatory and emulative impulses that Branford and Geddes diagnosed as central to the social malaise of contemporary modernity. These primitive instincts, then, must be converted to ideals of tenderness and workmanship that are central to a civilized—civic—life (Branford 1926b, 76). The concept of conversion was taken directly from Hall, who saw it as the process by which the intense emotional experiences inherent in primitive instincts are channeled and controlled in such a way that a person can move on to a new sense of self and social activity in civilized purposes. According to Branford and Geddes, emotions, ideas, and images—the three principal elements in mental life—could all be converted to alternative uses. They discovered, through Hall, similarities with the Freudian ideas of "repression" and "sublimation," which came to be seen as alternative ways of understanding the process of conversion (P. Geddes 1927b, 134–35; see also Branford 1912).[8]

Hall had invited Freud to lecture in the United States in 1909 and was a leading proponent of his views. From 1914 he became more particularly interested in the ideas of Alfred Adler and Carl Gustav Jung, drawing especially on the latter's emphasis on the inherited "racial" unconscious of primitive instincts (see Jung 1917). It was at this time that Geddes and Branford also began to draw on psychoanalysis and to combine it with their early developmental psychology. This was also the beginning of a wider engagement with new trends in social psychology through debates with the works of Trotter (1908, 1909), McDougall (1908), and, somewhat later, Rivers (1920), each of whom had adopted an instinct psychology and sought to integrate these ideas with the newer psychoanalytic ideas (see Richards 2000, 186–89). Geddes himself was particularly closely involved with the British Adlerians, along with other members of the Chandos Group (see chapter 8), while associates such as Arthur Tansley (1920) and Theodore Faithfull (1927, 1933), were drawn more closely to Jung.[9] Psychoanalysis was promoted through the Sociological Society, with the leading British Freudian, Ernest Jones, organizing a series of lectures at the Society in 1924 (Jones 1924).

THE DEVELOPMENTAL FRAMEWORK

Geddes and Branford used the psychological ideas of recapitulationism as the basis for their construction of a model of mental development from infancy through adulthood. They saw this as a sequence of five stages that correspond to the phases of the life cycle in contemporary societies. The movement from one stage to the next is conditioned by physiological maturation, but the ways in which each transition occurs reflect the accumulating life experiences of the person. At each stage, biological maturation and changing social circumstances jointly generate new powers and faculties and refine or subordinate old impulses and instincts as the new faculties are strengthened. The newly developed faculties are, at first, unfocused and inchoate and must be guided into maturity. Each stage exhibits a relative stability of instincts, habits, and motives, but each ends with a critical period of biological maturation or social change that radically transforms mentality. If movement through a particular stage of development is not properly negotiated, transition to the next stage may not occur or may occur in a distorted or unnatural way. Psychological development, then, involves a constant clash between cultural constraints and a variety of conflicting inherited forces and dispositions (Geddes 1904c, 85).

The stages of psychological development most typically identified by Branford and Geddes are shown in Table 6.1. These stages run from infancy through childhood and youth into adult maturity and old age.

Infancy is the stage in life at which purely natural impulses are strongest, the infant only slowly becoming aware of its own existence and of the world around it. Infants initially live in a world of disconnected sense impressions, and only gradually do they learn to unify these impressions into a coherent image of their world. Through months of trial-and-error encounters with their environment as they act on the basis of organized and instinctive purposiveness, they begin to act on the basis of "perceived purposiveness" and so act with conscious deliberation (Thomson 1920; V. V. Branford 1923, 43). Their engagement with the world takes the form of "play" as they explore both its features and their own powers and limitations. The stage of infancy ends at around age six to seven, when a critical period of biological growth triggers entry into the next stage: childhood.

Childhood lasts from age eight to twelve and Hall saw it as a sensual and materialistic period that corresponds to the savage or "pigmoid" stage of human evolution (Hall 1904: 1, x). It is psychologically equivalent to the cultural phase of pre-Christian barbarism. Geddes elaborated on this cultural

Table 6.1. The Stages of Development

Stages of development:	Biological transitions	Life projects
	BIRTH	
1. Infancy: The babe		PLAY
2. Childhood: The boy and the maiden		
	ADOLESCENCE	
3. Youth: The adolescent		QUEST
4. Maturity: The adult		MISSION
	SENESCENCE	
5. Old Age: Decline		PILGRIMAGE
	DEATH	

Source: Compiled from Hall (1904, Vol. 2, 50); Geddes (1904a, 1927b); Branford (1923, 33).

equivalence, claiming that early childhood embodies a mental outlook similar to the "Mohammedanism" of more primitive societies, with the later stages of childhood embodying "Confucian" or "Jain"-type mentalities (Geddes 1904a, 319). Rather than posing direct links, Geddes was here suggesting mental similarities with cultural traits that he assumed would be familiar to his audience. It is during childhood that the most primitive instincts must gradually be converted—through repression or sublimation—into more "civilized" forms of expression through indoctrination and habit formation. Psychologically, the child begins to move beyond a self-centered mentality. This is achieved through the play activities in which these instincts can be explored and expressed. The books and toys provided to children and the opportunities for exploration offered to them in play are means through which they can express their motor energies and developing interests in a safe context. This gives them an "apprenticeship to work" (Geddes and Thomson 1931, 1264) in which they playfully anticipate and prepare for adult activities.

The childhood stage ends at around age thirteen or fourteen, when puberty triggers the beginning of youth or adolescence. Youths show a growing interest in other people as they begin to interact more intensively with those beyond the immediate family circle. It is at this stage that sex, love, and social gregariousness develop as strong orientations, and adolescents tend to be driven by their concern for what others think of them. They may, for example, experience feelings of jealousy and a sense of rivalry. An integral aspect of this concern for others, however, is a strong "idealizing instinct" with "religious potentialities" that begins to grow and to swell within the personality (Branford 1914a, 152). It is for this reason that Geddes regarded youth as corresponding to the stage of social evolution in which idealistic Christianity is dominant. Youth is characterized by idealism, optimism, and religious impressionability: the "adolescent quest" and adventuring spirit impel youths to search for intellectual and moral answers to the questions of life (Hall 1904: 2, 363). Adolescents have strong aspirations, dreams, and ambitions and young people are fired by the "gleam" of spiritual light that drives purposive action. They experience both a growing interest in their personal "vocation" in life and optimism about the possibility of pursuing this. They may, in consequence, have a tendency toward hero worship and the desire to emulate or to excel others in their vocation. Youth was described as a "crisis" period marked by an idealism that is ripe for conversion to civic purposes, though this idealism can become misdirected if childhood instincts remain unconverted and opportunities for constructive personal development are not available:

> The hooligans of our city slums are adolescents awakened to great issues but unsupplied with great opportunities. It depends probably far less on hereditary instinct than on environment and the use

you make of it, whether the highlighting of the adolescent flame involves the hero or the devil, the poet or the drunkard, the lover or the lunatic. (Branford 1914a, 151; and see the argument in Branford 1912)

Variations in social circumstances mean that "the man-made organs devised for care, sifting, development and transmission of the social heritage are too easily diverted from divine to demonic service" (V. V. Branford 1923, 19). A similar point of view was taken by Jane Addams, who had also been inspired by Hall's ideas on adolescence, in her own study of urban youth (Addams 1910).

Youth ends at around age eighteen, the period of adolescence having been lengthened by contemporary patterns of education and a consequent later entry into work and marriage. The transition from youth to adulthood, then, is far more of a social transition than it is a simple biological maturation. Adult maturity or "manhood" is characterized by an outlook of realism and matter-of-factness that develops as people enter their vocations in life and pursue them as careers. They fall into habit and routine, losing sight of the spiritual quest that initially led them to it. This is, however, necessary if life is to continue. Maturity involves an acceptance of the "mission" in life to pursue one's goals systematically, and it is at this stage that "conceived purposiveness"—conscious scheming, planning, and designing—becomes central to human action (Thomson 1920; cited in V. V. Branford 1923, 21). Maturity is marked by the subordination of "vision" to social demands and expectations; the "still small voice" is ignored in the face of "the strident tones of Stentor in the Market, the suave oratory of Sophist in the Forum, the alluring notes of Phryne at the Fair" (V. V. Branford 1923, 19). In contemporary modernity people learn to adjust their actions to the demands of the economy and bureaucracy.

Adult maturity was seen as involving three substages. In the "early prime" phase the wisdom that has been built up during youth matures and the adult prepares for the middle phase of "the battlefield of life," in which the struggle to build a family and a career predominates. Finally, when "fully skilled," the adult is engaged in his or her life work and becomes aware of life's limited duration (1927b). It is in this final stage of adulthood that Geddes noted the possible adoption of a mental outlook, akin to that of Buddhism and Eastern spirituality, in which there is a stress on universal sympathy and peace.

Old age was given far less attention than the earlier stages. It is said to be a stage in which, once again, biological factors become central. As physical and mental faculties decline, people must come to terms with the problems of adaptation to which this decline leads. Withdrawal from work and the end of child rearing are associated with the prospect of continuing decline and, eventually, of death. The mental outlook of old age is marked by pessimism and by a concern for one's ultimate fate in life and death. The adult mission is replaced by the "pilgrimage" toward an acceptance of one's own mortality.

This developmental psychology rests on the now-disregarded recapitulationist assumptions, though the description of the various stages of human development has a great deal of plausibility and many similarities with later developmental ideas such as Erikson's (1950) account of life stages, Piaget's (1926, 1932) account of cognitive and moral development, and Bruner's (1960) emphasis on the importance of play in psychological development. There is, of course, a bias toward Western patterns of cultural and structural development, though they strive to construct their theory in universal terms. Of more significance is the rather forced attempt to find parallels between psychological ages and social stages of evolution, betraying an overstrong reliance on classical nineteenth-century evolutionary assumptions that all societies will inevitably undergo a transition from primitive savagery, through barbarism, to civilization. Both the inevitability and the unreality of this schema have been questioned and it clearly cannot be relied on as an explanatory device in a psychological theory. There is less harm in taking it as a heuristic framework for organizing psychological research and educational practice, which is very much what Geddes and Branford were attempting to do. So long as it is recognized that there is no inevitability in the movement from one psychological stage to the next, and that the timing and character of each stage and point of transition will depend upon the specific social contexts in which they occur, the framework proposed by Hall, Geddes, and Branford is a useful first approximation to a more adequate theory of psychological development—and this was, in fact, very much the role it played in relation to subsequent developmental theories.

GENDER AND WOMEN

Much sociology in the formative period of social science ignored gender as a dimension of analysis and so marginalized women in social analysis. This was not the case for Branford and Geddes, though their particular views of women can be, and have been, questioned. The basis of their view of sex and gender was the evolutionary theory set out by Geddes and Thomson (1889) and taken up in the influential ideas of Havelock Ellis (1894). They argue that all higher animals show a differentiation into male and female types that can be quite different in appearance and behavior. Male and female are distinguished biologically by essential and accessory sexual differences in morphology and physiology, and these sexual characteristics are seen as resulting from the Darwinian process of sexual selection—from competition among males for mates and the selective choices made by females. The genetic variations that determine whether a fertilized egg cell becomes an egg producer or a sperm provider also determine the development of these sexual characteristics (Geddes and Thomson 1931, 484, 487–88, 501; see also Geddes and Thomson 1889, 1914).[10] The less salient secondary characteristics, they argue, including characteristics that signal sexual attraction or readiness, result largely from hormonal differences.

Human males and females, like other mammals, show a marked sex-dimorphism and difference of constitution: "[T]he characteristic masculine and feminine features are part and parcel of the normal man and woman, deeply rooted, not tacked on, of ancient origin and therefore not likely to change quickly" (Geddes and Thomson 1931, 566). This argument is applied to both physical and mental characteristics and is supported by Karl Pearson's statement that "[w]e inherit our parents' tempers, our parents' conscientiousness, shyness, and ability, as we inherit their stature, forearm, and span" (cited in Geddes and Thomson 1931, 568). However, the expression of these characteristics depends on environmental conditions, including the cultural environment, which can determine whether they are triggered, fostered, or suppressed and so can produce considerable variation in their form and degree of expression (Geddes and Thomson 1931, 570). The social environment is especially important as an influence, and, "The mind is in great part a social product" (Geddes and Thomson 1931, 571). Thus, it is recognized that sexual characteristics can vary in their social expression according to physical and social environmental conditions.

It is on this basis that culturally formed characteristics of gender with a natural basis are said to arise. The specific characteristics of women and the qualities that they can bring to social life derive from their experience of involvement in the domestic sphere. The home and the domestic sphere of the family is the generating milieu of altruism and mutual aid. In making a home and sustaining a family they develop an "emotional" and altruistic character that allows them to make a distinctive and important contribution to social life. This character "is so partly by nature but even more by art, albeit an art which she has incorporated or translated into human nature itself" (Branford 1914a, 108).

Thus, initial bodily and mental differences are reinforced and magnified by social experiences, with the character produced being far more a cultural than a natural product.

On this basis, Geddes and Thomson see males as active and energetic, eager, egoistic and self-regarding, and having developed greater intelligence. Females, on the other hand, are passive, conservative, sluggish, altruistic, and marked by affection and sympathy (Geddes and Thomson 1889, 270).

It is possible, they hold, to divide activities into masculine and feminine types. Men are more concerned with material means and goals, and hence are the major participants in competition and combat and the temporal powers of machinery, imperialism, and finance. On the other hand, "It is in fact the natural task of women to safeguard life" (Geddes and Slater 1917, 131) and so to think in terms of the quality of life and of home rather than work and the requirements of health, education, and the upbringing of children. They held that it is the emotionality of women that makes them especially important contributors to both sociology and social reconstruction. This emotionality is rooted in their orientation toward family and communal solidarity:

> It seems consistent that men should fight, if there's fighting to be done; and that women should nurse, if there's nursing necessary. Man hunted and explored, woman made the home and brought up the children. Man sailed the seas, woman developed home industries. Woman is *naturally* a teacher of the young, a domesticator, a gardener, and so on. (Geddes and Thomson 1931, 571)

Lionel Tayler (1904) elaborated on this in his account of temperament. He, too, saw historical forces as amplifying the initial biological differences to produce largely arbitrary cultural differences of gender. He concluded, nevertheless, that in contemporary societies, women have become more emotional and altruistic in character, while men have become oriented to achievement, self-interest, and control. Men are "initiators" and women are "humanisers" and a socially binding force (Tayler 1904, 166):

> [A] woman's mind is generally attuned for both a higher and a more distant goal than that of a man. It is higher because she is less governed by animal cravings, and its ideals are more distant because the mind as a whole is moved by mental rather than physical feelings, and its aims are correspondingly raised, and because feelings direct woman by indefinite, but forceful, emotional promptings; whereas in man intellectual principles, less high, but more definite, largely govern. (Tayler 1904, 201–202)

These arguments amplify the view of Comte that "woman" as a social type corresponds to emotionality. Comte meant that emotionality defines a quality of femininity that is acquired by most women, but also by some men. It is a temperament that is central to "energizers," to such social types as the priest, the poet, and the artist. Womanhood is the impulse to realize an ideal of life and so to act it out (V. V. Branford 1923, 69), and these are all occupations that depend upon the expression of the emotionality epitomized in femininity. The particular contribution of women to social life is to infuse an emotional dimension to it. Emotionals, then, include all those in these occupations and also those women who have not entered the professions and higher education, such as housewives within the domestic sphere. Branford held that the contemporary divide between intellectual males and emotional women was a block to religious advance (V. V. Branford 1925, 512).

Tayler drew particularly conservative conclusions from his argument. He rejected the social constructionism that he found in Astell (1694) and Gilman (1898), arguing that substantial biological differences are relevant to mentality: "All women have distinctive and inherited qualities of mind which need healthy expression" (Tayler 1922, 38), and they can find this in domesticity and motherhood. Both male and female temperaments are essential to social life, he argued, and so sexual differences had to be maintained: "Without womanly ideals to bind those that are truly manly into a co-ordinated advancing whole, there can be no guarantee for social progress" (Tayler 1904, 182). For these reasons, Tayler opposed both coeducation and female employment.[11] Nevertheless, he did not simply seek to confine women to the home. He argued that a woman must have an understanding of the industrial activity in which men are involved and of "the collective realities around her" (Tayler 1904, 205). The key question for social policy, he held, was how to do this without undermining her "womanliness."

More radical were the views of Olive Schreiner (1911), intimate friend of Havelock Ellis, who held that it was the institutional arrangements of marriage and the involvement of women in mothering and domestic work that produced the characteristic "sex parasitism" responsible for distinct male and female personalities. By changing social institutions and relations, she argued, it is possible to change human character and to produce new men and new women. She did, however, see the involvement of women in care and domesticity as responsible for the highly valued characteristics of "ethical" ways of living—of altruism and social responsibility. Thus, women socialized under relations of sex parasitism nevertheless had an important contribution to make to social life.

The views of Geddes and Branford were closer to Schreiner's than to Tayler's. They argued that the biological predispositions of men and women toward, respectively, intellectuality and emotionality, have been exaggerated under contemporary social conditions to the point at which the structure of opportunities divides men and women too sharply into distinct spheres of activity and so becomes an obstacle to social reconstruction and the universal "brotherhood" of humankind. It is the historically established division of labor between men and women that shapes the differences and so there is no necessary confinement of women to the domestic sphere by nature.

Social roles must be constructed that allow human sexual differences to be expressed in undistorted ways while maximizing the opportunities for each sex. Women can pursue a different life if opportunities permit—as did Sybella Branford—and men might, it can be surmised, follow a domestic role and develop "feminine" characteristics if their opportunities for public participation are restricted. For this reason, Branford and Geddes encouraged female education and employment. Education, they held, must make the most of the complementary differences between men and women: "It profits national efficiency more when gifted women do what no man could do so well" (Geddes and Thomson 1931, 576). There had been a beginning to the opening up of more opportunities for women to participate in occupations where sexual differences are irrelevant as well as those, such as teaching and nursing, to which they are especially suited by nature and socialization, but there was a need for further change. Recognition of gender complementarity, they argue, challenges all forms of patrilineal and patriarchal organization.

ALIENATION AND MENTAL HEALTH

A striking application of some of the psychological ideas developed by Geddes and his associates was that of Arthur Brock (1923), a medical practitioner who worked alongside William Rivers in the treatment of World War I soldiers suffering from "shell shock" (see Barker 1992; Slobdin 1978). Brock worked on these issues at the military hospital at Craiglockhart War Hospital, where his best-known patient was the poet Wilfred Owen (Cantor 2005; Hibberd 1977). Brock later set up in private practice at Garth Hill, near Edinburgh, and worked in close association with the activities of the Outlook Tower.

Brock set out his ideas in a book originally intended for the "Making of the Future" series. His argument was that shell shock involved deep feelings of social detachment that could be treated by bringing about a reacquaintance with a proper sense of place and body (Brock 1923, 40). Shell shock was an extreme form of a more general social malaise, a widespread "mild neurasthenia" that he saw as resulting from contemporary industrialism. Brock followed Geddes and Branford in describing this as an age of finance and mass consumption that is dominated by a culture of "Mammonism" that alienates people from their properly human feelings. People are forced to engage in monotonous work, they must struggle to make ends meet, and they inhabit cramped housing and live under dull conditions that rob them of the joy of life. As a result, they experience a dissociation and disintegration of mind and can think only in fragmentary or segregated form. They may feel, for example, that they are mere cogs in a vast, impersonal machine. Typical responses to this are poor memory and a weakness of will, a loss of confidence and self-respect, depression, irritability, fatigue, and boredom. For most people there is a flight from reality, and many seek to avoid exertion and become "work-shy" (which Brock referred to as *ergophobia*). This flight from reality may involve a resort to excessive consumption or the seeking of a refuge in the sensuality of food and sex. For some, there is a resort to patent medicines and alcohol. Escapist and sentimental novels and music provide the illusion that dreams and desires can be realized. Such escapism allows people to become conformists in their everyday lives, bound by the herd mentality. This is the alienation and passivity of a mass society.

This state of mild neurasthenia or "civilian shell shock" (Brock 1923, 21), Brock argued, contributes to the causation of physical problems such as TB, gastric disorders, colds and flu, and even cancers. He went so far as to suggest that diseased systems may "symbolize" the structure of the disordered mind (Brock 1923, 46). More acceptably, perhaps, this implies that fatigue, exhaustion, and anxiety may predispose people to a susceptibility to certain physical diseases and disorders.

This generic condition of modern social life is rooted in and reinforced by conventional educational practices that prevent the recapitulation of primitive instinctive behavior. Contemporary industrialism is marked by the increasingly bureaucratic organization of work and by the growing commitment of political institutions to wardom (Brock 1923, 23, 235, 244), and there are few outlets for primitive instincts except in aggressive economic competition and state militarism. In actual time of war, this generalized mild neurasthenia becomes far more serious. The experience of shell fire can trigger a true shell shock and breakdown in those in whom civilian life has fostered a particularly extreme form of the neurasthenic personality.

Personality development and mental health were seen within the Geddes circle as crucially influenced by a sense of place and of embeddedness in a region. Knowledge and understanding of region gives people the sense of security and confidence that enables them to develop into full adult citizens able to contribute to the moral renewal of social life. Conversely, a detachment from place, or the destruction of place, could be a significant cause of mental stress, anxiety, and nervous breakdown. This underlined the importance of regional surveys, which must explore the culture and psychological state of a region as well as its material foundations. Community regeneration, inspired by a social survey, is a means to mental and moral betterment (Sandeman 1913).[12]

Brock's treatment for neurasthenia was to encourage the development of a more thorough knowledge and reflexive attitude toward the immediate environment. Sufferers must grasp their environment mentally so that they can more effectively act in and on it in terms of their deepened understanding. The means through which he sought to achieve this reintegration was the regional survey, which he saw as a means through which his patients could recapture what "every countryman of old" achieved intuitively but has been lost in industrial society (Brock 1923, 257). An individual can contribute to the survey from his or her own particular standpoint and so can achieve an understanding that reflects their particular interests and concerns. The treatment of shell shock involves bringing patients to a point at which they can recognize the need for such understanding and so begin to re-embed themselves in a civic community.

EDUCATION, SCHOOL, AND THE PLAY WAY

The developmental psychology of Branford and Geddes was the basis on which they set out their particular views on the nature and purpose of education and the part played by active engagement in "playful" leisure activities. Hall's theories of childhood and adolescence had led him to the view that educational practices had to build on children's natural, inherited tendencies and instincts. Schooling should be organized according to the nature of the child, allowing the child to develop his or her understanding and abilities at an appropriate pace and through close contact with the natural world. In primitive societies, instincts could be given a direct adult expression in hunting and pastoralism. In civilized societies, however, the primitive instincts of childhood had to be expressed and given their full realization in a safe and secure educational setting, as a means for their "conversion" into more adult—more civilized—forms of behavior. Disciplined schooling had to be combined with opportunities for the expression and exploration of the instincts developing in the child. This involved allowing children at school to engage with nature in ways that allow them to reacquire the skills appropriate to their natural tendencies. Children are able to do this through play, which gives them an opportunity to learn about the world in practical but safe ways. Childhood learning at school, Branford argued, ought to be structured around the "play way," which enables a "progressive mastery of its world by the child" (V. V. Branford 1924a, 82).[13]

A comprehensive account of the "play way" had been set out by Henry Caldwell Cook in a series of articles for *The New Age* during 1914. Although commissioned to convert these into a contribution to the series of "Papers for the Present," he produced instead a book-length study (Caldwell Cook 1917) that built on his experience of teaching at the Perse School in Cambridge. In this book he set out a method of education for boys aged eight to thirteen, though arguing that the general principles would apply also to older boys in early adolescence. Caldwell Cook candidly admitted that he knew nothing about girls!

Caldwell Cook's argument was that the tendency of modern life had been to build rational structures of work and systematic book learning that deny basic instinctive tendencies and so make proper learning difficult or impossible (1917, 5–6). If these instincts are not to be completely distorted, educational practices must take account of them. Schools organized around purely didactic instruction that ignores the actual expression of instincts are counterproductive. The natural way to learn about the world is through a practical engagement with it, and children at school must be encouraged to engage their interests in practical activity. Caldwell Cook saw this as achievable in the form of play, and held that schooling must be organized around the creation of numerous opportunities for play. Rather than eliminating play from a child's life, play must be used in order to gain his or her interest: "[W]ithout interest there is no learning, and since the child's interest is all in play it is necessary, whatever the matter in hand, that the method be a play-method" (Caldwell Cook 1917, 3–4). Learning is a natural result of the innate attempts made at imaginative operations on the world. The aim of schooling must be to create opportunities for such playful and imaginative engagement with the world. Children will find these activities pleasurable, and the inferences that they draw from their play activities can lead them to a genuine understanding of the nature of the world and a practical ability to cope with it. Drawing explicitly on the recapitulation theory, Caldwell Cook argued that learning involves the imaginative reliving of past ages, and education is most effective when this is *not* presented as summary knowledge in books but when the child can experience its imaginings in a play way. He stressed, in particular, the importance of drama as a means of understanding and learning, as it is in dramatic presentations that children learn what it means to act in specific ways.

Branford argued that existing elementary schools were integral elements in the established industrial system and were distorting child socialization through their strong commitment to competition and Mammonism. Education had to become, instead, a more constructive "play rehearsal for life" (Branford 1914a, 271, 255ff.). Central to this educational ideal were a high valuation of arts and crafts, nature study, local social studies, and civic involvement. Branford held that schools should involve local craftsmen and skilled workers, such as farmers, shepherds, craftsmen, and so on, in the work of the school as teachers. Schools must also create the conditions under which children could discover for themselves the stages through which rural and industrial skills had developed. This learning of craft skills was an essential element in a "rustic renewal," by which was meant "a real training of the young by aiding them successively to appropriate and to master the characteristic conditions of each form of primitive life" (Branford 1914a, 271; Branford and Geddes 1919a, 204). Branford argued that

> [b]y no other way than the trials, failures and triumphs of some real apprenticeship to the Masters of Crafts, may the youth of a nation

enter upon an elementary education that is at once technical and social, intellectual and moral. (Branford 1914a, 273)[14]

Geddes and Branford interpreted the education of the child somewhat simplistically in relation to the "valley section," which laid the foundations for the evolution of social life from rustic to civic occupations. Education should allow the child to participate playfully in all of the basic occupations in succession so that children and early adolescents can acquire the aptitudes and gain the experiences involved in each way of life (Branford 1912, 43). Rather idealistically, perhaps, they argued that

> [g]iven unhindered scope for natural impulse, the child will play its way up and down the valley section. By turn it will sample the characteristic life of each and all the rustic series. And something of occupational habit and cultural outfit of story, song, and dance, it will absorb, passing in easy sequence of Edenic innocence, from gentle shepherd to fearsome hunter, from patient peasant and forelocking gardener, to exploring sailor, ingenious woodman and dreaming miner. (Branford and Geddes 1919a, 317–18; 1919b, xix).

From these rustic pursuits the adolescent can go on to explore the civilized "civic" issues and activities, learning what it means to be a citizen. Play, properly structured and converted, has its part in adult life. Adult life builds on the experiences encountered through childhood play, and so an effective play-based education provides the foundation for a genuinely human and civilized adult life. In adult life, play should be expressed in truly creative work and in leisure activities. Degraded, routine work is oppressive and denies natural instincts. Genuine creative work, on the other hand, is playful in the sense that it allows the spiritual—intellectually and emotionally engaged—shaping of activity. There should, therefore, be no real division between work and leisure. Branford held that adult leisure should involve the play of the body, the mind, and the spirit. The play of the body allows the rhythmic use of muscles and nerves in dance and drill. The play of the mind allows the passive reveries of art, music, and literature and the dramatic make-believe of card and dice games that "simulate the adventure of life." Finally, the play of the spirit gives full rein to the imagination and makes possible an "integral life-play" in communal activities (V. V. Branford 1924a, 82–83). The latter can be undermined by watching or engaging in "mimetic combat" in sport and war games. Thus, adult leisure in the community is the counterpart to childhood play.

Educators influenced by Hall's psychology saw children as "social projects" whose proper education could produce well-balanced citizens (Noon

2005, 382). This was certainly the view of Geddes and Branford. Geddes outlined his educational project in his own publications (Geddes 1925a) and the Branfords' education of their adopted sons was also seen as a practical sociological project.[15] Critical of most existing British schools, Branford and Geddes had considerable sympathy with the emerging progressive school movement and with the educational ideas of Johann Pestalozzi, Maria Montessori, Rudolph Steiner, and Friedrich Froebel with which Hall's work resonated. Taking this view of psychology and the purpose of education, Branford and Geddes were drawn into a close involvement with the progressive school movement of the late nineteenth century. The first of these "new schools" to be founded in Britain at the end of the nineteenth century were Abbotsholme in 1889 and Bedales in 1893,[16] and Geddes and Branford were closely associated with each of these. Both schools had been set up by men committed to the principles of the Fellowship of the New Life, though only Bedales had any lasting success in promoting these principles.

Cecil Reddie, the founder of Abbotsholme, had been introduced into the Fellowship through his association with Edward Carpenter and with Geddes. After graduating from Edinburgh University he had worked with Geddes as a demonstrator before going into school teaching to apply the ideals of Ruskin and Morris (Stewart 1968, 8–13, 243–67; Searsby 1989; Ward 1934; Geddes 1905b). He moved to rural Derbyshire and founded Abbotsholme in order to further these hopes and to promote the communitarian ideals of the Fellowship. Both Geddes and Branford were appointed to the school's advisory council, and Geddes took on the role of Inspector. Reddie, in turn, taught at a number of Geddes's Summer Schools during the 1890s. Branford delivered a course of lectures on "The Making of Europe" to Abbotsholme pupils in 1895.[17]

Reddie initially worked very closely with Carpenter, establishing a curriculum that emphasized practical craft and agricultural skills and the importance of learning about the environment through visits to nearby towns. Craft and agricultural activities were seen as the playful engagement and exercise of hunting and farming instincts, while local fieldwork activity was seen as a way of developing a "regionalist" orientation among the pupils. However, the views of the two men soon diverged. Where Carpenter had hoped to see the school committed to equality, brotherhood, and practical community, Reddie increasingly saw participation in temporal power as a priority and aimed to make the school into a means of transforming the professional middle classes into a humane "Directing Class" (Reddie 1901). Nevertheless, Reddie continued to incorporate Hall's theories directly into the school's practices, and Geddes praised the school's focus on the moral question of the transition "from boyhood toward virility" in his inspector's report of 1905 (Geddes 1905b, 397). Although Abbotsholme initially prospered, Reddie moved toward the right in his politics and his approach and style no longer proved attractive to his small constituency of potential parents. The school declined rapidly after 1900, and by 1917 there were just thirteen pupils; by 1927 there were only two.[18]

Bedales founder John Badley was a supporter, though not a member, of the Fellowship of the New Life and was an active Fabian who later joined the Independent Labour Party (Stewart 1968, 13–17, 268–81; Badley 1923, 1937). He began his teaching career at Abbotsholme but left in 1893 to set up Bedales at Hayward's Heath in Sussex. Though inspired by the Fellowship, Badley also drew on the new educational ideas of Pestalozzi, Froebel, and Montessori, and was strongly committed to Hall's psychology of adolescence. In 1898, the school became the first coeducational progressive school in the country, and it moved in 1900 to a more permanent base in Petersfield, Hampshire. As at Abbotsholme, the curriculum stressed farm work and practical craft skills alongside academic work, though unlike Abbotsholme the school retained its communitarian and egalitarian outlook.

The educational philosophies underpinning these first generation progressive schools combined the ideals of Ruskin and the Fellowship of the New Life with recapitulationist theories of childhood and adolescence. The Garden City Theosophical School, formed at Letchworth in 1915, combined these with Theosophy. The Theosophical Society had been closely involved in the work of the Fellowship of the New Life, the Garden City movement, and with educational reformers such as Rudolf Steiner, who had been a member of the Theosophical Society until 1910 when he left to form his own Anthroposophy Society. Geddes had long been involved on the margins of the Theosophical Society, and both he and Sybella Branford had long been active in the Garden City movement, though they do not seem to have been actively associated with the school.[19] The Garden City at Letchworth had become the center for Theosophical Society activity outside London and was an obvious place for its first school to be located. The school, later renamed Arundale and then St. Christopher's, was firmly controlled by Beatrice de Normann (later Beatrice Ensor) through the Theosophical Educational Trust. It was, like Bedales, a coeducational school and was organized as a self-governing pupil community that followed an interdisciplinary curriculum combining academic with practical activities and promoting ideals of "brotherhood" and organic farming (Parker 1997).

There were, however, close links with the fourth of the major progressive schools, Bembridge. Formed by John Whitehouse, this was far more closely aligned with the Geddesian ideals. Heavily influenced by Ruskin, Whitehouse had become interested in youth work while working for Cadbury's in Birmingham (Stewart 1968, 97–103). After this time at Cadbury's he took a post as secretary to the Carnegie Trust in Dunfermline, in order to work with Geddes, and then spent some time working with William Beveridge at Toynbee Hall. Whitehouse and Beveridge served as joint editors of *St. George*, the magazine of the Guild of St. George, through which they became close to Branford as well as to Geddes. Following a brief period working for the Manchester University Settlement with Thomas Marr, Whitehouse entered Parliament as a Liberal in the 1910 election. It was the Liberal defeat in 1918 that led to his decision to form his own school at Bembridge, on the Isle of Wight, the following year.

Dedicated to the ideals of Ruskin and Geddes, Whitehouse's curriculum put great emphasis on natural history and on the arts and crafts. He involved his pupils in exhibitions of their work, some of which he published (Whitehouse 1928). Whitehouse stressed the importance of sociology in a humanist education and built the school's history curriculum around a sociological approach to contemporary issues. Less radical politically than De Normann's school, Bembridge was, nevertheless, highly progressive in its approach to the relationship between the school and its region. Taking seriously the regional approach of Geddes and Branford, Whitehouse proposed the building of "school bases": clusters of schools serving a town or part of a city, with each cluster being close to a library, gallery, concert hall, and swimming pool (Whitehouse 1908, 1943). Given the commitment of the school to these regional ideas, it is not surprising that Victor and Sybella Branford chose to send their son Archie to the school in the 1920s.[20]

Of the later postwar foundations, Summerhill, founded by A. S. Neill in 1924, and Dartington, founded by Leonard and Dorothy Elmhirst in 1926, became the best-known schools to build on this same complex of ideas. The schools that were most closely associated with the educational ideas of Geddes and Branford, however, were the Priory Gate School of Theodore Faithfull and the Forest School of Aubrey Westlake. Both were organized strictly along recapitulationist lines and their work was integrated with a national scouting movement that was similarly organized. It was widely held in Britain at this time that adolescent working-class behavior constituted a problem to be solved through youth organizations and education (Hendrick 1990). Scouting was described by Branford as "perhaps the most notable advance towards eutopia made in our times" (V. V. Branford 1923, 225; and see Geddes 1930).

WOODCRAFT AND SCOUTING

The scout movement originated in the United States from boys' clubs established on the basis of the theories of the child study pioneers (Schlossman 1973), its distinctive features being its organization around "woodcraft" ideas. In the late 1890s, Ernest Thompson Seton had formed a number of "tribes" for young people, intending that they should learn about and practice the hunting and survival skills of Native Americans. The tribes were later renamed the Woodcraft Indians and became the Boy Scouts of America in 1910 (Morris 1970). Seton's scouts were autonomous, democratic, and self-governing, reflecting his belief in the anarchist principles of Reclus and Kropotkin and which he saw as a means to build world peace and a new global order. Seton's commitment to recapitulationism led him to see the woodcraft skills of Native Americans as providing an essential preparation for a healthy and creative adult life. These most fundamental human traits of "manhood" were evident in the "noble savagery" of the North American Indian, but Seton held that his contemporaries had lost touch with them. Skills and knowledge that aid survival in the outdoors had atrophied, and public, civic life had been diminished as a result.

Seton's ideas were taken up in Britain by Robert Baden-Powell, who formed his first "Boy Scout" troop in 1907 with the intention of building a strong and active body of "good" citizens. Shortly after this, he set up a parallel organization of "Girl Guides," and both the Scouts and the Guides were given junior branches as, respectively, the "Wolf Cubs" and the "Brownies" (Evans 1930). Geddes, Branford, and many other advocates of the new psychology came to feel that, by the end of World War I, Baden Powell's scouts had taken an increasingly militaristic form and had subverted the original woodcraft principles. The scouts, they argued, had come to epitomize the very wardom that was supposed to be prevented by learning and practicing woodcraft skills (and see Geddes and Thomson 1931, 1357). Prominent among those who criticized scout militarism and aimed to recapture the spirit of the woodcraft idea were Ernest and Aubrey Westlake.

Ernest Westlake had studied with T. H. Huxley in London around 1876, when he may have met the young Patrick Geddes. Having undertaken geological research abroad, he lived in Hampstead until financial difficulties forced him to return to his family home at Fordingbridge in the New Forest. It was there, between 1905 and 1910, that he encountered Auberon Herbert of the Girlingite pagan group and his family Quakerism became increasingly leavened with elements of Paganism. Westlake felt a need to get closer to the natural spirit of all things in order to revivify Christianity (Hutton 1999, 165; Hoare 2005). Already influenced by Carpenter's (1889) critique of civilization and Ruskin's medievalism, he read the anthropologists Edward Tylor (1871) and James Frazer (1890) on myth, and was particularly influenced by Jane Ellen Harrison's (1913) account of Dionysius. Westlake saw Dionysius as the counterpart to the "Green Man" of the English May Day celebrations and developed a "green" Pagan spirituality that made him an enthusiastic supporter of Geddes's environmental biology and the politics of Orage's *New Age*. He saw contemporary civilization as a precarious veneer on a more primitive human nature, a veneer that had been shattered by the 1914–18 war. An overextension of civilization had disconnected people from their fundamental human nature and the result was contemporary wardom.

The authoritarianism and militarism of the Baden-Powell scouts also disheartened Westlake's son Aubrey, already a scout, and seemed to epitomize this state of alienation. Seeking to return scouting to its original love of nature and the countryside, the Westlakes set up the Order of Woodcraft Chivalry in 1916 as an alternative and rival to Baden-Powell's organization. The OWC brought together boys and girls, organized into age grades, as a democratically controlled and self-disciplined organization devoted to the "woodcraft way" and to pacific rather than militaristic goals.[21] The use of age grades to organize woodcraft scouting reflected Ernest Westlake's commitment to recapitulationism and developmental psychology. He held that the scouts should provide opportunities for children and young people to experience their developing instincts to the full. Linking this to Geddes's model of the valley section, Westlake wanted to establish "occupational camps" along a river valley where children could experience hill, upland, and coastal ways of life. A child who explores his or her primitive nature and develops practical skills, abilities, and interests will slowly and gradually build up a sound character structure that fits them to be good citizens in a reconstructed civilization. Drawing on both Native American and native English traditions, including woodcraft, agriculture, and such rural leisure time pursuits as folk song and folk dancing, allows a child to experience the primitive. Pagan religion was seen as a necessary step in the development toward Christianity, a view reinforced by the appearance of Edward Carpenter's *Pagan and Christian Creeds* (1920). Paganism was to be the means through which the overcivilized Christianity of the contemporary world could be revitalized and respiritualized.

These ideas were reinforced by a reading of *The Coming Polity* and its argument in support of a postwar cultural renewal of the civilized world (Westlake and Westlake 1918).[22] Branford and Geddes had argued that the scouting movement "in its origin and growth recapitulates with curious fidelity the natural divergences of the primitive hunting life" and the opportunities available through scouting "advance the process of converting the perennial hunter that is in every youth," giving direction to the combative hunting impulse (Branford and Geddes 1919a, 108, 110; Branford 1926b, 43). The Westlakes held that a child can best develop in a secure rural environment where their true potential could be recognized and encouraged and the foundations for participation in a more rounded urban life could be laid. Similarly, Branford argued that the scout playing up and down the river valley can acquire a synthetic picture of rural life that can be broadened by participation in "constructive city life" (V. V. Branford 1923, 226).

Ernest Westlake noted, however, a certain tension between his views and the regionalism of Branford, emphasizing that his own aim was to promote "woodcraft not citycraft" (quoted in Edgell 1992, 127).

The Westlakes promoted the OWC through Quaker and Theosophical progressive schools sympathetic to their aims, and the first OWC "lodge" was set up at Sidcot School in Somerset. A Council of Guidance and body of informal advisers for the OWC was set up, the Council including Patrick Geddes, Victor and Sybella Branford, Herbert Fleure, and the progressive educationalists Edmund Holmes, Beatrice de Normann, and Margaret McMillan (see Mansbridge 1932; Bradburn 1989). In recognition of its links with the American Boy Scouts, Seton was appointed as Honorary Grand Chieftain (Edgell 1992, 95–98; Prynn 1983). Toynbee Hall was used as a London base for meetings of the Order, and wider informal links were established through the circle around Orage's *New Age* and through Ernest Westlake's membership of the bohemian 1917 Club in Soho.

The aim of the Westlakes was to start the OWC as a camping organization and gradually build it into a more comprehensive system of socialization. In 1919, Ernest bought some land at Sandy Balls near his family home of Godshill at Fordingbridge, aiming to use this as a camping site for the growing number of OWC lodges. He hoped to raise a regular income from commercial camping, while making the site available for use by OWC groups.[23] Aubrey gave up his medical practice in London—where he and his partner Alfred Salter had formed the Bermondsey Lodge of the OWC—and took over the day-to-day running of both the OWC and the Sandy Balls estate.

The OWC was hugely successful through the 1920s, holding regular camps and an annual "folkmoot" at which policy issues were ritualistically debated. By 1924 its total membership had risen to 1,200. Fraternal relations were maintained with similar organizations in Britain and overseas. Chief among these was the Kibbo Kift Kindred ("Brotherhood of the Strong"), formed by John Hargrave in 1920. The Kibbo Kift, too, followed the recapitulationist philosophy of age grading and took as its mission the socialization of those able to establish a new stage of civilization marked by the universal brotherhood of humanity. Active members of the Kibbo Kift included Mabel Barker and Moya Jowitt, but not Geddes or the Branfords.[24] Rolf Gardiner of the Kibbo Kift attended the 1925 OWC folkmoot as a fraternal delegate to speak on the virtues of the German youth movements.

Rank and file membership of the OWC had initially been limited to young people, its membership structured into five age grades: Babes (under 5), Elves (5–8), Woodlings (8–12), Trackers (12–15), and Pathfinders (over 15). Adult members remained Pathfinders but served as "chiefs." In 1925, a separate adult section was formed, and there were eventually to be three adult sections: Waywardens (18–25), Wayfarers (25–60), and Witana (over 60). A leading Wayfarer was Henry Byngham, later known as "Dion" (short for Dionysius). Byngham was editor of the Order's magazine, *Pine Cone*, and became the focus of public controversy and undesired publicity for the OWC through his advocacy of nudism (which he called "gymnosophy"), sexual freedom, and Paganism. In 1928, Byngham stated, in explicit and forthright sexual terms, his view of the virile masculinity that he sought in the OWC: the OWC, he argued, is "the erect Penis of the social organism (nation or civilization) of which it is a part" (quoted in Edgell 1992, 279). For the most part, the mainstream rituals of the OWC drew from Masonic and Native American sources, the aim being to embody "a safe middle ground between religions" (Hutton 1999, 168). For Byngham, however, a stronger dose of Paganism was needed. His friend Victor Neuberg, the former lover of Aleister Crowley (see Fuller 1965), had introduced him to Crowley's ideas on magic and Byngham pursued ideas of nudity and magical ritual through a separate sect within the OWC, though his general ideas received some support from Aubrey Westlake.[25]

Others recruited as Wayfarers included psychologists Norman Glaister and Harold Jennings White (Jennings White 1925, 1928). Glaister had developed a form of psychoanalysis strongly influenced by Trotter's idea of the "herd instinct," published as articles in the *Sociological Review* (Trotter 1908, 1909). Glaister formed the concept of what he called the "resistive/sensitive team," applying this to the OWC as a "living social organism" (Glaister 1925). Within a social organism, he argued, there is a need for both resistive and sensitive leadership. The resistive leader is the technical, instrumental, or executive leader, while the sensitive leader is the thinking, creative, and spiritual leader. This distinction echoed the Comtean distinction between the intellectual "initiators" and the emotional "energizers," and Glaister sought to institutionalize these two aspects of leadership in the OWC, where they were formally adopted into the constitution in 1929.[26]

Aubrey Westlake had long proposed the introduction into the OWC of a system of "training" by using nonmembers as a "peace army" to contribute to community projects and community development. Growing unemployment in 1929–1930 made this idea attractive to many other members of the OWC who, echoing the earlier land colony schemes of Fels and Lansbury, felt that the Order ought to be doing something actively to help the unemployed. Aubrey's idea of a cooperative craft colony at Sandy Balls was actively supported by George Sandeman, who already lived on the estate and saw this as a means to realize something of the "practical community" that he and his wife Frances had earlier promoted (Sandeman and Sandeman 1919, 1929). The proposal to provide craft training at a work camp for the unemployed was seen as a "civic adventure" toward a "constructive peace," and in 1932 the Grith Fyrd (Anglo Saxon for "Peace Army") was established, with Glaister playing a key part from his base at Toynbee Hall (Edgell 1992, ch. 12). The camp aimed to train the unemployed in skills of building, farm work, and crafts, with the men having to first build their own accommodations and workshops. The OWC received the unemployment benefit paid to the men and, in return, provided them with their keep and lodgings as well as the training. Numbers attending averaged around twenty-five, with men staying at the camp for around eighteen months. The venture was so successful that a second camp was opened in Derbyshire in 1934 (see Field 2009).

PRIORY GATE AND FOREST SCHOOL

Two schools were closely associated with both the educational ideas of Geddes and Branford and the social organization of the OWC. These were Priory Gate and the Forest School. Priory Gate had been set up by Theodore Faithfull in Sudbury, Suffolk, in 1919, but was reorganized around the ideas of Ernest Westlake in 1923.[27] Faithfull integrated recapitulationism with Jungian psychoanalysis and the whole school was organized as a section of the OWC, all the staff becoming members of the Order. The school stressed informality, open air teaching between May and September, outdoor activities, nudity, and camping and, like Bedales and the Garden City School, it was coeducational. The school specialized in "difficult" or "problem" children aged between four and eighteen, taking around twenty pupils in all. Its aim was to free these children from repression and so allow them to grow naturally as individuals.

Dorothy Revel, a teacher at the Priory Gate, wrote a book in which she set out the recapitulationist principles behind the organization of the school, presenting these as a blueprint for the "school of the future." Such a school had to be a residential community in which full-time teachers work alongside practical craftsmen and children have the opportunity to choose to undertake paid craft work as well as their academic work. The school should include self-sufficient farms, forges, printing presses, and other artisan workshops as bases for craft work. Teachers and pupils should take on family roles in domestic, residential groups that may have either an intellectual or practical character according to the specialism and interests of the teacher. Children should be able to move from house to house during the day or over the course of their schooling as they explore different approaches and interests (Revel 1928, Part 2, ch. 1).

Faithfull took his staff and pupils to the 1924 OWC folkmoot at Godshill and met Norman Glaister, who had brought his own school group from Chertsey.[28] Over the following years, the two men discovered a mutual interest in Freudian ideas and in 1928 Faithfull recruited Glaister as psychiatric adviser to Priory Gate School. Glaister also worked as a psychiatrist at a London mental hospital and it was through him that John Bowlby was recruited to the school's staff (G. Faithfull 1991; van Dijken and others 1998, 251–53).[29] The school had only a limited success, and closed in the 1930s, when Theodore Faithfull decided to concentrate on his New Cavendish Street psychotherapy practice.

The Forest School was set up in 1928 by the Westlakes themselves and had its base at Sandy Balls. Formation of the school was part of the larger program of communitarian projects organized by the OWC leadership (Edgell 1992, ch. 10; van der Eyken and Turner 1969, 125–44). The directors of the school included Aubrey Westlake and Norman Glaister, with Westlake's cousin Cuthbert Rutter—previously a Toynbee Hall worker—as headmaster. The Forest School was largely self-governing, with classes being compulsory only for the over-twelves. Its principles were directly based on Ernest Westlake's ideas about the loss of "primitive" skills and on Geddes's views of craft skills, these being tied together through recapitulationism. Housed in a timber-built bungalow constructed by George Sandeman a few years previously, the school had recruited nine pupils and four staff by early 1930, though the number of pupils gradually rose to forty. Teachers were paid a mere £30 per year, plus board and lodgings, and the school was heavily dependent on the commitment of its staff to its communitarian goals. The emphasis of the curriculum was on learning through exploration and investigation: on "learning by doing."

Despite growing reservations among psychologists about the validity of strong recapitulationism as a scientific theory, it remained the basis for organizing the curriculum and schedules of the school. Children of ages four to eight were seen as requiring an education that encouraged "old stone age" skills. They played with sand, clay, and water and were encouraged to explore their emotions. From ages eight to twelve, they were taught skills appropriate to the "new stone age" and could both grow and make things for themselves. They were encouraged to develop their intuition by learning about myth and folklore. The early adolescent period from twelve to fifteen was a period when intellectual pursuits and an interest in communally relevant activism were encouraged. Finally, from fifteen to eighteen the stress was on the development of creativity and leadership, athletic abilities, and a preparation for romance. Many children were, however, withdrawn from the school at fifteen and transferred by their parents to more academic schools that could prepare them for university.

Dion Byngham's promotion of sexuality and Paganism within the OWC triggered a series of controversies around sex education and the promotion of sexual exploration. The "marriage" of Norman Glaister to

Dorothy Revel at the folkmoot of 1930 also aroused controversy over its sexual morality.[30] Many members and parents of potential pupils were alienated by these scandals: by the end of 1930, the number of members had fallen to four hundred, and by 1934 it had fallen to just 246 (Edgell 1992, 523). Much of the discontent focused on Aubrey Westlake himself, who was seen as too closely identified with Byngham and the radicals, and in 1933 he resigned his Chieftainship.[31] Aubrey had, in any case, become more closely involved with John Macmurray's Christian socialism and with the New Britain movement (see chapter 8). Though Macmurray was never a member of the OWC, he had financed and supported the Grith Fyrd as a communitarian venture.

Disputes deepened over the extent to which the OWC should exercise control over the Grith Fyrd and the Forest School. Matters came to a head at the 1934 folkmoot when a small clique maneuvered to reinstate Aubrey Westlake as the ultimate leader by suspending the constitution and establishing a "Group of Four" to support his leadership. Opposition to this was led by Glaister, who saw the move as reinforcing the ever-closer relationship that Westlake had established with social credit organizations: when New Britain broke up in 1934, Westlake had become involved with John Hargrave's Greenshirt Movement for Social Credit (formerly the Kibbo Kift). Glaister successfully mobilized a vote against the Westlake clique, and the eventual outcome was to establish an enlarged collective leadership group headed by Theodore Faithfull's son Glynn. However, the OWC had by this time ceased to be a major force in British scouting. Its pacifist aims were more successfully carried forward by the Woodcraft Folk, which had been formed as an adjunct of the cooperative movement in 1925.[32] The Forest School was seriously affected by these disputes and when Aubrey Westlake broke with the OWC the school was transferred to Norfolk, only to close in 1945.

THE UNIVERSITY MILITANT

The final element in the Geddes and Branford approach to education was a consideration of university-level education and the wider issues of the role of the university in its region. Industrialization had led to a massive growth in town life, but it did so without establishing any strong spiritual power to replace what was formerly provided by the monastery and the university in the medieval city. The university had been a central cultural and educational organ in the medieval city, but its decline along with the social role of the Catholic Church had left temporal power unchecked by spiritual power. Branford and Geddes saw the university as the base for this reconfiguration of power. The university must be the "supreme guardian of the social heritage," transmitting it from generation to generation, and a university education must direct "the path of youth to this Third Way of living a Man's life" (Branford 1914a, 287, 341). The wisdom of the older generation would be passed on to the younger one as a cumulative experience: "The essential function of the university is to bring together, for the transmission of experience and impulse, the sages of the passing and the picked youths of the coming generation" (Branford 1914a, 288). It would allow a "re-birth" into citizenship.

The proper cultural role of the city could be realized, Geddes argued, through its "civic organ of higher education"—its university. Universities can build and sustain a civic life; and without a vital university, no town can be a city. Geddes concluded that a eutopian strategy of urban renewal would convert conurbations into both the "city beautiful" and the civic community (Geddes 1915a, ch. 7). It was within the university that sociology was to be nurtured as the key means of civic reconstruction. The work of the universities must be firmly embedded in the traditions and practical needs of their regions, organized through regional surveys. Universities must be the basis for the reestablishment of spiritual power over temporal power, producing a "new Christendom" in which university and church can cooperate (Branford and Geddes 1919a, 237).

Geddes took a great interest in the development of the modern university, looking in particular at the new universities of Germany and the United States (Geddes 1890, 1906). State centralization had, however, ensured that the new universities were "national universities" rather than regional universities, and they had to be reconnected with their regions. This would require that they be freed from bureaucratic regulation and "examination torments" (Branford and Geddes 1919a, 228). Universities are overspecialized, with knowledge and ideas available only in limited and fragmented forms: "It is a practical impossibility under existing curricula for a student, within a measurable time, to achieve any adequate reading of the human record in its vital and essential aspects" (Branford and Geddes 1919a, 40). The spiritual disciplines, in particular, are fragmented and overspecialized, allowing no space for any synoptic account of humanity or culture except as highly abstract philosophy. Specialisms must be integrated and synthesized through broader curricula and through the key role of an "Institute of Synthesis" based on the idea of the Outlook Tower. This would serve as a "common signpost and center," a "spiritual telephone-station and conference room" for cultural development (Branford 1914a, 333).

Branford and Geddes also saw the national focus as an obstacle to wider cooperation and, inspired by the ideas of the American social thinker Charles Ferguson, they aimed to build the "university militant" as a federation of regional universities committed to serving a wider humanity. They saw this as occurring through the building of new universities that would play a global role as harbingers of a new society.

Such a prospect for a renewal of the university involved bringing together the best minds of war-torn Europe after World War I to renew the historic character of their universities. The constituent universities of the university militant must be "post-Germanic," building on the research specialization of the German universities but embodying a spiritual renewal based on a stronger emphasis on the humanities, with each specialism pursued in relation to a synthetic, encyclopedic integration of knowledge (Branford and Geddes 1919b, 339–40). They found emergent examples at the University of Clermont-Ferrand, the University of Michigan at Ann Arbor, the University of Wisconsin at Madison, and the University of Arizona and hoped to see the Collège des Écossais in Montpellier developing in this direction (Branford 1914a, 327 ff.; Branford and Geddes 1919b, 343).

A model for the university militant was provided in Benchara Branford's depiction of the "world university" (B. Branford 1916, 26). A world university would be a spiritual counterpart to the temporal institutions of the League of Nations and the International Tribunal (now the Court of Justice) at The Hague. Benchara Branford saw this world university as the builder and carrier of distinctively cosmopolitan ideas and values. It would be concerned with world history, rather than merely national histories, it would develop world science through the pioneering work of Reclus on the terrestrial globe, it would have a world library covering all the arts and sciences, and it would help to promote a world language and a world currency (B. Branford 1916, 30).

Benchara Branford held that the centrality of the world university to global culture and its independence from powerful states required that it be based on an island in the Eastern Mediterranean, and he hoped that the postwar peace treaty would allocate such an island to the new university (Branford 1916, 32–33). It is clear from his account that he had Cyprus in mind as the location, perhaps motivated by Geddes's own earlier involvement in Cypriot affairs. In the spirit of the Benedictine monastery, he saw the university as sustaining itself through "simple husbandry, art-crafts and healthy types of simple manufacture on a small-scale" (Branford 1916, 33). This would prevent it from becoming beholden to any nation state.

This view of the university placed it at the pinnacle of the educational system. Schooling prepared children through the following of the rustic process and on to the verge of civic participation in their society. The university completes a training in the civic process and is the means through which spiritual development can contribute to a morally informed social reconstruction.

A key feature of the university militant was that it should considerably enlarge the outreach activities that had begun to develop in the university settlement movement and so ensure that there was no gulf between the university and its surrounding region. The idea of involving university undergraduates and teachers in residential social work had been proposed by Ruskin as early as 1869 and the first products of this idea were the Oxford and Cambridge settlements in the East End—most notably Canon Barnett's settlement at Toynbee Hall in Whitechapel—and Geddes's own settlement in Edinburgh (Scotland 2007). The settlement, as proposed by Barnett, was not to be a church mission but a means of social reconstruction and class integration. Its success led to the similar efforts of Stanton Coit and Jane Addams in the United States (Briggs and Macartney 1984; Meacham 1987).

Branford and Geddes agreed on the need for university settlements with a specifically sociological orientation. This would involve a commitment to taking sociological knowledge out into the region and involving local residents in its research work (Branford and Geddes 1919b, 358; B. Branford 1916, 116). The settlement must be a "civic settlement," incorporating a "civicollege" and a "civicentre." As such, the university and its settlement would have a broader cultural role in spiritual and social renewal (Geddes 1906, 1907). University extension work involves seeing the university "as a whole community in its culture aspect" (Branford 1914a, 289), emphasizing what is now known as outreach, engagement, and university-community partnership. This vision of the university lay behind the huge efforts made at Crosby Hall in London and Geddes's later work at Montpellier.

SEVEN

COOPERATION, FINANCE, AND CAPITALISM

The sociological work and practical activities of the Geddes circle were inextricably linked with their commercial business undertakings. The development of their ideas on economic and material processes owed a great deal to their own economic activities in business. Their commitment to cooperative ideals found its expression in agricultural and housing cooperatives that nurtured those ideals and established personal connections that fed into their intellectual work. Victor Branford spent his life as an active businessman and saw a synergy between the various corporate enterprises in which he was involved and both the implementation of practical ventures inspired by Geddes and his sociological activity. In South America he supported agricultural colonies and the undertaking of social surveys linked to economic development and social reconstruction. Branford's business and personal resources also financed the sociological project and made possible the organizational framework of sociology in Britain.

Much of the money that financed Geddes's academic work and the early activities of the Sociological Society came from the personal wealth of Martin White. A boyhood friend of Geddes, his willingness to subsidize the eccentric figure that he so much admired was crucial for the development of British sociology. White's father had set up the firm of J. F. White and Co. in 1849, operating from Dundee and New York as merchants in linen and burlap. His partners were Bryce Gray in New York and David Martin in Dundee. White became more closely involved in the firm after his father's death in 1884, but he preferred to spend his time on social and political activities and the company seems largely to have been run on a day-to-day basis by its managers and by business associate George Bonar of Low and Bonar, jute merchants in Dundee.[1] This allowed White to indulge his admiration of Geddes through practical and financial support.

Geddes was involved in some commercial undertakings, though he regarded these as necessary evils if his work was to be pursued, and he gave them as little attention as possible. His businesses, unsurprisingly, were not conspicuously successful, and even Martin White seems to have been unwilling to put his money into financial ventures in which Geddes took a leading part. Branford, too, had entered business out of necessity. In his case, however, it was the necessity to earn a living that drove him. Unlike Geddes, Branford applied himself diligently to this work. Having failed to obtain an academic post, and recognizing that he was unlikely to enter a conventional academic career, he sought to pursue his business ventures, as far as possible, as a basis for academic research and as tools of social reconstruction.

ENTERPRISE AND COOPERATION IN HOUSING

All three of the key figures were involved in cooperative approaches to housing, agriculture, and community development. Geddes promoted tenant participation in university residences, forming a company to control the finances; Branford established cooperative trading enterprises to operate in overseas agriculture; and Gurney was an administrator for nascent cooperative ventures in housing and became a leading figure in their development into a social movement. They saw this involvement as an expression of their commitment to the cooperative politics of social reconstruction that they derived from Owen and Ruskin.

Geddes's first business venture was formed in order to control his mishandling of his personal finances. His involvement in buying, improving, and renting out houses in self-governing communities of students led him into a reckless acquisition of run-down property and so into serious financial difficulties. His friends and associates proposed a consolidation of the property holdings and debts into the Town and Gown Association, which was formed in 1886, and this eventually took over almost ninety apartments together with their furnishings and a rolling program of repair work. The key figure in its affairs was Thomas Whitson (later knighted), a Dundee accountant already involved in Geddes's educational work. Much of the finance came from Henry Beveridge of Pitreavie Castle in Fife, owner of the St. Leonard's Linen manufactory and who also served as a director of the Town and Gown company. Victor Branford and John Ross were involved in a minor capacity: it was the task of Ross, for example, to try to keep track of Geddes's chaotic finances and to ensure that his bills were paid.

The Edinburgh housing cooperative was an integral element in Geddes's strategy of urban regeneration and cultural development, and many of the same people, including Martin White, were drawn into the formation of Patrick Geddes and Colleagues in 1893. This was essentially a publishing company for the literary periodical *The Evergreen*, which had been launched in 1895 but appeared only for one year. It was intended to produce a number of other literary and sociological works that would further the vision of community development, and some publications did, erratically, appear under its imprint. It was the only one of Geddes's businesses in which Martin White seems to have invested, though White did make him a personal loan of £2000 in 1898.

Geddes became involved in a minor capacity as a member of an organization called the Labour Association for Promoting Co-operative Production Among the Workforce (later the Labour Co-Partnership Association), and it was through this organization that he first met Sybella Gurney. The Association had been formed in Derby to promote profit sharing and worker participation, and from the late 1880s the promotion of housing cooperatives had become its central purpose. Its key figure was Henry Vivian, who set up an associated cooperative building company—General Builders—to work under contract to cooperative housing schemes such as the 1901 cooperative Ealing Tenants (Reid 2000). Vivian formed a number of other associated businesses, including the Co-Partnership Tenants Housing Council of 1905, to which he appointed Sybella Gurney as secretary. In 1907, under the simpler name of Co-Partnership Tenants, this became the central coordinating body for cooperative housing schemes and began to acquire shares in a number of local societies.

Vivian and Gurney were both involved with Henrietta Barnett in the formation of the Hampstead Garden Suburb Trust and Hampstead Tenants (Miller and Gray 1992; and see Gurney 1907). This had been inspired by the work of Ebenezer Howard's Garden City Association, which was developing the first "Garden City" at Letchworth. Gurney was a member of the executive council, which took the successful Ealing Tenants as its model (Miller 1989; Hardy 2000, ch. 3). Sybella Gurney was an important link between the two companies, and connected them both to the Labour Co-Partnership Association. She provided the bulk of the capital for Garden City Tenants, the company formed to finance the development of Letchworth (Vivian 1906).

Victor Branford and John Ross formed their accountancy partnership in 1896. As well as the resources that Branford was eventually able to bring from his marriage to Bess Stewart, finance for the partnership is likely also to have come from Ross's father, James Ross, who had recently retired from the ownership of the Lochside Brewery in Montrose. Trading under the name of Ross, Branford & Co., they set up an Edinburgh office at 549 Castlehill—the address of the Outlook Tower. This convenient arrangement saved them the cost of a commercial rent and also allowed them to try to exercise a close supervision over Geddes's disorganized finances. They set up a London headquarters in Westminster, basing themselves initially at 28 Victoria Street and then in larger offices in a Queen Anne house at 5–7 Old Queen Street.[2] Ross was qualified as an accountant, serving his apprenticeship with William Melvill Sym of Edinburgh and passing the final examinations of the Society of Accountants in Edinburgh, at the second attempt, in December 1892. Branford, as was common among practicing accountants at the time (Walker 1988, 48), had no formal qualifications. The partners followed a clear division of labor: Branford undertook the general financial and investment work while Ross handled the detailed paperwork and the more routine work of auditing company accounts.

Ross and Branford were drawn into Geddes's business ventures in the early years of their partnership, though this was unlikely to have been lucrative for them. Their first substantial task was to form the Eastern and Colonial Association in 1897. Patrick and Anna Geddes had become closely involved in the problems of the Armenian minority in Turkey and the eastern Mediterranean, and especially with the refugees in Cyprus who had fled there from Turkish oppression and whose treatment had become a cause for public concern. A number of organizations had been set up to provide food and clothing aid to the Armenian refugees. Most notable among these were the Anglo-Armenian Society of 1879 (Fisher 1927, 183) and the attempt by Sarah Amos, widow of colonial lawyer Sheldon Amos, to set up an industrial farm (Cons 1896). Patrick and Anna Geddes visited the island in 1897 and proposed that the Armenians be provided with the means for agricultural development and economic autonomy through the establishment of small-scale cooperative ventures (see Geddes 1897; Geddes and Geddes 1897). Providing tools, seeds, and land, they argued, would be the most effective means of social development. To this end, the Geddeses helped set up two estates and a silk farm. They also proposed the establishment of an agricultural school to educate the Armenians in the use of these resources. Ross and Branford were asked to form Eastern and Colonial to take over these ventures and to facilitate other undertakings.

Based in the Ross, Branford offices, the principal shareholders in the Association were Henry Beveridge with 28 percent, Edith Rawnsley with 24 percent, and John Pennington Thomasson with 14 percent. Geddes himself held only 7 percent. Beveridge, of course, was already involved with Geddes in the Town and Gown Association, and the other large shareholders were drawn from Geddes's extensive circle of acquaintances: Thomasson was a Bolton cotton spinner, an amateur naturalist, and former MP; Rawnsley and her husband, a vicar in Keswick, had been friends of John Ruskin, had set up the National Trust and the Keswick School of Industrial Art (Bruce 2000), and were involved in the Garden City Association. The smaller shareholders, too, were of a similar character and included numerous lawyers, manufacturers, and clergymen. They included Harry Barker, a chemical manufacturer of Silloth in Cumbria and a childhood friend of Geddes, John Armour Brown, a corn-flour manufacturer in Paisley, and Sir Colin Campbell Scott-Moncrieffe, the undersecretary of state for Scotland. The board of directors included Geddes, Beveridge, and a selection of the middling shareholders. Branford had asked Geddes if Thomasson should nominate him as a director when Thomasson agreed to increase his investment in the company, but neither the increased funding nor Branford's nomination took place.[3] Andrew Dunlop, a colonial merchant in London and brother of a partner in Russell and Dunlop WS of Edinburgh, held just 1.4 percent, but early in 1898 he undertook a major reorganization through a reverse takeover. Under this arrangement, Eastern and Colonial acquired the business of Dunlop Brothers and moved to its offices at 49 Fenchurch Street. The Armenian problem in Cyprus had been eased through other means, and this transaction increased the Dunlop stake in the company and transformed it into a conventional mercantile business specializing in trade with Cyprus. It was not conspicuously successful and few of the shareholders took any significant interest in the company. For many years, after Geddes had moved on to other enthusiasms, it was run by Andrew Dunlop alone and was virtually moribund by World War I.[4]

A year after his involvement in the formation of Eastern and Colonial, Branford formed a company in which he was to be more centrally involved. Inspired by the agricultural cooperatives of Horace Plunkett in Ireland, Ross and Branford formed the West Indian Cooperative Union to carry through the cooperative ideas on which Geddes (1888) had been working. The Union was intended to promote investment in small-scale cooperative farming on the Caribbean islands, and this focus on colonial rather than domestic cooperatives seems to have come about through Branford's business connections in London with Malcolm Kearton, a West India merchant and legal agent for firms operating in the Caribbean. The principal aims of the company were educational and informative rather than trading in its own right, and Branford saw it as a means of promoting and diversifying small-scale agriculture through cooperation and credit banking. Financial backing for the company once again came from Henry Beveridge, who held 16 percent of the capital, but the single largest shareholding was the 49 percent held by George Mathieson and Alexander Horn of Clarke Nicholls and Coombs in Hackney. The latter firm was engaged in the production of candied peel and confectionery and had become involved because of its substantial interests in the Caribbean sugar trade. Smaller shareholders included Branford himself, his brother Jack, and the grandson of the first Lord Brassey. Its board of directors, effectively headed by Victor Branford, comprised Malcolm Kearton, Professor William Bottomley, and Norman Wyld. These men, officially described as the "London Board," secured the appointment of a number of the great and the good to honorary positions as presidents and vice presidents. These included Geddes, Earl Grey, Lord Stanmore, and the leading advocates of cooperatives and credit unions Horace Plunkett[5] and Henry Wolff. It was probably through the Cooperative Union that Branford first met Vernon Malcolmson, a West India merchant involved in the Trinidad sugar industry. Malcolmson was committed to the idea of the Cooperative Credit Bank and remained a lifelong associate with interests in Branford's social reconstruction work.

The Union was principally concerned with farms in Jamaica and Barbados. Branford seems to have investigated its agricultural development work in Barbados in a paper on the "areal farm" (Branford 1898),[6] and in its first annual report he made the case for higher levels of investment in Caribbean farming (Branford 1899). It may have been at this time that, while visiting Barbados, he first entered the United States and visited Philadelphia or Baltimore. The company achieved little, despite its substantial capital, and Branford's first annual report was also the last. Business had virtually ceased by 1901, and by 1903 Branford was reporting to the Registrar of Companies that all the funds had been exhausted, that the most active director had died, and that he was simply keeping the company ticking over by responding to requests for information from enquirers. Like Eastern and Colonial, the Union was largely moribund after its first few years and its affairs were largely forgotten, even by Branford.[7]

A BANKERS' AGENT AND THE RAILWAY SYNDICATE

The West Indian Cooperative Union and the Eastern and Colonial Association were ventures that Branford had hoped would promote Geddes's ideas on economic development and social reconstruction through cooperation. Other companies with which Branford was associated in the early years of the century were more prosaic domestic ventures for which Ross, Branford were auditors or accountants and offered few possibilities for developing their sociological ideas. Much of their business was undertaken in collaboration with the accounting firm of Edmund Hamilton Burton at 16 St. Helen's Place, London. Branford also lived in Burton's Chelsea apartment at 20 King's Mansions, just off Cheyne Walk, when visiting London. His introduction to Burton may, paradoxically, have come through the Edinburgh firm of lawyers who had been pursuing the payment of William Branford's debts. Impressed by the efforts that Victor had made to pay off the debts, they may have decided to put some business into the hands of the nascent London partnership of Ross, Branford through Burton and his associate William Borradaile. The latter was chairman of the Home and Colonial Assets and Debenture Corporation—largely Scottish in ownership and with James Mylne, of Mylne and Campbell, as a director—and both Burton and Borradaile were directors of the Cumberland River Estates, involved in farming, grazing, and mining in Tennessee.[8]

Branford's business activities were largely domestic, low key, and slow, and in early 1900 he reported to Geddes that business was very quiet and there was little prospect of improvement.[9] In 1902 he was still involved in the minutiae of rent collection and accounting for Geddes's Edinburgh apartments. He was, however, beginning to take on some business for overseas companies. There is some evidence that he may have played a small part in the financing of the Kansas City, Mexico, and Orient Railway, formed in 1902 by Arthur Stilwell to connect with the utopian community at Topolobampo on the Mexican coast (Moore 1975; Reynolds 1993).[10] Stilwell had previously formed the Missouri, Kansas and Texas Trust (later the Guardian Trust) and in 1893 he used this company to finance the Kansas City, Pittsburgh and Gulf Railroad through using the numerous Dutch connections of the Amsterdam East India merchant John de Goijen and brokers Tutein, Northenius and De Hann.[11] Branford was certainly involved with the Scheveningen development company *Exploitatie Maatschappij Scheveningen*, which was building hotels, restaurants, and a casino in the Hague's coastal resort. His Dutch connections were with S. F. van Oss, a railway investment banker (Veenendaal 1996, 1992),[12] and Branford reported to Geddes in September 1905 that his Dutch partner had called him to the Hague to discuss some railway business and that he was to travel to Amsterdam before returning to London.[13]

This call to the Hague led to a business relationship that was to decide the whole development of Branford's business career and enable him to try to link business ventures with economic development and social reconstruction. Branford was asked to handle some business for the Argentine North Eastern Railway, in which Manuel Antonio Rodríguez and Benito Villanueva were investing.[14] The intermediary seems to have been the grain merchant Charles Mendl, who had set up the South American branches of his family firm and had then become involved in Argentine railways before a later career in the British secret service (see Smith 1982). Rodríguez and Villaneuva were good clients of the London and River Plate Bank, and Branford's involvement with them may have been eased by the fact that his stepson-in-law, Adam Goodfellow, was a senior manager in the Buenos Aires branch of the bank.

Rodríguez had been born in Brazil and started his adult life as a cook, subsequently making a fortune in Argentina and Paraguay and acquiring an interest in the Monte Casera–based Argentine North Eastern Railway (Warren 1967b). Villanueva was an Argentine *hacendado*, a large landowner and one of the wealthiest people in the country. His three-story house was run by nine French servants and was valued at the time at $300,000 (Bower 2003, 397).[15] He was president of the Argentine Chamber of Deputies from 1901 to 1903, senator for Mendoza (his home province) and for the federal capital, and was president of the national senate on various dates. His business interests included the Córdoba Central Railway. Rodríguez and Villanueva were closely associated with each other in a number of land and railway investments and it was through these Argentine connections that Branford became involved with the Paraguay Central Railway Company during 1906. This was to become his principal business commitment for almost twenty years.

The Paraguay Central Railway Company had been formed in London in 1889 to take over an earlier business run by the Paraguayan government (Warren 1967a; Waters 1994, 1996; Brady 1926).[16] Financial backing for the new company came from Morton, Rose and Co., the London associate of Levi Morton's Morton Trust (Greenberg 1980; McElroy 1930), and from the London merchant bank of Perry, Cutbill de Lungo and Co.[17] The Paraguayan government held the preference shares, while the ordinary shares were held by Perry, Cutbill and the debentures were syndicated through the London stock market by Morton, Rose. This structure of control was unstable and there followed an eighteen-year period of struggle between the London company and the Paraguayan government over the terms of the reorganization. In 1891, the Paraguayan government defaulted on its agreed interest payments, forcing Perry, Cutbill into bankruptcy. The debenture holders in London, led by Henry Lawson White, put the railway into receivership and appointed two receivers: Emanuel Underdown, a London barrister and QC, and Walter J. Stride. Through Underdown the company was linked to a number of Cuban railway and telegraph concerns. The receivers, in turn, appointed White as the local manager and tasked him with a further reorganization of the company. White worked closely in this task with English expatriate Campbell Ogilvie and, in 1904, brought the company to the verge of a deal with the Paraguayan authorities (Ogilvie 1910). When this deal was set back by a change of government, White resigned.

Underdown and Alfred Frewin, the key directors, formed a joint committee of share and debenture holders to renegotiate the terms of the financial reorganization. The first achievement of the new controllers was to establish an administrative base in London at an office in New Broad Street House, shared with the Uruguay Northern Railway of which Underdown was also chairman.[18] William Lauber served as secretary to both companies,[19] and Cecil A. Grenfell, a stockbroker with Govett, Sons, was recruited to the PCRC board. A settlement was finally achieved when a new pro-Argentine government was elected in Paraguay and Argentine financial interests headed by Rodríguez and Villanueva were brought in to lead a controlling syndicate.[20] This syndicate included the new Paraguyan president Benigno Ferreira (Waters 1997).[21] By 1906, the Argentine syndicate and its British associates held 85 percent of the ordinary shares (Herken 1984, 1985), with the remaining shares being held by a U.S. syndicate managed by Levi Morton and held through Morton Rose.[22] The bulk of the capital, however, was the debenture stock issued through the London stock market, and the leading representative of these bond holders was Charles Mendl's brother Sigismund.[23]

Victor Branford, working closely with the Argentine investors, became involved in the company's affairs at this point. He was immediately involved with Rodríguez and Villanueva in promoting a railway bill in the Argentine Congress, a process held up by the death in office of President Manuel Quintana. Branford's concern about the finances of the company led him to speak witheringly of its former management. In his own records he noted that between 1890 and 1906 there had been a war of "recrimination, charging and countercharging" between the English shareholders and the Paraguayan authorities.[24] To remedy this, Branford felt it necessary to become closely involved in the day-to-day affairs of the railway. He was in Paraguay in January 1907, returned there in April, and in the summer he was advertising for a Spanish-speaking assistant to work at the London offices of Ross, Branford.[25] Rodríguez, a somewhat shady and suspicious financier, relied on Branford's solidity and probity as a front for business operations that involved deals and political negotiations that Branford, at the time, knew little about.[26]

The railway company reorganization was completed in November 1907 with the passing of a formal liquidation resolution, and the law firm of Ashurst, Morris and Crisp was appointed at the behest of Underdown to handle the claims against the company.[27] The preference shares held by the Paraguayan government were canceled and a committee of reconstruction was appointed in London, its key members being Cecil Grenfell, John Young (from the London Trust and associated with the company's lawyers), and the merchants Sigismund Mendl and John Heslop. In February 1908, the capital of the company was increased by the issue of 6 percent debentures floated in London through Chaplin, Milne, Grenfell and Co.[28] The offices of the company, and so Branford's London base, were moved to the main office building for Latin American companies in River Plate House at 13 South Place.

Branford took a broad view of his involvement in the railway, seeing his work as a further attempt—after those in Cyprus and the British West Indies—to apply scientific methods to regional development. He put the development case to the governments in both Argentina and Paraguay and in January 1906 had presented himself to the Paraguayan president as a representative of European banking interests and an associate—via the Sociological Society—of Lord Avebury, whose firm of Robarts, Lubbock were the London bankers to the Paraguayan government. It was also in 1906 that his friend Joseph Fels became involved in Paraguay. Joseph and his brother Samuel ran a very successful naphtha business in Philadelphia (Dudden 1971; Rosen 2000), and Joseph had become involved with Israel Zangwill in the search for a Jewish homeland, (see chapter 3). Fels hoped that Paraguay might be a possible location for the homeland and in correspondence during April and May 1907 he claimed that "overtures" to this effect had reached him from Rodríguez through Branford. He informed Zangwill that he "was preparing to send Branford to Paraguay as his agent" (Dudden 1971, 174).[29] Though Rodríguez was happy to discuss the ideas in London, he was unwilling to do anything to promote them lest the proposal threaten his existing business interests in Paraguay.

A construction contract to extend the PCRC line to Encarnación was awarded to Rodríguez in 1908, his aim being to convert the whole line to standard gauge and to connect it with the Argentine North Eastern and the Entre Rios railways as a unified system (Macdonald 1911, 10). To avoid any appearance of a conflict of interest, Branford became acting chairman and began to spend even more time on railway business. The partnership with John Ross came under increasing strain. Indeed, by 1906 Ross had already been looking to the future and had been considering an appointment with a new company in Canada or moving back to Edinburgh. The partnership between the two men was eventually dissolved in May 1908 to allow Branford to devote his time fully to the Latin American businesses.[30] Abandoning the idea of a new venture, Ross moved into an office at River Plate House in order to help Branford with his railway work.

Branford traveled frequently to Argentina and the United States, and much of his time in Britain was also spent traveling. In 1910, when he had reported "the most satisfactory year in the history of the [Paraguay] company,"[31] he spent some time visiting the workshops of the North British Locomotive Company in Springburn, Glasgow, to arrange the purchase of new locomotives. Through 1912 he became heavily involved in negotiations over the railway's acquisition of the Asunción tramways.

By March 1910, Branford was discussing with Rodríguez the possibility of commissioning surveys on behalf of the railway from Marcel Hardy, a Belgian botanist who had worked with Geddes in Dundee and was the principal promoter of a settlement colony at Las Palmas in the Canary Islands, operated partly with indigenous labor (Macdonald 1911, 55; Naylor and Jones 1997, 282). Hardy's surveys were to look at land values for timber, grazing, and crops with the aim of using the railway as a vehicle for economic development. Finance for the surveys was to come from a syndicate that included Chaplin, Milne Grenfell and Robert Fleming, though Rodríguez was wary of the venture and of Hardy's surveys. They were eventually carried out between April and December 1910 and in May 1913 with finance from Henry Pulley and with Hardy being instructed to misinform the Paraguayan authorities that he was merely acting on behalf of Kew Botanical Gardens and a group of geographers.

ELECTRICITY, TRAMWAYS, AND TELEPHONES: VENTURES IN MEXICO, CANADA, AND CUBA

Branford's business interests extended to Mexico, an involvement that came about through participation in the financing of Frederick Pearson's ventures. Pearson had formed the Mexican Light and Power Co. in 1902, and a dominant position was taken by a financial syndicate headed by Sir George Drummond and including the Bank of Montreal and its associates, together with a number of New York financial interests. Pearson went on to form the Mexico Tramways in 1906, this time with a Toronto syndicate headed by William Mackenzie and George Cox, but with the bulk of its funds raised through bonds issued in London. The underwriters for both companies were the Montreal stockbroking firm of Mackay Edgar and the London bankers Dunn, Fischer. "Mike" Mackay Edgar worked closely with Sperling and Co., a London outside broker and underwriter whose senior partner Monty Horne-Payne was already handling the finance for Pearson's Brazilian companies. In 1906, Edgar transferred his office to London from Montreal's CPR Building and the following year became a partner in Sperlings.[32] The other underwriter, Dunn, Fischer, had been formed in 1905 when Canadian company lawyer and stockbroker Jimmy Dunn moved to London to represent the Pearson interests that he had been involved with in both Mexico and Cuba. Dunn's partnership with Charles Fischer was initially based at 85 London Wall and he worked closely with the London stockbrokers Mendel and Myers (McDowall 1984; Aitken 1961; and see Mitchie 1988; McDowall 1984–86).[33] Mexico Light and Power suffered serious financial difficulties in the business recession of 1907, and Pearson pushed through an alliance with Mexico Tramways. Share purchases by Edgar and Dunn on the London and Canadian markets enabled Pearson to weld the Canadian syndicates into a single controlling group led by William van Horne, with whom Pearson had previously been involved in Cuba (Armstrong and Nelles 1984). Branford was asked by the Sperling interests to visit Mexico on tramway company business in 1906–07 (Mairet 1957, 128), and he became a close, if unlikely, friend of Edgar.

In Mexico, Branford may also have come into contact with John De Kay, who was involved in talks with Joseph Fels at this time about a possible

Jewish settlement in the country, Fels having begun these after the failure of his talks with Rodríguez. In March 1908, Fels visited Texas and Mexico with De Kay and while Branford was not in this case the intermediary his presence in Mexico would certainly have been useful. De Kay was the founder of the Mexican National Packing Company (known as "Popo"), formed in 1902 with backing from George Ham's United States Banking Company.[34] The packing company was expanded in 1906 with British finance, mobilized through the British-Mexican Trust, which held 80 percent of the MNP capital. The principal shareholders in the Trust were De Kay, Campbell Ogilvie, William Slaughter (lawyer and associate of Erlangers Bank), and the British refrigeration engineering firm of Farringdon Works.[35] The key board members were Ogilvie and the chairman Sir William F. Haynes Smith. Despite further funding from Britain in 1909, the company did not achieve a secure position, and the following year Ham's United States Banking Company was itself forced into bankruptcy (Pilcher 1998, 2004; Schell 2001).

Branford's banking connections also led to his involvement in Cuba through the Havana Telephone Company. This had originally been formed in New Jersey in 1900 and was based around an earlier company providing a telephone service to western Cuba (Rippy 1946).[36] Ownership of its ordinary shares rested with U.S. interests headed by Roland Ray Conklin, who began his business career in Kansas real estate and became involved in irrigation works and street railways through the Jarvis-Conklin Mortgage Trust. During 1891–92, Conklin drew up plans for the development of Roland Park, a model suburb of Baltimore, using British bond finance raised through the Lands Trust, a London associate of the JCMT and Conklin's North American Trust (Waesche 1987).[37] The largest backers of the Lands Trust were merchant Eli Lemon Sheldon and the Fryer family of Wilmslow, Cheshire, though other shareholders included the architect Alfred Waterhouse and his accountant brother Edwin.[38] When the JCMT was bankrupted in 1892, Conklin moved to New York and converted the North American Trust into a more general banking business. He was shortly, however, to make a major shift in direction, taking up investment opportunities in Cuba by forming the National Bank of Cuba and using this to mobilize a syndicate of Caribbean sugar estate owners and New York businesses to form the Havana Telephone Company.[39]

British finance was drawn into the Havana company in 1906 with the issue of debentures through F. J. Benson & Co and its associated trustee company the Prudential Deposit Trust.[40] The New York trustee for the bonds was Conklin's National Bank of Cuba, operating from 1 Wall Street.[41] Seeking to consolidate its interests in the nonagricultural sector of the Cuban economy, the Conklin group set up a Delaware company, the Cuban Telephone Company, to acquire the shares of both the HTC and a company promoted to build a Havana Subway. The group sought to use its government concession to extend and operate a telephone system across the whole of the island. The interests of the London bondholders were protected through the formation in 1908 of Havana Telephone Securities, which acquired the British interests in the HTC. The new company established its offices at River Plate House and its board consisted of Victor Branford and four stockbrokers. Branford's involvement with these Cuban interests may have been made possible by the fact that Emanuel Underdown, the associate of Rodríguez and chairman of the United Railways of the Havana, was a leading representative of Schroders and other British financial interests in Cuba. Underdown's general manager at the United Railways was American lawyer Walter E. Ogilvie, who was himself already involved in business schemes with Conklin.[42] HTS was, however, a totally separate venture from Underdown's involvement with the Rodríguez syndicate.[43]

CTC acted as a nominee or custodian for the bonds held by British participants in HTC, who transferred their holdings into the debentures of the CTC. Newly issued bonds in CTC itself were issued on the London market through Chaplin, Milne Grenfell & Co., acting as Conklin's London agent.[44] For some time after its takeover, the HTC maintained a separate London advisory board to which Victor Branford was appointed along with Lord Elcho (a partner in the Benson bank) and Cecil Grenfell.[45] Branford secured the services of Ralegh Phillpotts,[46] a partner in the company's lawyers, who traveled to Cuba and New York on company business during 1908. In 1910, the London business of the CTC was transferred from Chaplin, Milne, Grenfell to a separate London agency run by Branford from New Broad Street House, and from where he was running the PCRC. As London agent for both CTC and HTC, Branford wound up HTS when it completed the business of transferring the London interests to CTC. Branford's local links in Cuba were with the law firm of Valdes Pages and Co., a firm in which Andres Valdés-Pagés was most probably the senior partner.[47] In 1911, Branford handled Conklin's use of the CTC to acquire the mortgage bonds of the HTC and the Havana Subway Company through an issue of CTC bonds on the London market, Mike Edgar and Sperling taking the lead in registering London holdings in CTC ordinary stock.[48] By 1913, the Benson directors had withdrawn from the CTC and Branford was its sole London agent.

The CTC found its expansion constricted by interest payments that had to be made on the bonds issued in London. William Talbott, appointed in 1911 as manager by Conklin on behalf of the syndicate, was faced with a company that was virtually insolvent and by 1915 its share price was crashing. Later that year, Talbott returned to New York, and the National City Bank urged the directors to involve Sosthenes Behn in a corporate reorganization. Behn had branched out from a Puerto Rico sugar business into banking, brokerage, and the local telephone company and from this base he acquired the bulk of the CTC shares in 1916 and began to build his various businesses into International Telephone and Telegraph (ITT) in 1920 (Sobel 1982, 29–30). HTC was still only partly consolidated into CTC at this time, and Branford and Ross remained involved in its affairs for some time to oversee the continuing interests of the British debenture holders.

FINANCIAL ACTIVITIES IN LATIN AMERICA, LONDON, AND NEW YORK

Between 1903 and 1910, Branford, through his connections to Rodríguez, Edgar, and Underdown, became embedded in a nexus of business connections that formed a triangular relation between Britain, Latin America, and the United States. Branford's involvement in these railway and telephone businesses became so great that he was effectively a full-time participant, and Branford henceforth described himself as a banker's agent or a merchant. His growing business interests, coinciding with the breakup of his first marriage, forced him into a peripatetic life in which he moved among hotels, clubs, and company offices in London, Buenos Aires, Paraguay, New York, and other financial centers. It was in London and New York, however, that he maintained his principal bases and independent offices, and it was at this time that he may seriously have considered permanent residence in the United States.

He established a London base on the first floor of New Broad Street House, located above 25–35 Broad Street. This was the registered office for the Paraguay Central Railway, its associated company the Uruguay Northern Railway, and the London office of the Cuban Telephone Company. In addition to his continuing association with John Ross, he may also have worked with solicitor Charles George Scott.[49] Branford continued to spend some of his time at River Plate House, where he maintained contact with British financiers and engineers involved in the Paraguay and Argentine railways. His main contacts were with the Henderson brothers, Alexander, Brodie, and Frank. Alexander Henderson (later Lord Faringdon) was partner in stockbrokers Greenwood & Co., who financed many Argentine railways. Brodie Henderson was partner in Livesey, Sons, and Henderson, railway engineers in Argentina and Uruguay, who were associated with many of the Argentine railways financed by his brother. Frank Henderson was the manager of the Buenos Aires and Great Southern Railway and was also associated with the Central Uruguay railway (Wainwright 1985). Branford also maintained close contact with (Sir) Frank Crisp and his son at solicitors Ashurst, Morris and Crisp, who acted for such Argentine railways as the Entre Rios but were frequently at odds with Rodríguez. Under John

Morris, the firm had formed a number of specialist "River Plate" investment trust and mortgage agencies and these acted as trustees for debenture issues made by Schroders and other London banks (Slinn 1997; Jones et al. 1977). The business activities of Morris, Crisp, and the Hendersons were entwined through the Anglo-American banker Sir John H. Puleston: he had been a partner of Morris in the River Plate ventures, his daughter had married Morris's son, and one of Alexander Henderson's sons was given the second name Puleston.[50] Other businessmen closely associated with this cluster of interests were South America merchants Woodbine and Frank Parish, Jason Rigby, John Phillips, Campbell Ogilvie, Marcus and Jacques van Raalte, and Edward Norman.

In New York, Branford had his base in the Johnston Building at 30 Broad Street, a seventeen-story building on the southwest corner of Broad and Exchange, where he worked most closely with Frederick J. Lisman,[51] the head of an investment banking firm, and William Goodman, a real estate dealer and stockbroker. Lisman, with whom Branford had been associated since at least 1908, was involved in Cuban railways and had been an early associate of Fred van Oss. Lisman and Goodman specialized in railroad finance, and Branford worked with them in this business as well as in a number of mining and property ventures. A further associate in New York was Louis J. Vorhaus, senior partner in the legal firm of House, Grossman, and Vorhaus, who worked in Room 901 at 115 Broadway. Vorhaus was especially active in the theatre business and the newly emerging film industry, as were his main partners Moses and William Grossman. Branford's connections with Goodman, Vorhaus, and Lisman were close and, in the case of the latter, enduring, but all three were, like Branford himself, agents acting on behalf of more powerful principals.[52]

It is clear that by 1911 Branford and his associates were involved with one of the most famous—if not infamous—financiers in New York. The offices of Louis Vorhaus at 115 Broadway were, until the middle of 1911, the New York headquarters for the interests of railway promoter and financier Percival Farquhar.[53] Later in 1911, following press publicity about his growing interests, Farquhar established a larger U.S. base at 25 Broad Street, just across from the office used by Branford, Goodman, and Lisman. It seems very likely that Branford's work with Louis Vorhaus in the preceding years was connected with the growing financial interests of Percy Farquhar.[54]

Farquhar had begun his business career in his father's export firm but first made a name for himself in 1898 when he successfully bid for the Havana Electric Railway to electrify and operate Havana's streetcars. He then worked closely with Sir William van Horne in the formation of the Cuba Company to construct a trans-island railway.[55] With backing coming initially from United Fruit, various Indies merchants, and New

York bankers such as Levi Morton and Edward Harriman, the Cuba Company began to acquire land along the route of its planned line (Santamarina 2000; Knowles 2004).[56] Farquhar next moved into Brazil, where he became involved in the utility companies that Pearson and Mackenzie were forming and where he established, in 1906, his own railway business. Finance for Pearson's Brazilian ventures was mobilized in London by Monty Horne-Payne's British Empire Trust together with Sperling and Dunn, Fischer (McDowall 1988). Additional finance came from Belgium through Alfred Loewenstein of Stallaerts and Loewenstein. Dunn formed Canadian and General Finance Corporation, with Henry Hubbard as manager, to serve as the British office for the whole Pearson group. Farquhar saw Pearson's Brazilian system as the key to a north-south transcontinental railway, and he set about acquiring the various railroads that would comprise the links in such a system. His business interests went largely unnoticed in New York until his unsuccessful involvement in the Rock Island line led to the extent of his interests becoming public knowledge through a series of newspaper disclosures.[57] Farquhar operated through an enlarged New York base and interlinked offices in Paris, London, and Brussels. The key offices were Room 1501 of the Broad Exchange Building at 25 Broad Street (New York), 9 Rue Louis le Grand (the Paris office shared with Pearson), and 64 Cornhill (London), as well as a major office in Brazil. Farquhar's London office was managed by Bernhard Binder, who was soon to be joined by Ralph Hamlyn (Gauld 1964, n13 on pp. 104–105).

From this base, Farquhar began his expansion into Argentina, Uruguay, and Paraguay, though it is possible that he had already been working closely with the syndicates that had been building up their holdings in some of those countries.[58] Farquhar, like Branford, saw railway development as a means to broader economic development. When expanding into Brazil he commissioned Charles E. Akers, the Latin America correspondent of *The Times* to produce a survey of rubber production in the Amazon (Gauld 1964, 111; Akers 1914), and in 1910 he formed Paraguay Land and Cattle with the aim of developing the Paraguayan Chaco. This latter was a partnership with "Tex" Rickard, boxing promoter and saloon owner in Goldfield, Nevada, where Branford had received his divorce.[59] Branford's own surveys in Paraguay, and his involving of Marcel Hardy in survey activities, were directed toward similar purposes.

Manuel Rodríguez needed to raise money for a large loan to Eduardo Schaerer to finance the 1911 insurrection aimed at installing a pro-Argentine government in Paraguay and sold the syndicate's remaining 58 percent stake in the Paraguay Central to Farquhar's Brazil railways group (Waters 1998b). Late in 1912, the Argentine Railway Company was formed by George B.

Hopkins to consolidate the Farquhar syndicate's control of Argentine North Eastern Railway, the Entre Rios railway, and the Cordoba group, as well as the Paraguay Central Railway.[60] This consolidation brought Argentine Northern Land and Industrial Paraguay under the same control. The financial advisers to this consolidation were Speyer Brothers, who, together with Schroders, sold the bonds on the open market. Although Rodríguez had been left in place as Farquhar's representative on the ARC, he left its board in 1913 when Bernhard Binder was appointed as a director. The principal London interests represented on the board of the Argentine Railway holding company were Sigismund Mendl, F. W. Barrow, Farquhar executive A. H. A. Knox-Little,[61] and N. Smith.

The trade depression of 1913 and the deteriorating political situation in Europe in the lead-up to World War I resulted in great financial difficulties for many companies and by July 1914 PCRC was in serious trouble. Speyer Brothers, closely linked to the German members of the original Argentine shareholding syndicate, took the lead in putting the company into receivership and appointed Binder as receiver (Waters 1998a). In November of the same year, the whole Farquhar empire collapsed and both Binder and Branford became heavily involved in the reorganization and refinancing of the companies in receivership. This marked the beginning of a close relationship between Binder and Branford. The PCRC and various other Farquhar companies, as well as Cuban Telephone, had their London offices moved to 3 St. Helen's Place, from which the reorganization of the group was coordinated. This office was staffed by Branford and Ross, together with Alois Pfeiffer to advise on engineering issues.[62] Chaplin, Milne, and Grenfell, as representatives of the ordinary capital, still played a part in the company's affairs, while Sigismund Mendl continued to play a leading part representing the interests of the debenture holders.[63] Branford and Binder themselves remained on the company board specifically to represent the interests of the debenture holders, though Branford's physical breakdown through exhaustion possibly led to his absence from London in the winter of 1914–15 and in mid-1916.[64] When a special meeting of PCRC, chaired by Binder and Branford, was held at Winchester House in November 1918, Branford's office address was given as Exchange Chambers, St. Mary Axe, possibly the offices of F. Mendl & Co., the family firm of Sigismund and Charles Mendl. Branford had already by this time become a founding partner in the accounting partnership of Binder Hamlyn, constructed from their shared experience of salvaging the Farquhar empire.[65] Formed in 1918, the new partnership set up its principal office at 80 Bishopsgate,[66] with Branford henceforth working from that base and with his business interests almost exclusively London-based.

THE ROUTINIZATION OF INVESTMENT

After the end of World War I, Branford's business interests became more routine in nature, concerned largely with day-to-day financial advice and liquidation matters. He maintained a small number of company directorships and managed his own portfolio of shareholdings, but he no longer sought involvement in Latin America or in North American high finance. His normal practice through the 1920s was to spend Tuesday, Wednesday, and Thursday in London working at Binder Hamlyn and at the Sociological Society in Le Play House, and to spend the rest of the week at Hastings. Branford remained a director of the Paraguay Central Railway for the rest of his life, and his son Hugh emigrated to South America in the late 1920s to work for the railway or possibly for a bank in Argentina. The affairs of the company proved rather less pressing during the 1920s, though it was never a major success.

During the 1920s, Branford took on directorships in timber and oil companies that he began to deal with through Binder Hamlyn, and he was also a director of Sociological Publications, set up by the Sociological Society. The Argentine Paraguayan Timber Company, of which he was both a director and chairman of its London Committee, had obvious links with the Paraguayan railway, having been formed to hold its land acquisitions. The General Petroleum Company of Trinidad was a completely separate venture. It was formed by the Imperial and Foreign Corporation in 1919 to acquire certain rights of the Anglo-Caribbean Petroleum Syndicate, and in 1921 it acquired the Amalgamated Oilfields of Trinidad and various other Trinidad oil companies. Though not a cooperative, this company renewed Branford's links with the British West Indies. The key director was solicitor Herbert Guedalla of the Imperial and Foreign Corporation and a director of numerous mining, commodity, and oil companies. Branford secured the appointment of Sybella Branford's cousin, Harold Manby Gurney, to the board. Gurney was also involved in a number of financial matters for the Sociological Society. The company underwent a further reorganization in 1924, becoming the Orepuche (Trinidad) Oilfields and with close links to Apex (Trinidad) Oilfields. Branford remained a director until 1927.

Sybella Branford's mother had died in 1907, leaving her half of an estate of £5,048, the residue of a fortune earned from slave plantations in the West Indies. On the abolition of slavery in 1833, Sybella's great-grandfather had received £117,383 in compensation for 3,953 slaves owned on six islands. This inherited wealth allowed Sybella to fund a number of housing cooperatives and to invest in numerous companies.[67] The largest single shareholding that she owned, in terms of the number of shares, was that in Co-Partnership Tenants, which she had held since its formation. She was, in addition, a significant shareholder in First Garden City, Hampstead Tenants, Ealing Tenants, Leicester Anchor Tenants, and Ruislip Manor Cottage Society. At the time of her death, Sybella held a wider portfolio of shares including the brewing companies Barclay Perkins and Courage, British Cotton and Wool Dyers, the Grand Trunk Railway of Canada, and the London, Midland and Scottish Railway.

Victor Branford seems to have taken few opportunities to acquire substantial shareholdings in the companies with which he dealt. Although he had a large portfolio of shares, these did not form a significant personal fortune. He bought shares through a number of stockbrokers,[68] including his old friend Vernon Malcolmson, then a partner in Scrimgeours, and both John D. Laurie of Laurie Milbank and Edward Beddington-Behrens of Myers and Co. Beddington-Behrens was a particularly important contact for him in the latter years of his life. They had met in 1928 while Branford was staying at Territet, Switzerland, and discovered a common interest in social reform (Beddington-Behrens 1963). Hearing that Beddington-Behrens was seeking a position in the City, Branford put him in touch with his old friend R. C. Whitcroft of the Law Debenture Corporation. Whitcroft gave him an entrée to Myers, the successor firm to Mendel and Myers with which James Dunn had worked on the Mexican business.

The Branford papers report that the gross annual dividend income from the combined shareholdings of the Branfords in 1922 amounted to £1,807. This income was held in accounts with the Clydesdale and Westminster Banks and, in Buenos Aires, with the London and River Plate Bank (which became the Bank of London and South America in 1923). The core of Victor Branford's personal portfolio consisted of shares in Paraguay Central Railway, Cuban Telephone, Argentine Paraguayan Timber, the Consolidated Cities Light, Power and Traction, the Compañia de Electricidad de Buenos Aires, and the Le Play House Press, together with a number of gilt bonds issued in Paraguay, Brazil, Tokyo, and Romania.[69] At one time, Branford had owned shares in Reliance Trust, International Nickel, British Celanese, and Apex Trinidad, but he sold these and in 1928 acquired holdings in Argentine Land, Financial News, the British North Borneo Company, and the General Theatre Corporation (for which Beddington-Behrens was working at the time they met).

These shareholdings were the basis of the various bequests in the wills of Victor and Sybella Branford.[70] Probate on Sybella's will gave a valuation of her estate at £10,000, while that for Victor's estate in 1930 (including his inheritance from Sybella) was £11,692. There were complex linkages between the two wills, Sybella having left a lifetime interest in her estate to Victor and directing that after his death the money should be used, under trust, to provide for the two sons. She and Victor made a number of small bequests to relatives, friends, and associates, with the residue of the estate being left to the Sociological Trust under the trusteeship of Sybella's cousin Harold Gurney and others. Archie and Hugh would not reach the age of twenty-five—the age of maturity specified in Sybella's will—until 1937 and 1939, respectively, and this complicated the need to both provide for them and to leave funds to the Trust. At a rough estimate, almost £5,000 would have to have been found from the estate to meet the provisions for the boys. The Branfords had overestimated the value of their company shares, especially those in South America, not having foreseen a time of global economic depression. In a 1928 codicil, Victor recognized that the sum left to the Trust would be insufficient and hoped that other benefactors would be found to match the financial contributions that he had made over the course of his lifetime. In the event, insufficient sums were realized to meet in full the bequests to the sons and the Sociological Trust.

In the course of his business career, Branford worked with a great variety of investors, speculators, and financiers, gaining experience of corporate activity in a variety of countries and economic sectors. Although he proposed and sometimes managed cooperatives, most of his work was concerned with corporate capitalist enterprises, focusing especially on opening up new lands and expanding markets in an expanding world economy. He came into contact with some mercurial business visionaries with ideas to remake the world, notably Joseph Fels, Arthur Stilwell, and Percival Farquhar, but his own business dealings were characterized by a solid, sober, and trustworthy professionalism. He had a remarkable ability to focus on two separate objectives: making the money to support himself, his family, and the sociological project, and pursuing his intellectual vision of a new and different social system. He wrote little about his work in business, but he had an in-depth knowledge of the complex workings of contemporary capitalism and he drew on this in working with Geddes to develop a sociological model of the contemporary world and a vision of an alternative society.

EIGHT

FINANCIERS, THE CREDIT SYSTEM, AND THE THIRD ALTERNATIVE

The social theory that Branford and Geddes derived from Le Play and Comte was the basis on which they and their associates examined the structure of contemporary industrialism and drew up a political strategy for its transformation into a new and more humanitarian social order. Their general theory held that the overall power system of a society is unbalanced whenever the temporal and spiritual systems are dislocated and counteract each other. This is the situation in contemporary industrial societies, they argued. Basing their views on Branford's inside knowledge of finance and the financial system, they developed a view of financiers as the chiefs of temporal power who have usurped spiritual leadership, enshrined monetary calculations in the heart of their cultures, and driven their societies toward warfare and revolution. On the basis of Branford's business experience, he and Geddes proposed a root and branch reform of financial structures, advocating a cooperative banking system, a system of national credit, and corporatist structures that formed a "Third Way" in politics: a politics between capitalism and socialism. These were the means through which a reconstruction of temporal power could be achieved and spiritual reeducation and communal renewal could be ensured.

The late nineteenth century saw a radicalization of social thought as liberal and conservative views of the contemporary order came to be challenged by those who diagnosed fundamental contradictions or dislocations in its economic base. Principal among these radical social theories, of course, was the orthodox Marxism of the German social democrats, which had an influence in Britain through such political organizations as the SDF. Revisionist Marxists, however, had begun to explore the likely consequences of the growing monopolization and concentration of capital and the ever-tighter fusion of industrial and banking capital. Fabian socialists such as Bernard Shaw (1889) rejected Marxist economics but shared this view of contemporary economic conditions. They saw the concentration of industry as having produced an ever-starker polarization of classes between the wealthy controllers and the impoverished workers who produce the wealth. With the revisionist Marxists, they held that the Marxist orthodoxy had failed to take proper account of these changes in the mode of capitalist production and had drawn overoptimistic conclusions about the likelihood of spontaneous revolutionary change. The Fabians held that the state had to take a far more directive role in social transformation, guided by intellectuals who had seen and analyzed the true characteristics of contemporary capitalism.

A more unorthodox form of socialist radicalism was that of John Hobson (Mumery and Hobson 1889). This provided a strong strand in the New Liberalism and in labor politics, though its unorthodox conclusions limited its influence in the political mainstream. Hobson had originally developed his ideas on the economic consequences of financial concentration in his lectures to the London ethical societies, and it was there that Branford and Geddes encountered his work and recognized its affinity with the ideas of Ruskin that they had already imbibed.[1] Though modifying its details, they took over many of its tenets.

Hobson had first set out his account of *The Evolution of Modern Capitalism* in 1894, but it was in the revised edition of 1906—the edition most likely to have been used by Geddes and Branford—that he set out his key views on contemporary capitalist conditions (Hobson 1906, ch. 10; see also Hobson 1902).[2] He argued that new technologies of production and a huge increase in the scale of production resulted in far greater capital requirements than was the case for the entrepreneurial and family-owned firms of the nineteenth century. The greater scale of contemporary business enterprises had generated ever-greater opportunities of saving for the expanding middle classes. Innovations in the financial system made these savings available to business undertakings in a form that divorced the savers from any direct control over the uses of their savings.[3] New specialists in finance, Hobson claimed, allocate savings to companies as capital and pay interest to the small savers and distribute credit. Financiers exercise power through the promotion and acquisition of companies and through issuing their shares on the stock market. They are the operators of a vast credit system that integrates and coordinates business operations through transactions in stocks, shares, and loans. These transactions comprise a flow of monetary capital that circulates largely independently of the physical processes of production. Financial activities are inherently speculative and offer much scope for personal gain and for a dislocation of credit transactions from the "real" economy. Hobson also saw the financiers as the agents of imperial expansion and as driving the leading capitalist nations into deeper competition and conflict (Hobson 1902). The world had come to be divided between rival imperialist powers within which national monopolies and their financial controllers are supported by increasingly centralized states that promote national economic and military expansion.

Branford and Geddes enthusiastically took up the ideas of Hobson and the related work of Thorstein Veblen (1899, 1904),[4] who had influenced Hobson and who they later met on their visits to the United States.[5] They developed a distinctive account of contemporary capitalism and used this to formulate their alternative to the Fabian political strategy of state centralism.

THE FINANCIAL ERA AND PALEOTECHNIC INDUSTRIALISM

Modern industrialism was defined as the "paleotechnic" stage of industrial development, the age of "old" technology (Geddes 1905a, 170; Branford and Geddes 1919a, 239). It is based on the steam and coal technologies through which skilled workers and unskilled laborers can produce cheap and standardized machine-made products for a mass market. Industrial development in such a system can be measured in purely quantitative terms by the growth in wealth and population.

Industrialism, ushered in by an industrial revolution, had passed through three successive stages of development: the manufacturing, expansionist, and financial (Geddes 1904b, 82; Branford and Geddes 1919b, ch. 1.4). Each stage is marked by the dominance of a particular organizing class or elite that forms the "chiefs" of temporal power. First the manufacturer was the dominant force, then the bureaucrat rose to prominence, and finally the financier achieved a dominant position (Branford and Geddes 1919b, 42).

The era of the financier is the high point of the paleotechnic stage of standardization, mass production, and rational calculability. In the manufacturing or mechanical stage of industrialism production is the key social activity and the economy is organized around the factory and the machine. "Capitalist" manufacturers, as the owners and masters of industrial workshops and factories, are the dominating force and the mechanical age has as its central structural principle the opposition of capital to labor. The manufacturing capitalist—as the embodiment of monetary and physical capital—exercises power over labor through a coordinated division of labor and authority that ties the worker to the machinery (V. V. Branford 1919a, 7; Branford and Geddes 1919b, 38). The relations among individual capitalists, each pursuing their individual profit, are, on the other hand, regulated only through market exchange and the allocation of resources.

The movement of businesses into larger national and international markets, requires a greater scale of production and transforms the mechanical stage into the expansionist stage of industrialism. In this stage, the central economic activity is no longer production but market trading. Trade grows through the operations of large national enterprises and, as a result, the managers standing at the tops of their large centralized hierarchies of command and regulation became the dominant social force (Geddes and Slater 1917, 106–107). Their power base lies not in property per se but in bureaucratic structures of authority. In the second age of industrialism, then, the ruling elite comes to comprise an amalgam of bureaucrats and manufacturers, under the leadership of the former. Large mining and trading monopolies expand into the tropics and transform colonies from sources of luxury goods into sources of industrial raw materials.

The introduction and growing importance of financial devices in business organization initiates a third stage of industrialism. Shares, debentures, and other securities become the means through which productive and commercial units can be combined into monopolistic trusts that earn their profits from a flow of interest and dividend payments rather than directly from actual production or trading. This credit system has, in contemporary societies, become organized around loans and the hugely increased use of check payments and the clearing system. This has become the means through which large enterprises can coordinate the production and commercial activities that take place in geographically dispersed factories and offices. Large numbers of undertakings can be controlled through the manipulation of paper claims and concessions, underpinning the growing power of those who operate through the stock exchange, the banking system, and the ever more extensive system of credit and taxation (Branford and Geddes 1919b, 42). This involves critical changes in the financial system itself. Merchants who deal in goods and also handle bills of lading, warehouse warrants, and bills of exchange become merchant bankers. Merchant banks that abandon the trade in physical goods to concentrate exclusively on dealing in credit instruments become true bankers and begin to engage in share issuing, investment management, and other financial activities. Competition for business among bankers had led to a concentration of credit in the hands of a small number of large banks and the expansion of their securities business, along with the concentration and amalgamation of businesses of all types. This transforms the banker into a financier (V. V. Branford 1923, 139). Financiers and bankers exercise temporal power through their control over the credit system rather than through the direct personal ownership of capital. The spread of investments through the extensive networks of the financial system brings about a global interconnection that encourages a "cosmopolitanism" (Geddes and Slater 1917, 122) among financiers.

Directly echoing Veblen, Branford and Geddes saw the financiers as "pecuniary experts" involved in the strategic management of economy-wide "interstitial relations" among companies through interweaving shareholdings and interlocking directorships. In the financial stage, purely financial concerns in major enterprises are separated from the technical aspects of material production and their directors and top executives become concerned exclusively with the status of the balance sheet and the financial profitability of their businesses. The financiers and large investors operate through subordinate ranks of stockbrokers, solicitors, barristers, and smaller bankers who act as their agents but also benefit directly from the credit system.[6] They have no significant involvement in, or knowledge of, the production processes through which that profitability is generated and so have little concern for the actual products placed on the market. Purely technical matters are devolved to specialist engineers and technicians who must operate within the tight constraints of a pecuniary culture that subordinates their technical knowledge and skills to the requirements and interests of the financiers (V. V. Branford 1923, 151–52).

Branford saw the credit mechanism and accounting systems of the financial age establishing a system of social control through indebtedness (V. V. Branford 1919a, 44). The population as a whole is enmeshed in an extensive system of indebtedness that constitutes a predatory or "parasitic" system that secures the private advantages of a leisure class at the expense of ordinary workers. This class benefits disproportionately from the wasteful operations of the credit system (V. V. Branford 1923, 99). Those who benefit from the system form an extensive "leisure class" with the financiers at its core (Branford and Geddes 1919b, 45; Veblen 1899). This leisure class, as the chiefs of the paleotechnic age, comprises the ruling elite of chiefs: the dominant financiers, bureaucrats, and entrepreneurs in alliance with those who hold the top positions within the state. The balance between the various elements within the ruling elite varies from one society to another. In contemporary Germany they saw state officials holding the dominant position, while in the United States they point to the overriding dominance of big business.

The outlook of the financier comprises a systematic ideology of calculative, instrumental rationality, rooted in the larger rationality of the Western cultural tradition. Drawing on utilitarian philosophy, it is a cult of profiteering organized as a policy of laissez-faire (Branford and Geddes 1919a, v). Economic power is organized through a narrow, sectional profiteering that is itself rooted in the competitive drive to monopoly. According to Branford, the financier does not raise his or her mind above the level of everyday economic routine to consider anything properly spiritual. The financier "remains too much of a mere empiricist to be conscious of his mental processes, and so but half develops his coordinating powers: he is too intent on the making or maintenance of his private fortune to be free from bias in the allocation of credits, even if trained to scrutinize its social repercussions" (V. V. Branford 1923, 98).

The separation of science and religion in the Renaissance created the conditions for a growth in technical, instrumental knowledge and the building of a secular, pecuniary culture (V. V. Branford 1923, 37). The expansion of temporal power through the system of finance consolidated the pecuniary culture and finally undermined the autonomy and influence of spiritual reflection. The spiritual power of religion had been in decline since the medieval period and the church was no longer a vibrant source of spiritual values and ideas. Financiers had, in effect, usurped the cultural authority of the church by making their pecuniary culture the dominant cultural force in modern society. The financial system and its values become self-sustaining and lack any critical challenge from independent sources of spiritual power. It is difficult to escape the influence of this dominant cultural outlook; all personal values are measured in terms of material wealth, and society as a whole is marked by a materialistic "Mammonism." This pecuniary materialism limits the possibilities for any consideration of wider social goals.

Branford and Geddes diagnosed the early stages of a process described much later by Habermas (1981b) as the "colonization" of the institutions of spiritual power (the lifeworld) by the system of temporal power (the "system"). The temporal chiefs that comprise the ruling elite—the controllers of the state and capitalist enterprises—extend their influence over the institutions that nurture the initiators and the energizers. The school and university intellectuals who ought to initiate ideas and the emotionals of the arts and the press who ought to energize social motivations and commitments each lack any significant cultural influence. It is, instead, financiers who control newspapers through ownership and advertising revenue and education through the endowment of chairs in universities.[7]

Branford and Geddes paid particular attention to the direct financial influence over ideas that is made possible by the advertising system and the profits derived from the sale of advertising space. Newspapers aim to maximize their circulation among those who are the potential purchasers of the products advertised in their pages. This means that editorial and other staff are recruited in so far as they are "whole heartedly devoted to the maintenance, furtherance and development of the pecuniary culture" (V. V. Branford 1923, 142; 1919a, 36). Through an immense growth in consumer advertising in the press and on street hoardings, advertising has become the "characteristic spiritual institution" of the financial age. The purchasing of publicity and celebrity builds "an appeal to the will through the intellect and the emotions" (Branford and Geddes 1919b, 55).

Financial control over the press is manifest in the ways in which news and entertainment are presented. Newspaper coverage of sport, for example, places particular emphasis on the results of games and races and their implications for gambling, and the sports pages appear as extensions of the reports on the financial markets. Readers are encouraged to adopt a calculative, instrumental orientation in all matters, whether this be share prices, football results, or horse racing, and to see everything in relation to its financial implications: "Thus do preoccupations with the market picture spread and extend into hours of leisure and times of relaxation amongst all classes" (V. V. Branford 1923, 142). At the same time, news reports in the "yellow press" pander to the "herd instinct,"[8] introducing the emotional sway of opinion into press reports. Serious theatre had, in a similar way, been largely transformed into the populism of the music hall.

The intellectual, if dull, culture of the liberal age had been transformed into systematic, disciplined forms of education combined with irrational and emotionally charged leisure. This "debased" cultural outlook comes to be embedded in the practices of the educational system and is promoted through school and university curriculums (Branford 1926b, 57–58). Education is standardized and uniform, establishing a "disciplined docility" of the masses enforced by the school board and the school inspector.

In all these ways, financiers attain "a certain mastery of public opinion" (Branford and Geddes 1919b, 58). The mass of the working people are socialized into the social outlook of the financier and the legitimacy of the financial system. In "demanding" the products of the industrial system because of their socialization into consumer "acquisitiveness," they reinforce the tenets of its utilitarian, pecuniary culture (V. V. Branford 1923, 37). Thus, people live wastefully as they consume indiscriminately and in unfocused ways. They collect fancy bric-a-brac, insist on an unnecessary high quality finish in goods, require irrelevant standards of service and richness in food, fill their time with trivial clubs and leisure pursuits, and read poor-quality books and magazines that convey mere titbits of knowledge. These rather puritan judgments on the growth of mass culture were, as they were later to be seen by Adorno and Horkheimer (1944), grounded in a recognition of the standardizing and alienating effects of the nascent system of mass communications.

POLITICAL FORCES IN THE FINANCIAL ERA

In their contribution to the "Making of the Future" series, Branford and Geddes traced the consequences of these cultural changes for the development of contemporary political forces. In the manufacturing stage, they held, liberalism was the political counterpart of the economic laissez-faire of the entrepreneurs. Relations among capitalists and between capitalists and workers were expressed in a competitive system of party politics in which politicians competed through an electoral mechanism for seats in parliamentary assemblies. The expansionary phase of industrialism saw the development of a political strategy of imperialism as national business interests extended their interests across the globe and expanded the influence of their nation-states. This massive expansion of state power led to a decay in civility and a decline in the regional influence of cities as centralized structures of political administration consolidated the ascendancy of national ministers over regional politicians. This was a tendency for which they adopted the current term of "Zabernitis."[9]

Branford and Geddes saw the emergence of a "Party of Order" or "Party of Convention" during the first decades of the twentieth century as the liberal and imperialist chiefs coalesced with the financial organizers to form a single political force (Branford and Geddes 1919b, 62; V. V. Branford 1923, 101). This, they argue, is a political movement of the Right, which follows a conservative strategy of reaction and readily resorts to repression to pursue its interests. The exercise of political power tends ever more toward coercion, force, and despotism, a "cult of force" epitomized in the "Prussianism" of statecraft and the Machiavellianism of international diplomacy. Prussianism—"Hegelian Caesarism"—might be "taken neat or diluted with the muddy waters of the Isis" (V. V. Branford 1919a, 28). That is, it might appear in its original German form or in the justifications of the imperial state produced by Oxford idealist social philosophers and New Liberals such as Green (1879), Bosanquet (1899), and Jones (1910). A similar political outlook is apparent in the state socialism of Fabians and other progressive politicians. The groups and organizations that make up the Party of Order, Branford and Geddes argue, are driving the industrial system toward militarism and aggressive "wardom." The major cities become "war capitals," foci of economic and political power through which taxes and interest payments are mobilized to sustain the war machines of the financiers (Geddes and Slater 1917; Geddes 1915b). Paleotechnic society comes to be organized around *Kriegspiel*—war games—and the destructive tendencies of greed, competition, ignorance, and hate (Branford and Geddes 1919a, 60).

Each temporal elite arouses characteristic forms of political opinion among the "people." When opposition can be organized as "insurgent" groups that stand in the vanguard of social change, the chiefs must face a challenge from outside the sphere of conventional politics. During the manufacturing stage, liberal capitalists were opposed by "radical" factory workers who were excluded from conventional electoral politics and had organized themselves into trades unions. During the imperialist stage, political opposition entered the state itself, with "socialists" such as the Fabians pursuing the interests of labor through centralized policies of collectivist administration that appealed to populations organized as taxpayers and standing armies. In the financial stage, the principal focus of opposition shifts to the proletarianized and financially subordinate workers who are politically organized as "anarchists" and Bolsheviks. As a Party of Order is formed from the dominant political forces, so radicals, socialists, and anarchists are increasingly fused into a single opposition movement as a rival "Party of Progress" or "Party of Insurgence" (Branford and Geddes 1919b, 59, 62; V. V. Branford 1919a, 38). This is a movement of the Left that tends increasingly to pursue nihilistic, negative opposition toward the dominating power of the Party of Order (see Table 8.1).

The political alignments of the financial age, then, involve a polarization between reactionary and revolutionary movements, each formed into parties and organizations that carry forward their projects. This polarization is the basis of the economic and political crisis that Branford and Geddes diagnosed as the cause of contemporary social breakdown and disequilibrium. The outcome of this clash of social tendencies varies with the balance of power between the two political forces. When the balance shifts toward order, a drift toward warfare is most likely. When the balance shifts towards insurgency, on the other hand, the drift is toward revolution. The financial age, then, is marked by a "tendency to explosive disintegration" through war or revolution. It was in this light that Branford and Geddes interpreted the drift toward European warfare in 1914 and the outbreak of the revolutions in Central Europe and Russia toward its end (V. V. Branford 1919a, 43; Branford and Geddes 1919b, 64, 65–67).

Branford anticipated that Britain could avoid social disintegration if a leading role could be taken by a party committed to a route that is neither capitalist nor socialist. Such a "Party of the Third Alternative" would be oriented to "peacedom" rather than wardom and so could promote an "eirenicon"—a concrete peace proposal—to moderate between the negative and destructive poles of revolution and reaction (Branford 1920; V. V. Branford 1923, 101). This conception of a "Third Way" had been identified some

Table 8.1. Temporal Power Alignments

Chiefs: conventional politics	Workers: insurgent politics	Structural principle
Liberals	Radicals	Manufacturing age: profit
Imperialists	Socialists	Imperial age: organization
Financiers	Anarchists	Financial age: credit
Party of Order (Reaction)	Party of Progress (Revolution)	

years before by Branford (1914a). He was the first person to use the phrase in this way, using it in a discussion of university education in which he argued for the need to avoid the "fictitious dilemma" of choosing between private and public careers.[10] In characteristic prose, and citing a verse remembered from his childhood, he wrote that

> there is open for travel that Third Way that was shown to Thomas Rhymer. He was shown the two Ways we know so well—"the narrow road, so thick beset wi' thorns and briers" and "the braid, braid road"—but also a third:—
>
> > And see ye not that bonny road
> > That winds aboot the ferny brae?
> > That is the road to fair Elfland
> > Where thou and I this night main gae!
> > (Branford 1914a, 341).[11]

The social basis of the Third Alternative is to be found neither in the temporal chiefs nor in the mass of workers. Rather, it is provided by four groups: the mass of the "dispossessed poor" who stand outside the ranks of organized labor, the professional classes who stand outside the sphere of speculative investment, the clergy, intellectuals, artists, and other "emotionals," and women working at home who are excluded from temporal power and referred to as the "queens of home" (V. V. Branford 1919b, 144; 1926b, 95). The temporally dispossessed and their rising spiritual inspirers and mobilizers are the key agents of rational social change.

The social change sought by the carriers of the Third Alternative is rational because it is scientifically guided. A scientific understanding of the actual tendencies of social change allows a eutopian vision of the future and a realistic assessment of the mechanisms of reconstruction and renewal. In the political context of the financial age, Branford and Geddes saw the organizations and agencies of the Third Alternative building on existing social tendencies and bringing into being a "neotechnic" age that resolves the crisis of paleotechnic industrialism. Actual tendencies in this direction were seen as inherent in the greater command over national energies that have been made possible by the use of electricity and by its implications for the organization of work. In its turn, education and civic solidarity can be transformed through the technically and creatively skilled work of the designer and the engineer, the architect, and the improver. These tendencies of change are not confined by existing national boundaries but are global in character, and the global orientation of the protagonists of the new age will ensure that it is a truly "Geotechnic" age (Geddes 1905a, 171).

THE SEARCH FOR A MIDDLE WAY

The politics of the Third Alternative was one of a number of political doctrines that drew inspiration from Ruskin's medievalism (V. V. Branford 1919a, 30). Many on the Left in Britain had become disenchanted with Fabian socialism and the bureaucratic and centralized administrative mechanisms being pursued through the Labour Party. Many sought a more pluralistic and less state-centered socialism that would provide a middle or third way between liberal individualism and state centralism. The Independent Labour Party provided an attractive alternative for some, but those who had come to Labour politics through their commitments to the ideals of Ruskin and Morris were more attracted by the renewed interest in medievalism introduced in Arthur Penty's (1906) book *The Restoration of the Guild System*.

Penty was an architect involved in the Garden Cities movement who, inspired by Ashbee's adoption of Ruskin's values, enthused over the aesthetic ideals he found in medieval guild craftsmanship. The social problems generated by industrial technology, he held, were incapable of solution under the existing economic conditions. Stability and social order could be reestablished only if the complex division of labor were to be abandoned and a return made to medieval practices of small-scale craft work. This led him to advocate "guild socialism" as a pluralistic alternative to Fabianism. Guild socialism developed as a recognizable political doctrine from 1912 after Alfred Orage launched a debate on Penty's ideas in his periodical *The New Age*.[12] Recognizing some parallels with French syndicalism, Orage saw the guild idea as providing an alternative to centralized policies of economic reorganization. It was, therefore, a middle way between centralized socialism and individualistic capitalism that was compatible with the values of Ruskin, Carlyle, and Morris. Orage commissioned a series of anonymous articles—actually written by Sam Hobson—that were republished in book form (Hobson 1914). G. D. H. Cole worked towards similar ideas, setting these out in a series of influential books on the political role of trades unions (Cole 1913, 1917). In 1915, together with Maurice Reckitt, he formed the National Guilds League to promote these new ideas (see Bechhofer and Reckitt 1918).[13]

The guild socialists proposed the formation of autonomous guilds of specialized producers as the collective organizations through which work could be moralized and workers would be able to contribute creatively to communal life. National politics was to be reconstructed through the direct "functional" representation of these guilds in corporatist chambers. Functional associations based in productive, civic, cultural, and other social activities were to be organized on a local basis into "communes," each sending its representatives to regional and national chambers. These chambers were to be the foundations of a pluralistic system of power in which central government was limited to the role of regulator or arbitrator among the independent chambers and guilds. Cole made this the basis of a comprehensive social theory that saw any society as "a complex of associations" (Cole 1920a, 12). Guild socialism, in this strong form, proved a short-lived political movement and many of its main proponents moved further leftward during the 1920s. It was abandoned by Cole who, along with Raymond Postgate and Rajani Palme Dutt, became a prominent advocate of Leninist communism, and established the Communist Party of Great Britain.

Penty's ideas had also proved attractive to those on the Right whose strong religious commitments had led them to see this medievalism and its encouragement of small-scale property ownership as the basis for a reestablishment of a distinctively Catholic social order. The roots of this Catholic social doctrine are to be found in the social policy that Cardinal Henry Manning had urged on Pope Leo XIII for his landmark encyclical of 1891 that advocated the recognition of trades unions and the granting to them of autonomous powers on a principle of subsidiarity.[14] Manning himself had translated and popularized the papal teachings (Manning 1891) and exercised a strong influence in wider Christian circles. The Spanish writer Ramiro de Maeztu produced a fusion of this doctrine with elements of guild socialism in a series of articles for *The New Age* (1916).[15] De Maeztu's ideas influenced Reckitt and Penty to modify their national guilds policy into a form of Christian socialism (Penty 1923; and the later Reckitt 1932; see also Peart-Binns 1988),[16] but the key thinkers to develop these ideas were Hilaire Belloc and G. K. Chesterton, whose emphasis on the redistribution of property led to their doctrine being called "distributism,"

Belloc had visited Manning frequently as a young man, and after Manning's death in 1892 he felt obliged to carry forward Manning's social ideas. He saw the principles of the medieval church, as formulated by Manning, as a necessary condition for the construction of a new social order. These ideas were developed after a brief and disillusioning parliamentary career as a Liberal MP from 1906 to 1910. Belloc developed his critique of party politics with Cecil and Gilbert Chesterton, two Anglo-Catholic brothers who later converted to Roman Catholicism. A general social critique (Chesterton 1910) was followed by a critique of the parliamentary system as dominated by a financial oligarchy that blocks any chance of real freedom and democracy (Belloc and Chesterton 1911). However, it was in Belloc's *Servile State* (1912) that the distributist solution was most fully developed (Carlson 2007; Corrin 1987).

Belloc argued that the Christianization of Europe had made possible the medieval society of free peasant proprietors—a societal condition that Belloc called the distributive state. He argued that property was distributed such that most families are property owners and production is regulated by self-governing corporations of property-owning producers. The slow and gradual development of capitalism had reconcentrated property in the hands of the few and had destroyed the autonomy and liberty of the producers (Belloc 1912, 51–52). The growth of monopolies and trusts in the late nineteenth century had enlarged the gulf between the wealthy few of truly free individuals and the degraded mass of producers. The concentration of property under capitalism generates advantages for the leisured few at the expense of the many who work on their behalf. Belloc concluded that capitalism tends toward the establishment of a "servile state" in which labor is reduced to a state of slavery (1912, 17). This tendency toward servility, he argued, was most marked in Prussia and England, where the Protestant Reformation had had its greatest effects. It was least marked in strongly Catholic countries such as France and Ireland. Belloc anticipated an outbreak of war between these two variants of capitalism and hoped that such a war would seriously weaken the move toward the servile state.

The distributists held that Fabian opposition to capitalism was merely reinforcing its tendency toward servility through the creation of a centralized command system. For this reason, the collectivist response of transferring property to the state and its political officers offered no real solution to the social crisis. Only a distributist solution in which property is transferred directly to individual citizens could offer any realistic chance of ending the drift toward servility. Distributism, like guild socialism, was presented as a third way between the capitalist and collectivist routes to the servile state. The foundations of the new social order were to come about through a huge increase in the numbers of independent and autonomous shopkeepers, craft workers, and farmers. The distributist strategy was to bring about a redistribution of property from the few to the many not through coercive expropriation but through modifications to the credit and taxation systems. By subsidizing small savings and taxing large-scale ownership there would, over time, be a shift in the pattern of ownership and so an alteration in the structure of opportunities open to the mass of the people (Belloc 1912, 110–11).

These distributist views were promoted through the National League for Clean Government—set up shortly after the publication of Belloc's book—which was renamed the New Witness League and then, in 1926, the Distributist League.[17] Concrete policy details had been in rather short supply in Belloc's work, and the League was the means through which there was an attempt to formulate more specific proposals. Its membership was, however, quite diverse, including advocates of credit unions and cooperatives together with activists in rural communes such as that at Ditchling in Sussex. Although they were united by the view that property distribution and the system of credit were the basic problems to be addressed, they differed as to whether reform should be implemented through guilds, cooperatives, or communes. Penty himself had moved from guild socialism to a position much closer to that of the distributists, describing his new position as an advocate of "post-industrialism" (Penty 1922).

Guild socialists and distributists seemed to offer a radical alternative to both Fabian socialism and Soviet communism, both of which placed their hopes in large organizations and state collectivism. Indeed, the affinities were such that many Fabians were attracted to the communist solution (Webb and Webb 1920, 1935). The new programs were united by the desire for a middle way politics in which the pluralism and autonomy of small producer and retailer collectives was guaranteed through larger-scale organizations responsive to their interests and requirements.

COOPERATION AND CREDIT

These "third way" or "middle way" approaches to politics resonated directly with the ideas on the collective organization of consumers into cooperatives that Patrick Geddes and Victor Branford had long advocated. As they developed their Third Alternative, they drew on both guild socialist and distributist ideas, stressing the overriding need for a collective reorganization of the financial system into a system of social credit and cooperation. Parallel views on social reconstruction as an expression of spiritual renewal were outlined by associates within the Theosophical Society (Guest 1912; Besant 1914) and by Rudolf Steiner (1919).

Central to the Third Alternative was the "resorption" of government through the transfer of power to the lowest level possible, allowing authority to be built up from the bottom. Thus, power is to be distributed to localities and work organizations, to cities and guilds, and these are all to participate in national and international federations. This devolution of power is to be complemented by a transformation of private credit into social credit through making finance available at lower rates for public investment and with the allocation of credit being administered but not controlled by bankers. These temporal reforms, taken together, were seen as the bases on which cities would be able to plan improvements in the environment and could encourage the renewal of community spirit by institutionalizing the ethos of the town planner and the "spirit creative" that ensures the aesthetic principles of design are followed. If civic politics were to be the means for humanizing the environment, then guilds and professional associations were to be the means through which work could be humanized and made into a meaningful activity. There would be a shift from a "money-economy" to a "life-economy," with individuals becoming more fully social in their activity through adopting the ethos of the artist-craftsman. Finally, education would be organized in relation to civic organization and civic purpose, enabling people to learn from their region and contribute to its development. This is the key to the renewal and extension of spiritual power that underpins all other aspects of social reconstruction (V. V. Branford 1921b, xiv–xv).

The view that Branford and Geddes developed of the need to reform the credit system was rooted in the economic theories they had set out around the turn of the century. Geddes (1881) had begun to explore the foundations of economics when, in 1883, he came across the work of the leading marginalist economist Leon Walras, with whom he subsequently corresponded. Through Walras he discovered the work of both Stanley Jevons and Carl Menger. Geddes (1884a) rejected the marginalist avoidance of physical, biological, and psychological mechanisms and their reliance on exclusively formal, hypothetical models of action. He sought, instead, an invariant measure of value—as had Marx—and could not be satisfied with a focus simply on "exchange value." Utility theory, he argued, had to be based on an understanding of the physiology of human labor and he began to draw ideas from Peter Tait's (1864) summary of the work of Clausius and Joule that had stimulated a school of "social energetics."[18] Geddes combined this approach with what he had learned from Ruskin (1861, 1862; see Geddes 1884b), who had criticized economics for ignoring human aesthetic needs and who had argued that the intrinsic value of an object is to be found in its ability to support life both in its physical and its aesthetic or cultural dimension.

Economic value, for Geddes, reflects the contribution of an object to subsistence and the satisfaction of culturally formed desires. He thus distinguished between the "necessary" (physical) and "super-necessary" components in consumption (Geddes 1888b). Taking up a classification of the sources of energy, he showed that the amount of energy varies directly with the stage of material production, from the Stone Age through the Bronze and Iron Ages to the industrial "Age of Energy." The combination of the physical and cultural dimensions of labor was later to reappear in the distinction between the "rustic" process and the "civic" process in human development. This view of the stages of production, he argued, could be combined with a sectoral classification of economic activity to produce physical input-output tables in which the physical and the culturally variable aspects of labor were combined.

Branford drew on this argument in his attempt to articulate a theoretical basis for accountancy in constructing national accounts. He proposed that accountants devise ways of measuring changes in "social value" by "the sum of mechanical energy expended directly on matter by the collective efforts of a given nation during the year" (Branford 1901b, 399; 1901c, 29). Such a measure, he held, would make it possible to use units of energy to calculate the distortions introduced into systems of production by capital organized as credit. To eliminate the reliance on private credit, Branford advocated the formation of small-scale credit societies able to mobilize the available savings of the working classes and small savers and so to build up a "national banking fund" (Branford 1901a).

Branford developed these ideas further in 1910, when he proposed a central cooperative credit agency as a mechanism for coordinating national credit. Reflecting on the success of the cooperative principle in the Irish Agricultural Organisation Society, he argued for a unification of landholding societies, trading societies, and credit unions within a Central Cooperative Credit Agency. The agency was to be owned by the constituent cooperative societies, whose holdings would be underwritten by long-term government credit and who would use the agency to provide for their credit needs (Branford 1910).[19] In 1914, Branford argued that an extension of the system of national credit set up in Britain in the early months of World War I could bring about a larger postwar mobilization of the credit system for social investment by effectively turning the credit system "inside-out" as a means of promoting small-scale enterprise (Branford 1914b). This wartime system made the Bank of England responsible for managing state guarantees that would underwrite the creditworthiness of the private banking system and so maintain levels of investment and productivity in the socially necessary industries unable to secure commercial funding. Branford proposed the establishment of a similar system based on cooperative guarantees to mobilize credit for small-scale undertakings. This would, he argued, allow the "organisation of credit for small people" and the "financing of *petite culture*" (Branford 1914b, 309–10).

The "sporadic initiatives" of the wartime system included the grants, loans, and scholarships given for activities that were not immediately or sectionally profitable, and Branford identified these as illustrating the possibilities that would be offered by a system of national credit. His main examples of the mechanisms through which these could be delivered came from the cooperative movement. He highlighted both the cooperative credit systems operated by the Agricultural Organisation Societies set up in Ireland by Horace Plunkett and Thomas Finlay and in England by Nugent Harris, and the cooperative housing schemes, Garden Cities, and co-partnership schemes with which Sybella Branford had been involved. The cooperative and commune savings banks of rural Germany, he held, also provided a powerful example of what could be achieved through such means. Branford's (1899) report on the West Indian cooperatives had shown that producer cooperatives could provide credit for investment in further production, but he now also saw the need for a more extensive cooperative system that could compete with capitalist enterprises. Sybella Branford was, in parallel, developing some ideas about national credit based on her involvement in rural cooperatives. Noting that the real demand for housing in rural areas greatly exceeded the supply, she aimed to rectify the failure of existing commercial mechanisms and proposed a trades union–guaranteed investment fund that would allow "a return to something corresponding to the guild system of the middle ages" (S. Branford 1915, 50). Short accounts of developments in rural credit were produced by Victor Branford's business associates John Ross (1921) and Frederick Lisman (1922) in support of this view.

The wartime crisis, Branford argued, had highlighted the need to integrate the earlier credit initiatives with the system of financial regulation operated by the Bank of England. He argued that a national council of bankers should be supplemented by a council representing the cooperative system. This mechanism of corporatist, functional political representation would be the basis for a "socialising of finance" (Branford 1914b, 310). The returns to capital, whether as profit, interest, or rent, would be limited and this would free up credit for public purposes. The system would bring together representatives of the workers and the professionals who supply goods and services, the accountants who record and balance credits and debits,[20] and the bankers who allocate credit to alternative uses (Branford 1914b, 312–13). Bank credit would be issued at low "insurance" rates, rather than conventional high interest rates. Key agencies in this reconstructed system would be cooperative banks that "manufacture credit not for sale, but for use, and moreover for direct use by the productive group" (V. V. Branford 1919b, 149; 1917). Bankers have typically been concerned with promoting the well-being of one particular kind of "society"—the joint stock company—but they must become involved also in promoting the well-being of such societies as the village, the town, the city, and the nation. The pioneering cooperatives were concerned with the reconstruction and improvement of the environments within which people lived, and this had to be made the aim of the whole national credit system. The system must promote not merely economic efficiency but also an "ennobling and dignifying of life" that furthers "genuinely creative work" (Branford 1914b, 311). By expanding education for citizenship, the Third Alternative creates the possibility for a "resorption" of government into society, achieving the goals of local and regional autonomy pursued by the anarchists (Branford 1914a, 319). This involves a "renewal" of society (Sandeman 1913).

While Branford was clear about the general principles involved in a democratic and cooperative system of credit, he was less clear about the specific mechanisms through which these could be implemented. Indeed, his proposals for the immediate postwar situation were rather naive and unrealistic. He proposed that postwar social reconstruction could be financed through the public use of all private investment income for one year: in effect, a one-off supertax on property ownership (V. V. Branford 1921a, 88–89). This capital, he held, could be used for social betterment and for building an awareness of working toward the common good. Needs in housing, industrial development, and social welfare could be met from allocations to individuals and enterprises made by local boards of accountants, bankers, and social workers. Needs for cultural improvement, aesthetic and scientific, could be met through boards recruited from the energizers and intellectuals. Scientific and intellectual advances would be furthered through capital allocations made by a board of critical intellectuals willing to break with current schools of thought and to consider novel approaches. Aesthetic improvement was to be controlled by artists and craftsmen, together with "a motherly woman of the people, one of the humbler clergy, and, perhaps a civic sociologist" (V. V. Branford 1921a, 91). Branford saw the two spiritual boards also taking on a broader remit and being organized as, respectively, a council of recreation and a council of social survey. The two councils would work jointly with the temporal powers in regional "soviets."

This quaint and, so far as women are concerned, rather patronizing view reflected Branford's naivety in practical political matters. His adoption of the terminology of the "soviet" reflected the wide recognition of the progressive features of the Russian revolution then current on the Left. However, the broad conclusion is clear: the allocation of credit should not be seen in merely financial terms and had to be seen in a wider context of those who are the stakeholders in the eutopian future of humanity. There needed to be a moderating of the temporal interests of the financiers and a complementing of this through a newly constituted system of spiritual boards. While Branford abandoned the idea of the one-off supertax in his subsequent writings, the organizational framework for the "expert" allocation of funds was retained.

Branford and Geddes also saw social renewal as something that might, paradoxically, develop out of the experience of war. In time of war, the army recruit feels part of a social organization geared toward collective ends and so is able to transcend the individualism of ordinary economic and political life. War appeals to the soldier's incipient sense of idealism and calls him to duties and sacrifice in the name of a greater good:

> An army in action is an extraordinary synergy, a solidarity of feeling, a combination of individual action all dramatically intensified, of which peace has not yet found the secret. (Geddes and Slater 1917, 48)

The building of a lasting peace requires a mobilization of this idealism and altruism and the "spiritual awakening" fostered by war, using them as a means to both social reconstruction and spiritual renewal (Geddes and Slater 1917, 60). Peacetime reconstruction requires the "moral equivalents of war" that can bring about a spiritual "conversion" of wardom into the altruism and social solidarity that would ensure a successful reconstruction of the credit system (V. V. Branford 1919a, 45) and would enhance "social uplift" through the arts and sciences, recreation, and leisure as well as through production. The key thing, he held, was to move from a centralized credit system, to a decentralized, regional one. There must be local credit associations, housing associations, and cooperative retailers (Branford 1926b, 102, 104). Sybella Branford echoed these ideas, holding that the crucial question was: "[C]an the general character of our civilization be changed to one in which the energies of all the more active participants are more or less consciously directed to social ends" (S. Branford 1924, 128). This "social vision," she argued, must come through the building of a social consensus that would inform the use of social resources.

Victor Branford's brother Benchara set out an alternative view of the institutional organization of the Third Alternative (B. Branford 1919). He saw the coming polity as one that would combine "occupational" and "geographical" principles of political representation in a bicameral system of representation, and advocated the establishment of a parliament or grand council comprising an occupational chamber of production and a geographical chamber of consumption. The chamber of production was to be elected by occupational guilds while the chamber of consumption would represent people as individual consumers in geographical constituencies of cities and regions. The idea was that diverse occupational interests in a particular locality or region would be integrated through the geographical constituency, while geographical differences would be integrated through the functional chamber that brings together all those in a particular occupation, regardless of their geographical location (B. Branford 1919, 103).

The Sandemans (1919) drew on the experience of Ashbee's communal workshops and saw the cooperative principle at work as involving communal property in workshops, offices, clubrooms, and dwellings, run by workers elected to a committee responsible for the organization of work and all activities of the community, including schools and leisure activities. The occupational and geographical unity depicted by Benchara Branford is the federation of such cooperative work communities.

Within this overall structure, Benchara Branford held that the guild of bankers should hold a key role. In a reorganized system of national credit, bankers, as technical experts, would be liberated from the control of the financiers and could play the social role set out for them by Saint-Simon and Comte. Bankers, involved in each chamber, are to be the managers of the system of taxation and credit, operating according to evolving ideas of "public credit that renew medieval principles of distribution" (B. Branford 1919, 111–12).

Benchara Branford thought that this structure should be repeated at each political level from the regional through the national to the international. He placed particular emphasis on the formation of a world parliament that would, as an enlarged League of Nations, be representative of all nations, and he held that emerging geopolitical blocs—European, Asian, and African—must be organized into the larger global body. In this way, individuals are able to act as true "Cosmopolitans" or world citizens (B. Branford 1919, 155).

FROM NATIONAL CREDIT TO SOCIAL CREDIT

An important influence on the politics of Geddes and Branford was the emerging doctrine of social credit that had begun to appear in the pages of *The New Age* (See Hutchinson and Burkitt 1997).[21] Orage's commitment to guild socialism had weakened during World War I, and the trade depression and unemployment that followed seemed to him to expose the limits of any political strategy that failed to address the issue of the aggregate level of demand and investment in an economy. He explored the early underconsumptionist arguments of Hobson (Mumery and Hobson 1889) and Arthur Kitson (1894) and was attracted to the arguments of Clifford Douglas, which he published in a series of articles on credit during 1919. It was through these articles that Branford first got to know Douglas. The articles were soon reprinted in book form (Douglas 1921a,b) and were rapidly followed by a much fuller statement (Douglas 1924). Where distributism came to be seen during the 1920s as an increasingly right-wing form of Third Way, medievalist corporatism and Douglas's social credit came to be seen as the more progressive strands in this complex of ideas.

Douglas's ideas were forged through his reflections on wartime conditions. He saw the years leading up to World War I and the wartime period itself as having significantly expanded the productive capacity of the factory system. Once the war was over, he felt, it would be possible to shift this productive capacity to peaceful purposes and to produce, on a huge scale, almost any article that it was possible to imagine. However, the total of articles that could potentially be produced could not actually be absorbed by consumers, as the financial resources available for the purchase of the goods is insufficient.

This argument rested on the view that the use of advanced technology in the production of any commodity increases overheads (selling costs, advertising, profits) relative to the direct labor costs involved in production. In an industrial economy, then, the "factory cost" is always greater than the cost of labor and raw materials, and the ratio of overheads to direct costs is always increasing. At an aggregate economic level, total overheads increase relative to total labor inputs. However, purchasing power is directly proportional to labor costs—it represents the money wages received—so it will always fall below the level necessary to buy the produced goods on the open market. For this reason, "the world's production is continuously growing more and more in excess of the capacity to absorb or liquidate it" (Douglas 1918, 151); there is always a tendency to underconsumption.

Douglas concluded that there is inevitably a structural contradiction between centralized technology and centralized capital. The technological advance of the forces of production, to use Marxian terminology, generates crises of underconsumption because the structure of control over capital distributes purchasing power inappropriately. Bankers use other people's money to lend to producers and earn a profit that they can then lend again. The depositors are denied any substantial return on their own money and so are defrauded of its potential purchasing power. The financial structure of the credit system—the "ticket system"—generates an artificial scarcity and establishes a "society of restriction." Capital is mobilized and controlled in such a way that there is a "constant filching of purchasing power" from the individual citizen to the financier (Douglas 1921b, 79; 1924, 88). The fact that individual borrowers have to repay loans and pay interest reduces their purchasing capacity.

Douglas saw the specific credit mechanisms required by this new system as a citizenship stakeholder model of national resources (see Douglas 1924). According to this model, all individuals, as citizens, are stockholders in the material and cultural resources on which the productive capacity of their society depends.[22] Individual citizens have a stake in the "inalienable and unsaleable" stock of resources. Such resources are their common property and so they are entitled to a "dividend" on their virtual share in the cultural heritage. This dividend, he argued, represents the surplus appropriated by the financiers as overheads and if distributed to individual citizens would enable them to purchase the whole of the society's production.

The key issue in politics, therefore, is one of distribution, as it was for Belloc and Chesterton (Douglas 1921b, 91–92). Nationally available credit must be removed from the control of the financiers and administered in more effective ways. The centralized, pyramidal system of credit through which financiers and their bureaucratic machines can distort the system had to be abandoned and replaced by a combination of the coordinated organization of technique and the decentralization of "initiative" (Douglas 1921b, 98, 55, 63). This would involve a national bank making available the total amount appropriated in savings as a single national credit fund. In allocating the national credit fund, the bank was to make democratic rather than sectional decisions.²³ Douglas agreed with Benchara Branford that this must form part of a strong "functional" system of governance, with power distributed according to functional responsibility and, therefore, according to expert knowledge and competence (Douglas 1921b, 143). Political decision making in a system of social credit, Douglas held, was to be dominated by the expert, the technocrat making decisions on the basis of purely technical considerations. The "economic democracy" that Douglas advocated rested on this decentralized authority, but his relative neglect of "spiritual" power meant that his solution had a more technocratic orientation than that sought by Geddes and Branford. Indeed, Sybella Branford criticized this aspect of the "Douglasite" position for its focus on underconsumption and failure to address the "social question" resulting from the "blind direction of our credit resources without any moral consideration" (S. Branford 1924, 127).

SOCIAL CREDIT AND CORPORATIST POLITICS

Until the 1920s, Branford and Geddes relied almost exclusively on Le Play House and the Cities Committee of the Sociological Society to promote their ideas on the Third Alternative. All their key works were published as books and pamphlets under the Le Play House imprint or as articles in the *Sociological Review*. They tried to influence mainstream politics through the occasional letter to a politician, but they were far from being political activists. During the 1920s, however, they began to engage with some of the political groups that they felt might give organizational form to their ideas. For the most part, this was limited to participation in small discussion groups where they hoped that their style of political discourse might have an effect and stimulate others to carry it forward. Their naive assumption was that their strategy would be adopted as soon as political and business leaders realized the logic and force of their argument.

Douglas, too, had taken a similar point of view about the implementation of social credit. His ideas were, in fact, considered by the Labour Party—and rejected by them—in 1922, and interest in them began to wane in the mainstream of labor politics. The crisis years of 1925–26, however, led many who feared the collapse of social order to propose private initiatives and private militia groups, and it was in these groupings that Douglas's ideas began to find fertile ground. The scouting movements discussed in chapter 6 were the primary bases for this subpolitics. Aubrey Westlake, John Hargrave, and Rolf Gardiner—leaders of the Order of Woodcraft Chivalry and the Kibbo Kift Kindred—discussed the possible amalgamation of their groups into a single body tasked with meeting the national crisis that had been brought on by the run up to the General Strike. Hargrave had met

Douglas in 1923 and, encouraged by Rolf Gardiner who had been a member of a social credit study group at Cambridge, he took the lead in advancing social credit ideas. The new organization was seen as a possible social credit body and the presence of Geddes as a key and influential member of both organizations was seen as a fruitful basis for their possible cooperation around a middle way solution to the crisis. Le Play House members were soon drawn into crisis planning discussions at a meeting held under the auspices of a "Centre Party" at the Chertsey home of Norman Glaister of the Order of Woodcraft Chivalry (Edgell 1992, 348). Reservations about the politicization of the movement, however, led Glaister to soften its focus by renaming it from a "Centre Party" to the "Midfolk." It was through the Midfolk that Glaister proposed a "New Commerce Guild" for the woodcraft group at Sandy Balls (see chapter 6). He proposed that people should offer labor skills as a service to the community and without regard for monetary return. The exchange of services was to be regulated by "certificates" issued to participants in a local credit union—effectively creating social credit—and it was intended that this altruism and self-expression would weaken the cash nexus, However, only fifty people signed up for this and the experiment was abandoned.

Cooperation between the two scouting groups broke down in 1927, however, and it was the Kibbo Kift alone that formed the heart of the emerging social credit movement. Hargrave formed the Crusader League and in 1932 merged it into the Kibbo Kift, which he then renamed the Green Shirts (Finlay 1970, 60–64). The change of name—unfortunately leading the group to be linked in the public mind with the fascist Black Shirts—was intended to mark the ecological concerns fostered by the woodcraft ideals that Hargrave saw as closely linked with social credit. Critical of democracy, which he saw as an all too easily manipulated mass society, Hargrave advocated strong leadership exercised through militaristic, but nonviolent, means. He saw formal politics as a purely technical matter of choosing the correct policy and proposed the closure of Parliament, holding that discussion and debate were unnecessary in matters of technical administration. Rejecting conventional electoral politics and stressing instead street marches as a way of demonstrating popular views, he hoped to mobilize the unemployed and the workers to combine against the bankers and in support of "the people's credit." He proposed to make the Bank of England the heart of a new system of national dividend and national credit. Many at the time saw Italian fascism as a positive example of the third way, and Rolf Gardiner became an active supporter of German fascism. In 1935, the Green Shirts were once more reformed as the Social Credit Party of Great Britain, inspired by the example of the Alberta Social Credit Party (Finlay 1970; Drakeford 1997; Macpherson 1953).

Another, smaller grouping active in this area in the 1920s was the Economic Freedom League of Frederick Soddy and Arthur Kitson. Soddy was a Sociological Society activist and had become involved in debates around Douglas's papers in *New Age*, but he had become disillusioned with Douglas's emphasis on central state power. He and Kitson formed the League to focus attention on economic theories of monetary reform similar to the "energetics" of Geddes and Branford. They set out these ideas in a journal called *The Age of Plenty* and in two key works (Kitson 1921; Soddy 1926; see also Soddy 1922, 1924). Breaking with Douglas's idea of the national dividend, they proposed instead that the Gold Standard be abandoned and the issue of "national money" be related, instead, to a retail price index based on the working-class household budget. On this model, aggregate purchasing power would be regulated by changes in money supply that were automatically linked to changes in prices. They combined this with the argument that a nonnationalized banking system should operate on a not-for-profit basis to maximize the level of national investment.

The social credit groups in which Geddes became most actively involved were a cluster of organizations formed by Bosnian émigré Dimitrije Mitrinović, who had fled to London in 1914 and began to write for Orage's *New Age*. An admirer of Hélène Blavatsky and Annie Besant for their advocacy of the spiritual basis of universal brotherhood, Mitrinović aimed to provide social credit with a broader spiritual basis than had been provided by its principal advocates. Mitrinović held to the Comtean vision of the global unity of humanity, though he saw this in rather mystical terms and emphasized the importance of the spiritual "soul" of Europe as the basis for its unity. He developed an idealist account of a universal cultural spirit manifested in the various nations of the world and shaping their historical development. The purpose of political action, Mitrinović argued, should be to overcome the division of this universal spirit and to forge the whole of humanity into a cohesive, solidaristic, and self-conscious social organism (Rigby 1984).

Mitrinović called a meeting of influential writers at the Chandos Hotel in May 1926 to discuss a possible way forward from the current crisis. Those attending the meeting included Maurice Reckitt and Philip Mairet. The latter, who had met Mitrinović in 1914, developed a specifically psychological dimension to Mitrinović's work from the psychoanalysis of Alfred Adler. Both Douglas and Geddes joined the Chandos Group[24] in 1927 and contributed to a collective volume on the coal crisis in which the group reiterated some guild socialist ideas on the reestablishment of a "real" community. In this community, the creativity that had been lost with the degradation of work under capitalism was to be fully realized. Such a community would have its political expression in economic and cultural councils organized into a corporate structure that regulated the allocation of social credit (Porter 1927; see also Delahaye 1929).

Mairet had formed a psychoanalytic study group and had, in 1927, formally convened the British branch of the International Society for Individual Psychology (Mairet 1928). The Chandos Group formally allied itself with the Adler Society in 1928, aiming to promote "absolute and eternal principles of true sociology" alongside principles of individual character (Rigby 1984, 96). Adler, however, became disenchanted with this use of his work and Mitrinović began to restructure his organizations. In 1931 he formed two new organizations, each of which operated through semiautonomous local "clubs" from an office at 60 Gower Street. The so-called Eleventh Hour Flying Clubs were to carry forward the political project of the Chandos Group through the redistribution of property and credit within a European federation. The Women's Guild for Human Order was specifically charged with the distinctively Comtean task of renewing the idea of womanhood as the emotional support for male public participation. Later in the year the Eleventh Hour groups were recast as a national organization with the name New Europe Group.[25] Geddes was appointed as its first president and speakers at its meetings included Soddy and Kitson, whose Economic Freedom League had collapsed in 1930, together with Raymond Postgate and philosopher John Macmurray. Fringe supporters included Ellen Wilkinson and John Strachey. The NEG promoted autonomous worker-regulated enterprises, social credit, and regionally devolved power, seeing a "New Britain" at the heart of a New Europe and the New Europe as the first step toward a new world order.

The *New Britain Quarterly*, later made into a weekly, was launched to promote these ideas and in 1932 it became the basis for a partially separate New Britain Movement. Alfred Orage became the editor of these magazines and helped to set up the *New English Weekly* as a successor to the *New Age*.[26] Contributors to the journals included Philip Mairet, Frederick Soddy, Sam Hobson, Montague Fordham, and John Macmurray, as well as Mitrinović himself, and the enlarged membership included Theodore Faithfull (see Faithfull 1925), Norman Glaister, and Aubrey Westlake. New Britain proposed a "Social State" along the lines suggested by Benchara Branford. The social state would comprise an economic chamber organized along functional lines, a political chamber based on regional representation, and a cultural chamber concerned with intellectual and emotional renewal. The *New English Weekly* followed an editorial line that aimed at a broadly Christian approach to economic and social matters, especially as these could be achieved through social credit and organic farming. The stress on organic farming was aimed at enhancing agricultural productivity, reducing reliance on imported food, and protecting rural communities in ways set out by Lord

Lymington (1932). Promotion of organic farming became an increasingly important element in Third Way politics as it came to espouse a strong ecological commitment.

New Britain presented itself as an antifascist Third Way organization, though some of its supporters did espouse more extreme views. Kitson (1933), for example, was explicitly anti-Semitic and alleged that the dominance of financiers was the result of a Jewish conspiracy (Hammes and Wills 2005). Douglas also began to exhibit similar tendencies. This became a strong element in "English Mistery," formed in 1936 as a nationalist party promoting "Anglo-Saxon virtues" through agricultural reform and rural reconstruction. Its leading members—Rolf Gardiner, Henry Massingham, and Lord Lymington—were firmly on the political Right, with Lymington being overtly anti-Semitic and pro-Nazi (see Massingham 1944; Gardiner 1943). Its ideology stressed rural themes from Ruskin and Morris and the financial ideas of Chesterton and Belloc, linking the Catholic idea of the organic community with the use of organic farming, and equating "natural" with "national."[27] Before internal divisions brought New Britain to an end in 1935 its membership had included such advocates of Third Way politics as the future prime minister Harold Macmillan (1938) and T. S. Eliot. New Europe itself continued for much longer and Geddes was succeeded as its president by other architects of the Third Way and social credit, most notably Kitson, Soddy, and Sam Hobson. The NEG was finally disbanded in 1957, having been actively involved in the early debates over the formation of a European Common Market.

Victor Branford was also actively involved in social credit and corporatist organizations during the 1920s, though his participation was limited by the illnesses of himself and Sybella. He seems mainly to have been concerned with those organizations that were developing corporatist strategies for Britain's industrial problems, and mainstream opinion in business had, indeed, come to abandon laissez-faire in favor of planning and coordination in industry (Pemberton 2006). Branford was in close contact with Norman Wyld, his old friend and associate from the West Indian Cooperative Union and a regular visitor to Branford's Hastings home. Wyld had become secretary of the Society of Technical Engineers, later reformed as the Industrial Institute and with offices in Belgrave Road close to Le Play House. Another visitor to his home was Arthur Salter, a civil servant and director of the economic section of the League of Nations. At the height of the coal crisis of 1926 Salter organized an economics conference on reconstruction at the Royal Institute of International Affairs, Chatham House, that was attended by Wyld—in all probability Victor Branford would also have participated.

In 1928, Wyld was involved in the Mond Conference, organized by Sir Alfred Mond (Lord Melchett) to bring together the major employers and trades unions to discuss the prospects for corporatist cooperation with organized labor. Wyld was used by Mond as an unofficial channel to labor opinion (McDonald and Gospel 1973, 818), though one participant in the conference noted the widespread view that the Industrial Institute was currently ineffective because of the "unacceptability" of Wyld to both employers and unions.[28] Even Branford was concerned that Wyld was getting too closely associated with the "currency cranks" Soddy and Kitson.[29] The ideas promoted in the Mond Conference were echoed by Lyndall Urwick and others who produced the Liberal Industrial Inquiry report (Liberal Party 1928) and in Max Nicholson's *National Plan* (1931), the latter inspiring the formation of the think tank Political and Economic Planning by Leonard Elmhirst and others in 1931.

Shortly after Branford's death, Salter produced a corporatist manifesto based on lectures that he had given at Cambridge University (Salter 1934). This embodied ideas that had been emerging through the Mond Conference and various international bodies sponsored by the League of Nations. Salter argued for a decentralized system of "institutional self-discipline," by which he meant self-regulation by economic interests such as the chambers of commerce, the Federation of Industry, employers organizations, trades unions, and professional organizations such as the General Medical Council. These, he argued, must adopt a less "defensive" and more "professional" stance and must be drawn directly into the formulation of economic policy. At the heart of this system would be a transformed Bank of England, a National Investment Board (as advocated by Maynard Keynes), and specialized mortgage-lending bodies for agriculture and each of the major industrial sectors. In a move beyond the ideas of Geddes and Branford, he argued for comprehensive national economic planning through a National Economic Council, but he did not pursue the mechanisms of spiritual renewal that Branford and Geddes had seen as an essential counterpart to economic reconstruction. His model of the corporate state was enthusiastically cited by Oswald Mosley in his book *The Greater Britain*,[30] but its lasting legacy was, perhaps, the establishment of the corporatist planning system of the 1960s.

This form of corporatism, shorn of its spiritual dimension, was also taken forward by Sir Richard Acland's Common Wealth Party, which Norman Glaister joined in 1941 (Prynn 1972). Acland, J. B. Priestley, and others later broke with the Labour Party over its role in the wartime coalition, arguing for an extension of collective ownership and for a greater role for morality in politics. Although it was effectively dissolved in the 1950s, the party strengthened the case for a managerialist form of socialism that combined central economic coordination with the collective self-management of industry. It maintained close links with Glaister's School of Interpretive Social Research at Brazier's Park, in which Theodore Faithfull's son Glynn was involved as a teacher.

The interwar years of 1918–1939 were a period of intense discussion and creative thinking about third way approaches to banking, credit, political representation, and economic planning. Victor Branford, Patrick Geddes, Sybella Branford, and their associates all made contributions alongside those of other social reconstructionists and social-credit advocates. The period was, however, dominated by the Great Depression and the growing global polarization between communism and fascism. Especially in Europe, the increasingly polarized politics of the 1930s created a very negative atmosphere for the development of broad reformist coalitions of the type that would have been needed to implement a "third alternative." Despite the obvious lessons of the Great Depression and the failings of contemporary capitalism, reforms to capitalist structures did not occur until after World War II, and only then in a more limited form than that envisaged by Branford and Geddes. More centralized practices of state intervention and planning were built, but these did not take the cooperative and democratic forms for which Branford and Geddes had argued.

NINE

FAILURE OF A SOCIOLOGICAL PROJECT

In this book we have analyzed the work and ideas of the Geddes circle. Many of these people, however, have been marginalized and their ideas forgotten. An important question to ask, therefore, is *why* they should have been forgotten. Why did a collaborative circle with a clear vision and organizational base come to be such a prime case of professional failure? Of course, Geddes, Branford, and their associates deserve recognition for their crucially important role in the history of the Sociological Society, but it is their intellectual contribution that requires reassessment.

It might, perhaps, seem obvious to say that they were forgotten because their ideas were wrong and so have been rightly rejected and ignored. However, things are not so simple. Many theorists who espouse wrong or incorrect ideas are remembered in disciplinary histories, so it cannot simply be the content of their ideas that explains the failure of the Geddes circle. We have shown, in any case, that their ideas are often of considerable importance and that they are deserving of continuing recognition in sociological practice. Indeed, many of their ideas have been independently rediscovered by more recent sociologists, often in complete ignorance of the earlier discussions. Much time has been lost and much intellectual effort has been wasted by the failure to explore and develop the intellectual content of these ideas as originally formulated. It is, surely, more productive to improve on existing arguments than it is to completely reinvent their key ideas from scratch. How, then, is the failure of the sociological project initiated by Geddes and Branford to be explained?

Some of the most important factors responsible for this intellectual failure must lie within the social organization of the collaborative circle itself. The circle was organized around Patrick Geddes as its inspirational and charismatic leader. This was clearly one of its strengths, as it provided the core set of ideas that went largely unchallenged among his followers. This structure was also, however, a source of weakness. Geddes's charisma as a teacher attracted those who were seeking an answer to fundamental questions. His synoptic vision and the apparent completion of his theoretical system tended to ensure that his followers were immediately and absolutely committed to furthering his work. They believed they had discovered "the truth" and so felt an almost religious obligation to bring this truth to those who had not yet encountered it. They became disciples with a commitment to proselytize on behalf of the master and to take his words to the ignorant masses. As convinced believers, they felt that it was necessary only to bring these ideas to the attention of others for them to recognize and accept their truth. Argument and persuasion were felt to be unnecessary, given the "obviousness" of the ideas once stated. Hence, they emphasized didactic education rather than persuasive discussion.

For some of the key figures—and most notably for Victor Branford and his brothers—a further factor reinforced the master-disciple relationship. The Branford brothers were the academically brilliant sons of a disreputable, but also brilliant, scientist. All showed some of their father's eccentricities and, more importantly, believed that Geddes was more completely the inspirational father figure than their own father had been. Seeking intellectual comradeship in their father, but finding him seriously flawed, they attached themselves almost unquestioningly to Geddes. Victor Branford, in particular, found it hard to question Geddes's intellectual views. Often exasperated by his practical and financial incompetence, this exasperation rarely extended to any intellectual questioning of the fundamental ideas.

The members of the circle therefore felt no real need to enter into proper dialogue with advocates of other positions. Their absolute certainty—often perceived as arrogance—was viewed with suspicion by their intellectual rivals, who simply ignored what they had to say. Other sociologists felt alienated from the Geddes circle and refused to cooperate in any venture that they thought might be a mere pretense at cooperation designed to impose the Geddes viewpoint. Excluded from expanded professional activities, the Geddes circle became increasingly inward looking. Its members tended to overpromote the work of very minor members of the group, further undermining their credibility in the eyes of others.

This was the reason for their failure to establish the Sociological Society as the primary basis for the professional development of sociology in Britain. This failure was reinforced by their lack of any strong university base from which they could deliver their ideas. Until his move to India, Geddes held only a part-time post in botany, having failed to gain the chair at the LSE that had been designed especially for him. Branford had applied for chairs in commerce at Birmingham and Manchester, where he would have been responsible for the teaching of social studies, but he spent most of his adult life in business and was, for much of this time, unable to participate in mainstream sociological activities. As sociology slowly became established within the London University system and in social work and teacher training in London and the provinces, it was Hobhouse's view of the subject that prevailed and became the principal basis of a textbook tradition in British sociology.

The Geddesian view of sociology was in many ways grander and more ambitious than Hobhouse's view, or even the academic sociology that emerged after World War II, with the establishment of the British Sociological Association. However, at the critical moments in the first three decades of the twentieth century it was not presented with sufficient force, conviction, or widespread diffusion. The times were difficult, punctuated by World War I, the influenza pandemic, and the Great Depression, and publications were often cancelled or reduced to low print runs and cheap, dull formats. Meanwhile, Geddes spent a great deal of his time away from Britain, and Geddes, Branford, and others in the circle faced various health and family crises.

Geddes's international absences, with extended periods in India and France, were further complicated by his "disciplinary absences." He was never clearly and solely committed to sociology. Instead, he floated in and out of the emerging discipline, appearing at meetings and in publications as a sage and celebrity, but then disappearing for long periods and often presenting himself as a biologist, a city planner, an educationalist, a specialist in civics, or a general promoter of culture and learning. Geddes, like his younger contact Lewis Mumford, was one of the few twentieth-century Renaissance men and public intellectuals, unwilling to renounce fields of study to others, and unwilling to commit to one academic discipline or to define limits to his expertise. He was a professor of sociology in Bombay, but he spent a lot of his time in India serving as a city planning consultant. Victor Branford and other members of the Geddes circle started and stalled projects in the hope of having Geddes's full participation, but that full participation was little more than a dream. Geddes was pulling in many different directions, and was increasingly unwilling to commit to a single objective for any significant period. His co-authors had to do more and more of the work, trying to imagine what the great man himself would have written. After Branford's death, Geddes had the opportunity to focus on sociology and to finally bring the grand sociological project to fruition in Branford's memory, but instead he focused on his biology textbook with J. Arthur Thomson and on his new educational project at the Collège des Écossais in Montpellier. Quite soon, of course, his own death further complicated the sociological project, leaving it in the hands of Alexander Farquharson, a second-tier figure who lacked the intellect, networks, and funding to bring the grand Geddesian vision to fruition. Under Farquharson, the Sociological Society emphasized regional surveys that were more akin to geographical fieldwork of the pre-computer era than to anything practiced in the emerging academic discipline of sociology. Any last opportunity to vindicate a Geddesian vision of sociology, or to give sociology leadership among the social sciences, was frittered away in the interwar period.

It has to be recognized that the writings of those within the Geddes circle were not written in such a way that they could have a maximum intellectual impact. Influenced by Ruskin, Morris, and the Arts and Crafts movement, they sought a literary style of presentation that would evoke these influences. However, the key figures simply did not have the literary skills to deliver this. Their texts come across as obscure, dense, and often pretentious. The impenetrable character of the texts did not encourage a wide readership. Texts were also produced as partial drafts and fragments that were inexpertly bolted together to meet publication schedules, and many of Geddes's works appeared only because Victor Branford or Arthur Thomson took control and made efforts to complete the works. While Thomson had some success with Geddes's biology texts, Victor Branford's efforts with the sociology texts were less successful. Many of their works achieved few sales and had correspondingly little influence.

The work of the circle cannot be regarded as having been a complete failure. Geddes had a major influence in urban planning, both in Britain and overseas, and his ideas were also central to the development of urban studies as a distinct discipline. The emphasis of the circle on the social survey method had a more diffuse influence with the establishment of statistical surveys in university sociology and social science departments and in the development of fieldwork survey methods in school and university geography teaching. These were, however, less political and more technical forms of survey than the members of the circle had advocated. In sociology, however, they were almost completely superseded and, eventually, forgotten. In sociology it was the speculative evolutionism of Hobhouse (1924) and the structural-functional approach of MacIver (1917, 1921) that came to form the disciplinary core. The insights and innovations of the Geddes circle disappeared along with their errors and eccentricities.

We should not imply that because the members of the Geddes circle have been forgotten within sociology they deserve to be forgotten. It should be apparent from the whole of our book that we believe that they had a great deal to offer and that much of what they said has a continuing relevance today. They were unsuccessful in competition with Hobhouse and his supporters at the London School of Economics, but they could, in fact, have made a substantial difference to the shape of British sociology if there had been a proper engagement with their ideas.

The dominant Hobhouse school established a wide-ranging evolutionism, cast at a very general level, with empirical research taking the form of comparative cross-cultural investigations. Detailed studies of contemporary society were largely seen as the province of social policy and administration specialists who approached this in the spirit of the centralized administrative socialism of the Webbs and the Fabians. The work of Branford and Geddes suggested a very different, and more fruitful focus.

Their work was, first of all, strongly interdisciplinary. They articulated a view of the social as comprising economic and political processes as well as the cultural framework of social institutions. These could not be studied in isolation, and while disciplinary specialisms were important, they should not preclude an exploration of the interdependence of factors in a social whole. They also recognized the importance of psychological processes in understanding the social, seeing a developmental social psychology as an integral feature of the sociological approach. While they mapped out the disciplinary relations of sociology, geography, anthropology, economics, etc., these were analytical distinctions that highlighted ways of thinking and were not intended to establish rigid subject and departmental boundaries. Their vision of sociology was that it had to be the central social science that brought to a focus these special disciplinary concerns. In this respect, they speak directly to current debates about disciplinarity, interdisciplinarity, and postdisciplinarity.

The particular view of modern society was also far more in line with contemporary concerns than was that of Hobhouse. Where Hobhouse constructed a grand scheme of evolution from simpler to more complex societies and saw this as a movement of "progress," Geddes and Branford focused on the specific transition from medieval to modern societies and explored this transition and its consequences through a clear awareness of the fundamental importance of scientific knowledge and industrial technology.

Their model of modernity was one in which the political economy ("temporal power") was in a state of constant tension and imbalance with cultural concerns ("spiritual power") and in which competing classes and elites drove societies forward and determined whether this movement was toward wardom, collapse, and oblivion or toward a "larger modernity" in which the forces of technology could be harnessed to meet autonomously determined human needs. Their emphasis on social reconstruction was precisely related to this diagnosis; there was no inexorable movement of progress, and the future is what is chosen and made by people themselves. A scientific understanding of society was seen as the essential requirement for this choice to be a realistic one, to be "eutopian" rather than "utopian."

A key feature of their sociology was its emphasis on the "region," which was the means through which they were able to theorize the effects of the natural environment on human activities. This very contemporary focus on environmental issues was largely absent from Hobhouse's view of sociology. While it was fundamental to the work of MacIver and, through him, became a central element in the textbook tradition through which students were trained in sociology (see Scott 2013), it barely figured in the professional practice and research of those who entered academic sociology. Despite the production of a number of "community studies," a consideration of the environment was largely left to the geographers. Geddes and Branford saw this differently and in ways that are far more in accord with the contemporary concern for environmental issues in sociology. Their argument was that the material environment had to be understood in all its complexity as setting limits within which certain forms of action and ways of life are possible, but not inevitable, and thereby shape the social structure of the naturally constituted region. They recognized, however, that more complex forms of social life, such as those that arise first in cities, are the bases for an autonomous flow of cultural concerns that exert a reciprocal influence on the region and so transform the material environment. Social development is the outcome of this interplay between nature and culture.

Their conception of the region did not, however, lead them to an extreme localism. They were among the first social theorists to recognize the inherently global character of human activity. Social life cannot be understood as purely localized in its region but must be seen as embedded in natural and transnational interchanges that fundamentally affect it. There is a real interdependence of the local and the global, and they saw social reconstruction itself as requiring a global reach if it was to bring about the unity of humanity that Comte advocated and anticipated. This underpinned their conception of the world city and the world university, and it was the basis of a view of the "cosmopolitan" character of truly modern orientations.

Methodologically, too, Geddes and Branford were ahead of their time. The social surveys with which they were associated tended to be small-scale and largely limited to school field trips, but their aspiration was to establish comprehensive surveys that integrated physical mapping, economic and political charts and tables, and cultural ethnographies into an all-encompassing model that they sought to give physical expression in the Outlook Tower, as an "index museum" serving as an archive, museum, observatory, and university. Their mapping and charting ideas anticipated possibilities that would become realities only with post-code mapping and small-area statistics, and their view of the index museum as the repository and source of sociological understanding could be realized only with the archival and search facilities offered by the development of the Internet. All this they combined with a view that the division between social scientist and human subject must be abandoned in favor of a view of the human subjects of research as active participants in that research.

They proposed a view of politically directed social reform that was fundamentally different from that of the Webbs. Where the Webbs and other Fabians proposed the centralized administrative socialism that became a key element in the Labour Party's establishment of a bureaucratic welfare state, Branford and Geddes were pioneering advocates of decentralized and cooperative organizations that could associate autonomously in democratic federal and functional bodies. This "third way" was rediscovered only in the 1980s—without any recognition of the pioneers—and it is only in the second decade of the twenty-first century that politicians are again emphasizing cooperation, voluntarism, and localism. Where politicians of the political Right see this "Big Society" as a means of fragmenting the central state and, in particular, of reducing levels of public expenditure, Geddes and Branford saw it as a central element in truly democratic participation and as a means through which centralized democratic agencies could utilize ever greater amounts of capital in projects of planned social reconstruction and human betterment.

Whenever concepts such as participatory action research, bio-regionalism, sustainability, engaged universities, historic preservation, neighborhood upgrading, lifelong education, alternative schools, and experiential learning are used, the pioneering works of the Geddes circle are pertinent. The members of the circle often used different terms to illustrate the same ideas, but it is their ideas that matter, and they were often ahead of their time. The reinvention of many of the key ideas pioneered by Geddes, Branford, and their associates makes imperative a rediscovery and reconsideration of their thought. This book is a contribution to that reconsideration. Perhaps Alfred North Whitehead's famous dictum that "a science that hesitates to forget its founders is lost" must be recast as the statement that a science that hesitates to *remember* its founders is lost.

APPENDIX A

WILLIAM BRANFORD

William Catton Branford was born in Thetford, Norfolk, in 1837 but moved to London to train at the Royal College of Veterinary Surgeons, qualifying in 1857. He set up practice at 15 West Street in Oundle, specializing in the treatment of horses. In September 1858, he married Mary Kitchen, ten years his senior and the daughter, or possibly stepdaughter, of William Kitchen, a small farmer of ninety-three acres in Upton, Nottinghamshire.[1] The marriage was in haste—it was by license rather than banns—and Mary died of consumption just one month later. Although this may have been a love match arranged while Mary was on her deathbed, William lost little time in securing a new partner and housekeeper for his home in Oundle. Within months, Ann Kitchen, Mary's younger sister, had moved into the house to take Mary's place and in November 1860 a daughter, Mary, was born. William and Ann seem never to have married—and until 1907 there was a legal prohibition on marriage to a deceased wife's sister.[2] When William Kitchen died during the 1860s, William Branford became the owner of the farmland in Upton and combined the income from this with the profits from his veterinary practice. It was in Oundle that six children were born to William and Ann, one of whom survived for fewer than three months.[3]

William Branford was ambitious, self-assured, and litigious. He achieved a degree of local notoriety in March 1869, when he sought damages from the Great Eastern Railway for injuries to one of his colts. Branford had claimed that a colt that he bought at the Bury Agricultural Show in 1867 had been injured during the shunting of its horsebox and that it died eight weeks later. The jury found for Branford and awarded him £4 damages.[4] He was dissatisfied with life as a mere country vet and within weeks of the court case he applied for the post of professor of anatomy in the veterinary college in Edinburgh, mobilizing the support of a local landowner and politician, and making the most of a fleeting acquaintance with Lord Chief Justice Bovill, who had highly praised the medical evidence that he had given in his claim against the railway.[5] Despite some reservations about his age and experience—he was just thirty-two—the trustees appointed him to the post, though this reflected their inability to attract better-qualified candidates to the poorly paid position.

William took up the post in 1869 but was almost immediately thrust into confrontation with his students and the college management. Students claimed that he did not seem to have prepared his lectures and that he generally arrived fifteen to twenty minutes late and left fifteen to twenty minutes early. They raised questions over the extent of his knowledge—including a dispute over the fibula, subsequently referred to as the "bone of contention." Students formally complained in a petition that Branford was unfit for his position, that he did not understand his work, and that he had "degraded" a student by sitting them in the dunce's position. When Branford heard about the students' petition he berated them in a lecture and the student protest escalated into riotous disturbances. Sticks and stones were thrown at his windows, and swan-shot and other objects were thrown in his face. Branford was reduced to tears in front of his students. The students hung an effigy of him outside his parlor window and put another effigy, labeled "Pity the insane anatomist," on a roof in the college quadrangle. Branford refused to lecture or to provide a substitute, refused to have his competence examined by experts, demanded the expulsion of the critical students, and withheld the key to the bone-room. He was suspended without pay and a replacement teacher was appointed. In November 1870, following a committee of investigation, his appointment was terminated. Though fighting his dismissal, and accusing the principal of having connived with the students in the disorder, William Branford returned south.

Now in Upton, he took over the running of Ann's family farm—then around seventy-one acres[6]—and managed a stable of cross-country race horses. In 1871, he secured a mortgage of £400 from Alissimon Bradley, an ironmonger's widow of Newark, to purchase the Bugle Horn Inn in Battlesbridge Close, Upton. The strain of the events of the previous two years proved too much for Ann, who died in 1871 of "nervous fever"—a depressive exhaustion brought on by her experiences, and the official cause of death perhaps masking a suicide. William sought to claim £600 on a life insurance policy, though this was opposed by the Liverpool, London, and Globe Insurance Company on the grounds that the policy had been fraudulently obtained. Not until 1876 did William win his claim and secure the funds.

William Branford's persistence with his claim against the veterinary college paid off when the principal was dismissed and its management was reorganized.[7] Branford was offered the post of professor of veterinary medicine and surgery at the newly named Dick Veterinary College in 1874. Although he continued to describe himself as "Professor" Branford throughout his life, he held the post for only two years before taking up an appointment in the Cape of Good Hope as colonial veterinarian.

He held his post in the Cape from 1876–79 and was a prominent and outspoken veterinarian, making important contributions to the environmental explanation of virus diseases. He made enemies easily and became involved in numerous disputes with the Crown Agents over the payments of his expenses and the level of his salary. He remained in South Africa after the ending of his contract but became involved in a horse lottery that led to his trial in 1880 for fraud. Found guilty and imprisoned for fourteen days, he was, as a result, struck off the register of the Royal College.[8]

He returned to Edinburgh in 1880 and must have secured some income from the racing stables he maintained while in Edinburgh, but he seems never to have had any further full-time employment. Much of his life revolved around horses. He raced horses in the Midlands and had won the Southwell Cup, he hunted with the Linlithgow and Stirlingshire Hounds, and in 1884 he received a good mention for a five-year-old mare that he had entered into the Highland Show.[9] He maintained some intermittent contact with his cousin Edgar Branford of Norfolk, the two of them being involved in racing at Newmarket, where they lost a great deal of money. William maintained a stable of seven horses in Pitt Street, Edinburgh, and in June 1887 he and his sons were charged at the Burgh Court with cruelty toward one of the horses. He claimed that he had been away in London at the relevant time. His son Ben was found guilty of failing to provide proper veterinary treatment and was fined £2.[10]

Protesting his innocence of the South African lottery fraud, Branford pursued a lengthy appeal that caused him financial difficulties, though the appeal was eventually found in his favor.[11] Simultaneously, he was engaged in a struggle with lawyers over his failure to meet the interest payments on his Upton mortgage since 1878.[12] In 1886, the Bradley lawyers sought to recover the sum owed, but their associates in Edinburgh—Mylne and Campbell WS—reported that his circumstances were such that they would be unlikely to recover anything at all. The Bradley family were advised to give Branford time to sell what he claimed to be his sole asset—a thoroughbred mare called the Countess Viola. Branford feared bankruptcy for the sake of his children and was forced to hide from the summons server who called on his house. By the middle of 1888, the lawyers felt that there was little chance of recovering the debt at all.

In 1889, William Branford set up the Zout Kom Nitrates Company to handle the exploitation of his land in Calvinia and he traveled back to the Cape, leaving his family to handle his debt to the Bradleys. William had, in November 1888, declared himself bankrupt from a false address in London.[13] The Zout Kom company itself proved to have little substance behind it and it was wound up with an undertaking to repay the money subscribed by its shareholders.

William Branford's exoneration of fraud in 1890 was short-lived: less than a year later he was to die in a London hotel, aged fifty-four, during the influenza epidemic of 1891.

APPENDIX B

THE BRANFORD, GURNEY, AND GEDDES FAMILIES

Allardyce, Lady. See Elsie Stewart.

Branford, Archer Robert Francis (1912–1957). Born, in Fulham, Robert Francis Bailey on April 25, 1912. Natural son of Francis Robert Bailey (reputedly an illegitimate member of a branch of the Gurney family) and his wife Poppy Gwendoline Bailey (neé Hyde). He and his brother were adopted by Victor and Sybella Branford because the parents were unable to look after them, and he was given the name Archer. Victor Branford expressed a wish that his Archie should be given a secretarial position within the Sociological Society and put him through training in bookkeeping. By 1931, however, he was a civilian clerk at the RAF Depot, Uxbridge. In 1936, he married Gertrude McCoy, though the marriage broke up during the war, when Archie was in the RAF and serving in India. He married Winifred Ethel Cooper in 1946 and, once again divorced, he married Barbara Wilby in 1952. For a while he worked as a "private secretary," but then became a truck driver for a London sugar refinery. He had four children by his third wife and died from Hodgkin's Disease.

Branford, Benchara Bertrand Patrick (1868–1944). Brother of Victor Branford. Appointed as assistant lecturer in pure and applied mathematics in Yorkshire College, Leeds, and promoted after seven years to degree-level teaching for Victoria University. In 1901 appointed principal of Sunderland Technical College. Later, divisional inspector and adviser on mathematics for the London County Council. Married his cousin Edith Baker of Cambridge, 1892, and had one daughter, Violet (Violet Branford 1939). See *Scotsman*, July 1884 and May 3, 1901.

Branford, Frederick Victor. See Frederick Powell.

Branford, Hugh Sydney (1913–?). Born on March 23, 1913, to the same parents as Archer Branford. Known as Hughie, he may have gone to work in South America for one of the railway companies with which his father was involved, as he sailed for Buenos Aires, aged fifteen, on the *Deseado* from Liverpool in August 1928. Paraguay was recorded as his place of future permanent residence.

Branford, John Frederick Kitchen (1869–1946). Brother of Victor Branford. Successively deacon at St. Andrew's, Edinburgh, priest at St. Andrew's, Brechin, curate of Callander for the Railway Mission, Crianlarich, and chaplain of St. Ninian's Cathedral, Perth. Married Annie More (d. 1936) at Edinburgh, St. George's in 1893 and immediately took up appointment as curate of Bulwell, Nottinghamshire. Returned to Scotland in 1898 as rector of All Saint's Mission, Jordanhill, Glasgow, succeeding his brother Lionel. Rector of All Saint's Challoch, Newton Stewart from 1913 to 1938, though retaining a London home at 5 Hornsey Lane Gardens, Highgate. Retired to Bristol.

Branford, Lionel William Ernest Catton (1866–1947). Brother of Victor Branford. Returned to Scotland, in 1892, to marry Dorothy Cuthbertson, the daughter of a wealthy Edinburgh lawyer and fourteen years his senior. Held missionary posts in Auchterarder and Glasgow and by 1900 was living at Lye, in Binley, St. Mary Bourne, Hampshire, as vicar of Ashmansworth. Dorothy had married Lionel "in a moment of unguardedness" and the marriage was never consummated. She abandoned him in 1903–05 to live in Ardgay with her herd of goats and her nephew Freddie (Macgregor 1951). Lionel was priest-in-charge at St. Columba's on Islay in 1909. From 1913 to 1921, private chaplain to the Marquess of Breadalbane and then a short period in the Mission to Seamen in Leith. Formally divorced in 1921 and married, three months later, Mary Mitchell. In the 1920s he adopted the additional surname Somers-Cocks and took a series of parish posts in Renfrew, Challacombe, Whissonsett, and Great Hampden. Collapsed and died in the street in High Wycombe.

Branford, Mary Ann Kitchen (1861–1907). Sister of Victor Branford. Took up acting and made a short stage career. In 1891, immediately after the death of her father, she married another actor, J. Frederick Powell, who later achieved some fame under the stage name Joynson Powell. Mary had some West End success in 1902 at Charles Hawtrey's Avenue Theatre, in Northumberland Avenue, playing "Mrs. Daly" in "After All," by Freeman Wills and Frank Longbridge, and "Akulina" in "A Cigarette Maker's Romance," by Charles Hannen, listed in both playbills as "Mrs. Frederick Powell." Mary died from lung cancer in 1907, aged forty-five. While the actors were traveling away from their Fulham home, their son, Freddie (Frederick Victor Powell), was looked after by Lionel Branford and his wife Dorothy.

Branford, Matilda Elizabeth ("Bess") (1852–1915). Daughter of Isaac Smith, manager of Josiah Mason steel products firm. Sister of Martyn Josiah Smith. Married firstly James Farqharson Stewart in 1874, two sons (Martyn and Arthur), one daughter (Elsie); secondly, as his first wife, Victor Branford in 1897. Divorced by Branford in 1910, following the breakdown of the marriage, and lived in the care of Lionel Branford near Andover, Hampshire, where she died.

Geddes, Alasdair C. B. (1892–1917). Son of Patrick Geddes. Worked with his father on town planning exhibitions. Served during World War I in RNAS Balloon Corps on reconnaissance work. Awarded Military Cross but killed in action in 1917.

Geddes, Arthur A. F. (1895–1968). Son of Patrick Geddes. Studied for PhD at Montpellier. Married Jeannie Colin, niece of Elisée Reclus. Professor of geography at Edinburgh University, specializing in the geography of South Asia where he had spent much time with his father.

Geddes, Norah. See Norah Mears.

Gurney, Archer Thompson (1820–1887). Father of Sybella Gurney. On return from Paris worked as curate in Westminster (1872–74), Brighton (1874–75), Hastings (1877–78), Regent's Park (1879–1880), Rhyador (1880–81), and Brecon (1882–83). Retired to Keble Terrace, Oxford and died on a visit to his doctor in Bath (WT 1887).

Gurney, Gerald (1860–?). Brother of Sybella Gurney. Clergyman who became actor with the Bensonian Shakespeare Players and with the Howard and Wyndham Players. Credits include "The Taming of the Shrew" (1889), "The Merry Wives of Windsor" (1890), and "The Lady of the Lake" (1890). Married Dorothy Frances Bloomfield in 1897. Resigned his living in 1919 on conversion to Roman Catholicism. Sometime actor-manager at Globe Theatre, Plymouth.

Gurney, Harold Manby (1874–1969). Cousin of Sybella Branford (*née* Gurney) and excutor to the wills of Victor and Sybella Branford. On staff of

Cecil Rhodes in South Africa, worked for *The Times* and for Incandexcent Fittings Co., and a stockbroker. Involved in businesses associated with Victor Branford.

Gurney, Vivian (1865–1935). Brother of Sybella Gurney. Suffered from congenital mental disability. Cared for by Sybella following his mother's death but lodged with family of Harry Yeo, a professional singer, in Boldre close to Sybella's Hampshire home. Died in Cornwall.

Mears, Frank (1880–1953). Trained as architect. Worked for Geddes as secretary at the Outlook Tower 1908–1910 but continued association with Geddes after setting up his own practice. Married Norah Geddes in 1915. Served with Alastair Geddes in RNAS Balloon Corps in World War I. Knighted 1946. Died on a visit to New Zealand.

Mears, Norah (1888–1967). Daughter of Patrick Geddes. Married to Frank Mears. Worked at Outlook Tower and became a landscape gardener.

Powell, Frederick Victor Rubens Branford (1892–1941). Son of Mary Branford, nephew of Victor Branford. Known as "Freddie." Brought up by his aunt Dorothy and, after her separation from Lionel Branford, they lived in Ardgay, Scotland. An RNAS Captain in the 1914–18 war, he was shot down over the Belgian coast and swam ashore to Holland. Interned, but supported by Fred van Oss. Treated at Craiglockhart Hospital. Lived on a disability pension for the rest of his life. A war poet of repute, publishing under the name Frederick Victor Branford. He stopped writing poetry in 1923, disillusioned with the prospects for future peace. In 1937, he eloped with and married, as his second wife, his cousin Margaret Branford, playwright daughter of John Branford.

Smith, Martyn Josiah (ca. 1854–1930). Brother of Elizabeth Branford (*née* Smith). Related to Sir Josiah Mason. Chairman of Perry and Co., pen manufacturers, and founding trustee of Mason's College, later University of Birmingham.

Stewart, Elsie Elizabeth (Lady Allardyce) (1875–1962). Daughter of Victor Branford's first wife. Married Adam Goodfellow in 1897. Subsequently married (in 1920 as his second wife) Sir William Allardyce (d. 1930), governor of the Falkland Islands, Tasmania, and Newfoundland.

Stewart, Elizabeth ("Bess") See Matilda Elizabeth Branford.

NOTES

CHAPTER ONE. VICTORIAN AND EDWARDIAN SOCIOLOGY

1. A useful overview of statistical survey work in Britain can be found in Kent (1981).

2. The *AJS* is still associated with the University of Chicago Press, though less directly with the department. The *American Sociological Review* was formed in 1936 and the ASS was renamed the American Sociological Association in 1959.

3. On Spencer's life and work see Peel (1971) and Spencer's own autobiography (Spencer 1904). See also Turner (1985) and Offer (2010).

4. On Kidd's life and works see Crook (1984).

5. A similar recognition of Spencer's ideas was set out by Charles Cooley (1902) in the United States, Cooley's ideas generally being seen, however, as an extension of the symbolic interactionism of G. H. Mead (1927) and the Chicago sociologists.

6. Somewhat later, Peter Winch (1958) elaborated on these ideas and combined them with those of Wittgenstein to develop a view of social life as organized through shared rules and practices.

7. Edward Pease was a socialistically inclined stockbroker; Hubert Bland was a journalist and the husband of the children's author Edith Nesbit.

8. Besant left the Fabians in 1891 to join the Theosophists. Later members of the Fabian Society included H. G. Wells (for a short while), Leo Chiozza Money, and Richard H. Tawney.

9. Similar views were promoted in the United States by Henry George (1879).

10. Its first directors were W. A. S. Hewins, Sir Halford Mackinder, and, from 1908–1919, William Pember Reeves.

11. The continuing influence of these ideas was apparent in the later political sociology of Ralph Miliband (1961, 1969) and at Oxford in the work on social class undertaken by G. D. H. Cole (1955). The Webbs wrote much of the new program for the Labour Party in 1918, including the famous Clause Four on the nationalization of the means of production. Sidney became a Labour MP in 1922, was a minister in the first Labour government, and took a seat in the House of Lords as Lord Passfield. Although the Webbs remained in the Labour Party they moved closer to orthodox Marxism and to an acceptance of the Soviet regime from the early 1930s. Beatrice died in 1943, and Sidney in 1947.

12. It is unclear why MacIver came to be interested in Durkheim and Simmel. MacIver's son-in-law, Professor Robert Bierstedt, said that he knew of no reason other than "intense intellectual curiosity" why MacIver should have read these writers so

closely (personal communication to John Scott, March 23, 1998). MacIver's own account (MacIver 1968) gives little insight. MacIver's books of 1917 and 1921 can be regarded as texts in British sociology (Scott 1913). As he remained for the whole of the rest of his life in North America, his later works show greater influence of trends in American sociology. MacIver joined Columbia University in 1927 and was appointed a year later to head the Department of Sociology, which had been run down under the ineffective leadership of Franklin Giddings. MacIver's later works include *The Modern State* (1926), *Society* (1937), *Social Causation* (1942), and *The Web of Government* (1947). He retired from Columbia in 1950 but remained active in sociology until the 1960s.

13. McDougall expanded his general psychology in a text written in England but published just after his arrival in the United States (McDougall 1923). McDougall's approach to psychology was further developed in England by Jack Sprott, who had been a student of Myers at Cambridge (see Sprott 1937; and see the later Sprott 1952). McDougall's work and influence are discussed in Hearnshaw (1964, ch. 12).

CHAPTER TWO. GEDDES, BRANFORD, AND GURNEY

1. Parts of this chapter draw on the discussion in Scott and Husbands (2007). In the initial character sketches we draw on the various sources cited in greater detail in the later sections of the chapter.

2. Geddes has been well supplied with biographers. The first attempt to present an account of his life and work was produced by Amelia Defries (1927) during his own lifetime. This was followed by a more comprehensive assessment in Philip Boardman's 1936 PhD thesis at Montpellier and its conversion and subsequent enlargement in book form (1944; 1978). The final book to be produced by someone with personal knowledge of Geddes was that of Philip Mairet (1957). Later biographies include those of Paddy Kitchen (1975), Helen Meller (1990), and Walter Stephen (2004), together with the material in Novak (1995). These are the sources from which we have drawn much of the information not attributed to other sources in the notes to this chapter. We do not cite specific pages from these sources except where they concern particularly important issues or where the sources are ambiguous or contradictory. The papers of Patrick Geddes are held in archives at Strathclyde University, the National Library of Scotland, and Dundee University. Where letters have been reprinted in Novak (1995) we cite that source. Much information on all those people discussed comes from registration data, census returns, street directories, and passenger records, and we have not generally cited these numerous sources individually.

3. Geddes's actual place of birth was finally established by Stephen (2008, 2007). He was christened Peter but adopted the name Patrick in his early teens.

4. It was also in 1881 that John Geddes visited London in search of business connections.

5. Summons of Miss Helen or Ella Guillan Grant, 1896, National Archives of Scotland NAS02023 CS248-2390/1.

6. In his letters to Lilian, Geddes rather uncomfortably referred to himself as "Uncle" and "Daddy" (Boardman 1978, 363–64) and invited her to confess her

emotional concerns as if he were a psychoanalyst. In 1927, he opened up about his own feelings and proposed marriage.

7. Sources on Branford and his family are few and far between. The only discussion of any length is the overadmiring account produced by Amelia Defries (1928). The Sociological Society archives and the papers of Victor Branford are held (largely unsorted) at Keele University in the series VB. These are now being reorganized and reclassified, but our sources give the original classification by which they were filed. Some further information comes from the diaries of Benchara Branford (in the possession of John Scott), which will be transferred to the Keele University archive.

8. William Branford's life and character were crucial in shaping the life and vision of his son Victor. A full account of William himself is given in Appendix A to this book.

9. His year of birth is usually given as 1864, but it was in fact 1863. The birth was registered in 1864 and the register notes a correction to the original entry. His full name is Victor Verasis Branford, and the second name is often spelled "Veracis," the Latin word for "the true thing." However, the only examples that we have seen of his own signature spell it "Verasis." Although this may have been a misspelling by his father, it seems more likely that the name was deliberately used. It can be speculated that the two forenames may have been given because his father aspired to a connection with the Count Verasis di Castiglione, cabinet advisor to King Victor Emmanuel. The latter became king of a unified Italy just two years before the birth of Victor Branford.

10. Information from Stephen Forge, Oundle School archivist.

11. *Scotsman*, April 22 and November 2, 1882.

12. These were produced at his own expense and the *Hand-Book of Animal Classification*, to which his father contributed a diagram of animal evolution, was successful enough to run to a third edition in 1890. A copy of this edition at the British Library seems to be the only surviving example of the booklet.

13. Nottinghamshire Archives DD/H/149/89.

14. Nottinghamshire Archives DD/H/149/92.

15. Immediately before the death of William, he and all his children except Lionel were living at 22 Clarence Street, Edinburgh, paying a rent of £32. Information from the Census and *Scotsman*, February 4, 1888.

16. One son, Martyn Mason Stewart, settled in Seattle, living at 519 People's Savings Bank Buildings. Bess traveled to see him in May 1907. The other son, Arthur Bradford Stewart, was a private in an Australian regiment and served in South Africa, last heard of sailing from London on the SS *Inkosi* bound for Port Natal in 1905.

17. Adam Goodfellow died in 1913 and Elsie later married Sir William Allardyce.

18. Declaration of Intention, No. 60032, April 11, 1910, U.S. Immigration Service records. The declaration, in which Branford claimed to be a resident of Goldfield, Nevada, was supported by his business associates William Goodman and Louis Vorhaus.

19. Divorce petition, State of Nevada and County of Esmeralda, Case No. 271, 1910.

20. The Chelsea apartment was at 7 King's Mansions, Lawrence Street.

21. There are no published biographical sources on Sybella Gurney apart from obituaries and material in the sources given in note 7 for Victor Branford. The history of her family was privately produced in a manuscript by her uncle Augustus Gurney (1887), now held at the British Library at Add. 81597. We are grateful to Gerald Gurney for permission to make use of a typed copy of this manuscript. Other information has been provided by David Gurney of Norwich.

22. Though her will and some other sources name her as Nina, the official birth record and the memorial tablet arranged by Victor give Sybella's middle name as "Nino."

23. There is a Gurney Row in Tregony, named after a nineteenth-century member of the family.

24. The early years of Archer Gurney and his family are recounted in Gurney (1887). See also "WT" (1887).

25. Gurney Drive in Hampstead Garden Suburb was later named in memory of her involvement in the founding of the suburb.

26. See ship manifest for SS *Cedric*, December 4, 1910, at www.ellisisland.org.

27. Marriage Record, State of Pennsylvania, Philadelphia County, License no. 259316, 1910. We are grateful to Halyna Myroniuk for providing information on the background of Krohmalney. Hugh Vivian (1927) correctly gives 1910 as the date of the marriage but is misleading in suggesting that Sybella Gurney was unknown to him before her marriage. In fact, they had been closely associated for some time (Reid 2000, 28).

28. Victor Branford returned alone to the UK on January 13, 1911, docking at Plymouth. He seems to have been sufficiently ill with his chest condition (most probably asthma) to take a cure in the relatively warm and sunny private nursing home "Hygeia" in Belle Vue Road, Ventnor, on the Isle of Wight. He returned to New York later in the year. Hygeia is now the Burlington Hotel.

29. Certificate of Naturalization 399047, November 12, 1913. Victor Branford was readmitted to British citizenship on February 6, 1923 (National Archives HO 144/2646). The Branfords lived in temporary accommodation owned by the National Arts Club at 119 E. 19th Street and then at 124 or 128 E. 24th Street.

30. Draft deposition, Keele Archive VB 301.

31. See http://www.hgs.org.uk/tour/tour00017000.html. The house was on the market for £3.5 million in 2005, then named Wyld's Close Corner.

32. In fact, no baptismal record can be found for either son. It is possible that the baptism was privately carried out by Victor's brother Lionel and may have been recorded, if at all, at his parish church in Hampshire.

33. Correspondence in Keele Archive, VB 51.

34. Information from inscription in a copy of Branford's *St Columba* owned by his niece Violet Branford and in the possession of John Scott.

CHAPTER THREE. ORGANIZING AN INTELLECTUAL VISION

1. Ashbee's Guild moved to Chipping Campden, Gloucestershire, in 1902, but it soon ran into financial problems (Hardy 2000, 112 ff.).

2. Carpenter, along with Geddes's Edinburgh student Cecil Reddie, later founded the Fellowship School at Abbotsholme to apply some of these ideas in an educational context (Armytage 1961, 327 ff.; Ward 1934). This is discussed in chapter 6 below.

3. Branford remained active in the Guild of St. George for many years. From 1920 Alexander Farquharson became the dominant figure and in 1933 the guild was formally moved to Le Play House.

4. Some aspects of this biography of Wood are conjectural on the basis of partial evidence, but seem to be consistent with what is known. See Rimmington (2005) and Gould (1900).

5. Early English Positivism is discussed in Kent (1978), Wright (1986), and Bryson (1936).

6. Congreve established branches of the church in Birmingham, Cambridge, Leeds, Leicester, Liverpool, and Newcastle. His Church of Humanity survived after his death in 1899 and was eventually reunited with the Positivist Society in 1917.

7. See the discussions in MacKillop (1986) and Sylvester Smith (1967).

8. Coit's centralized and theistic approach encountered opposition from the increasingly secular membership, and he was forced to resign in 1891. He formed the West London Ethical Society, which took a much more churchlike form, and later worked closely with the Ethical Church in Bayswater.

9. On Hobson's life and work see Hobson (1938) and Townshend (1990). On Robertson see Herrick (1987a,b).

10. The LES had close links with the School of Sociology, set up by the COS to train social workers, and that was run from the Women's University Settlement.

11. Besant's booklet originally appeared in *The Theosophist* magazine in 1912 and 1913.

12. Edmund Gurney was a member of the Norfolk Gurney family, associated with Barclays Bank, and was not close kin to Sybella Gurney.

13. At this time, the most influential of Comte's works in Britain were Martineau's (1853) condensation of his argument and Bridges's 1865 translation of the *General View* (Comte 1848), the Introduction to the *Positive Polity*. Other works of Comte were largely unknown.

14. It is unclear whether Branford visited Philadelphia at this time, as no evidence of a transatlantic sailing can be found. His article was probably compiled from discussions with Geddes and from secondary sources.

15. Papers by Branford (1902), and Geddes (1902) were published in the *Scottish Geographical Magazine* to promote this venture. On Geddes's work in Scottish geography and his sponsorship of the botanical mapping of Scotland by Robert and Willam Smith see Mather (1999).

16. Elder lived at 11 Dudley Gardens, Leith, McGegan lived at 31 Royal Park Terrace.

17. In later life, Branford claimed that the Edinburgh School of Sociology had been formed in the 1890s and had been the basis of all he had done for more than thirty years (Branford 1926: Appendix B). This romantic reflection perhaps confused the short-lived organization with the larger and longer-lasting intellectual

circle formed around Geddes from the summer schools through to the numerous sociological ventures of the 1920s.

18. Some discussion of the founding of the Sociological Society can be found in Halliday (1968) and Evans (1986).

19. Branford set out a charter statement for the society in Branford (1905).

20. The sources for this and the following discussion of membership are the printed membership lists and constitutions of the Sociological Society.

21. John C. Medd was a cousin of Walter H. Medd, who, in 1911, married Sybella Gurney's goddaughter Muriel Beatty.

22. Mavor had gone to Toronto at the suggestion of W. J. Ashley, who had moved to Harvard. Ashley was subsequently appointed to the chair at Birmingham for which Branford had applied. Mavor set out an account of his own life in Mavor (1923).

23. On Letchworth see Miller (1989) and Jackson (1985).

24. An interesting discussion of urban planning and postwar reconstruction ideas and debates is Slavitt (1994). Nettlefold's planning ideas were set out in Nettlefold (1905).

25. Built by Thomas Cubitt, Le Play House was at 65 Belgrave Road. This is now part of the Victoria Hotel.

26. The checkered history of the Le Play Society and the eventual demise of the Institute are recounted in Evans (1986). The *Sociological Review* became more academic and more successful and the LSE sociologists wanted to take it over completely (Harper 1933, 341). This was refused and in 1948 they left the *Review* and drew up plans for both the *British Journal of Sociology* and the British Sociological Association.

27. Hull House had been set up in 1887 by Jane Addams and Ellen Gates Starr.

28. For a later reflection on Laindon see Walker (2007).

29. They may also have had contact with each other through their mutual acquaintance with Earl Barnes, who knew Geddes through his involvement in the Child Study movement and who met Fels sometime after 1902. Child Study is discussed further in chapter 6.

30. Kropotkin lived at 6 Crescent Road, Bromley. Fels later acquired an additional London home at 10 Cornwall Terrace, Regent's Park.

31. NLS MS10571.

32. NLS MS10570, 90–93.

33. Mumford's life and work are discussed in Miller (2002) and also in his own autobiography (Mumford 1982). The correspondence between Mumford and Geddes held at the University of Pennsylvania is usefully collected in Novak (1995).

34. See the discussion of this debate in McBriar (1987).

35. The paper had been read at a meeting of the Sociological Society in October 1909.

36. Branford to Geddes, undated, NLS MS10557, 58.

37. Practical organization of the symposium had been undertaken by Mabel Barker. The book was based on lectures given by Geddes that were reworked by Slater and then completely rewritten by Victor Branford.

38. Branford to Geddes, May 5, 1917, NLS MS10557, 25.

39. A brief note on Le Play was omitted from the revised edition.

40. The *Handbook of Animal Classification* includes a diagram of animal evolution drawn by Branford's father. This is incorrectly bound in the British Library copy of the *Handbook*.

41. This viewpoint was later to be developed systematically by Frederick Soddy (1922, 1924, 1926; and see Merricks 1996; Martinez-Alier 1987).

42. *Ideas at War* (Geddes and Slater 1917) originated in a summer school on wardom and peacedom organized in 1915 by Gilbert Slater at Ruskin College, Oxford. Geddes's contribution appeared in the *Sociological Review* (Geddes 1915b) and was later compiled with other material to form the book.

43. See Scott (2009). Copies of the manuscript of *Orpheus and Eurydice* are held at the University of Keele and at the British Library. Unfortunately, proof corrections to Scott (2009), including a report on the British Library copy, were not incorporated into the published version.

44. Ben Branford's wife, Edith Dagmar Branford, and his daughter, Violet, produced short volumes of prose and poetry exploring moral themes (Mrs. B. Branford 1923; Violet Branford 1939).

45. A list of some of the geographers influenced by Geddes can be found in Maclean (2004, 95).

46. Dorothy Herbertson wrote her account of Le Play between 1897 and 1899, passing it to Victor Branford for possible publication around the time of World War I. Branford edited and published the first three chapters in *Sociological Review* in 1920 but was depressed at the lack of response. Farquharson published the whole (minus Branford's edits to the final chapters) in *Sociological Review* in 1946. This was the version published in book form in 1950.

47. Fawcett's statement of federalism was presented as a paper in 1916 and was published in the *Geographical Journal* (Fawcett 1917) before its publication in book form.

48. MacIver was a Scottish expatriate and an early member of the Sociological Society. See his own account of his life in MacIver (1968).

49. Mumford's work from the later 1950s (1956, 1961, 1967) took a more pessimistic view of the future.

CHAPTER FOUR. ENVIRONMENT, REGION, AND SOCIAL RECONSTRUCTION

1. These ideas were developed in the second edition of Le Play's work, published in 1877–79.

2. Lord Avebury's *Scenery in England* (Lubbock 1906) is cited as an example of the mapping of places from a geological standpoint, and Hilaire Belloc's *The Old Road* (Belloc 1904) is given as an example of the documentation of transport patterns. More generally the works of Herbert Fleure (see, for example, Fleure 1919) were invoked as exemplifying this approach.

3. This descriptive framework and general approach was very influential for the social investigations carried out by Charles Booth (1901–02) and Seebohm Rowntree (1901).

4. This cultural formation is seen as involving the "recapitulation" during socialization of the evolutionary achievements of the species. We discuss this developmental psychology in chapter 6 below.

5. Branford and Geddes refer to Alfred Zimmern's discussion of the relationship between nation and state, later published in the *Sociological Review* (Zimmern 1915).

6. The same distinction appears more recently in Jürgen Habermas's (1981a,b) distinction between the steering "system" and the sociocultural lifeworld.

7. This possibly refers to the novel *The Pretty Lady* (Bennett 1918), though they refer to a wartime essay. The Arnold Bennett Society has been unable to identify a definite source in Bennett's work.

8. This article of Branford's originally appeared in the *Encyclopaedia Britannica* (1926).

9. Geddes first introduced the word *megalopolitan* (Geddes 1904) and then *conurbation* (Branford and Geddes 1917). He finally settled on *megalopolis* (Geddes 1927).

10. The book was actually written in 1909–1910 and was republished in a shorter edition in 1949 by cutting some of the more historically specific sections.

11. In support of their argument they cite the work of Jane Addams (1910).

12. On John Macmurray see Costello (2002).

13. Branford paid particular attention to the relationship between sociologists and the theatre, his interest perhaps strengthened by the fact that both his own sister and Sybella's brother had been actors.

14. Percey Mackaye, the playwright, dramatist, and poet, was the brother of Benton Mackaye, a close friend of Lewis Mumford, and who is discussed in chapter 5.

15. The studios of the GPO Film Unit were based at 47 Bennett Park, Blackheath.

16. On the Philadelphia study see Bulmer (1991, 173). The Pittsburgh study was published in six volumes in 1908–09, the best-known being that by Elizabeth Butler (1909). The Russell Sage Foundation had been organized by lawyers Robert and Henry De Forest.

17. Crawford was a boyhood friend of Harold Peake. His general approach was set out in his *Man and His Past* (Crawford 1921). See Hauser (2008).

18. Later attempts at such a project were the descriptions of the one-inch sheets published by the Geographical Association in its series "British Landscape through Maps." Particularly notable is Fleure's report on Guernsey (Fleure 1961).

19. Marr's survey was undertaken for the Ancoats university settlement and Walker's survey on behalf of the Dundee Social Union. On Walker's survey see Lenman and Carroll (1972). Early surveys are discussed in Freeman (2002).

20. Presidents of the section at various times included Branford, Geddes, Fagg, Geoffrey Hutchings, Farquharson, Fleure, and Peake.

21. Branford's Paraguay reports are all held in the Keele archives with the reference number shown: "British and Germans on the River Plate" (1906, VB279), "Regional Sociology: The Region of the River Plate" (1906, VB96), and "Paraguay Central Railway" (1912, VB32).

22. Hardy's surveys at the Keele archive are: "Paraguay—Rediscoveries in South America" (1910, VB279) and "Notes on Agriculture in Paraguay" (1913, VB165). The 1910 survey is the survey that Branford had told his business associate

Rodriguez must be kept secret. During the discussion of Barclay's 1909 survey at the Royal Geographical Society, Follet Holt referred to the need for geographical surveys to lead the way for railway development and colonization, proposing that the RGS organize an expedition to connect the Paraguay railway into a transcontinental system.

23. The study of the *War Factory* is largely a participant observation study undertaken by Celia Fremlin.

24. On Geddes's influence in geography, see Bell (1998).

CHAPTER FIVE. PLANNING THE BUILT ENVIRONMENT

1. For a vigorous refutation of conservative surgery and upgrading, see Davis (2006).

2. On contemporary bioregionalism and sustainability, see McGinnis (1998), Sale (2000), Thayer (2003), and Berg (2009).

3. Examples of Geddes's writings on regionalism include Geddes (1902; 1915), Geddes and Branford (1919), and his "Talks from the Outlook Tower" reproduced in *The Survey (Survey Graphic)* for 1925 and in Stalley (1972, 289–380).

4. As examples of the utopian thought that influenced Branford and Geddes, and the work of several close associates, see the volume edited by Hollins (1908).

5. The original Megalopolis was an ancient Greek city that was not large or polycentric enough to correspond to the meaning that Geddes gave to the term *megalopolis*. Gottmann (1961) further elaborated on the concept of megalopolis, associating it with an archetypal case, the urbanized northeastern seaboard of the United States.

6. See especially Galton (1904) and Geddes (1905). Both papers were delivered at the first meeting of the Sociological Society, held at the London School of Economics in April 1904.

7. By far the most sophisticated analysis of Geddes's vitalism is Welter (2002), a very thorough exploration of how Geddes interlinked his activism with his scholarship on social and environmental sciences. For other insights, see Dehaene (2002) and Studholme (2007).

CHAPTER SIX. SOCIALIZATION, CITIZENSHIP, AND THE UNIVERSITY MILITANT

1. Related work on child study by Hall's colleagues at Clark University included Chamberlain's *Child* (Chamberlain 1903), Hodge's *Nature Study* (Hodge 1902), Starbuck's *Religion* (Starbuck 1899), and Sanford's *Psychology* (Sanford 1897).

2. This is also the judgment of his biographer Dorothy Ross (1972). See also Pruette (1926).

3. The founders John Heyl Vincent and Lewis Miller outlined its aims in their book published early in the history of the circuit (Vincent and Miller 1886).

4. We are grateful to Kevin Brehoney for information on these points.

5. A useful critical assessment can be found in Arnett (2006).

6. Through Hall's sometime colleague Franz Boas, the book influenced the more cultural approach to adolescence undertaken by Margaret Mead in Samoa (1928)

and New Guinea (1930). It also influenced the later developmental psychology of Erik Erikson (1950, 1968).

7. Though he was not himself a recapitulationist, the social behaviorism of George Mead (1910, 1927) also owed a great deal to Baldwin's emphasis on child development and the importance of play. Hall also drew on the English-born psychologist Preyer (1893), who spent most of his career in Germany. On the general approach see Noon (2005).

8. Freud, Jung, and Piaget all drew on recapitulationist ideas in constructing their developmental psychologies. See Sulloway (1979).

9. Theodora Thompson set out a psychology of the unconscious spirit, but saw this as the divinely inspired emotional "Light Within" (Thompson 1928, 2, 5). On Tansley see Cameron and Forrester (2000).

10. Modifications to the theory of sexual selection are discussed in Geddes and Thomson (1931, 102 ff).

11. Tayler partially justified the exclusion of women from employment on the grounds that they tire more easily than men and cannot sustain constant attention to any task. "Women naturally require frequent intervals of rest, and this explains why housework, which supplies varied employment and opportunity of little pauses, is so readily accomplished by women" (Tayler 1904, 223). Few today would accept such arguments.

12. This argument is elaborated in Lineham and Gruffudd (2001).

13. The recapitulation theory in relation to education was most influentially set out in Benchara Branford's text on mathematical education (B. Branford 1908). He discussed the relevance of Le Play to the school curriculum in a later book (B. Branford 1916, 141ff.). On educational psychology and the advocacy of responsible citizenship see Roberts (2004).

14. In support of their position Branford and Geddes (1919, 206) cite a report by Henry Wilson (1918) to the Montessori Conference held at Oxford.

15. According to his daughter Sabita, Archie Branford was rather critical of his parent's apparent experimentation on him. His uncle Jack, however, felt that this view, derived from Defries's biography (1928, 95), seriously misrepresented the project as if it were cold and manipulative (letter of Jack Branford to Violet Branford, in the possession of J. Scott).

16. On the rise of progressive schooling see Selleck (1972), Pekin (1934), and Stewart (1968).

17. Keele archives VB42.

18. One of the best-known pupils was the publisher Stanley Unwin, who attended the school between 1897 and 1899. His brother Sidney was a teacher at the school and a cousin was head boy (Unwin 1960, ch. 4). Geddes remained in contact with Reddie into the 1920s, when Reddie was living in Welwyn Garden City at 1 High Oaks Road.

19. Geddes was for a time president of the Governors of King Alfred School in Hampstead Garden Suburb.

20. Archie Branford was not academic and did not thrive at school. He and his younger brother Hugh completed their education at a small private school in Bletsoe, Bedfordshire.

21. The idea of a chivalrous order was heavily influenced by such Romantic novels as Maurice Hewlett's *The Forest Lovers* (Hewlett 1898).

22. Their presentation of their psychological arguments rested also on the views of William James (1890) and William McDougall (1908) on habit and instinct.

23. The initial plan had been to also open a school on the site, but financial problems following Ernest's death in a motor accident in 1922 meant that this plan was postponed.

24. In 1924 the Kibbo Kift, took a more political direction in support of social credit and corporatist, expert control of the state and economy (Moore-Colyer 2003). It was in this year that the Woodcraft Folk seceded and built on its links to the cooperative movement.

25. There is no evidence that the mainstream of the Order were involved in witchcraft or magic. It is clear, however, that Byngham's activities and the fact that the Order did employ Pagan ideas and rituals gave it a particular reputation locally. When, in the 1950s, Gerald Gardner created his story of witchcraft initiation rites in a New Forest coven—the basis of contemporary Pagan Wicca—it is likely that he drew on this reputation to give credence to his story.

26. This view of leadership has some similarities to that of the American social psychologist Robert Bales (1950), who drew on the arguments of Talcott Parsons to distinguish the "adaptive" task leader and the "integrative" socio-emotional leader. See also Parsons and Bales (1956).

27. The school later moved to Walsham-le-Willows and then to Hazeleigh, near Malden, Essex.

28. Also taken to the 1924 folkmoot was Theodore Faithfull's son Glynn, then aged twelve. Glynn's daughter Marianne Faithfull, later a popular singer, was a visitor to Sandy Balls in her childhood during the 1950s.

29. Bowlby became an influential child psychologist and produced a number of key child studies (1965, 1969–80).

30. Glaister and Revel in fact went through a civil ceremony in Islington, London, in the late spring of 1930.

31. Byngham had left the order in 1931.

32. Aubrey resigned from the OWC in 1935 and started charging for the use of the camping facilities at Sandy Balls. Folkmoot moved to Brockenhurst, to Savernake, and then to Abergavenny. The Grith Pioneers—the renamed Grith Fyrd—concentrated their activities at a site in Derbyshire, where the folkmoot eventually settled.

CHAPTER SEVEN. COOPERATION, FINANCE, AND CAPITALISM

1. Further information on Bonar and other Scottish businessmen mentioned in this chapter can be found in Scott and Hughes (1980).

2. The address in 1907 is given in *Scotsman*, August 31, 1907. Information on companies and business addresses, except where indicated, comes from the various annual volumes of the *Stock Exchange Yearbook*, the *Stock Exchange Official Intelligence*, and the *Directory of Directors*. Address information also appears in *Kelly's London Directory*. Further information on office addresses comes from dated letterheads in the Keele archives and the National Library of Scotland.

3. National Library of Scotland, MS 10556, 8–9.

4. The company was eventually wound up in 1933. See National Archives BT 31/31563/54294.

5. Plunkett was a pioneer of agricultural cooperatives in Ireland but had spent many years on the Powder River in the United States where his path had crossed with that of Dundee financier and newspaper proprietor Sir John Leng. There may well have been a Dundee connection involved in his association with Geddes.

6. Branford's authorship of this article on the areal farm, a copy of which was retained by him in his files, is uncertain. However, its ideas clearly influenced his thinking.

7. Following several letters of default from the Registrar of Companies, sent to an out-of-date address, it was struck off the register in 1911 (National Archives BT 31/8091/58334).

8. National Archives BT 31/4263/27639 and BT 31/6783/47737.

9. National Library of Scotland, MS 10556, 18.

10. The Branford papers at Keele include a copy of the 1902 prospectus and a newspaper cutting about Stilwell.

11. In 1908, J. de Goijen was a banker in Amsterdam and his offices were bases for the Amsterdam representation of the Guardian Trust and the Missouri, Kansas and Texas Trust.

12. This was a suggestion of Guus Veenendaal, confirmed by the inclusion of van Oss bankers in Branford's business address book (Keele Archives VB 48). We are grateful to Guus Veenendaal and Bert Schijf for archival help in tracing possible associates for Branford.

13. National Library of Scotland, MS 10556, 90.

14. The ANR had been formed in 1887 to operate in the northern "Mesopotamia" region of Argentina. Its chairman from 1897–1913 was W. Bailey Hawkins. The ANR cooperated with the neighboring Entre Rios Railway, whose chairman from 1891–1903 was R. J. Neild. He was succeeded by Jason Rigby (Stones 1993).

15. Villanueva was also a horse breeder at Los Arenales and Chapadmalal and was a president of the Jockey Club. On his death in 1933 he received a state funeral.

16. General information on foreign and domestic capital in Paraguay in this period can be found in Abente (1989).

17. Fred Perry's company also acted as contractors to the railway.

18. Underdown had for long been a director of the Argentine North Eastern Railway. Warren (1967, 40) has suggested that Rodríguez may have begun to buy shares in the PCRC as early as 1899. He had already bought into the original syndicate controlling the ANER and had become a major shareholder in that company. In 1901 the ANER was based at 13 Devonshire Square and had as directors, in addition to Underdown, William Bailey Hawkins (chairman since 1897 and trustee for bondholders, based at 39 Lombard Street), Harry Gibbs (of Antony Gibbs), G. Zwilgmeyer (London manager of the Deutsche Bank), L. Cahers d'Anvers (of Paris), Sir Charles Arthur Turner, and Harrison Hodgson (civil engineer). Anvers had extensive interests in Paraguay and later became a close associate of Percival Farquhar.

19. The other directors of Uruguay Northern were Charles E. Gunther (of Corneille David and Co., 4 Fenchurch Avenue, and a director of Liebig's Extract of

Meat), Frederick C. Norton (barrister of Lincolns Inn), and Colonel Ernest Villiers (of 44 Lennox Gardens and chairman of Hotel Cecil and Birmingham Mint). All the ordinary shares were held by Livesey, Son and Henderson, engineers, who were contractors to the line.

20. Rodríguez had spent some time in London where he already had business connections with Underdown.

21. Ferreira, a pro-Argentine, came to power with a liberal coalition in 1906, succeeding two short-lived presidencies initiated in coups.

22. The Paraguayan government's interests were represented by its holding of the preference shares.

23. Rodríguez seems to have been suspicious of Sigismund Mendl's motives, despite his own close association with Charles.

24. "British and Germans on the River Plate," Keele archives VB 279.

25. *Scotsman*, August 31, 1907.

26. An unknown hand, most probably Alexander Farquharson, has annotated the relevant file at the Keele Archive (VB 254) with the statement that "Rodríguez cuped him in the end."

27. On the reconstruction see *London Gazette*, Nov. 26, 1907. And see *London Gazette* February 7, 1908, and March 13, 1908. The offices of Ashurst, Morris and Crisp were at 17 Throgmorton Avenue.

28. The original New York and London interests of Levi Morton had been completely separated in 1899. In London Morton Rose & Co. had been reformed as Chaplin, Milne Grenfell by 1900. In New York Morton, Bliss had been reformed as the Morton Trust.

29. Dudden confuses Manuel Rodríguez with a Paraguayan president of the same surname.

30. *London Gazette*, June 11, 1908. John Ross took offices at 5 Victoria Street, Westminster and became involved in the auditing of Victor Branford's Latin American work.

31. *Scotsman*, November 3, 1910.

32. In 1910, Edgar called H. E. Borradaile from Canada to become a partner in Sperling. Borradaile was almost certainly related to Branford's early associate William Borradaile.

33. In 1907–08, the firm's offices moved to 41 Threadneedle Street and were linked to those occupied by the Law Debenture Corporation, managed by R. C. Whitcroft.

34. In 1906 the United States Banking Company became a correspondent bank of the Bank of Montreal.

35. National Archives, BT 31/31981/95881.

36. The origins of this earlier company are unclear, but they may lie with a subsidiary of the Continental Telephone Company that had been organized by the Bell group to operate across Latin America (Rippy 1946).

37. The North American Trust itself was merged into the Mexican Trust Co. by Parker H. Sercombe, with William H. Hunt as president, and eventually became part of the International Banking Trust. The bank collapsed in 1903 and Hunt was jailed in 1905 (Schell 2001, 93–94).

38. National Archives BT 31/4141/26712.

39. In 1911, Conklin merged various Cuban sugar businesses into Central Cuba Sugar, obtaining financial backing from the United Railways of the Havana (Roberts 1992, 136). He went on to form the Jucaro and Moron Railway. The activities of the other major business interest operating in Cuba—the Cuba Company of William van Horne and his assistant Percival Farquhar—are discussed in Santamarina (2000) and Sibley (1913). See also Zanetti and García (1987).

40. F. J. Benson and Co were based at 11–12 Bloomfield Street; Prudential Deposit was at 16–17 Broad Street Avenue. The principal partner, and sometimes sole partner, in the company was Frederick Jessel Benson, a merchant living at 15 Belsize Avenue.

41. Solicitors for the trustees were Norton, Rose, Barrington & Co., of 57½ Old Broad Street. The accountants for HTC were Haskins and Sells, operating in both New York and London.

42. Ellis Island records show that a sailing from Havana in February 1907 included Roland Conklin and his wife, Emanuel Underdown, Walter Ogilvie, Frank Tiarks from Schroders of London, and John Orr. On Walter Ogilvie see van Ness (1986).

43. Underdown was associated with Schroders in the Chilean railways and was placed on the board of the United Railways when Schroders masterminded a reorganization of the company in 1897 (Roberts 1992: 104). See also letter of Rodríguez to Branford, July 14, 1907, at Keele Archives, VB 254.

44. Chaplin, Milne, Grenfell & Co., was the successor company to the London operations of Morton Rose. It was also described as the Canadian agent.

45. The directors of Prudential Discount Trust were Frederick Benson, Lord Elcho, John Archibald Grove, and Sir John Fowke Rolleston. In 1910, PDT changed its name to Brazilian, Canadian and General Trust.

46. Ralegh Buller Phillpotts, partner in Surtees Phillpotts and Co. Phillpotts had close business links with Speyer and Co. Information on travel to Cuba and the United States from the Ellis Island records.

47. National Archives BT 31/12364/97712.

48. *Scotsman*, January 26, 1911. Keele Archive, VB 168.

49. See *Kelly's London Directory*, 1910.

50. His eldest son was given the name Greenwood, after another business associate.

51. The telegraphic address of Lisman's company in 1908 was FARBRANG, suggesting a possible link with FARquhar and the BRAzil railway at that date, though "Farbrang" is also Yiddish for a joyful communication and gathering.

52. The New York offices of the Cuban Telephone Company were at 60 Broadway, from which office its affairs were managed by Daniel Boissevain, an affiliate of Gideon Boissevain's Amsterdam firm Gebr. Boissevain. Boissevain in New York was run by David Boissevain, son of Gideon, and was involved in the reconstruction of the Kansas City railway (Veenendaal 1996, 19, 148–51). Gideon's cousin Athanase Adolphe Henri Boissevain (1843–1921) operated in London as Blake, Boissevain and Co until 1901, after which he worked as sole partner.

53. 115 Broadway was a large office building with many companies located in it and these often had little or no connection with each other. One other company

located there and that may have been of relevance to the Branford interests was Alliance Realty, a property, mining, and railway investment company. Two of the directors of this company also sat on the board of the North America Company, based at 30 Broad Street. The latter, associated with General Electric and contractors J. G. White, was to become one of the largest utility holding companies in the United States.

54. Branford's Argentine syndicate, headed by Manuel Rodríguez, had been involved in negotiations with Farquhar for some time, even acting as a front for Farquhar, and in February 1911, Farquhar acquired the syndicate's holding in PCRC. Letter of B. G. Mummery to Branford, referring to letter of Branford to Rodríguez, February 15, 1911, Keele Archive VB 254.

55. For the interlinked histories of Percival Farquhar and William van Horne see Gauld (Gauld 1964), Armstrong and Nelles (1988), and Hanson (1937). Earlier in the century Percival Farquhar had shared a New York office with Sir William van Horne at 80 Broadway. The general pattern of British investment in North and South American railways is discussed by Jenks (1951).

56. Financial difficulties in the Cuba Company in 1902 led Farquhar to negotiate the sale of a substantial stake in the company to Scottish financier Robert Fleming. The company was then renamed the Cuba Railroad Co.

57. See especially *New York Times*, August 7, 1910.

58. Nickson (1993, 217) suggests that Farquhar began to invest in Paraguay in 1908 as an associate of Rodríguez but this seems unlikely.

59. Paraguay Land and Cattle later became part of International Products and then came under the umbrella of South American Assets as part of the rescue package for Farquhar's businesses.

60. MacDonald (1911) notes that by 1911 the ANER, Entre Rios, and PCRC were operating in combination to provide a through service from Buenos Aires to Asunción. See also Lewis (1968, 209). In 1901 Farquhar and van Horne were involved in the formation of a company of the same or similar name to the Argentine Railway, the finance organized by George B. Hopkins and a ten-member syndicate (Knowles 2004).

61. Appointed by Farquhar as European manager of the Brazil Railway in 1911.

62. *Kelly's Directory of London*, 1915. There is a reference in a Scots Canadian genealogy to an Alois Pfeiffer as son-in-law of Francis W. Newman (brother-in-law of Cardinal Newman). He may be connected with a company also in the offices: Alliance Investment Company (Canada) Ltd.

63. Other representatives of the debenture holders were Bernard Crisp, stockjobber associated with the lawyers Ashurst Morris and Crisp, Cecil Grenfell, stockbroker, and John Heslop.

64. Draft response of Branford to U.S. Embassy in connection with his U.S. citizenship in Keele Archives VB 301.

65. In August 1918, Asuncion Tramway, of which Victor Branford was chairman, went into liquidation. Creditors were to send claims to Bernhard Binder at 80 Bishopsgate, with Ashurst Morris and Crisp acting as lawyers. See *London Gazette*, August 16, 1918, and November 5, 1918.

66. Its offices by this time were at 80 Bishopsgate.

67. Letter of Druces and Attlee, Solicitors, to Eliza Gurney, October 2, 1894, in Keele Archives, Sybella Gurney Box 1; Probate of will Eliza Gurney, 1907; http://www.brh.org.uk/articles/scandle.pdf.
68. Strathclyde University archives T-GED 9/1669, 9/1672, 9/1688/1, 9/1681, 10/2/1, and 10/2/2.
69. Keele archives VB168 and VB 48.
70. Probate copies of the wills, Probate Registry.

CHAPTER EIGHT. FINANCIERS, THE CREDIT SYSTEM, AND THE THIRD ALTERNATIVE

1. See also Hobson's (1898) own account of Ruskin.
2. The book on modern capitalism was originally intended to be written by William Clarke as an extension of his Fabian essay (see Shaw 1889), but he passed the contract over to Hobson.
3. The subsequent debate over the relationship between ownership and control is reviewed and assessed in Scott (1997).
4. References to these works by Veblen are given in Branford (1914, 241) and Geddes (1915a, ch. 6).
5. Hobson met Veblen on a trip to the United States and hoped to build a British audience for Veblen's work. See Rutherford (1994, 188–89); Edgell and Tilman (1994); and Edgell and Townshend (1992).
6. There is, surprisingly, no mention of the accountant as an agent of the financier. However, Victor Branford probably saw himself, as an accountant and bankers' agent, as a mere technician constrained to act in the interests of the financiers with whom he dealt.
7. Branford failed to reflect on the fact that he had been involved in persuading the financier Martin White to endow a chair in sociology at the London School of Economics (Husbands 2005a).
8. They are referring here to Trotter's (1908, 1909) analysis of the so-called herd instinct.
9. Zabern (or Saverne) is a small town in Alsace, occupied by German forces prior to World War I. It came to prominence in 1913 when a German officer insulted the local population. The name became a byword for the abuse of military authority.
10. Those who discuss the more recent origin of the idea of the Third Way generally trace the term to Mussolini in the 1920s—the prior works of Branford and Geddes are generally ignored. A recent discussion traces the idea only to the period after World War I (Bastow and Martin 2003, ch. 1).
11. Branford appears to be citing the traditional Scottish ballad "Thomas Rymer and the Queen of Elfland."
12. Orage had first met Penty when working in Leeds and had moved with him to London in 1905. Orage and *The New Age* are discussed in Mairet (1936) and Martin (1967).
13. Cole (1920) set out a general social theory as a foundation for this political position. Hirst (1994, 1997) has described this emerging politics as "associationalism" and presents a statement of its contemporary relevance.

14. Pope Leo XIII's encyclical *Rerum Novarum* is available at http://www.vatican.va/holy_father/leo_xiii/encyclicals/documents/hf_l-xiii_enc_15051891_rerum-novarum_en.html.

15. Ramiro de Maeztu (1875–1936) His book was first published in English while he was London correspondent for a Spanish newspaper. It was translated into Spanish in 1919.

16. Other influential guild socialist work that stressed a religious, but non-Catholic, dimension included that of Neville Figgis (1913) and Richard Tawney (1921).

17. It was in this year that Chesterton (1926) restated the basic principles of distributism.

18. See the discussion of this approach in Mirowski (1989) and Martinez-Alier (1987).

19. Branford brought together two articles as a privately printed pamphlet in 1911. "Banks and Social Selection" was reprinted from *The Statist*, circa 1901, while "Memorandum *Re* Proposed Central Co-operative Credit Agency" had been written in the previous year. The pamphlet was produced in connection with a proposed cooperative credit bill in Parliament.

20. Branford had proposed a mechanism for achieving this through Le Play's categories in an early paper (Branford 1901).

21. The first statement of Douglas's position was in an influential article for the *English Review* (Douglas 1918).

22. Douglas draws specifically on Veblen (1921) on this point.

23. Douglas did not see the nationalization of banking as essential. His emphasis was purely on the distributive mechanism.

24. Other members included the social credit writer Maurice Colbourne (1935; a revision of his 1933).

25. On the New Europe Group see Passerini (1999, ch. 3).

26. The editorship of the original *New Age* magazine had passed in the mid-1920s from Orage to Arthur Brenton, editor of a magazine called *Credit Power*, which had published the social credit work of Marshall Hattersley (see 1922, 1929). In 1934, Philip Mairet became editor of *New English Weekly*, following the death of Orage.

27. This group and its later development are discussed in Cornford (2002, 2001); Reed (2001); Moore-Colyer (2001a,b); and Brace (2003).

28. R. G. Casey to Prime Minister of Australia, February 28, 1928; http://www.info.dfat.gov.au/info/historical/HistDocs.nsf/2ecf3135305dccd7ca256b5d007c2afc/e44f29c818fcfc36ca256d9400823bb1?OpenDocument.

29. National Library of Scotland MS 10559, 101–102.

30. http://www.oswaldmosley.com/buf/corporate_state.html.

APPENDIX A. WILLIAM BRANFORD

1. Marriage registration, Southwell, September Quarter 1858, 7b 367. Mary's mother, Ann Barlow from Lambley, may have given birth to her daughters as a result of a prior relationship, though this cannot be established with any certainty.

2. There is no sign of any fraudulent marriage by the pair. Unless they traveled abroad to marry, it must be presumed that they were unmarried.

3. John William Tennant Kitchen Branford, born and died 1862.

4. Case heard Northampton, on Norfolk Circuit, March 16, 1869.

5. This account of William Branford draws on the *Scotsman* of July 13 and November 2, 1869, September 6, November 22, and November 24, 1870, June 30, 1873, August 4 and 17, 1874, April 28, 1881. Some additional information is reported in Bradley (1923). Information on Branford's time in Edinburgh was provided from the Edinburgh University archives by Irene Ferguson, Assistant to the Archivist.

6. Return of Owners of Land, 1873.

7. In 1873 the trustees formally required the principal, William Williams, to resign. His response was to establish a rival college, the New Veterinary College, to which he took a majority of the students and the whole of the library. The original college responded by adopting the name Dick Veterinary College and completely reorganizing its management.

8. We are grateful to Brendon McDonagh, Librarian at the RCVS, for archive information about William Branford's qualifications and career. See also Beinart (1997a,b; 2003, ch. 4).

9. *Scotsman*, July 23, 1884.

10. *Scotsman*, June 25, 1887.

11. *Veterinary Record*, April 5, 1890, 543–44. *Times*, November 3, 1888, 11.

12. Papers in Nottinghamshire Archives: Newton and Wallis papers in the series DD/H/149.

13. 125 Sinclair Road, Hammersmith.

REFERENCES

All sources are cited by the date of first publication. Where a second date is shown, this is the date of a later reprint or translation.

Abente, D. 1989. Foreign capital, economic elites, and the state in Paraguay during the Liberal Republic (1870–1936), *Journal of Latin American Studies* 21, no. 1: 61–88.
Abercrombie, P. 1926. *The preservation of rural England*. London: Hodder and Stoughton.
———. 1934. *Country planning and landscape design*. Liverpool: University of Liverpool Press.
———. 1944. *Greater London plan*. London: HMSO.
Abrams, P. 1968. The origins of British sociology. In *The Origins of British Sociology, 1834–1914*, ed. P. Abrams. Chicago: University of Chicago Press, 1968.
Adair-Toteff, C. 2005. *Sociological beginnings. The first conference of the German Society for Sociology*. Liverpool: Liverpool University Press.
Adams, T. 1932. A communication in defense of the Regional Plan, *New Republic* 71, July 6, 207–10.
———. 1934. *The design of residential areas*. Cambridge: Harvard University Press.
———. 1935. *Outline of town and city planning, A review of past efforts and modern aims*. New York: Russell Sage Foundation.
Addams, J. 1910. *The spirit of youth and the city streets*. London: Macmillan.
Adorno, T., and M. Horkheimer. 1944. *Dialectic of enlightenment*. London: Verso, 1979.
Aitken, I. 1990. *Film and reform: John Grierson and the documentary film movement*. London: Routledge.
Aitken, M. 1961. *Courage. The story of James Dunn*. London: Collins.
Akers, C. E. 1914. *The rubber industry in Brazil and the Orient*. London: Methuen.
Anderson, L. 2002. *Benton MacKaye: Conservationist, planner, and creator of the Appalachian Trail*. Baltimore: Johns Hopkins University Press.
Anderson, P. 1968. Components of the national culture. In *Student power*, ed. R. Blackburn and P. Anderson. Harmondsworth: Penguin.
Anderson, V. 1980. *Friends and relations*. London: Hodder and Stoughton.
Anonymous. 1888. *Alphabetical list of graduates of the University of Edinburgh, from 1859 to 1888*. Edinburgh: James Thin.
Appleton, L. E. 1910. *A comparative study of the play activities of adult savages and civilised children*. Chicago: University of Chicago Press.
Armstrong, C., and H. V. Nelles. 1984. A curious capital flow: Canadian investment in Mexico, 1902–1910, *Business History Review* 58, no. 2: 178–203.

———. 1988. *Southern exposure: Canadian promoters in Latin America and the Caribbean, 1896–1930.* Toronto: University of Toronto Press.
Armytage, H. 1976. Educational research: A tercentenary romp, *Research Intelligence* 2, no. 2: 5–13.
Armytage, W. H. G. 1961. *Heavens below. Utopian experiments in England, 1560–1960.* London: Routledge and Kegan Paul.
Arnett, J. J. 2006. G. Stanley Hall's *Adolescence*: Brilliance and nonsense, *History of Psychology* 9, no. 3: 186–97.
Ashton, T. S. 1934. *Economic and social investigations in Manchester 1833–1933.* London: P. S. King.
Ashworth, W. 1954. *The genesis of modern British planning.* London: Routledge and Kegan Paul.
Asquith, H. H. 1924. *Studies and sketches.* London: Hutchinson.
Astell, M. 1694. *A serious proposal to the ladies for the advancement of their true and greatest influence.* London: Richard Wilkin.
Badley, J. H. 1923. *Bedales: A pioneer school.* London: Methuen.
———. 1937. *A schoolmaster's testament: Forty years of educational experience.* Oxford: Basil Blackwell.
Bailey, W. B. 1906. *Modern social conditions.* New York: The Century.
Baldwin, J. M. 1893. *The mental development of the child and the race.* New York: Macmillan.
Bales, R. F. 1950. *Interaction process analysis.* Cambridge, MA: Addison-Wesley.
Balfour, F. M. 1880. *A treatise in comparative embryology.* London: Macmillan.
Bannon, M. J. 1999. Dublin town planning competition: Ashbee and Cheltte's "New Dublin—A Study in Civics," *Planning Perspectives* 14, no. 2: 145–62.
Barclay, W. S. 1909. The River Parana: An economic survey, *Geographical Journal* 33, no. 1: 1–40.
Barker, P. 1992. *Regeneration.* Harmondsworth: Penguin.
Barnes, E. 1896 and 1902. *Studies in education, Two volumes.* Stanford: Stanford University Press.
———. 1899. Methods of studying children, *Paidologist* 1, no. 1: 9–17.
———. 1901. A forgotten student of child study, *Paidologist* 3, no. 3: 120–23.
Barrows, H. 1923. Geography as human ecology, *Annals of the Association of American Geographers* 13: 1–14.
Bastian, A. 1881. *Die Vorgeschichte der Ethnologie.* Berlin.
Bastow, S., and J. Martin. 2003. *Third way discourse. European identities in the twentieth century.* Edinburgh: Edinburgh University Press.
Beaver, S. H. 1962. The LePlay Society and fieldwork, *Geography* 47: 225–40.
Bechhofer, C. E., and M. B. Reckitt. 1918. *The meaning of national guilds.* London: Cecil Palmer and Haywood.
Beddington-Behrens, E. 1963. *Look back, look forward.* London: Macmillan.
Beinart, W. 1997a. Vets, viruses, and environmentalism: The Cape in the 1870s and 1880s, *Paideuma* 43: 227–52.
———. 1997b. Vets, viruses, and environmentalism at the Cape. In *Ecology and empire. The environmental history of settler societies*, ed. T. Griffiths and L. Robbin. Edinburgh: Keele University Press.

———. 2003. *The rise of conservation in South Africa.* Oxford: Oxford University Press.
Bell, Lady. 1907. *At the works.* Newton Abbott: David and Charles, 1969.
Bell, M. 1998. Reshaping boundaries: International ethics and environmental consciousness in the early twentieth century, *Transactions of the Institute of British Geographers* 23, no. 2: 151–75.
———, and C. McEwan. 1996. The admission of women Fellows to the Royal Geographical Society, 1892–1914. The controversy and the outcome, *Geographical Journal* 162, no. 3: 295–312.
Belloc, H. 1902. *The path to Rome.* Harmondsworth: Penguin, 1958.
———. 1904. *The old road: From Canterbury to Winchester.* London: Constable.
———. 1912. *The servile state.* London: T. N. Foulis (Third Edition: London: Constable, 1927).
———, and C. Chesterton. 1911. *The party system.* London: Stephen Swift.
Benjamin, F. A. 1974. *Ruskin linen industry of Keswick.* Beckermet: Michael J. Moon.
Bennett, A. 1918. *The pretty lady.* London: Cassell.
Bentham, J. 1789. Introduction to the principles of morals and legislation. In *A fragment on government and An introduction to the principles of morals and legislation,* ed. W. Harrison. Oxford: Basil Blackwell, 1948.
Berg, P. 2009. *Envisioning sustainability.* San Francisco: Subculture Books.
Besant, A. 1914. Theosophy and social reform. In *Theosophical ideals and the immediate future,* ed. A. Besant and others. London: Theosophical Publishing Society, 1914.
———. 1916. *The bearing of religious ideas on social reconstruction.* London: Theosophical Publishing.
———. 1925. *Shall India live or die?* Madras: National Home Rule League.
Blumer, H. 1937. Social psychology. In *Man and society,* ed. E. P. Schmidt. Englewood Cliffs: Prentice-Hall.
Boardman, P. 1944. *Patrick Geddes: Maker of the future.* Chapel Hill: University of North Carolina Press.
———. 1978. *The worlds of Patrick Geddes.* London: Routledge and Kegan Paul.
Booth, C. 1901–02. *Life and labour of the people of London.* 17 Volumes. London: Macmillan.
Booth, W. 1890. *In darkest England and the way out.* London: Salvation Army.
Bosanquet, B. 1897. *Psychology of the moral self.* London: Macmillan.
———. 1899. *The philosophical theory of the state.* London: Macmillan.
Bosanquet, H. 1898. *Rich and poor.* London: Macmillan.
———. 1902. *Strength of the people.* London: Macmillan.
———. 1906. *The family.* London: Macmillan.
Bourdieu, P. 1972. *Outline of a theory of practice.* Cambridge: Cambridge University Press, 1977.
Bower, S. 2003. Political and socio-economic elite: The encounter of provincials with porteños in fin-de-siecle Buenos Aires, *The Americas* 59, no. 3: 379–403.
Bowlby, J. 1965. *Child care and the growth of love.* 2nd Ed. Harmondsworth: Penguin.
———. 1969–80. *Attachment and loss,* Three volumes. London: Hogarth Press.
Bowley, A. L. and A. R. Burnett-Hurst. 1915. *Livelihood and poverty.* London: Bell.

Bowley, A. L., and M. H. Hogg. 1924. *Has poverty diminished?* London: P. S. King.
Brace, C. 2003. Envisioning England: The visual in countryside writing in the 1930s and 1940s, *Landscape Research* 28, no. 4: 365–82.
Bradburn, E. 1989. *Margaret McMillan. Portrait of a pioneer.* London: Routledge.
Bradley, F. H. 1876. My station and its duties. In *Ethical studies*, ed. F. H. Bradley. New York: Bobbs-Merrill, 1951.
Bradley, O. C. 1923. *A history of the Edinburgh Veterinary College.* Edinburgh: Edinburgh University Library, 1988.
Brady, G. S. 1926. *Railways of South America.* For the Department of Commerce. Washington, DC: Government Printing Office.
Brakarz, J. 2002. *Cities for all: Recent experiences with neighborhood upgrading programs.* Washington, DC: Inter-American Development Bank.
Branford, B. 1908. *A study of mathematical education.* Oxford: Clarendon Press.
———. 1916. *Janus and Vesta: A study of the world crisis and after.* London: Chatto and Windus.
———. 1919. *A new chapter in the science of government.* London: Chatto and Windus.
———. 1934. *Eros and Psyche.* London: University of London Press.
Branford, F. V. 1918. *Titans and gods.* London: Christophers.
———. 1922. *Five poems.* Edinburgh: The Porpoise Press.
———. 1924. *The white stallion.* London: Christophers.
Branford, Mrs. B. 1923. *The wheel of life.* Whitstable: The Whitstable Times.
Branford, S. 1915. The relation of capital to credit, *Sociological Review* 8, no. 1: 48–51.
———. 1916–17. The arts and crafts exhibition: I. What the city might do for the craftsman, *Sociological Review* 9, no. 1: 49–52.
———. 1919. The new Jerusalem, *Sociological Review* 11, no. 2: 141.
———. 1921. In defence of the English cottage, *Town Planning Review* 9, no. 1: 41–46.
———. 1923. Labour Co-partnership and the guild movement, *Co-partnership* (March): 36–37, 44.
———. 1924. Social credit, *Sociological Review* 16, no. 1: 126–30.
———. 1925. The red peril—or the peril of big words? *The Crusader* (October 30): 692–93.
———. 1927. Co-operators and the community, *Sociological Review* 19: 228–33.
———, and A. Farquharson. 1924. *An introduction to regional surveys.* London: Le Play House.
Branford, S. (writing as Mrs. V. Branford). 1913. The revival of the village, *Sociological Review* 6: 1143–46.
Branford, V. V. 1888. *Hand-book of animal classification.* Edinburgh: E and S Livingstone.
———. 1889. *Atlas of chemistry [inorganic and organic].* Edinburgh: E and S Livingstone.
———. 1898. The areal farm. *Barbados Globe* (November 30).
———. 1899. *An undeveloped estate of the empire.* London: West Indian Cooperative Union (Appendix to the First Annual Report).

———. 1901a. Banks and social selection. In *Co-operative credit societies and the joint stock banks*. London: privately printed, 1911.

———. 1901b. On the calculation of national resources, *Journal of the Royal Statistical Society* 64, no. 3: 380–414.

———. 1901c. *On the correlation of economics and accountancy*. London: Gee and Co. (Originally a lecture delivered at the London Economic Club.)

———. 1902. The Philadelphia Commercial Museum, *Scottish Geographical Magazine* 18: 243–52.

———. 1903a. Accountancy in its relation to the economic theory of value. *Encyclopaedia of accounting*.

———. 1903b. On the origin and use of the word "sociology" and on the relationship of sociological to other studies and to practical problems, *American Journal of Sociology* 9, no. 2: 145–62.

———. 1904. The founders of sociology, *American Journal of Sociology* 10, no. 1: 94–126.

———. 1905. Sociology in some of its educational aspects, *American Journal of Sociology* 11, no. 1: 85–89.

———. 1906. Science and citizenship, *American Journal of Sociology* 11, no. 6: 721–62.

———. 1909. Comment [On the River Parana survey by William Barclay], *Geographical Journal* 33, no. 1: 38.

———. 1910. Memorandum re proposed central co-operative credit agency. In *Co-operative credit societies and the joint stock banks*, ed. V. V. Branford. London: privately printed, 1911.

———. 1911. Comment on "Things one expects of a Sociological Society," *Sociological Review* 4, no. 3: 247–52.

———. 1912. *St. Columba: A study of social inheritance and spiritual development*. Edinburgh: Patrick Geddes and Colleagues.

———. 1914a. *Interpretations and forecasts: A study of the survivals and tendencies in contemporary societies*. New York: Mitchell Kennerley.

———. 1914b. The mobilisation of national credit, *Sociological Review* 7, no. 4: 307–14.

———. 1917. The banker's part in reconstruction, *Sociological Review* 9: 149–81.

———. 1918. *A citizen soldier: His education for war and peace, being a memoir of Alasdair Geddes*. London: Le Play House.

———. 1919a. The drift to revolution. In *Whitherward: Hell or eutopia*, ed. V. V. Branford. London: Le Play House, 1921.

———. 1919b. The third alternative, *Sociological Review* 11, no. 2: 142–51.

———. 1919c. Towards the third alternative, *Sociological Review* 11, no. 1: 62–65.

———. 1920. The war-mind, the business-mind, and a third alternative. In *Whitherward? Hell or eutopia*, ed. V. V. Branford. London: Williams and Norgate, 1921.

———. 1921a. Hell, earth, and the third alternative [A new year's message]. In *Whitherward? Hell or eutopia*, ed. V. V. Branford. London: Williams and Norgate, 1921.

———. 1921b. *Whitherward?: Hell or eutopia*. London: Le Play House.
———. 1923. *Science and sanctity: A study in the scientific approach to unity*. London: Le Play House Press and Williams and Norgate.
———. 1924a. *Living religions: A plea for the larger modernism*. London: Williams and Norgate.
———. 1924b. A view of Hastings, *Observation* 1: 31–34.
———. 1925. General survey. In *Religions of the Empire*, ed. W. L. Hare. London: Duckworth, 1925.
———. 1926a. The background of survival and tendency exposed in an exhibition of modern ideas. In *Coal: Ways to Reconstruction*, Ed. V. V. Branford. London: Le Play House, 1926.
———. 1926b. The conditions of eutopian repair and reconstruction. In *The coal crisis and the future: A study of social disorders and their treatment*, ed. P. Abercrombie, V. V. Branford, C. Desch, P. Geddes, C. W. Saleeby, and E. Kilburn Scott. London: Le Play House and Williams and Norgate, 1926.
———. 1928. Sociology: Its past, present, and future, *Sociological Review* 20, no. 4: 322–39.
———. 1930. A more realistic approach to the social system, *Sociological Review* 22, no. 3: 195–218.
———, and P. Geddes. 1917. *The coming polity*. London: Williams and Norgate.
———. 1919a. *The coming polity*. Revised edition. London: Williams and Norgate.
———. 1919b. *Our social inheritance*. London: Williams and Norgate.
Branford, V. 1939. *Songs from a Kentish garden*. Oxford: Shakespeare Head Press.
Brehoney, K. 2004. From kindergarten to the English nursery school: The role of the Pestallozzi-Froebel House. *European Conference on Educational Research*: Photocopy.
———. 2009. Transforming theories of childhood and early childhood education, *Paedogogica Historica* 45: 585–604.
Briggs, A., and A. Macartney. 1984. *Toynbee Hall. The first hundred years*. London: Routledge and Kegan Paul.
Brock, A. 1923. *Health and conduct*. London: Le Play House.
Bromley, R. 2001. Metropolitan regional planning: Enigmatic history, global future, *Planning Practice and Research* 16, no. 3–4: 233–45.
———. 2003. Peru 1957–1977: How time and place influenced John Turner's ideas on housing policy, *Habitat International* 27, no. 2: 271–92.
Bruce, I. 2000. *The loving eye and the skilful hand: The Keswick School of Industrial Arts*. Carlisle Bookcase.
Bruner, J. 1960. *The process of education*. Cambridge: Harvard University Press.
Bryson, G. 1936. Early English positivists and the religion of humanity, *American Sociological Review* 1, no. 3: 343–62.
Bukharin, N. I. 1921. *Historical materialism: A system of sociology*. New York: International Publishers, 1925.
Bulmer, M. 1991a. The social survey in historical perspective. In *The social survey in historical perspective, 1880–1914*, ed. M. Bulmer, K. Bales, and K. K. Sklar. Cambridge: Cambridge University Press.

---. 1991b. W. E. B. Du Bois as a social investigator. In *The social survey in historical perspective 1880–1940*, ed. M. Bulmer, K. Bales, and K. K. Sklar. Cambridge: Cambridge University Press.

Burawoy, M. 2005. For public sociology, *British Journal of Sociology* 56, no. 2: 259–94.

Burnham, D. H., and E. H. Bennett. 1909. *Plan of Chicago*. Chicago: Commercial Club of Chicago.

Butler, E. B. 1909. *Women and the trades*. New York: Russell Sage Foundation.

Calder, A. 1985. Mass-Observation 1937–1949. In *Essays in the history of British sociological research*, ed. M. Bulmer. Cambridge: Cambridge University Press.

Caldwell Cook, H. 1917. *The play way*. London: William Heinemann.

Cameron, L., and J. Forrester. 2000. Tansley's psychoanalytic network: an episode of the early history of psychpoanalysis in England, *Psychoanalysis and History* 2, no. 2: 189–256.

Cantor, D. 2005. Between Galen, Geddes, and the Gael: Arthur Brock, modernity, and medical humanism in early twentieth-century Scotland, *Journal of the History of Medicine and Allied Science* 60, no. 1: 1–41.

Caradog Jones, D. 1934. *Social survey of Merseyside*. London: Hodder and Stoughton.

---. 1941. Evolution of the social survey in England since Booth, *American Journal of Sociology* 46, no. 6: 818–25.

Carey, H. C. 1858–89. *The principles of social science*. Three vols. New York: Augustus Kelley, 1963.

---. 1872. *The unity of law: As exhibited in the relation of physical, social, mental, and moral science*. New York: Augustus M. Kelley, 1967.

Carlson, A. C. 2007. *Third ways*. Wilmington, DE: ISI Books.

Carpenter, E. 1884. *England's ideal*. London: Swann and Sonnenschein.

---. 1889. *Civilization*. Revised and enlarged edition (1906). London: Swann and Sonnenschein.

---. 1894. *The art of creation*. London: George Allen and Unwin.

---. 1908. *The intermediate sex: A study of some transitional types of men and women*. London: George Allen and Unwin.

---. 1920. *Pagan and Christian creeds*. New York: Harcourt, Brace.

Chabard, P. 2009. Competing scales in transnational networks: The impossible travel of Patrick Geddes' Cities Exhibition to America, 1911–1913, *Urban History* 36, no. 2.

Chamberlain, A. 1903. *The child: A study of the evolution of man*. New York: Charles Scribner's Sons.

Chambers, C. A. 1971. *Paul U. Kellogg and the survey: Voices for social welfare and social justice*. Minneapolis: University of Minnesota Press.

Cherry, G. E. 1979. *The evolution of British town planning*. Leighton Buzzard: Leonard Hill.

Chesterton, G. K. 1910. *What's wrong with the world*. London: Cassel.

---. 1926. *The outline of sanity*. London: Methuen.

Cities-Committee 1911. *City survey preparatory to town planning*. London: Sociological Society Cities Committee.

———. 1918. *A rustic view of war and peace.* London: Sociological Society Cities Committee.

Clapperton, J. H. 1885. *Scientific meliorism and the evolution of happiness.* London: Kegan Paul, Trench.

Clavel, P. 1971. Introduction to the Torchbook Edition. In *Cities in evolution*, ed. P. Geddes, vii–xxiii. New York: Harper and Row.

CNHSS. 1936–1962. *Regional survey atlas of Croydon and District.* Croydon: Croydon Natural History and Scientific Society.

Colbourne, M. 1933. *Economic nationalism.* London: Figurehead.

———. 1935. *The meaning of social credit.* London: Figurehead.

Cole, G. D. H. 1913. *World of labour.* London: Bell.

———. 1917. *Self-Government in industry.* London: Bell.

———. 1920a. *Guild socialism restated.* London: Parsons.

———. 1920b. *Social theory.* London: Methuen.

———. 1955. *Studies in class structure.* London: Routledge and Kegan Paul.

Coleridge, S. T. 1830. *On the constitution of church and state, according to the principles of each.* London: William Pickering.

Collingwood, R. G. 1923. *Roman Britain.* Oxford: Oxford University Press.

Comte, A. 1848. *General view of positivism.* London: Trübner, 1865.

Conn, S. 1998. *Museums and American life, 1876–1926.* Chicago: University of Chicago Press.

Cons, E. 1896. Armenian exiles in Cyprus, *Contemporary Review* 70 (July-December): 88–95.

Cook, H. C. 1917. *The play way.* London: Heinemann.

Cooley, C. H. 1902. *Human nature and the social order.* New York: Scribner's.

Conford, P. 2001. *The origins of the organic movement.* Glasgow: Floris Books.

———. 2002. Finance versus farming: Rural reconstruction and economic reform, *Rural History* 13, no. 2: 225–41.

Corrin, J. P. 1987. *G. K. Chesterton and Hilaire Belloc, The battle against modernity.* Athens, OH: Ohio University Press.

Costello, J. E. 2002. *John Macmurray: A biography.* Edinburgh: Florris Books.

Coudenhove-Kalergi, R. N. 1943. *Crusade for pan-Europe: Autobiography of a man and a movement.* New York: G. P. Putnam.

Crawford, A. 1985. *C. R. Ashbee.* New Haven: Yale University Press.

Crawford, O. G. S. 1921. *Man and his past.* London: Oxford University Press.

Creedon, A. 2002. A benevolent tyrant? The principles and practice of Henrietta Barnett (1851–1936), *Women's History Review* 11, no. 2: 231–52.

Crook, D. P. 1984. *Benjamin Kidd: Portrait of a Social Darwinist.* Cambridge: Cambridge University Press.

Das Gupta, U., ed. 2006. *Rabindranath Tagore: My life in my words.* New Delhi: Viking Penguin.

Davies, M. 1909. *Life in an English village.* London: T. Fisher Unwin.

Davis, M. 2006. *Planet of slums.* London: Verso.

de Tourville, H. 1904. *The growth of modern nations.* London: Edward Arnold, 1907.

Defries, A. 1927. *The interpreter. Geddes, the man and his gospel.* London: G. Routledge and Sons.

———. 1928. *Pioneers of science*. New York: Book For Libraries Press, 1970.
Dehaene, M. 2002. Survey and the assimilation of a modernist narrative in urbanism, *Journal of Architecture* 7: 33–55.
Delahaye, J. V. 1929. *Politics: Discussion of realities*. London: C. W. Daniel.
Demolins, E. 1897. *Anglo Saxon superiority: To what is it due?* New York: Charles Scribner's Sons, 1898.
Dewey, J. 1922. *Human nature and conduct*. New York: The Modern Library, 1929.
Dickinson, R. E. 1934. *The Le Play method in regional survey*. London: Le Play Society.
———. 1947. *City, region, and regionalism. A geographical contribution to human ecology*. London: Kegan Paul, Trench, Trubner.
Dilthey, W. 1883. *Introduction to the human sciences*. Princeton: Princeton University Press, 1989.
Disraeli, B. 1845. *Sybil*. Oxford: Oxford University Press, 1998.
Dodson, E. J. 2005. In the footsteps of Henry George. The Philadelphia geologist story. Phliadelphia: Council of Geologist Organizations: http://www.cooperativeindividualism.org/dodson-edward_in-the-footsteps-of-henry-george-the-philadelphia-georgist-story-2005.html.
Dole, C. F. 1899. *The young citizen*. Boston: D. C. Heath.
Douglas, C. H. 1918. The delusion of super-production. In *Economic democracy*, 5th ed., ed. C. H. Douglas. Sudbury: Bloomfield Books, 1974.
———. 1921a. *Credit-power and democracy*. London: Stanley Nott.
———. 1921b. *Economic democracy*. Sudbury: Bloomfield Books, 1974.
———. 1924. *Social credit*. London: Eyre and Spottiswoode.
Drakeford, M. 1997. *Social movements and their supporters. The Green Shirts in England*. Houndmills: Macmillan Press.
DuBois, W. E. B 1899. *The Philadelphia negro*. Philadelphia: University of Pennsylvania Press, 1996.
Dudden, A. P. 1971. *Joseph Fels and the single-tax movement*. Philadelphia: Temple University Press.
Durkheim, E. 1892. Montesquieu's contribution to the rise of social science. In *Emile Durkheim: Montesquieu and Rousseau*, ed. H. Peyre. Ann Arbor: University of Michigan Press, 1965.
———. 1893. *The division of labour in society*. London: Macmillan, 1984.
———. 1895. *The rules of the sociological method*. London: Macmillan, 1982.
———. 1897. *Suicide: A study in sociology*. London: Routledge and Kegan Paul, 1952.
———. 1912. *Elementary forms of the religious life*. London: George Allen and Unwin, 1915.
———, and M. Mauss. 1903. *Primitive classification*. London: Cohen and West, 1963.
Eden, Sir F. M. 1797. *The state of the poor: A history of the labouring classes in England*. London: Frank Cass, 1966.
Edgell, D. 1992. *The Order of Woodcraft Chivalry 1916–1949 as a New Age alternative to the Boy Scouts*. Lewiston: Edwin Mellen Press.
Edgell, S., and R. Tilman. 1994. John Hobson: Admirer and critic of Thorstein Veblen. In *J A Hobson after 50 years*, ed. J. Phoeby. Houndmills: Palgrave, 1994.

Edgell, S., and J. Townshend. 1992. John Hobson, Thorstein Veblen, and the phenomenon of imperialism: Finance capital, patriotism, and war, *American Journal of Economics and Sociology* 51, no. 4: 401–20.

Ellis, H. 1889. *The new spirit*. London: George Bell and Sons.

Ellis, H. 1894. *Man and woman: A study of secondary and tertiary sexual characteristics*. London: Walter Scott.

Ellwood, C. A. 1917. *An introduction to social psychology*. New York: Appleton.

———. 1922. *The reconstruction of religion. A sociological view*. New York: Macmillan.

Engels, F. 1845. *The condition of the working class in England in 1844*. Oxford: Basil Blackwell, 1958.

Erikson, E. 1950. *Childhood and society*. New York: W. W.Norton.

———. 1968. *Identity, youth, and crisis*. New York: W. W. Norton.

Espinas, A. 1877. *Des sociétés animals*. Paris: G. Baillière.

Evans, D. F. T. 1986. *Le Play House and the regional survey movement in British sociology 1920–1955*. Birmingham: City of Birmingham Polytechnic. M. Phil. thesis (available at http://www.dfte.co.uk/ios).

Evans, I. O. 1930. *Woodcraft and world service. Studies in unorthodox education*. London: Noel Douglas.

Fagg, C. C. and G. E. Hutchings. 1930. *An introduction to regional surveying*. Cambridge: Cambridge University Press.

Faithfull, G. 1991. Memories of Norman Glaister, *Research Connections* [Braziers Park School of Integrative Research] 13: 3–11.

Faithfull, T. 1925. *The king's prerogative and other undelivered addresses on the new socialism*. London: C. W. Daniel.

Faithfull, T. 1927. *Bisexuality*. London: John Bale, Sons and Danielsson.

———. 1933. *Psychological foundations*. London: John Bale, Sons and Danielsson.

Farrell, M. P. 2001. *Collaborative circles. Friendship dynamics and creative work*. Chicago: University of Chicago Press.

Fawcett, C. B. 1917. Natural divisions of England, *Geographical Journal* 49: 124–41.

———. 1918. *Frontiers: A study in political geography*. Oxford: Clarendon Press.

———. 1919. *The provinces of England*. London: Hutchinson, 1960.

———. 1933. *A political geography of the British Empire*. London: University of London Press.

Febvre, L. 1922. *A geographical introduction to history*. Westport, CT: Greenwood Press, 1974.

Ferguson, C. 1900. *The religion of democracy*. New York: Funk and Wagnalls.

———. 1911. *The university militant*. New York: M. Kennerley.

Ferguson, M. 2004. "Dear Guru"—John Duncan and Patrick Geddes. In *The artist and the thinker*, ed. M. Jarron. Dundee: University of Dundee Museum Service, 2004.

Field, J. 2009. *Able bodies: Work camps and the training of the unemployed in Britain before 1939*. Stirling: Stirling Institute of Education.

Figgis, J. N. 1913. *Churches in the modern state*. London: Longmans Green.

Finlay, J. L. 1970. John Hargrave, the Green Shirts, and social credit, *Journal of Contemporary History* 5, no. 1: 53–71.

Fisher, H. A. L. 1927. *James Bryce, Volume 1*. London: Macmilan.

REFERENCES

Fitzhugh, G. 1854. Sociology for the south. In *Ante-bellum*, ed. H. Wish. New York: G. P. Putnam's Sons, 1960.
Fleure, H. J. 1918. *Human geography in Western Europe: A study in appreciation.* London: Williams and Norgate.
———. 1919a. Human regions, *Scottish Geographical Magazine* 35: 94–105.
———. 1919b. Regional surveys, *Sociological Review* 11: 28–33.
———. 1922. *The peoples of Europe.* Oxford: Oxford University Press.
———. 1928. Regional surveys and welfare, *South-Eastern Naturalist* 33: 73–82.
———. 1947. *Some problems of society and environment* London: George Philip.
———. 1961. *Guernsey.* London: Geographical Association.
Flugel, J. C. 1933. *A hundred years of psychology, 1833–1933.* London: Gerald Duckworth.
Ford, P. 1934. *Work and wealth in a modern port.* London: George Allen and Unwin.
Fowle, F. 2004. The Franco-Scottish alliance: Artistic links between Scotland and France in the late 1880s and 1890s. In *Patrick Geddes: The French connection*, ed. F. Fowle and B. Thompson. Oxford: White Cockade Publishing, 2004.
Fraser, B., ed. 2005 *A meeting of two minds: Geddes, Tagore: Letters.* Edinburgh: Word Power Books.
Frazer, J. 1890. *The Golden Bough.* London: Macmillan.
Freeden, M. 1979. Eugenics and progressive thought: A study in ideological affinity, *Historical Journal* 22, no. 3: 645–71.
Freeman, M. 2002. The provincial social survey in Edwardian Britain, *Historical Research* 75, no. 187: 73–89.
Fuller, J. O. 1965. *The magical dilemma of Victor Neuberg.* Oxford: Mandrake of Oxford.
Gardiner, R. 1943. *England herself: Ventures in rural reconstruction.* London: Faber and Faber.
Gauld, A. 1968. *The founders of psychical research.* London: Routldge and Kegan Paul.
Gauld, C. A. 1964. *The last titan.* Stanford: Stanford University Press.
Geddes, A. 1927. *Au pays de Tagore: La civilisation rurale du Bengale occidental et ses facteurs géographiques.* Paris: A. Colin.
Geddes, P. 1881. *The classification of statistics and its results.* Edinburgh: A. and C. Black (Reprint of the Proceedings of the Royal Society of Edinburgh).
———. 1884a. *An analysis of the principles of economics.* London: Williams and Norgate (Reprint of the Proceedings of the Royal Society of Edinburgh).
———. 1884b. *John Ruskin: Economist.* Edinburgh: Brown.
———. 1888a. Co-operation versus socialism, *Co-operative Wholesale Societies' Annual.*
———. 1888b. *Every man his own art critic.* Glasgow: William Brown.
———. 1890. Scottish university needs and aims, *Scots Magazine* (August).
———. 1897a. Cyprus actual and possible. A study in the Eastern question, *The Contemporary Review* 71: 892–908.
———. 1897b. *Cyprus and its power to help the East*: Report of the International Committee on Armenian Aid.
———. 1902. Edinburgh and its region, *Scottish Geographical Magazine* 18, no. 6: 302–12.

———. 1904a. Adolescence, *Saint George*, October 7: 303–27.
———. 1904b. *City development. A study of parks, gardens, and culture-institutes*. Edinburgh: Patrick Geddes and Company.
———. 1904c. Civics as applied sociology, Part 1. In *The ideal city*, ed. H. Meller. Leicester: University of Leicester Press, 1979.
———. 1904d. An educational approach—A technical approach. In *Ideals of science and faith*, ed. J. E. Hand. London: George Allen.
———. 1905a. Civics as applied sociology, Part 2. In *The ideal city*, ed. H. Meller. Leicester: Leicester University Press, 1979.
———. 1905b. The school at Abbotsholme, conducted by Dr. Cecil Reddie, *Elementary School Teacher* 5, no. 7: 396–407.
———. 1905c. *The world without and the world within: Sunday talks with my children*. Bournville: Saint George Press.
———. 1906. University studies and university residence, *University Review* (July).
———. 1907. A suggested plan for a civic museum (or civic exhibition) and its associated studies, *Sociological Papers* 3: 197–236.
———. 1908. Chelsea, past and present. In *Utopian Papers*, ed. D. Hollins. London: Masters.
———. 1909. City deterioration and the needs of a city survey, *Annals of the American Academy of Political and Social Science* 34 (July): 54–67.
———. 1911. *Civic survey of Edinburgh. Transactions of the Town Planning Conference*. London: Royal Institute of British Architects.
———. 1913a. *The masque of ancient learning and its many meanings: A pageant of education from primitive to Celtic times*. Edinburgh: Patrick Geddes and Colleagues.
———. 1913b. *The masque of learning: Medieval and modern: A pageant of education through the ages*. Edinburgh: Patrick Geddes and Colleagues.
———. 1915a. *Cities in evolution*. London: Williams and Norgate.
———. 1915b. Wardom and peacedom: Suggestions towards an interpretation, *Sociological Review* 8: 15–25.
———. 1917. *Town planning in Lahore: A report to the municipal council*. Partially reprinted in *Patrick Geddes: Spokesman for man and the environment*, ed. M. Stalley, 387–449. New Brunswick, NJ: Rutgers University Press.
———. 1918. *Town planning towards city development. A report to the Durbar of Indore*. Indore: Holkar State Printing Press.
———. 1919. *Jerusalem actual and possible: A preliminary report to the chief administrator of Palestine and the military governor of Jerusalem on town planning and city improvements*. Jerusalem.
———. 1920a. Essentials of sociology in relation to economics. Part 1, *Indian Journal of Economics* 3, no. 1: 1–56.
———. 1920b. Essentials of sociology in relation to economics. Part 2, *Indian Journal of Economics* 3, no. 3: 257–305.
———. 1920c. *The life and work of Jagadis C. Bose*. London: Longmans Green.
———. 1924a. The mapping of life, *Sociological Review* 16, no. 3: 193–203.
———. 1924b. A proposed coordination of the social sciences, *Sociological Review* 16, no. 1: 54–65.
———. 1925a. The education of two boys, *Survey* 54: 571–75, 587–91.

———. 1925b. Valley plan of civilization, *Survey* 54: 288–90, 322.
———. 1926. Coal: ways to reconstruction: Part II: The background of survival and tendency exposed in an exhibition or modern ideas, *Sociological Review* 18, no. 3: 207–30.
———. 1927a. The charting of life, *Sociological Review* 19, no. 1: 40–63.
———. 1927b. The notation of life (condensed by Amelia Defries). In *The interpreter*, ed. A. Defries. London: George Routledge.
———. 1930. Scouting and woodcraft—Present and possible, *Sociological Review* 22: 274–77.
———. 1931. Towards a theory of life. In *Life. Outline of general biology*, ed. P. Geddes and J. A. Thomson. London: Williams and Norgate.
Geddes, P., and A. Geddes. 1897. Cyprus and its power to help the East. *Report of the International Conference on Armenian Aid.*
Geddes, P., and G. Slater. 1917. *Ideas at war.* London: Williams and Norgate.
Geddes, P., and J. A. Thomson. 1889. *The evolution of sex.* London: Walter Scott.
———. 1893. *Chapters on modern botany.* London: John Murray.
———. 1911. *Evolution.* London: Williams and Norgate.
———. 1914. *Sex.* London: Williams and Norgate.
———. 1931. *Life. Outlines of general biology.* London: Williams and Norgate.
George, H. 1879. *Progress and poverty.* London: Hogarth Press, 1966.
Giddings, F. H. 1896. *Principles of sociology.* New York: Johnson Reprint, 1970.
Gilman, C. P. 1898. *Women and economics: A study of the economic relations between women and men as a factor in social evolution.* London: Prometheus Books, 1994.
———. 1911. *The man-made world, or our androcentric culture.* New York: Humanity Books, 2001.
Ginsberg, M. 1921. *The psychology of society.* London: Methuen.
Glaister, N. 1925. The order as a social organism, *Pine Cone* (October).
Goldman, L. 2002. *Science, reform, and politics in Victorian Britain: The Social Science Association 1857–1886.* Cambridge: Cambridge University Press.
Gottmann, J. 1961. *Megalopolis: The urbanized northeastern seaboard of the United States.* New York: Twentieth Century Fund.
Gould, F. J. 1900. *The history of the Leicester Secular Society.* Leicester: Leicester Secular Society. Available at http://www.leicestersecularsociety.org.uk/history_gould.htm.
Gould, P. C. 1988. *Early green politics: Back to nature, back to the land, and socialism in Britain, 1880–1900.* Brighton: Harvester Press.
Green, T. H. 1879. *Lectures on the principles of political obligation.* London: Longmans, Green, 1911.
Greenberg, D. 1980. *Financiers and railroads, 1864–1889. A study of Morton, Bliss and Co.* Newark: University of Delaware Press.
Griggs, E. H. 1935. *Earl Barnes. A life sketch and an address.* New York: Orchard Hill Press.
Gruffadd, P. 1994. Back to the land: Historiography, rurality, and the nation in interwar Wales, *Transactions of the Institute of British Geographers* 19: 61–77.

Guenon, R. 1921. *Theosophy: History of a pseudo-religion*. Hillsdale, NY: Sophia Perennis, 2004.
Guest, H. 1912. *Theosophy and social reconstruction*. London: Theosophical Publishing.
Gurney, A. W. 1887. Memoir of Archer Thompson Gurney. Unpublished manuscript. British Library: BL ADD81597.
Gurney, S. 1896. *Sixty years of co-operation*. London: Labour Association for Promoting Co-operative Production based on the Co-partnership of the Workers.
———. (anon.) 1907. *Cottages with gardens for Londoners*. London: Hampstead Tenants.
———. 1909. *Co-partnership in housing, as a method of physical and social reconstruction*. London: Co-partnership Tenants.
———. 1910. Civic reconstruction and the Garden City movement, *Sociological Review* 3, no. 1: 35–43.
Habermas, J. 1981a. *The theory of communicative action, Volume One: Reason and the rationalisation of society*. London: Heinemann, 1984.
———. 1981b. *The theory of communicative action, Volume Two: The critique of functionalist reason*. London: Heinemann, 1987.
Haddon, A. C. 1887. *An introduction to the study of embryology*. London: Charles Griffin.
Hall, G. S. 1904. *Adolescence. Its psychology and its relation to psychology, anthropology, sociology, sex, crime, religion*. Two Volumes. New York: D. Appleton.
———. 1909. Evolution and psychology. In *Health, growth, and heredity*, ed. G. S. Hall. New York: Teachers College Press, 1965.
———. 1923. *Life and confessions of a psychologist*. New York: D. Appleton.
Halliday, R. J. 1968. The sociological movement and the genesis of academic sociology in Britain, *Sociological Review* 16, no. 3: 377–98.
Hammes, D., and D. Wills. 2005. Thomas Edison's "Except One": The money views of Arthur Kitson revisited, *Journal of Economic Studies* 32, no. 1: 33–46.
Hand, J. E. 1899. *Good citizenship*. London: George Allen and Unwin.
———. 1904. *Ideals of science and faith*. London: George Allen and Unwin.
———. 1906. *Science in public affairs*. London: George Allen and Unwin.
Hanson, S. G. 1937. The Farquhar syndicate in South America, *Hispanic American Historical Review* 17, no. 3: 314–26.
Hardy, D. 2000. *Utopian England: Community experiments, 1900–45*. London: Routledge.
Hardy, M. 1906. Botanical survey of Scotland, *Scottish Geographical Magazine* 22 (May): 229–41.
Hardy, M. E. 1902. *Geography of plants*. Oxford: Clarendon Press.
Hare, W. L., ed. 1925. *Religions of the empire*. London: Duckworth.
Harper, E. B. 1933. Sociology in England, *Social Forces* 11, no. 3: 335–42.
Harris, R. 2003. A double irony: The originality and influence of John F. C. Turner, *Habitat International* 27, no. 2: 245–69.
Harrison, F. 1877. *Order and progress*. Brighton: Harvester Press, 1975.
Harrison, J. E. 1913. *Ancient art and ritual*. London: Williams and Norgate.
Hattersley, C. M. 1922. *The community's credit: A consideration of the principles of the social credit movement*. London: Credit Power Press.

———. 1929. *The age of plenty: Its problem and the solution*. London: Pitman.
Hauser, K. 2008. *Bloody old Britain: O. G. S. Crawford and the archaeology of modern life*. London: Granta.
Hawkins, C. B. 1910. *Norwich: A social study*. London: P. L. Warner.
Hearnshaw, L. S. 1964. *A short history of British psychology, 1840–1940*. London: Methuen.
Hecht, J. S. 1920. *The real wealth of nations. or A new civilization and its economic foundations*. London: G. G. Harrap.
Hegel, G. W. F. 1821. *Hegel's philosophy of right* [*Naturrecht und Staatswissenschaft im Grundrisse/Grundlinien der Philosophie des Rechts*]. London: Oxford University Press, 1952.
———. 1831. *Philosophy of history*. New York: P. F. Collier and Son.
Hendrick, H. 1990. *Images of youth: Age, class, and the male youth problem, 1880–1920*. Oxford: Clarendon Press.
Herbertson, A. J. 1905. The major natural regions, *Geographical Journal* 25: 300–12.
———, and F. D. Herbertson. 1899. *Man and his work: An introduction to human geography*. London: A. and C. Black.
Herbertson, F. D. 1897–99. *The life of Frédéric Le Play*. Ledbury: Le Play House, 1950.
Herder, J. G. 1784–1791. Reflections on the philosophy of the history of man. In *On world history*, ed. H. Adler and E. A. Menze. New York: M. E. Sharpe, 1997.
Herken, J. C. 1984. *Ferrocarriles, conspiraciones, y negocios en el Paraguay, 1910–1914*. Asunción: Arte Nuevo Editores.
———. 1985. Financistas en el Paraguay, 1907–1920, *Jahrbuch für Geschichte von Staat, Wirtschaft und Gesellschaft Lateinamerikas* 22: 423–55.
Herle, A., and S. Rouse, eds. 1998. *Cambridge and the Torres Strait. Centenary essays on the 1898 anthropological expedition*. Cambridge: Cambridge University Press.
Herrick, J. 1987a. A biographical introduction. In *J. M. Robertson (1856–1933): Liberal, rationalist, and scholar*, ed. G. A. Wells. London: Pemberton, 1987.
———. 1987b. The politician. In *J. M. Robertson (1856–1933): Liberal, rationalist, and scholar*, ed. G. A. Wells. London: Pemberton, 1987.
Hewlett, M. 1898. *The forest lovers*. Harmondsworth: Penguin, 1945.
Hibberd, D. 1977. A sociological cause for shell shock: Dr. Brock and Wilfred Owen, *Sociological Review* 25, no. 4: 377–86.
Hirst, P. Q. 1994. *Associative democracy. New forms of economic and social governance*. Cambridge: Polity Press.
———. 1997. *From statism to pluralism*. London: Routledge.
Hoare, P. 2005. *England's lost Eden*. London: Harper Perrenial.
Hobhouse, L. T. 1893. *The labour movement*. London: T. Fisher Unwin.
———. 1896. *Theory of knowledge: A contribution to some problems of logic and metaphysics*. London: Methuen.
———. 1901. *Mind in evolution*. London: Macmillan.
———. 1906. *Morals in evolution*. London: Macmillan.
———. 1911. Liberalism. In *Liberalism and other writings*, ed. L. T. Hobhouse. Cambridge: Cambridge University Press, 1994.
———. 1924. *Social development: Its nature and conditions*. London: George Allen and Unwin, 1966.

———, G. C. Wheeler, and M. Ginsberg. 1914. *The material culture and social institutions of the simpler people*. London: Routledge and Kegan Paul, 1965.
Hobson, J. A. 1891. *Problems of poverty*. New York: Augusts M. Kelley, 1971.
———. 1894. *The evolution of modern capitalism*. London: George Allen and Unwin.
———. 1898. *John Ruskin: Social reformer*. Boston: Dana, Estes.
———. 1901. *The social problem: Life and work*. London: J. Nisbet.
———. 1902. *Imperialism: A study*. London: George Allen and Unwin.
———. 1906. *The evolution of modern capitalism, Revised edition*. London: George Allen and Unwin.
———. 1938. *Confessions of an economic heretic*. London: George Allen and Unwin.
Hobson, S. G. 1914. *National guilds. An enquiry into the wage system and the way out*. London: Bell.
Hodge, C. F. 1902. *Nature study and life*. New York: Ginn.
Hollins, D., ed. 1908. *Utopian papers: Being addresses to the utopians*. London: Masters.
Howard, E. G. and M. Wilson. 1907. *West Ham; A study in social and industrial problems; being the report of the Outer London inquiry committee*. London: J. M. Dent.
Hubback, C. 1927. A note on student days, *Sociological Review* 49, no. 2: 140–42.
Hughes, H. 1854. *Treatise of sociology: Theoretical and practical*. New York: Negro Universities Press, 1968.
Hutchinson, F., and B. Burkitt. 1997. *The political economy of social credit and guild socialism*. London: Routledge.
Hutton, R. 1999. *The triumph of the moon*. Oxford: Oxford University Press.
Hysler-Rubin, N. 2009. The changing appreciation of Patrick Geddes: a case study in planning history, *Planning Perspectives* 24, no. 3: 349–66.
———. 2011. *Patrick Geddes and town planning: A critical view*. London: Routledge.
Irving, R. G. 1981. *Indian summer: Lutyens, Baker, and imperial Delhi*. New Haven: Yale University Press.
Izoulet, J. 1927. *Paris la capitale des Religions*. Paris: Alban Michel.
Jackson, F. 1985. *Sir Raymond Unwin: Architect, planner, and visionary*. London: Zwemmer.
Jackson, K. 2004. *Humphrey Jennings*. London: Picador.
James, W. 1890. *The principles of psychology*. New York: Dover, 1950.
Jenks, L. H. 1951. Capital movement and transportation: Britain and American railway development, *Journal of Economic History* 11, no. 4: 375–88.
Jennings, Hilda. 1934. *Brynmawr: A study of a depressed area*. London: Allenson.
Jennings, Humphrey, and C. Madge. 1937. *May the twelfth*. London: Faber and Faber.
Jennings White, H. D. 1925. *Psychological causes of homoerotism and inversion*. London: J. E. Francis.
———. 1928. *The biological principles of education (Woodcraft series, No. 14)*. Salisbury: Order of Woodcraft Chivalry.
Jevons, W. S. 1871. *The theory of political economy*. Harmondsworth: Penguin, 1970.
Johnson, R. A. 2006. *Full moon over Washington. Charles Ferguson and the religion of democracy*. PhD dissertation. Union Theological Seminary.
Jolly, W. P. 1974. *Sir Oliver Lodge: Psychical researcher and scientist*. London: Constable.
Jones, E., ed. 1924. *Social aspects of psycho-analysis*. London: Williams and Norgate.

Jones, H. 1883. The social organism. In *The British idealists*, ed. D. Boucher. Cambridge: Cambridge University Press, 1997.
———. 1910. *The working faith of the social reformer*. London: Macmillan.
———. 1919. *The principles of citizenship*. London: Macmillan.
Jones, L., C. Jones, and R. H. Greenhill. 1977. Public utility companies. In *British imperialism, 1840–1930*, ed. D. C. M. Platt. Oxford: Clarendon Press, 1977.
Jung, C. G. 1917. The psychology of unconscious processes. In *Collected Works of C. G. Jung*, Vol. 7. 2nd ed. Princeton: Princeton University Press, 1966.
Kant, I. 1784. Idea for a universal history from a cosmopolitan point of view. In *Immanuel Kant on history*, ed. L. W. Beck. Indianapolis: Bobbs-Merril, 1963.
Karen, R. 1998. *Becoming attached*. Oxford: Oxford University Press.
Kearton, M. 1898. Incendiary fires, *Port of Spain Gazette*, June 17.
Kent, C. 1978. *Brains and numbers. Elitism, Comtism, and democracy in mid-Victorian England*. Toronto: University of Toronto Press.
Kent, R. 1981. *A history of British empirical sociology*. Aldershot: Gower.
Keynes, J. M. 1936. *General theory of employment, interest, and money*. London: Macmillan.
Kidd, B. 1894. *Social evolution*. London: Macmillan.
———. 1898. *The control of the tropics*. London: Macmillan.
Kitchen, P. 1975. *A most unsettling person: The life and ideas of Patrick Geddes, founding father of city planning and environmentalism*. New York: E. P. Dutton, Saturday Review Press.
Kitson, A. 1894. *A scientific solution to the money question*. Boston: Arena Publishing.
———. 1921. *Unemployment: The cause and a remedy*. London: Cecil Palmer.
———. 1933. *The banker's conspiracy*. London: Elliot Stock.
Klaus, S. L. 2002. *A modern Arcadia: Frederick Law Olmsted Jr. and the plan for Forest Hills Gardens*. Amherst: University of Massachusetts Press.
Knowles, V. 2004. *From telegraph to titan. The life of William C. van Horne*. Toronto: Dundura Group.
Kropotkin, P. 1899. *Fields, factories, and workshops, or Industry combined with agriculture and brain work with manual work*. London: Swann and Sonnenschein.
———. 1902. *Mutual aid*. London: William Heinemann.
Kuklick, H. 1998. Fieldworkers and physiologists. In *Cambridge and the Torres Straits*, ed. A. Herle and S. Rouse. Cambridge: Cambridge University Press.
Lanchester, H. V. 1925. *The art of town planning*. London: Chapman and Hall.
Laski, H. J. 1919. *Authority in the modern state*. New Haven: Yale University Press.
Law, A. 2005. The ghost of Patrick Geddes: Civics as applied sociology, *Sociological Research Online* 10, no. 2.
Le Play, F. 1855. Les ouvriers Européens. In *Family and society (condensed translation)*, ed. C. C. Zimmerman and M. Frampton. New York: D. van Nostrand, 1935.
Leary, D. 1987. Telling likely stories: The rhetoric of the new psychology, 1880–1920, *Journal of the History of the Behavioural Sciences* 23, no. 4: 315–31.
———. 2009. Between Peirce (1878) and James (1898): G. Stanley Hall, the origins of pragmatism, and the history of psychology, *Journal of the History of the Behavioural Sciences* 45, no. 1: 5–20.

Lenman, B., and W. D. Carroll. 1972. Council housing in Dundee, *Town Planning Review* 43, no. 3: 275–85.

Leonard, S. 2007. Through a glass clearly. In *A vigorous institution*, ed. W. Stephen. Edinburgh: Luath Press, 2007.

———, and J. M. Mackenzie. 1989. *Ramsay Gardens*. Edinburgh: Patrick Geddes Centre.

Levi, J. 2006. *And nobody woke up dead. The life and times of Mabel Barker—Climber and educational pioneer*. Bury St. Edmunds: Ernest Press.

Lewes, G. 1853. *Comte's philosophy of the positive sciences*. London: George Bell and Sons, 1878.

Lewis, C. 1968. Percival Farquhar and the Argentine railways, 1912–14, *Transport History* 1, no. 3: 209–31.

Lineham, D., and P. Gruffudd. 2001. Bodies and souls: Psycho-geographical collisions in the South Wales coalfield, 1926–39, *Journal of Historical Geography* 27, no. 3: 377–94.

Lisman, F. J. 1922. Rural credit in the United States, *Sociological Review* 14, no. 3: 224–25.

List, F. 1841. *The national system of political economy*. London: Longman's Green, 1904.

Llewellyn Smith, H. 1930–35. *New survey of London life and labour, nine volumes*. London: P. S. King.

Lodge, O. 1916. *Raymond: Or life After death*. London: Methuen.

Lubbock, J. 1865. *Prehistoric times*. London: Williams and Norgate.

———. 1870. *The origin of civilization and the primitive condition of man*. Chicago: University of Chicago Press, 1978.

———. 1906. *The scenery of England and the causes to which it is due*. London: Macmillan.

Lymington, Viscount. 1932. *Horn, hoof, and corn. The future of British agriculture*. London: Faber and Faber.

Macdonald, A. K. 1911. *Paraguay: Its people, customs, and commerce (a.k.a. Picturesque Paraguay)*. London: Charles H. Kelly.

Macdonald, M. 2000. The patron, the professor, and the painter. Cultural activity in Dundee at the turn of the nineteenth century. In *Victorian Dundee: Image and realities*, ed. L. Miskell, C. A. Whatley, and B. Harris. East Linton: Tuckwell Press.

———. 2004a. Patrick Geddes—Science and art in Dundee. In *The artist and the thinker. John Duncan and Patrick Geddes in Dundee*, ed. M. Jarron. Dundee: University of Dundee Museum Service.

———. 2004b. Patrick Geddes. Environment and culture. In *Think global, act local: The life and legacy of Patrick Geddes*, ed. W. Stephen and others. Edinburgh: Luath Press, 2004.

Macgregor, A. A. 1951. *The goat wife. Portrait of a village*. London: Museum Press.

MacIver, R. 1917. *Community: A sociological study*. London: Macmillan.

———. 1921. *Elements of social science*. London: Methuen.

———. 1926. *The modern state*. Oxford: Oxford University Press.

———. 1937. *Society*. New York: Rinehart.

———. 1942. *Social causation*. New York: Harper and Row.
———. 1947. *The web of government*. New York: Macmillan.
———. 1968. *As a tale that is told*. Chicago: University of Chicago Press.
MacKaye, B. 1921. An Appalachian trail: A project in regional planning, *Journal of the American Institute of Architects* 9 (October): 325–30.
MacKaye, P. 1912. *The civic theatre*. New York: Mitchell Kennerley.
MacKillop, I. 1986. *The British ethical societies*. Cambridge: Cambridge University Press.
Maclean, K. 2004. Patrick Geddes: Regional survey and education. In *Think global, act local*, ed. W. Stephen. Edinburgh: Luath Press.
Macmillan, H. 1938. *The middle way*. London: Macmillan.
Macmurray, J. 1935. *Reason and emotion*. London: Faber and Faber.
———. 1957. *The self as agent*. London: Faber and Faber.
———. 1961. *Persons in relation*. London: Faber and Faber.
Macpherson, C. B. 1953. *Democracy in Alberta: Social credit and the party system*. Toronto: University of Toronto Press.
Maeztu, R. de. 1916. *Authority, liberty, and function in the light of war*. London: George Allen and Unwin.
Mairet, P. 1928. *ABC of Adler's psychology*. London: Kegan Paul, Trench Trubner.
———. 1936. *A. R. Orage*. London: J. M. Dent.
———. 1957. *Pioneer of sociology. The life and letters of Patrick Geddes*. London: Lund Humphries.
Malcolmson, V. A. 1920. *Rural housing and public utility societies*. London: John Murray.
Malinowski, B. 1922. *Argonauts of the western Pacific*. London: G. Routledge.
Malthus, T. R. 1798. *Essay on the principles of population*. Harmondsworth: Penguin, 1970.
———. 1820. *Principles of political economy*. Cambridge: Cambridge University Press, 1989.
Manning, H. E. 1891. Leo XIII on The Condition of Labour, *Dublin Review* (July): 153–67.
Mansbridge, A. 1932. *Margaret McMillan, prophet and pioneer: Her life and work*. London: J. M. Dent.
Marr, T. R. 1904. *Housing conditions in Manchester and Salford*. Manchester: Sherratt and Hughes at the University Press.
Marshall, A. 1890. *Principles of economics*. London: Macmillan.
Marshall, T. H. 1949. Citizenship and social class. In *Sociology at the crossroads*, ed. T. H. Marshall. London: Heinemann, 1963.
Martin, W. 1967. *The new age under Orage*. Manchester: Manchester University Press.
Martineau, H. 1831. *Illustrations of political economy, Nine volumes*. London: Charles Fox.
———. 1837. *Society in America*. New York: Doubleday, 1962 (abridged edition edited by S. M. Lipset).
———. 1838. *How to observe manners and morals*. London: Charles Knight.
———. 1853. *Comte's positive philosophy, Three volumes*. London: George Bell, 1896.
Martinez-Alier, J. 1987. *Ecological economics. Energy, environment, and society*. Oxford: Basil Blackwell.

Marx, K., and F. Engels 1848. *The communist manifesto*. Harmondsworth: Penguin, 1967.
Mass-Observation. 1939. *Britain*. Harmondsworth: Penguin.
———. 1943a. *The pub and the people*. London: Victor Gollancz.
———. 1943b. *War factory*. London: Victor Gollancz.
Massingham, H. J., ed. 1944. *The natural order*. London: Dent.
Mather, A. S. 1999. Geddes, geography, and ecology: The golden age of vegetation mapping in Scotland, *Scottish Geographical Journal* 115, no. 1: 35–52.
Matless, D. 1992. Regional surveys and local knowledges: The geographical imagination in Britain, 1918–39, *Transactions of the Institute of British Geographers* 17, no. 4: 464–80.
Matthews, E. C. 1910. *The highlands of south-west Surrey*. London: A and C Black.
Mauss, M. 1902. *A general theory of magic*. London: Routledge and Kegan Paul, 1972.
———. 1904–05. *Seasonal variations of the Eskimo*. London: Routledge and Kegan Paul, 1979.
———. 1925. *The gift*. London: Routledge and Kegan Paul, 1966.
Mavor, J. 1923. *My windows on the street of the world, Two volumes*. New York: E. P. Dutton.
Mayhew, H. 1849–1850. *The Morning Chronicle survey of labour and the poor*. Firle, Sussex: Caliban Books.
———. 1861. *London labour and the London poor, 4 volumes*. New York: Dover Publications.
McBriar, A. M. 1987. *An Edwardian mixed-doubles: The Bosanquets versus the Webbs*. Oxford: Oxford University Press.
McDonald, G. W., and H. F. Gospel. 1973. The Mond-Turner talks, 1927–1933: A study in industrial co-operation, *Historical Journal* 16, no. 4: 807–29.
McDougall, W. 1908. *An introduction to social psychology*. London: Methuen, 1923.
———. 1920. *The group mind*. Cambridge: Cambridge University Press, 1939.
———. 1923. *An outline of psychology*. London: Methuen.
McDowall, D. 1984. *Steel at the Sault. Francis H. Clergue, Sir James Dunn, and the Algoma Steel Corporation, 1901–1956*. Toronto: University of Toronto Press.
———. 1984–86. James Hamet Dunn. In *Dictionary of business biography*, ed. D. J. Jeremy. London: Butterworths.
———. 1988. *The light. Brazilian Traction, Light and Power Co*. Toronto: University of Toronto Press.
McElroy, R. 1930. *Levi Parsons Morton. Banker, diplomat, and statesman*. New York: G. P. Putnam's Sons.
McGinnis, M. V., ed. 1998. *Bioregionalism*. London: Routledge.
McIntyre, A. 2007. *Participatory action research*. Thousand Oaks, CA: Sage.
Meacham, S. 1987. *Toynbee Hall and social reform, 1880–1914*. New Haven: Yale University Press.
Mead, G. H. 1910. *Essays in social psychology*. New Brunswick: Transaction Publishers, 2001.
———. 1927. *Mind, self, and society from the standpoint of social behaviourism*. Chicago: University of Chicago Press, 1934.

Mead, M. 1928. *Coming of age in Samoa: A study of adolescence and sex in priimitive societies.* Harmondsworth: Penguin, 1943.
———. 1930. *Growing up in New Guinea: A study of adolescence and sex in primitive societies.* Harmondsworth: Penguin, 1942.
Mearns, A. 1883. *The bitter cry of outcast London.* London: Frank Cass, 1970.
Mehra, A. K. 1991. *The politics of urban redevelopment: A study of old Delhi.* New Delhi: Sage.
Meller, H. 1990. *Patrick Geddes: Social evolutionist and city planner.* London: Routledge.
———. 1995. Philanthropy and public enterprise: International exhibitions and the modern town planning movement, 1889–1913, *Planning Perspectives* 10: 295–310.
Merricks, L. 1996. *The world made new. Frederick Soddy, science, politics, and environment.* Oxford: Oxford University Press.
Mess, H. A. 1928. *Industrial Tyneside: A social survey.* London: Benn.
Miliband, R. 1961. *Parliamentary socialism. A study in the politics of labour.* London: Allen and Unwin.
———. 1969. *The state in capitalist society.* London: Weidenfeld and Nicolson.
Mill, H. R. 1896. Proposed geographical description of the British Islands based on the Ordnance Survey, *Geographical Journal* 7, no. 4: 345–56.
Mill, H. R. 1900. A fragment of the geography of England: South-west Sussex, *Geographical Journal* 7 (March and April): 1900.
Mill, J. 1821. *Elements of political economy.* New York: G. Olms, 1971.
Mill, J. S. 1843. *The logic of the moral sciences.* London: Duckworth, 1987.
———. 1848. *Principles of political economy.* Harmondsworth: Penguin, 1970.
———. 1865. *Auguste Comte and positivism.* Bristol: Thoemmes Press, 1993.
———. 1869. *On socialism.* New York: Prometheus Books, 1976.
Miller, D. L. 2002. *Lewis Mumford: A life.* New York: Grove.
Miller, M. 1989. *Letchworth: The first Garden City.* Chichester: Phillimore.
———. 1992. *Raymond Unwin: Garden Cities and town planning.* Leicester: Leicester University Press.
———, and A. S. Gray. 1992. *Hampstead garden suburb.* Chichester: Phillimore.
Mirowski, P. 1989. *More heat than light.* Cambridge: Cambridge University Press.
Mitchell, M. 2010. *Learning from Delhi: Dispersed initiatives in changing urban landscapes.* Farnham, Surrey: Ashgate.
Mitchie, R. 1988. Dunn, Fischer & Co in the City of London, 1906–14, *Business History Review* 30, no. 2: 195–218.
Montesquieu, Baron de 1748. *The spirit of laws.* Cambridge: Cambridge University Press, 1989.
Moody, W. D. 1912. *Wacker's manual of the plan of Chicago.* Chicago: Chicago Plan Commission.
Moore-Colyer, R. J. 2001a. Back to basics: Rolf Gardiner, H. J. Massingham, and "A Kinship in Husbandry," *Rural History* 12, no. 1: 85–108.
———. 2001b. Rolf Gardiner, English patriot and the Council for the Church and Countryside, *Agricutural History Review* 49, no. 2: 186–209.
———. 2003. A northern federation? Henry Rolf Gardiner and British and European youth, *Paedagogica Historica* 39, no. 3.

Moore, C. W. 1975. Paradise at Topolobampo, *Journal of Arizona History* 16, no. 1: 1–28.
Morris, B. 1970. Ernest Thompson Seton and the origins of the Woodcraft movement, *Journal of Contemporary History* 5, no. 2: 183–94.
Muirhead, J. H. 1892. *Elements of ethics*. London: John Murray.
Mumery, A. F. and J. A. Hobson. 1889. *The physiology of industry*. New York: Kelley and Millman.
Mumford, L. 1922. *The Story of Utopias*. New York: Boni and Liveright.
———. 1926. Science and sanctity, *The Commonweal*, June 9, 126–28.
———. 1932. The plan of New York, *New Republic* 71, June 15, 122–26; and June 22, 207–10.
———. 1934. *Technics and civilization*. New York: Harcourt Brace.
———. 1938. *The culture of cities*. New York: Harcourt Brace.
———. 1944. *The condition of man*. New York: Harcourt Brace.
———. 1947a. *Green memories: The story of Geddes Mumford*. New York: Harcourt Brace.
———. 1947b. Introduction. In *Patrick Geddes in India*, ed. J. Tyrwhitt. London: Lund, Humphries.
———. 1948. Patrick Geddes, Victor Branford, and applied sociology in England: The social survey, regionalism, and urban planning. In *An introduction to the history of sociology*, ed. H. E. Barnes, 370–88. Chicago: University of Chicago Press.
———. 1951. *The conduct of life*. New York: Harcourt Brace.
———. 1956. *The transformations of man*. New York: Harper and Brothers.
———. 1961. *The city in history*. London: Secker and Warburg.
———. 1966. The disciple's rebellion: A memoir of Patrick Geddes, *Encounter* 27, no. 3: 11–21.
———. 1967. *The myth of the machine. Technics and human development*. New York: Harcourt Brace Jovanovich.
———. 1982. *Sketches from life*. New York: Dial Press.
Naylor, S., and G. A. Jones. 1997. Writing orderly geographies of distant places: The regional survey movement and Latin America, *Ecumene* 4, no. 3: 273–99.
Nelson, G. K. 1969. *Spiritualism and society*. London: Routledge and Kegan Paul.
Nettlefold, J. S. 1905. *A housing policy*. Birmingham: Cornish Brothers.
New York State. 1926. *Report of the Commission of Housing and Regional Planning to Governor Alfred E. Smith and to the legislature*. Albany: New York State.
Newbigin, M. 1912. *Man and the conquest of nature*. London: Adam and Charles Black.
———. 1914. *The British empire beyond the seas: An introduction to world geography*. London: Bell.
———. 1924. *Commercial geography*. London: Hutchinson.
Nicholson, M. 1931. A national plan for Britain, *Week End Review* (February).
Nickson, R. A. 1993. *Historical dictionary of Paraguay*. London: Scarecrow Press.
Noble, M. E. 1904. *The web of Indian life*. London: William Heinemann.
Noon, D. H. 2005. The evolution of beasts and babies. Recapitulationism, instinct, and the early discourse of child development, *Journal for the History of the Behavioural Sciences* 41, no. 4: 367–86.

Novak, F. G., ed. 1995. *Lewis Mumford and Patrick Geddes: The correspondence*. London: Routledge.
Odum, H. W., and H. E. Moore. 1938. *American regionalism*. New York: H. Holt.
Offer, J. 2010. *Herbert Spencer and social theory*. London: Palgrave.
Ogilvie, C. P. 1910. *Argentina from a British point of view, and Notes on Argentine life*. London: Wertheimer, Lea.
Olivier, S., ed. 1889. *Fabian essay in socialism*. London: Fabian Society.
Park, R. E., and E. W. Burgess. 1925. *The city*. Chicago: University of Chicago Press, 1967.
Parker, D. 1997. "For the common good of all": Education and the Hertfordshire garden cities, 1904–1939, *Journal of Vocational Education and Training* 49, no. 2: 283–310.
Parsons, K. C. 1994. Collaborative genius: The Regional Planning Association of America, *Journal of the American Planning Association* 60, no. 4: 462–82.
Parsons, T., and R. F. Bales. 1956. *Family, socialization, and interaction process*. London: Routledge and Kegan Paul.
Party, Liberal. 1928. *Britain's industrial future being the report of the Liberal industrial inquiry of 1928*. London: E. Benn.
Passerini, L. 1999. *Europe in love, love in Europe*. London: I. B. Taurus.
Payne, G. K. 1977. *Urban housing in the third world*. London: Leonard Hill.
Peake, H. and H. J. Fleure. 1927–1956. *The corridors of time, Ten volumes*. Oxford: Clarendon Press.
Pearsall, R. 1972. *Table rappers: The Victorians and the occult*. Stroud: Sutton.
Peart-Binns, J. S. 1988. *Maurice B. Reckitt*: Bowerdean.
Peel, J. D. Y. 1971. *Herbert Spencer: The evolution of a sociologist*. London: Heinemann.
Pekin, L. B. 1934. *Progressive schools*. London: Hogarth Press.
Pemberton, J. 2006. The middle way: The discourse of planning in Britain, Australia, and at the League in the interwar years, *Australian Journal of Politics and History* 52, no. 1: 48–63.
Penstone, M. M. 1910. *Town study*. London: National Society's Depository.
Penty, A. J. 1906. *The restoration of the guild system*. London: Swann and Sonnenschein.
———. 1922. *Post-industrialism*. Whitefish, MT: Kessinger, no date.
———. 1923. *Towards a Christian sociology*. London: George Allen and Unwin.
Piaget, J. 1926. *The child's conception of the world*. New York: Harcourt Brace, 1929.
———. 1932. *The moral judgement of the child*. London: Routledge and Kegan Paul, 1975.
Pilcher, J. M. 1998. Mad cowmen, foreign investors, and the Mexican revolution, *Journal of Iberian and Latin American Studies* 4, no. 1: 1–15.
———. 2004. *Fajitas* and the failure of refrigerated meat packing: Consumer culture and Porfirian capitalism, *The Americas* 60, no. 3: 411–29.
Porter, A. 1927. *Coal. A challenge to the national consciousness*. London: Hogarth Press.
Preyer, W. T. 1893. *Mental development in the child*. New York: D. Appleton.
Pruette, L. 1926. *G. Stanley Hall. A biography of a mind*. New York: D. Appleton.
Prynn, D. L. 1972. Common wealth—A British "Third Party" of the 1940s, *Journal of Contemporary History* 7, no. 1/2: 169–79.
———. 1983. The Woodcraft folk and the labour movement, 1925–70, *Journal of Contyemporary History* 18, no. 1: 79–95.

Pugh, C., and G. E. Hutchings. 1928. *Stockbury: A regional study in north-east Kent.* Stockbury: Hill Farm.
Putnam, R. D. 2000. *Bowling alone: The collapse and revival of American community.* New York: Simon and Schuster.
Quesnay, F. 1758. *Tableau économique.* London: Macmillan, 1972.
Radcliffe-Brown, A. R. 1922. *The Andaman islanders.* New York: Free Press, 1964.
Ratzel, F. 1882–1891. *Anthropogeographie: Die geographische Verbreitung des Menschen.* Darmstadt: Wissenschaftliche Buchgesellschaft.
Rauschenbusch, W. 1907. *Christianity and the social crisis.* New York: Macmillan.
———. 1914. *Theology for the social gospel.* New York: Abingdon Press.
Read, J. 2003. Froebelian women: Networking to promote professional status and educational change in the nineteenth century, *History of Education* 32, no. 1: 17–33.
Reckitt, M. B. 1932. *Faith and society.* London: Longmans.
Reddie, C. 1901. *John Bull: His origin and character.* London.
Reed, M. 2001. Fight the future! How the contemporary campaigns of the UK organic movement have arisen from their composting of the past, *Sociologia Ruralis* 41, no. 1: 131–45.
Regional Plan of New York and its Environs. 1929. *The graphic regional plan: Regional plan, Volume I.* New York: Regional Plan.
———. 1931. *The building of the city: Regional plan, Volume II.* New York: Regional Plan.
Reid, A. 2000. *Brentham: A history of the pioneer garden suburb 1901–2001.* Ealing: Brentham Heritage Society.
Renwick, C., and R. C. Gunn. 2008 Demystifying the machine: Patrick Geddes, Lewis Mumford, and classical sociological theory, *Journal of the History of the Behavioural Sciences* 44, no. 1, 59–76.
Residents of Hull House. 1895. *Hull-House maps and papers.* New York: Thomas Y. Crowell.
Revel, D. 1928. *Cheiron's cave. The school of the future.* London: William Heinemann.
Reynolds, R. 1993. Catspaw utopia: Alfred K. Owen, the adventurer of Topolobampo Bay, and the last grand utopian scheme, *West Coast Studies* 4.
Reynolds, S. 2004. Patrick Geddes' French connections in academic and political life: Networking from 1878 to the 1900s. In *Patrick Geddes: The French connection*, ed. F. Fowle and B. Thompson. Oxford: White Cockade Publishing, 2004.
Ricardo, D. 1817. *Principles of political economy and taxation.* London: J. M. Dent, 1911.
Richards, G. 2000. Britain on the couch: The popularization of psychoanalysis in Britain 1918–1940, *Science in Context* 13, no. 2: 183–220.
Richardson, A. 2000. The eugenization of love: Sarah Grand and the morality of genealogy, *Victorian Studies* 42, no. 2: 227–55.
Richardson, B. C. 2004. *Igniting the Caribbean past.* Chapel Hill: University of North Carolina Press.
Rieser, A. C. 2003. *The Chautauqua movement. Protestants, progressives, and the culture of modern liberalism.* New York: Columbia University Press.

Rigby, A. 1984. *Initiation and initiative. An exploration of the life and ideas of Dimitrije Mitrinovic*. New York: Columbia University Press.

Rimmington, G. T. 2005. Joseph Wood: Preacher of sweetness and light, *Leicestershire Historian* 41: 22–25.

Rippy, J. F. 1946. Notes on the early telephone companies of Latin America, *Hispanic America Historical Review* 26, 1: 116–18.

Ritchie, D. G. 1895. *Natural rights*. London: Allen and Unwin, 1924.

Rivers, W. H. R. 1920. *Instinct and the unconscious*. Cambridge: Cambridge University Press.

———. 1924. *Social organisation*. London: Dawsons of Pall Mall, 1968.

Roberts, N. 2004. Character in the mind: Citizenship, education and psychology in Britain, 1880–1914, *History of Education* 33: 177–97.

Roberts, R. 1992. *Schroders. Merchants and bankers*. Houndmills: Basingstoke.

Robertson, J. M. 1895. *Buckle and his critics. A study in sociology*. London: Swan Sonnenschein.

———. 1897a. *The dynamics of religion*. London: Watts. Revised edition 1926.

———. 1897b. *The Saxon and the Celt. A study in sociology*. London: University Press.

———. 1904. *Essays in sociology, Two volumes*. London: A and H. B. Bonner.

———. 1911. The sociology of race, *Sociological Review* 4: 1911.

———. 1912. *The evolution of states*. London: Watts.

Rocquin, B. 2006. The floating discipline: British sociology and the failure of institutional attachment, 1911–38. MA thesis, Oxford University; available at www.britishsociology.com.

Romanes, G. J. 1885. *Mental evolution in animals*. London: Kegan Paul, Trench and Trubner.

———. 1889. *Mental evolution in man*. New York: D. Appleton.

Root, J. D. 1978. Science, religion, and psychical research: The monistic thought of Sir Oliver Lodge, *Harvard Theological Review* 71, no. 3/4: 245–63.

Rosen, W. B. 2000. *The Philadelphia Fels, 1880–1920. A social portrait*. Cranbury, NJ: Associated University Presses.

Ross, D. 1972. *G. Stanley Hall. The psychologist as prophet*. Chicago: University of Chicago Press.

Ross, E. 1901. *Social control*. New York: Macmillan.

———. 1920. *Principles of sociology*. New York: The Century Co.

Ross, J. A. 1921. Rural finance, *Sociological Review* 13, no. 3: 168–76.

Rowbotham, S. 2008. *Edward Carpenter. A life of liberty and love*. London: New Left Books.

Rowntree, S. 1901. *Poverty: A study of town life*. London: Longmans Green.

Roy, P. E. 1973. Direct management abroad. The formative years of the British Columbia Electric Railway, *Business History Review* 47, no. 2: 239–59.

Ruskin, J. 1862. *Minerva Pulveris*. London: Smith, Elder, 1872.

———. 1861. *Unto this last*. Harmondsworth: Penguin, 2005.

Rutherford, M. 1994. J. A. Hobson and American institutionalism: Underconsumption and technological change. In *J. A. Hobson after 50 years*, ed. J. Phoeby. Houndmills: Palgrave, 1994.

Saint, A. 1991. Ashbee, Geddes, Lethaby and the rebuilding of Crosby Hall, *Architectural History* 34: 206–23.
Sale, K. 2000. *Dwellers in the land: The bioregional vision.* Athens: University of Georgia Press.
Saleeby, C. W. 1905. *Sociology.* London: T. C. and E. C. Jack.
———. 1909. *Parenthood and race culture.* London: Cassell.
———. 1911. *Woman and womanhood. A search for principles.* London: Mitchell Kennerley.
Salter, A. 1934. *The framework of an ordered society.* Cambridge: Cambridge University Press.
Sandeman, F., and G. Sandeman. 1919. *The community of work.* London: Arthur H. Stockwell.
———. 1929. *Practical community.* Fordingbridge: Godshill Press.
Sandeman, G. 1896. *Problems of biology.* London: Swan Sonnenschein.
———. 1909. *Uncle Gregory.* London: Heinemann.
———. 1913. *Social renewal.* London: William Heinemann.
———. 1915. *Agnes.* London: Chatto and Windus.
———. 1916–17. Spirit creative: a study in social renewal, *Sociological Review* 9: 139–48.
Sanford, E. C. 1897. *A course in experimental psychology.* Boston: Heath.
Santamarina, J. C. 2000. The Cuba Company and the expansion of American business in Cuba, 1898–1915, *Business History Review* 74 (Spring): 41–83.
Schell, W. 2001. *Integral outsiders: The American colony in Mexico City, 1876–1911.* Wilmington, DE: Scholarly Resources.
Schlossman, S. L. 1973. G. Stanley Hall and the Boys' Club: Conservative applications of recapitulation theory, *Journal of the History of the Behavioural Sciences* 9 (April): 140–47.
Schreiner, O. 1899. The woman question. In *An Olive Schreiner reader,* ed. C. Barash. London: Pandora Press, 1987.
———. 1911. *Women and labour.* London: Unwin.
Schulte Fischedick, K. 2000. From survey to ecology: The role of the British Vegetation Committee, 1904–13, *Journal of the History of Biology* 33, no. 3: 291–314.
Scotland, N. 2007. *Squires in the slums. Settlements and missions in Victorian London.* London: I. B. Tauris.
Scott, E. H. 1931 *Ruskin's Guild of St. George.* London: Methuen.
Scott, J. 1997. *Corporate business and capitalist classes.* Oxford: Oxford University Press.
———. 2009. Life, the universe, and everything. An undiscovered work of Benchara Branford, *Journal of the History of the Behavioural Sciences* 45, no. 2: 181–87.
———. 2013. Sociology textbooks, 1900–1968. In *The history of sociology in Britain,* ed. J. Holmwood and J. Scott. London: Palgrave, 2013.
———, and M. Hughes. 1980. *The anatomy of Scottish Capital.* London: Croom Helm.
Scott, J., and C. T. Husbands. 2007. Victor Branford and the building of British sociology, *Sociological Review* 55, no. 3: 460–85.
Searsby, P. 1989. The new school and the new life: Cecil Reddie (1858–1932) and the early years of Abbotsholme School, *History of Education* 18, no. 1: 1–21.

Selleck, R. J. W. 1972. *English primary education and the progressives, 1914–39*. London: Routledge and Kegan Paul.
Semple, E. C. 1911. *Influences of geographic environment. On the basis of Ratzel's system of anthropo-geography*. London: Constable, 1933.
Shaw, G. B., ed. 1889. *Fabian essays in socialism*. London: Fabian Socirty.
Sherwell, A. 1897. *Life in West London*. London: Methuen.
Shoshkes, E. 2006. Jaqueline Tyrwhitt: A founding mother of modern urban design, *Planning Perspectives* 21, no. 2: 179–97.
———. 2009. Jaqueline Tyrwhitt and transnational discourse on modern urban planning and design, 1941–1951, *Urban History* 36, no. 2: 263–83.
Sibley, C. L. 1913. Van Horne and his Cuban railway, *Canadian Magazine* 41 (May): 444–51.
Sidgwick, H. 1891. *The elements of politics*. London: Macmillan.
Simpson, M. 1985. *Thomas Adams and the modern planning movement: Britain, Canada, and the United States, 1900–1940*. London: Mansell.
Sinclair, Sir J. 1791–92. *The statistical account of Scotland (The old statistical account)*. Edinburgh: A. Constable, 1825.
Sklar, K. K. 1985. Hull House in the 1890s: A community of women reformers, *Signs: Journal of Women in Culture and Society* 10: 658–77.
Slater, G. 1901. Co-operators, the state, and the housing question, *Contemporary Review* 79: 254–63.
———. 1902. Rural Housing—A lesson from Ireland, *Contemporary Review* 82: 401–10.
———. 1915. *The making of modern England*. New York: Houghton Mifflin.
———. 1918. *Some South Indian villages*. Oxford: Oxford University Press.
———. 1924. *The Dravidian element in Indian culture*. London: Ernest Benn.
———. 1930. *Poverty and the state: A study of English conditions*. London: Constable.
Slaughter, J. W. 1909–1910. Selection in marriage, *Eugenics Review* 1: 150–62.
Slavitt, L. D. 1994. Reconstruction and World War One: Internationalism and the idea of the expert. MSc dissertation, Graduate School of Architecture, Planning, and Preservation, Columbia University.
Slinn, J. 1997. *Ashurst Morris Crisp: A radical firm*. Cambridge: Granta Editions.
Slobdin, R. 1978. *W. H. R. Rivers*. Stroud: Sutton, 1997.
Smith, E. 1910. *The Reigate sheet of the one-inch Ordnance Survey*. London: A and C Black.
Smith, J. 1982. *Elsie de Wolfe. Life in the high style*. New York: Atheneum.
Smuts, A. B. 2005. *Science in the service of children*. New Haven: Yale University Press.
Sobel, R. 1982. *I.T.T.: The management of opportunity*. New York: Truman Talley.
Soddy, F. 1922. *Cartesian economics*. London: Henderson's.
———. 1924. *The inversion of science and a scheme of scientific reformation*. London: Henderson's.
———. 1926. *Wealth, virtual wealth, and debt*. London: George Allen and Unwin.
Sombart, W. 1902. *Der modernen Capitalismus*. Berlin: Duncker und Humblot.
Spencer, H. 1873. *The study of sociology*. London: Kegan Paul, Trench, 1889.
———. 1873–93. *Principles of sociology, Three volumes*. London: Williams and Norgate.

———. 1904. *An autobiography, Two volumes.* London: Williams and Norgate.
Sprott, W. J. H. 1937. *General psychology.* London: Longmans.
———. 1952. *Social psychology.* London: Methuen.
Stacey, M. 1960. *Tradition and change: A study of Banbury.* Oxford: Oxford University Press.
Stalley, M., ed. 1972. *Patrick Geddes: Spokesman for man and the environment.* New Brunswick: Rutgers University Press.
Stamp, L. D. 1931. The Land Utilization Survey of Britain, *Geographical Journal* 78, no. 1: 40–47.
———. 1948. *The land of Britain: Its use and misuse.* Harlow: Longman.
Starbuck, E. D. 1899. *The psychology of religion: An empirical study of the growth of religious consciousness.* New York: Scribner's.
Stein, C. 1951. *Toward new towns for America.* Liverpool: Liverpool University Press.
Steiner, R. 1919. *The threefold commonwealth (Towards social renewal).* London: Anthroposophical Publishing, 1923.
Stephen, W. 2004. Patrick Geddes—The life. In *Think global, act local,* ed. W. Stephen. Edinburgh: Luath Press, 2004.
———. 2007. Where was Peter Geddes born? In *A vigorous institution,* ed. W. Stephen. Edinburgh: Luath Press, 2007.
———. 2008. *Where was Patrick Geddes born? The last word?* Edinburgh: Hills of Home.
Stewart, W. A. C. 1968. *The educational innovators, Volume 2.* London: Macmillan.
Stilwell, A. E. 1911. *Universal peace—War is Mesmerism.* New York: Bankers Publishing Co.
Stones, H. R. 1993. *British railways in Argentina, 1860–1948.* Bromley: P. E. Waters and Associates.
Strobel, M. 2002. Hull House and women's studies. Parallel approaches for first- and second-wave feminists, *Women's Studies Quarterly* 30, nos. 3 and 4: 52–59.
Studholme, M. 2007. Patrick Geddes: Founder of environmental sociology, *Sociological Review* 55: 441–59.
Sulloway, F. J. 1979. *Freud. Biologist of the mind.* New York: Basic Books.
Sumner, W. G. 1883. *What social classes owe to each other.* New York: Arno Press, 1972.
———. 1906. *Folkways.* Boston: Ginn.
Swann, P. 1989. *The British documentary film movement, 1926–1946.* Cambridge: Cambridge University Press.
Sylvester Smith, W. 1967 *The London heretics, 1870–1914.* London: Constable.
Tait, P. G. 1864. The dynamical theory of heat and energy, *North British Review* 40: 21–37.
Tansley, A. G. 1920. *The new psychology and its relation to life.* London: George Allen and Unwin.
Tarde, G. 1890. *The laws of imitation.* New York: H. Holt, 1903.
Tawney, R. H. 1921. *The acquisitive society.* Brighton: Wheatsheaf, 1982.
Tayler, J. L. 1904. *Aspects of social evolution. First series: Temperaments.* London: Smith, Elder.
———. 1921a. *Social life and the crowd.* Boston: Small, Maynard.

———. 1921b. *The stages of human life.* London: John Murray.
———. 1922. *The nature of woman.* London: Jonathan Cape.
———. 1931. *The story of a life.* London: Williams and Norgate.
Thayer, R. L. 2003. *LifePlace: Bioregional thought and practice.* Berkeley: University of California Press.
Thomas, W. I., and F. Znaniecki. 1918–19. *The Polish peasant in Europe and America.* New York: Dover, 1958.
Thompson, E. P. 1955. *William Morris: Romantic to revolutionary* New York: Pantheon Books, 1976.
Thompson, T. 1918. *The coming dawn.* London: The Bodley Head.
———. 1928. *The world without and the world within.* London: The Bodley Head.
Thomson, J. A. 1920. *The system of animate nature.* London: Williams and Norgate.
———, and P. Geddes. 1912. *Problems of sex.* London: Cassel.
Tönnies, F. 1889. *Community and association.* London: Routledge and Kegan Paul, 1955 (based on the 1912 edition).
Townshend, J. 1990. *John Hobson.* Manchester: Manchester University Press.
Trotter, W. 1908. Herd instinct and civilized psychology. In *Instinct of the herd in peace and war, 1917 edition,* ed. W. Trotter. London: Ernest Benn, 1947.
———. 1909. The psychology of herd instinct. In *Instinct of the herd in peace and war, 1917 edition,* ed. W. Trotter. London: Ernest Benn, 1947.
Tsuzuki, C. 1980. *Edward Carpenter, 1844–1929: Prophet of human fellowship.* Cambridge: Cambridge University Press.
Turner, J. F. C. 1967. Barriers and channels for housing development in modernizing countries, *American Institute of Planners Journal* 32: 167–81.
———. 1976. *Housing by people: Towards autonomy in building environments.* London: Marion Boyars.
———. 1982. Issues in self-help and self-managed housing. In *Self-help housing: A critique,* ed. P. M. Ward, 99–113. London: Mansell.
Turner, J. H. 1985. *Herbert Spencer: A renewed appreciation.* Beverly Hills: Sage.
Tylor, E. 1871. *Primitive culture,* Two volumes. London: John Murray, 1920.
Tyrwhitt, J. 1976. Patrick Geddes's "University of Central India." In *The Outlook Tower: Essays on urbanization in memory of Patrick Geddes,* ed. J. V. Ferreira and S. S. Jha. Bombay: Popular Prakashan.
———, ed. 1947. *Patrick Geddes in India.* London: Lund, Humphreys.
Unwin, R. 1909. *Town planning in practice.* London: Ernest Benn.
Unwin, S. 1960. *The truth about a publisher.* London: George Allen and Unwin.
van der Eyken, W., and B. Turner. 1969. *Adventures in education.* London: Allen Lane The Penguin Press.
van Dijken, S., and others. 1998. Bowlby before Bowlby: The sources of an intellectual departure in psychoanalysis and psychology, *Journal for the History of the Behavioural Sciences* 34, no. 3: 247–69.
van Ness, C. 1986. The Braga brothers collection at the University of Florida, *Latin American Research Review* 21, no. 2: 142–48.
Veblen, T. 1899. *The theory of the leisure class: An economic study of institutions.* New York: Macmillan.
———. 1904. *The theory of business enterprise.* New York: Scribner, 1915.

———. 1918. *The higher learning in America*. New York: Sagamore Press, 1965.
———. 1921. *The engineers and The price system*. New York: B. W. Huebsch.
Veenendaal, A. J. 1992. An example of "other people's money": Dutch capital in American railroads, *Business and Economic History* 21: 147–58.
———. 1996. *Slow train to Paradise: How Dutch investment helped build American railroads*. Stanford: Stanford University Press.
Vidal de la Blache, P. 1922. *Principles of human geography*. New York: H. Holt, 1926.
Vignes, J. B. M. 1897. *La science sociale d'après les principes de Le Play, Two volumes*. Paris: V. Giard et E. Brière.
Vincent, J. H., and L. Miller. 1886. *The Chautauqua movement*. Boston: Chautauqua Press.
Vivian, H. 1906. *Report of a conference of the Garden City Association*. London: Garden City Association.
———. 1927. Tributes from colleagues, *Sociological Review* 49, no. 2: 143–44.
Waesche, J. F. 1987. *Crowing the Gravelly Hill: A history of the Roland Park-Guildford-Homeland District*. Baltimore: Maclay and Associates.
Wainwright, D. 1985. *Henderson: A history of the life of Alexander Henderson, first Lord Faringdon*. London: Quiller Press.
Walker, D. 2007. *Basildon plotlands: The Londoners' rural retreat*. Chichester: Phillimore.
Walker, M. L., and M. Wilson. 1905. *Report on housing and industrial conditions and medical inspection of children*. Dundee: Leng.
Walker, S. P. 1988. *The society of accountants in Edinburgh, 1854–1914*. New York: Garland.
Ward, B. M. 1934. *Reddie of Abbotsholme*. London: George Allen and Unwin.
Ward, L. 1883. *Dynamic sociology*. New York: D. Appleton, 1913.
Warren, H. G. 1967a. The Paraguay Central Railway, 1856–1889, *Inter-American Economic Affairs* (Spring): 3–22.
———. 1967b. The Paraguay Central Railway, 1889–1907, *Inter-American Economic Affairs* (Spring): 31–48.
Waters, P. E. 1994. Paraguay Central Railway. Ferro-carril del estado before the war of triple alliance, *British Overseas Railway Journal* 11 (Summer): 159–61.
———. 1996. Paraguay Central Railway. British ownership before gauge conversion, *British Overseas Railway Journal* 13 (Autumn): 5–8.
———. 1997. Paraguay Central Railway. Argentine ownership: Gauge conversion, *British Overseas Railway Journal* 14: 24–27.
———. 1998a. Paraguay Central Railway. Control by bond holders, *British Overseas Railway Journal* 17 (Autumn): 84–87.
———. 1998b. Paraguay Central Railway. Control by Percival Farquhar, *British Overseas Railway Journal* 16 (Spring): 63–67.
Webb, S. and B. Webb. 1920. *A constitution for the socialist commonwealth of Great Britain*. London: Longmans Green.
———. 1935. *Soviet communism*. London: Longmans Green.
Weber, A. 1920–21. *Fundamentals of culture-sociology: Social process, civilization process, and cultural movement*. New York: Columbia University Press, 1939.

Weber, M. 1904. "Objectivity" in social science and social policy. In *The methodology of the social sciences*, ed. M. Weber. New York: Free Press, 1949.
———. 1904–05. The protestant ethic and the spirit of capitalism. In *Max Weber: The protestant ethic and the "spirit" of capitalism, and other writings*, ed. P. Baehr and G. C. Wells. Harmondsworth: Penguin, 2002.
Wells, A. F. 1935. *The local social survey in Great Britain*. London: George Allen and Unwin.
Wells, H. G. 1905. *A modern utopia*. Harmondsworth: Penguin, 2005.
Welter, V. M. 2002. *Biopolis: Patrick Geddes and the city of life*. Cambridge: MIT Press.
Wenley, R. M. 1913. *The anarchist ideal and other essays*. Boston: Richard G. Badger.
Westlake, E., and A. Westlake. 1918. *Primitive occupations as a factor in education*. London: Woodcraft Way Series, Number 4.
Westlake, J. 2000. *Seventy years a-growing*. Stroud: Hawthorn Press.
White, J. 2001. *London in the twentieth century*. London: Viking.
White, S. H. 1990. Child study at Clark University: 1894–1904, *Journal of the History of the Behavioural Sciences* 26, no. 2: 131–50.
Whitehouse, J. H. 1905. *Problems of a Scottish provincial town*. London: George Allen and Unwin.
———. 1908. article. *Toynbee Record*.
———. 1928. *Creative education at an English school*. Cambridge: Cambridge University Press.
———. 1943. *The school base*. Oxford: Oxford University Press.
———, N. Malcolmson and others. 1908. *Report of an enquiry into working boys' homes in London*. London: Andrew Fairbairns.
Wiese-Becker 1932. *Systematic sociology, On the basis of the Beziehungslehre and Gebildelehre of Leopold von Wiese, adapted and amplified by Howard P. Becker*. New York: Wiley.
Wilson, H. 1918. The value and importance of handicraft in education. In *Report of the conference on new ideals in education*. London: Women's Printing Press, 1918.
Wohlgelernter, M. 1964. *Israel Zangwill: A study*. New York: Columbia University Press.
Wood, G. A. (as "Members and friends of the Geography Club of Hockerill Training College"). 1929. *Bishop's Stortford. A regional study Bbased on the Le Play formula*. Ledbury: Le Play House Press, Revised edition 1948.
Wood, J. 1895. *Wealth and commonwealth*. New York: Commonwealth Library.
Woods, L. M. 2012. *Horace Plunkett in America: An Irish aristocrat on the Wyoming range*. Norman, OK: Arthur H. Clark.
Wooldridge, A. 1994. *Measuring the mind: Educational psychology in England, 1860–1990*. Cambridge: Cambridge University Press.
Worley, W. S. 1993. Development of industrial districts in the Kansas City region: From the close of the Civil War to World War II. *Midcontinent Perspectives Perspectives Lecture* (available at http://www.umkc.edu/whmckc/publications/MCP/MCPLecturer.htm). Kansas City.
Worms, R. 1896. *Organisme et société*. Paris: V. Giard et E. Brière.

Wright, T. R. 1986. *The religion of humanity: The impact of Comtean positivism in Victorian Britain*. Cambridge: Cambridge University Press.
Wrigley, G. M. 1950. Hugh Robert Mill: An appreciation, *Geographical Review* 40, no. 4: 657–60.
WT. 1887. In Memoriam. Archer Gurney, *The Guardian*. Manchester.
Wundt, W. 1912. *Elements of folk psychology*. London: George Allen and Unwin, 1916.
Young, C. 2004. In search of John Duncan. In *The artist and the thinker*, ed. M. Jarron. Dundee: University of Dundee Museum Service, 2004.
Zanetti, O., and A. García. 1987. *Sugar and railroads. A Cuban history, 1837–1959*. Chapel Hill: University of North Carolina Press, 1998.
Zimmern, A. E. 1915. Nationality and government, *Sociological Review* 8: 213–33.
Zueblin, C. 1899a. Industrial democracy, *Journal of Political Economy* 7, no. 2: 182–203.
———. 1899b. The world's first sociological laboratory, *American Journal of Sociology* 4, no. 5: 577–92.
———. 1905. *A decade of civic development*. Chicago: University of Chicago Press.

INDEX

Abbotsholme School, Derbyshire, 148–49, 229
Abercrombie, Patrick, 2, 58–59, 67, 79, 104
Aberdeen, Lord and Lady (John and Ishbel Hamilton-Gordon), 57, 59
Acland, Richard, 207
Adams, Thomas, 79, 108–109
Addams, Jane, 2, 12–14, 62–63, 96, 160, 230, 232
Adler, Alfred, 135, 204
Adler, Felix, 48, 63
Adler Society, 205
adolescence, 132–39, 145–50, 233
Adorno, Theodore, 187
Age of Plenty, 204
Alberta Social Credit Party, 203
allotment schemes and farm colonies, 63, 154, 164, 170
American Journal of Sociology, 11, 64, 225
American Sociological Society (renamed American Sociological Association in 1959), 11, 65, 225
Amos, Sarah, 164
anarchism and anarchists, 43–46, 83, 114–17, 121–22, 151, 188–89, 197
Année Sociologique, 9
anti-Semitism, 206
Appalachian Trail, 107
Appleton, Estelle, 133
Argentina, 167–71, 174–77, 222, 236, 239
Argentine Paraguayan Timber Company, 178–79
Armenia and Armenian refugees, 31, 73, 116, 164–65

Armes, Sarah, 34
Arnold, Matthew, 52
Arts and Crafts movement, 12, 31, 37–38, 43–46, 76, 113, 191–92, 212
Ashbee, Charles, 2, 44, 57, 63, 104, 191, 199
Ashurst, Morris and Crisp, 169, 174, 237
Asquith, Herbert, 57
Association for Planning and Regional Reconstruction (APRR), 121
Atterbury, Grosvenor, 108
Avebury, Lord (John Lubbock), 170, 231
Aveling, Edward, 45

Baden-Powell, Robert, 151; *see also* scouting
Badley, John, 149
Bahá'í religion, 13, 26, 50
Bailey, William, 64
Baker, Herbert, 118
Bakunin, Mikhail, 50
Baldwin, James, 133
Balfour, Arthur, 51
Ballater, Aberdeenshire, 29
Barclay, William, 99, 233
Barker, David, 30
Barker, Harry, 30
Barker, Mabel, 59, 112, 153, 230
Barnes, Earl, 132, 230
Barnes, Harry Elmer, 67
Barnett, Henrietta, 12, 45, 49, 163
Barnett, Samuel, 12, 44, 49, 57
Barrows, Harlan, 11
Bartholomew, John G., 54, 79
Bastian, Adolph, 10

275

Bauer, Catherine, 107
Beadle, Elspeth, 40
Bedales School, Sussex and Hampshire, 148–49, 155
Beddington-Behrens, Edward, 179
Beesley, Edward, 47
Behn, Sosthenes, 173
Bell, Valentine, 59–60, 112
Belloc, Hilaire, 57, 96, 192–93, 201, 231
Bembridge School, Isle of Wight, 40, 149–50
Bennett, Arnold, 88, 232
Bentham, Jeremy, 14
Benthamism and Benthamites, 7, 14–15
Bergson, Henri, 51, 120, 124
Besant, Annie, 13, 20, 50, 114, 120–21, 204
Beveridge, Henry, 56, 78, 150, 162, 164–65
Beveridge, William, 57, 66
Binder, Bernhard, 40, 176–77
Binder Hamlyn, 40, 176–78
bioregionalism, *see* environmentalism
Bing, Alexander, 107
Bland, Hubert, 20, 225
Blavatsky, Helena, 50, 204
Blumer, Herbert, 11
Bonar, George, 161, 235
Boardman, Philip, 226
Booth, Charles, 7, 20, 57, 231
Booth, John B., 56, 96
Borradaile, William, 166–67, 237
Bosanquet, Bernard, 18–19, 21, 48, 57, 67
Bosanquet, Helen, 19
Bose, Jagadish Chandra, 60
Bourdieu, Pierre, 83
Bowlby, John, 156, 235
Bowley, Arthur, 96
Boy Scouts, *see* scouting
Brabrook, Edward W., 56
Bradley, Francis, 48
Branford, Archer ("Archie"), 28, 39–40, 150, 179–80, 221, 234

Branford, Benchara, 2, 33–35, 49, 76–77, 159, 199–200, 202, 205, 219, 221, 227, 231, 234
Branford, Frederick Victor, 2, 78, 222, 224
Branford, Hugh ("Hughie"), 28, 39–40, 178–80, 234
Branford, John ("Jack"), 2, 33–34, 49, 165, 222, 234
Branford, Lionel, 2, 33–34, 37, 41, 49, 222
Branford, Mary ("Mollie"), 33–34, 222
Branford, Matilda Elizabeth, *see* Stewart, Bess
Branford, Sybella, *see* Gurney, Sybella
Branford, Victor Verasis: career, 3, 35–37, 161–80; death and will, 41, 179–80; early life, 33–35; first marriage, 35–37, 163; in New York, 39, 59, 64–65, 161, 171–75, 227, 228; Nevada divorce, 37, 116, 176, 227; personality, 26–28, 162, 180; second marriage, 39–41, 64, 116; United States citizenship, 39, 228; writing and editing, 67–76
Branford, William Catton, 33–35, 166, 217–20, 227, 231
Brazil, 167, 171, 176, 179, 238, 239
Brentham Garden Suburb, Ealing, 28
Bridges, John, 47, 56–57
British Child Study Association, 131
British Psychological Society, 55
British Sociological Association, 211, 230
Brock, Arthur, 70–71, 77, 143
Brown, Lilian, 33, 226
Bruner, Jerome, 139
Bryce, James, 54–55, 57
Buckle, Henry Thomas, 83
Buckton, Alice, 50
Buddhism, 13, 138
Burns, John, 20
Burrows, Herbert, 48
Burton, Edmund Hamilton, 166–67
Byngham, Henry "Dion," 154–57, 235

Cadbury's, 149
Caird, Edward, 18, 48
Carey, Henry, 10
Carlyle, Thomas, 52, 191
Carnegie, Andrew, 32, 58
Carnegie Trust, 32, 58, 105, 149
Carpenter, Edward, 20, 44–45, 48, 58, 148, 151–52, 229
Carr-Saunders, Alexander, 61
Carter, Huntly, 93
Census, use of, 6, 38, 98, 226–27
Centre Party (renamed Midfolk), 203
Chadwick, Edwin, 6
Chamberlain, Alexander, 132
Chandos Group, 135, 204–205
Charity Organisation Society (COS)
  London, 19–20, 48, 55, 229
  New York, 11, 108
Chautauqua, 11, 53, 131–32
Chelsea, London, 33, 37, 46, 49, 56–58, 73, 97, 166, 228
Chesterton, Cecil, 192
Chesterton, Gilbert K., 192, 201, 241
Chicago World's Fair (1893), see World's Columbian Exposition
childhood, 136–37, 145–50, 233, 234
children's play, see play, children's
child study movement, 131–32, 150, 230, 233
Christian socialism, 28–29, 49–50, 115, 157, 192
Cities and Town Planning Exhibitions, 32, 58–59, 79, 108, 111
Cities Committee of the Sociological Society, 59–60, 66, 104, 108, 121, 126, 202
Civic Education League, 59–62, 112
civic process, 82, 85–87, 195–97
civics, 52–62, 66–67, 101, 110–17, 126–27, 157–60
civic theatre, see dramatization
cloister, 114
Clouston, Thomas, 132
Coates, Henry, 56
Cobden-Sanderson, Thomas, 58
Cockrill, J. W., 108

Coit, Stanton, 48, 57, 160, 229
Cole, G. D. H., 191–92, 225, 240
Coleridge, Samuel Taylor, 89
collaborative circles (definition) 2
collectivism, 192–94
Collège des Écossais (Scots College), Montpellier, 33, 60, 159, 211
Collet, Clara E., 56
Collingwood, Robin, 19
Collins, Howard, 57
Columba, St., 73, 75, 114–16, 222, 228
Common Wealth Party, 207
communism, 12–13, 43, 76, 192, 194
Communist Party of Great Britain, 192
community development and regeneration, 12–13, 86, 89–93, 110–11, 144–45, 157–60, 162–63, 181
comparative religion, 50, 71, 114–15
Comte, Auguste, 7, 9–10, 47, 81, 87–88, 91, 99, 120, 124, 141, 181, 199, 229
Comteans and Comtism, 12–15, 20, 46–49, 62–63, 72, 154, 204–205, 229
Congreve, Richard, 47, 229
Conklin, Roland Ray, 172–74, 238
conservative surgery, see also neighborhood upgrading, 118–23, 233
conurbations, 91–92, 105, 107, 123
Cook, Henry Caldwell, 68, 77, 95, 145–46
Cooperatives: banking, 181; farming, 44, 162; housing, 25, 31, 38, 45–46, 110, 162, 196; movement, 12–14, 19–21, 113; principles, 76, 83, 93, 196–97
Co-Partnership, see Labour Co-Partnership Association
Co-Partnership Tenants, 163, 178
corporatism, 181, 191, 197, 200–208, 235
Coudenhove-Kalergi, Richard, 116
Crawford, Osbert, 98
Craig, Gordon, 93

INDEX

Craiglockhart War Hospital, Edinburgh, 77–78, 143, 224
Crane, Jacob, 122
Crisp, Frank, 169, 174, 175, 237, 239
Crosby Hall, Chelsea, 58, 94, 104, 160
Crowley, Aleister, 154
Cuba, 168, 171–77, 238
Cuban Telephone Co., 37, 172–74, 179, 238
Cumberland River Estates, Tennessee, 167
Cyprus, 31, 73, 113, 116, 159, 164–65

Darby, H. Clifford, 67
Dartington Hall and School, 44, 120, 150
Darwin, Charles, 16–17, 77, 83, 120
Darwinism and Darwinists, 16–18, 140
Davies, Maud, 96
Dawson, Christopher, 67, 71
De Bonald, Louis Gabriel Ambroise, 9
decentralization and devolution, 116, 194, 201, 215; *see also* distributism
De Forest, Robert, 108, 232
Defries, Amelia, 58, 226, 227
De Kay, John, 171–72
De Maetzu, Ramiro, 192, 241
De Maistre, Joseph, 9, 51
De Normann, Beatrice, 149
De Tocqueville, Alexis, 92
Demolins, Henri, 72, 81–82, 84
Dewey, John, 11, 62
Dickinson, Robert, 80
Dilthey, Wilhelm, 10
distributism, 192–94, 200, 241
Disraeli, Benjamin, 7
Ditchling, Sussex (commune), 44, 193
Douglas, Charles MacKinnon, 49, 55, 57
Douglas, Clifford, 200–206, 241
Doxiadis, Constantinos, 121
drama and dramatization, 58, 93–95, 146, 222–23, 232
Du Bois, W. E. B., 67
Duncan, John, 78
Dundee, 30–31, 35–36, 62, 78–79, 99, 103, 161–62, 170, 226, 232, 236

Dunfermline, 32, 58, 73, 79, 105–106, 114, 118, 126, 149
Dunlop, Andrew, 165
Durkheim, Emile, 6, 9, 22, 57, 66, 124, 225
Dutt, Rajani Palme, 192

Ealing Tenants, 163, 178
Eastern and Colonial Association, 113, 116, 164–65
Economic Freedom League, 204–205
Eden, Frederick, 6
Edgar, Mackay 171
Edinburgh School for Promoting the Study of Ethical, Social, and Economic Subjects, 54
Edinburgh Secular Society, 48
Edinburgh Social Union, 52–54, 78, 110
Edinburgh Summer Schools, 35, 44, 53, 93, 114, 132, 148
Edinburgh University 30–31, 34, 54, 76, 79, 110, 148, 223, 242
Ekistics, 121
Elder, George, 54
Eleventh Hour Flying Clubs, 205
Eliot, George, 52
Eliot, T. S., 206
Elmhirst, Dorothy, 44, 120, 150
Elmhirst, Leonard, 44, 120, 150, 207
Ellis, Havelock, 45, 139, 142
Ellwood, Charles, 3, 65, 94
Ely, Robert, 62
Emmott, Alfred, 57
Engels, Friedrich, 7, 10
English Mistery, 206
environmentalism, 104, 126, 203, 215
Environment Society, *see* Edinburgh Social Union
Erikson, Erik, 139
eugenics, 64, 66, 78, 127
Eugenics Education Society, 64, 78
eutopia, 46, 52, 68–69, 74–75, 90, 95, 114, 124, 150, 158, 198, 213
Evans-Pritchard, Edward, 19
Evergreen, 72–73, 78, 110, 163

INDEX

Exposition Universelle, Paris (1900), 32, 50, 53–54, 111
Eyre, Penelope, 37

Fabian socialism and Fabian Society, 8, 13, 19–21, 45, 63, 149, 181–82, 191–94, 213, 215, 225
Fagg, Christopher, 59–60, 99, 112, 232
Faithfull, Glynn, 157, 207, 235
Faithfull, Theodore, 133, 135, 150, 155–57, 205, 207, 235
farm colonies, *see* allotment schemes and farm colonies
Farquhar, Percival, 175–77, 180, 238, 239
Farquharson, Alexander, 60–62, 113, 211–12, 229, 231, 232, 237
Farquharson, Dorothea, 62
Farr, William, 6
fascism, 117, 203, 206, 208
Fauconnet, Paul, 67
Fawcett, Charles, 59–60, 70, 79, 97, 113, 231
federalism, *see also* decentralization and subsidiarity, 76, 79, 116, 215, 231
Fellowship of the New Life, 45, 148–49
Fels, Joseph, 39, 63–64, 154, 170, 180, 230
Fels, Samuel, 39, 64, 170
Ferguson, Adam, 14
Ferguson, Charles, 65, 158
Ferguson, Munro, 57
finance and financiers, 166–208
financialization, 184–87
financial takeover of media and advertizing, 186–87
Finlay, Thomas, 196
Fisher, Irving, 67
Fleming, Robert, 171, 239
Fleure, Herbert, 67–71, 79, 98, 113, 231, 232
Fordham, Montague, 205
Foerster, Friedrich, 51
Forest Hills Gardens, Queens, NY, 108
Forest School, Hampshire, 150–57
Foster, Walter, 57

Fourier, Charles, 10
Franklin, Henrietta, 57
Frazer, James, 17, 151
Freud, Sigmund, 130, 135, 156
Froebel, Friedrich, 132, 148–49
Fry, T.C., 57

Galton, Francis, 57, 66, 124, 127, 233
Garden Cities movement, 12, 25, 38, 45, 58, 67, 76, 126, 149, 196
Garden City Association, 108, 163–64
Garden City Theosophical School, 149, 155
Gardiner, Rolf, 153, 202–203, 206
Geddes, Alasdair, 31, 33, 59, 65, 223
Geddes, Alexander, 29
Geddes, Anna, *see* Morton, Anna
Geddes, Arthur, 31, 79, 120–21, 223
Geddes circle, 1–4, 26, 43–80, 161–66, 209–20
Geddes, Jessie ("Mousie"), 29
Geddes, John ("Jack"), 29
Geddes, Norah, 31, 223–24
Geddes, Patrick: and planning, 103–13; career, 31–33; character, 3, 25–26, 71, 103–104, 121–23, 162–63, 209–10; early life, 29–31; first marriage, 30–31, 33; second marriage, 33
Geddes, Robert, 29–30
gender, 139–43
General Petroleum Company of Trinidad, 178
George, Henry, 8, 63, 225
Georgism (the single tax), 63
German Sociological Society, 10
Giddings, Franklin, 11, 57
Gide, Charles, 124
Gill, Eric, 44
Gilman, Charlotte Perkins, 11, 63
Ginsberg, Morris, 22, 61
Girl Guides, *see* scouting
Glaister, Norman, 154–57, 203, 205, 207, 235
González Posada, Adolfo, 57
Goodfellow, Adam, 36, 167, 224
Goodman, William, 175, 227

Gould, Frederick, 46–47, 60
government, relocation of, 117
Grant, Helen ("Ella"), 31–32
Great Depression, 117, 180, 208, 211
Green, Thomas Hill, 18, 48
Greenshirts and Greenshirt Movement for Social Credit, 157, 203
Grenfell, Cecil A., 168–69, 171, 173, 239
Grierson, John, 94–95
Grith Fyrd (Peace Army), 155, 235
Guild of Handicraft, 44, 63, 228
Guild of St. George, 44, 150, 229
guild socialism, 191–94, 200, 204
Gumplowicz, Ludwig, 57
Gurdjieff, Georg, 51
Gurney, Archer Evelyn, 38
Gurney, Archer Thompson, 37–38, 223, 228
Gurney, Edmund, 51, 229
Gurney, Gerald, 38, 223
Gurney, Harold Manby, 178, 180, 223–24
Gurney, Sybella: career, 2–3, 38, 46, 67, 70, 76, 113, 163, 196, 202; death and will, 40, 178–80; early life, 37–38, 49, 228; marriage, 39–41, 64, 228; personality, 28–29
Gurney, Vivian, 38, 224

Habermas, Jürgen, 186, 232
Haddon, Alfred, 22, 55–56, 133
Haeckel, Ernst, 124, 132
Haggard, Rider, 66
Hall, G. Stanley, 3, 62, 76, 80, 120, 131–39, 145–48, 233, 234
Hammett, Elise, 38
Hammett, Sybella, 38
Hampstead Garden Suburb, 39–40, 46, 58, 108, 151, 163, 234
Hand, James, 49, 57
Hardy, Lavinia, 98
Hardy, Marcel, 64, 97, 99, 170–71, 176, 232
Hare, Loftus, 71
Hargrave, John, 153, 157, 202–203

Harris, Leverton, 57
Harris, Nugent, 196
Harrison, Frederick, 20, 47, 66
Harrison, Jane Ellen, 151
Harrison, Tom, 99
Havana Telephone Co., 172–74
Hebrew University of Jerusalem, 33, 60, 76, 119
Hecht, Charles, 57
Hecht, John, 65
Hegel, Georg, 9–10
Hegelian thought/ Hegelians, 18–19, 21, 52
Henderson, Alexander, 174–75
Henderson, Brodie, 174–75
Henderson, Frank, 174–75
Herbert, Auberon, 151
Herbertson, Andrew, 2, 54, 79, 98, 113
Herbertson, Dorothy, 79, 231
Herder, Johann, 9–10
Heslop, John, 2, 169
Hill, Octavia, 45, 52
Hinduism, 13
Hobbes, Thomas, 14
Hobhouse, Leonard, 1, 21–23, 38, 48, 55–57, 66–67, 211–13
Hobhouse, Nora, 38
Hobson, John, 47, 49, 56–57, 66–67, 124, 182–83, 200, 229, 240
Hobson, Samuel G., 191, 205–206
Hollins, Dorothea, 46, 56
Horkheimer, Max, 187
Horne-Payne, Monty, 171, 176
Horsfall, Thomas, 58
housing, see cooperatives, housing; neighborhood upgrading; self-help housing
Howard, Ebenezer, 45, 65, 108
Hughes, Henry, 10
Hull House, 13, 62, 96, 230
Hume, David, 14
Hutchings, Geoffrey, 112, 232
Huxley, Thomas H., 30, 47, 120, 151
Hyndman, Henry, 19, 44
Hysler-Rubin, Noah, 126

imperialism, 181–83, 188
Independent Labour Party, 149, 191
Index Museum, see museums, and International Index Museum project
India, 32–33, 50–51, 59–60, 103–104, 111, 116, 118–21, 126, 210–11
industrialism (paleotechnic), problems of, 91–92, 95, 143–45
influenza pandemic, see Spanish Flu pandemic
Institute of Sociology, 61–62, 74
International Cooperative Alliance, 113
International Index Museum project, 53–54, 111, 214
International Society for Individual Psychology, 205
International Telephone and Telegraph (ITT), 174
Irish Agricultural Organisation Society, 196
Izoulet, Jean, 77

James, William, 3, 11, 51, 62, 67, 120, 124, 131, 235
Jefferson, Thomas, 117
Jennings, Humphrey, 94–95, 99
Jevons, Stanley, 15, 195
Jewish Territorial Organisation, 63–64
Jones, Caradog, 99
Jones, Ernest, 135
Jones, Henry, 18
Jowitt, Moya, 153
Jung, Carl Gustav, 135, 155

Kant, Immanuel, 9–10
Kearton, Malcolm, 165–66
Keele University, 62, 113, 227, 228
Kellogg, Paul, 108
Keltie, J. Scott, 55–56
Keswick School of Industrial Art, 45, 164
Keynes, John Maynard, 15
Kibbo Kift Kindred, 153, 157, 202, 235
Kidd, Benjamin, 17–19, 55–57, 127
Kitchen, Ann, 33, 217

Kitchen, Paddy, 126, 226
Kitson, Arthur, 200, 204–207
Krishnamurti, 51
Krohmalney, John, 39, 228
Kropotkin, Pyotr, 43–44, 51, 55, 63, 83, 121, 151, 230

Labour Co-Partnership Association, 38, 46, 58, 76, 113, 163
Labour Party (Great Britain), 8, 63, 182, 191, 202, 207, 215, 225
Lafitte, Pierre, 47
Lamarck, Jean-Baptiste, 17, 124, 133
Lanchester, Henry, 59, 79, 121
Lands Trust, 172
Lansbury, George, 63, 154
Laski, Harold, 20
Lasswell, Harold, 94
League of Nations, 68, 117, 159, 200, 206–207
Ledbury, Herefordshire, 62
leisure class, 185, 193
Leng, John, 35, 236
Leo XIII, Pope, 13, 192, 241
Le Play, Frédéric, 6–8, 30, 53, 72, 79, 81–84, 97, 124, 181, 231, 241
Le Play House, London, 40, 60–61, 65, 71, 75, 79, 112–13, 178, 202–203, 206, 229, 230
Le Play Society, 61, 230
Letchworth Garden City, 58, 149, 163, 230
Lewes, George, 46
Liberal Party (Great Britain) 20, 48–49, 57, 150, 182, 207
Lilley, Alfred, 56
Lindsay, Alexander, 94
Lisman, Frederick J., 175, 197, 238
List, Friedrich, 10
Living Religions Conference, 71
Loch, Charles S., 55
Locke, John, 14–15
Lodge, Oliver, 49–51, 77
London and River Plate Bank, 167, 179
London Ethical Society (LES), 46, 48, 229

INDEX

London Positivist Society, 46–47, 56–57, 182
London School of Economics and Political Science (LSE), 2, 19–23, 54, 57, 60–61, 210, 212, 230, 233, 240
Loria, Achille, 57
Lutyens, Edwin, 118
Lymington, Lord (Gerard Wallop), 206

Macdonald, Ramsay, 57
MacIver, Robert, 22, 67, 80, 212, 214, 225, 231
MacKaye, Benton, 107, 232
MacKaye, Percy, 94, 232
Mackie, Charles, 78
Mackinder, Halford, 54, 57, 225
MacLeod, Josephine, 50
Macmillan, Harold, 206
Macmurray, John, 92, 157, 205, 232
Madge, Charles, 99
Mairet, Philip, 2, 204–205, 226, 240, 241
Making of the Future book series, 69–71, 115, 143, 187
Malcolmson, Vernon, 2, 166, 179
Malinowski, Bronislaw, 22
Malthus, Thomas, 6
Malvern, Worcestershire, 62
Manchester University Settlement, 150
Mann, Tom, 20
Manning, Cardinal Henry, 192
Marr, Thomas, 98–99, 150, 232
Marrett, Robert R., 61
Marsh, George Perkins, 121
Marshall, Alfred, 15
Marshall, Thomas H., 22
Martineau, Harriet, 11, 14–15, 46
Marx, Eleanor, 19–20, 45
Marx, Karl, 10
Marxism, 7, 10, 19–20, 43–44, 181–82, 225
Mason, Josiah, 36
masques, *see* drama and dramatization
Massingham, Henry, 206
Mass-Observation, 99, 233

Maudesley, Henry, 57
Mauss, Marcel, 3, 9
Mavor, James, 57, 62, 230
Mawson, Thomas, 32
Mayhew, Henry, 7–8
McDougall, William, 22, 57, 67, 135, 226
McGegan, Edward, 54
Mead, George, 11
Mears, Frank, 65, 104, 119, 224
Medd, John C., 56
megalopolis, 123, 232, 233
Meller, Helen, 126, 226
Mendl, Charles, 2, 167, 169, 177
Mendl, Sigismund, 169, 177, 237
Menger, Carl, 195
Mexican Light and Power Co., 171
Mexico, 29–30, 63, 167, 171–72
micro-credit, 196
Mill, Hugh Robert, 98
Mill, James, 14–15
Mill, John Stuart, 7, 15, 46, 52
Millar, John, 14
Mitrinović, Dimitrije, 204–205
Mond, Alfred (Lord Melchett), and Mond Conference, 206–7
Montesquieu, Charles-Louis, 9–10, 82–83
Montessori, Maria, 51, 148–49, 234
Montpellier, 33, 60–61, 159–60, 211, 223, 226
More Hall, Chelsea, 58
Morris, George, 59
Morris, John, 169, 174–75, 237, 239
Morris, William, 19–20, 44, 95, 124, 191, 206, 212
Morton, Anna, 30–31, 33, 47, 59–60, 110–11, 164
Morton, Frazer, 30
Morton, Levi, 168, 169, 176, 237
Mosley, Oswald, 207
Muirhead, John, 48–49
Mumford, Geddes, 110, 125
Mumford, Lewis, 3, 28, 40, 65, 67, 74, 80, 94, 104, 107, 110, 121, 123, 125, 211, 230, 231, 232

Mumford, Sophia, 110
museums, 53–54, 97–98, 105, 110–11, 119–20, 214
Myers, Frank, 51

national accounts, 195–200
National Arts Club, New York, 39, 64–65, 228
National Association for the Promotion of Social Science (SSA), 7
national credit fund, 201–202
National Geographical Institute project, 54
nationalism, 86–87, 206, 232
National League for Clean Government (later renamed Distributist League), 193
national planning, 207
National Trust, 45, 164
neotechnic, see paleotechnic and neotechnic
neighborhood upgrading, 104, 118–23, 126, 215, 233
Neill, A. S., 150
Nettlefold, John, 58
Neuberg, Victor, 154
neurasthenia, 143–45
New Age, 51, 65, 145, 151, 191–92, 200, 204, 240, 241
Newbigin, Marion, 79
New Britain movement, 157, 205–206
New Britain Quarterly, 205
New English Weekly, 205, 241
New Europe Group (NEG), 205–206, 241
Newman, Cardinal John H., 49
Nicholson, Joseph Shield, 54
Nicholson, Max, 207
Noble, Margaret, 50, 77, 114, 132

occupational differentiation, 84–85, 88–90, 139–43
Odum, Howard, 80
Ogilvie, Campbell, 168, 172, 175, 238
Oliphant, James, 30, 47, 52
Olivier, Sydney, 20

Olmsted, Frederick Law, 106
Olmsted, Frederick Law, Jr., 108
Oppenheimer, Max, 10
Orage, Alfred, 51, 95, 151, 191, 200, 204, 240
Order of Woodcraft Chivalry (OWC), 152–57, 202-203, 235
Ordinance Survey, 97
organic farming, 205–206
Oundle, 33–34, 217, 227
Outlook Tower, 2, 53–54, 77, 96–98, 110, 143, 158, 214
Owen, Robert, 10, 19, 46, 52, 113, 162
Owen, Wilfred, 77, 143

Paganism, 151–54, 235
Paidologist, 131–32
paleotechnic and neotechnic, 91–92, 123–25
Palestine, 33, 60, 73, 116, 126
Pan-European Movement, 116
Pankhurst, Emmeline, 20
Papers for the Present series, 67–69, 73, 115, 145
Paraguay, 64, 99, 167–71, 176–77, 222, 232, 236, 237, 239
Paraguay Central Railway Company (PCRC), 64, 99, 168–71, 174–79, 232, 236, 239
Paris Exposition (1900), see *Exposition Universelle*
Park, Robert, 11, 94
Parker, Barry, 2, 39, 58
parks and gardens, 105–106
participatory action research, 97, 214–15
Passmore Edwards Settlement, London, 50
Paxton, Joseph, 106
Peake, Harold, 69–70, 79, 232
Pearson, Frederick, 171, 176
Pearson, Karl, 48, 140
Pease, Edward, 20, 225
Penstone, Maria, 99
Pentland, Lord (John Sinclair, 1860–1925), 59, 111

Penty, Arthur, 191–94, 240
Perry, Cutbill de Lungo and Co., 168
Perse School, Cambridge, 145
Pestalozzi, Johann, 148–49
Philadelphia Commercial Museum, 53
Philadelphia Vacant Lots Cultivation Association, 63
Piaget, Jean, 76, 130, 139
Pittsburgh Survey, 96, 108, 232
play, children's, 68, 77, 101, 119, 136–39, 145–50, 156, 234
Plunkett, Horace, 113, 124, 165–66, 196, 236
Political and Economic Planning, 207
positivism, see Comteans and Comtism
Positivist Review, 47
Postgate, Raymond, 192, 205
Potter, Beatrice, see Webb, Beatrice
poverty
  activism, 12–14, 18–20
  research, 6–8, 20, 67
Priestley, J. B., 207
Priory Gate School, Suffolk, 133, 150, 155–56
Progressive Association, 45
progressive school movement, 129–57
psychoanalysis, 135, 155, 204–5, 227
Pullar, Robert, 62
Putnam, Robert, 92

Quesnay, François, 6
Quetelet, Adolphe, 6

Radburn, New Jersey, 107, 109
Radcliffe-Brown, Alfred, 22
Ramsay Gardens, 110
Rashdall, Hastings, 49
Ratcliffe, Sam, 66–67
Ratzel, Friedrich, 10
Rauschenbusch, Walter, 12
Rawnsley, Edith, 164
Rawnsley, Hardwicke, 45, 164
recapitulationism, 135, 146, 149, 151–52, 155–56, 232, 234
Reckitt, Maurice, 191–92, 204

Reclus, Elisée, 44, 53, 62, 83, 114, 151, 159, 223
reconstruction/reconstructionism, see social reconstruction
Red Cross, 111–12
Reddie, Cecil, 148–49, 229, 234
Regional Association, 59–62
Regional Plan Association, 108
Regional Planning Association of America (RPAA), 3, 104, 107, 109
regionalism and regional planning, 59–62, 67, 83–84, 90, 104–10, 153, 213, 233
Regional Plan of New York and its Environs, 107–109
Rerum Novarum, encyclical, 13, 241
Revel, Dorothy, 133, 155–57, 235
revolutions and revolutionary movements, 12, 14, 66, 68–69, 113, 117, 181–82, 187–89, 198
Ritchie, David, 18
Rivers, William H.R., 22, 67, 143
Roberts, R.D., 55–56
Robertson, John, 48, 57, 67
Rodríguez, Manuel, 64, 167–71, 174, 176, 232, 236, 237, 239
Romanes, George, 48, 133
Ross, Branford & Co, 36, 163, 169, 170
Ross, John, 36, 54, 57, 59, 162–66, 170, 174, 197, 237
Rousseau, Jean-Jacques, 9
Rowntree, Seebohm, 8, 57, 96, 231
Royal Geographical Society, 54–55, 59, 232
Royal Institute of British Architects, RIBA, 59
Royal Institute of International Affairs, 206
Royal Scottish Geographical Society, 54
Royal Statistical Society, 7, 55
rural reconstruction, 113, 120, 206
Ruskin, John, 19, 43–45, 51–52, 72, 95, 124, 149–51, 162, 182, 191, 195, 206, 212

Ruskin School, Wimbledon, 132
Russell, Bertrand, 49
Russell, George, 49, 65
Russell Sage Foundation, 96, 108, 232
rustic process and renewal, 82–85, 146–49, 195–97
Rutter, Cuthbert, 156

Saint-Simon, Henri de, 9, 199
Sage, Margaret Olivia, 108
Saleeby, Caleb, 57
Salter, Arthur, 206–207
Salvation Army, 12
Samuel, Herbert, 57
Sandeman, Frances, 92, 154, 199
Sandeman, George, 2, 68, 77, 92, 154, 199
Scheveningen development, 167
School of Industrial Art, Keswick, 45
School of Interpretive Social Research, Oxfordshire, 207
Schreiner, Olive, 45, 142
Scottish Enlightenment, 14
scouting, 150–52
self-help housing, 104
Semple, Ellen Churchill, 11
Sesame Club, 132
Seth, James, 54
Seton, Ernest Thompson, 150–53
Settlement House movement, 12, 62, 111–12, 160
sexuality, 45, 72, 139–43, 153–57
Sharp, William (Fiona McLeod), 78
Shaw, George Bernard, 20, 57, 182
Sidgwick, Henry, 15, 51
Siepmann, Otto, 56
Simiand, François, 9
Simmel, Georg, 22, 225
Sinclair, John, 6
Sister Nivedita, see Noble, Margaret
Slater, Gilbert, 2, 70, 77–78, 116–17
Slaughter, John W., 46, 64, 78, 132
Small, Albion, 2, 11, 13, 57, 62
Smith, Adam, 10, 14
Smith, Isaac, 35–36
Smith, Martyn Josiah, 37, 56, 224

Smith, Matilda Elizabeth, see Stewart, Bess
Smith, William Robertson, 49
social credit, 65–67, 195–208, 235
Social Credit Party of Great Britain, 203
Social Democratic Federation (SDF), 8, 19, 44–45, 48, 181
Social Doctrine of the Catholic Church, 13, 192
social evolution, 16–18, 21–23
social finance, see social credit
Social Gospel of Protestant churches, 12, 115, 131
socialism, 8, 10, 19–20, 43–49, 181–82, 187–89
Socialist League, 8, 19, 44, 58
socialization of individual personality, 129–35
social policy and planning, 10–11, 18–19, 49, 90, 92
social psychology, 21–22, 129–50, 155–57, 213
social reconstruction, 3, 12–14, 26, 43, 46–47, 52, 62–66, 73, 90–95, 115–17, 127, 157–60, 181–83, 194–200, 213–15
social solidarity, 18–19
Social Science Associations, 7, 10
social work, 13, 18–19, 30, 44, 57, 108, 126, 160, 198, 211, 229
Society for Ethical Culture, New York, 48, 63
Society for Psychical Research, 51
Society of Technical Engineers, 206
Society of the Eagar Heart, 50, 93–94
Sociological Papers, 36, 66, 127
Sociological Review, 23, 61–62, 65–67, 73, 77, 113, 154, 202, 230, 231
Sociological Society, 2–3, 20–23, 25, 27, 32, 36, 41, 51. 62–63, 66–80, 113–14, 135, 161, 178, 209–11, 227, 230, 231, 233
Sociological Trust, 60, 180
Sociology: as omnibus discipline, 2, 100–101, 158, 213; Britain, early

Sociology (continued)
  development, 5–23; business networks, 3–4; Chicago School, 11–13, 62, 86, 94, 131; Encyclopaedias, 17; France, early development, 9; Germany, early development, 9–10; Public sociology, 92–93; United States, early development, 10–14
Soddy, Frederick, 204–207, 231
Sombart, Werner, 10
South Africa, 34–35, 219, 224
South Place Ethical Society, 46, 48, 57, 182
Spanish Flu pandemic, 117, 211
Spencer, Herbert, 1, 7, 11, 16–18, 52, 57, 81, 120, 225
Speyer Brothers, 177
spiritual powers, systems and hemispheres, *see* temporal and spiritual powers, systems and hemispheres
spiritualism, 51
spirituality, 26, 28, 43, 49–51, 73, 86, 114–16, 127, 137
spiritual renewal, 3, 14–18, 51–52, 92–95, 157–60, 181, 194–200
Stamp, L. Dudley, 98
state, role of the, 17–18, 92–93, 114–17, 187–89, 192–94, 215
statistical societies, 6
Statistical Society of London, *see* Royal Statistical Society
Stein, Clarence, 107
Steiner, Rudolph, 148–49, 194
Stevenson, Janet, 29
Stewart, Arthur, 36, 227
Stewart, Bess (née Matilda Elizabeth Smith), 35–37, 163, 223
Stewart, Dugald, 14
Stewart, Elsie (later, Lady Allardyce), 36–37, 221, 224, 227
Stewart, James Farquharson, 36
Stewart, Martyn, 36, 227
Stilwell, Arthur, 167, 180, 236
Strachey, John, 205

Straight, Dorothy Whitney, *see* Elmhirst, Dorothy
structural functionalism, 23
subsidiarity, 116
Sully, James, 55
Summerhill School, Suffolk, 150
Sumner, William, 11
Sunnyside Gardens, Queens, NY, 107
Survey Graphic, 108
Surveys: civic, 96–98; diagnostic, 119; regional, 59–62, 96, 144, 158, 161; rustic, 96–97; social, 93, 95–100, 198, 212, 214
survey then plan, 112–13
sustainability, *see* environmentalism
Swinny, Shapland, 46–47, 56
Switzerland, 40

Tagore, Rabindranath, 13, 50, 114, 120
Tait, Peter, 195
Tansley, Arthur, 135
Tatton, Margaret, 60–61, 112–13
Tawney, Richard, 22, 57, 67
Tayler, Lionel, 2, 46, 57, 98, 141, 234
Taylor, Rachel Annan, 71, 78
temporal and spiritual powers, systems and hemispheres, 87–90, 148, 157–60, 181–87, 194–202, 213
Theosophical Society, 50, 149, 194
Theosophy, 13, 26, 48–51, 78
thinking machines, 104
third alternative, *see* third way
third way, 13, 181–208, 240
Thomas, William, 11
Thomasson, John Pennington, 164
Thompson, Theodora, 68, 77
Thomson, J. Arthur, 49, 56, 71–72, 79, 133, 139–43, 211–12
Tillett, Ben, 20
Tolstoy, Leo, 124
Tönnies, Ferdinand, 10, 57
Topolobampo, 167
Town and Gown Association, 57, 111, 162, 164
Town Planning Institute, 108
Toynbee, Arnold, 38, 44

Toynbee, Charlotte, 38
Toynbee Hall, 44, 48–49, 57, 62, 150, 153, 155–56, 160
Tregony, Cornwall, 37
Trotter, Wilfred, 135, 154, 240
Turner, John F.C., 104, 122–23
Twelves, Marion, 45
Tylor, Edward, 17, 151
Tyrwhitt, Jaqueline, 104, 121

Underdown, Emanuel, 168–69, 173–74, 236, 237, 238
United States, 3, 11–12, 36–37, 39–40, 62–65, 174–77
university militant, 129, 157–60
university outreach, engagement and community partnership, 104, 110, 126, 157–60, 215
University of Central India project, Indore, 119–20
Unwin, Raymond, 2, 39, 58, 67, 79, 104, 108
Uruguay Northern Railway, 168, 174, 236
Urwick, Edward, 55–56, 67
Urwick, Lyndall, 207
utilitarian economics, 14–15
Utopians, renamed the Chelsea Association, 44, 46, 49, 56, 58, 73
utopian thought, *see* eutopia

Vaccaro, Michaelangelo, 57
valley section, 84–85, 105, 147, 152
Van Horne, William, 171, 175, 238, 238, 239
Van Oss, S. Frederik, 167, 175, 224, 236
Vaux, Calvert, 106
Veblen, Thorstein, 3, 11, 62, 65, 109, 183, 240, 241
Vidal de la Blache, Paul, 9
Villanueva, Benito, 167–69, 236
Vincent, George, 11, 131
Visva Bharati University, 120
vitalism, 124
Vivekananda, Swami, 13, 50

Vivian, Henry, 28, 45–46, 163
Vorhaus, Louis J., 175, 227

Walker, Mary, 99, 232
Wallas, Graham, 20, 48, 56, 67
Walras, Leon, 195
Ward, Lester, 10, 63
war capitals 116–17, 188
wardom and peacedom, 33, 73, 76, 144, 151–52, 188–89, 199, 213, 231
Webb, Beatrice, 20, 66, 213, 215, 225
Webb, Sidney, 20, 55, 67, 213, 215, 225
Weber, Max, 10
Welby, Charles, 57
Wells, Alan, 99
Wells, H.G., 56–57, 88
Welter, Volker, 126, 233
Wenley, Mark, 2, 62, 64, 66
Westermarck, Edvard, 57, 66, 124
West Indian Cooperative Union, 113, 165–66, 196, 206
Westlake, Aubrey, 150–57, 202, 205, 235
Westlake, Ernest, 2, 77, 151–57, 202
Westminster, 36, 56, 70, 74, 75, 164, 239
Wharton, Susan, 96
White, Harold Jennings, 154
White, Martin, 30–31, 35, 55–56, 161–63, 240
Whitehead, Alfred North, 215
Whitehouse, John, 149–50
Whitson, Thomas, 162
Whyte, Alexander, 49–50
Whyte, Jane, 50
Wilkinson, Ellen, 205
Wilson, Mona, 99
Wolff, Henry, 113, 166
Women's Guild for Human Order, 205
Woodcraft Folk, 157, 235
woodcraft ideas, 150–55, 203; *see also* Seton, Ernest Thompson
Wood, Edith Elmer, 107
Wood, Joseph, 46, 229
world university, 159, 214

World War I, 32–33, 58–60, 77–78, 92, 103, 110, 115–18, 152, 177–78, 189, 196, 200, 223, 224, 231, 240
World War II, 23, 79, 109–10, 121–22, 125, 208, 211
World's Columbian Exposition (1893 Chicago World's Fair), 53, 71, 131
Worms, René, 57
Wright, Henry, 107

Wundt, Wilhelm, 10, 124, 131
Wyld, Norman, 57, 166, 206–207

YMCA, 12, 111–12
Younghusband, Francis, 71, 113

Zangwill, Israel, 13, 63–64, 170
Zionism, 13, 33
Zueblin, Charles, 11, 54, 58, 62, 111